Topics in Regulatory Economics and Policy

Series editor

Michael A. Crew, Newark, NJ, USA

More information about this series at http://www.springer.com/series/6646

Pier Luigi Parcu • Timothy Brennan • Victor Glass
Editors

The Contribution of the Postal and Delivery Sector

Between E-Commerce and E-Substitution

Springer

Editors
Pier Luigi Parcu
European University Institute
RSCAS, Florence School of Regulation
Communication & Media
Florence, Italy

Timothy Brennan
School of Public Policy
UMBC
Baltimore, MD, USA

Victor Glass
Rutgers Business School
Newark, NJ, USA

Topics in Regulatory Economics and Policy
ISBN 978-3-030-09980-0 ISBN 978-3-319-70672-6 (eBook)
https://doi.org/10.1007/978-3-319-70672-6

Printed on acid-free paper

This Springer imprint is published by Springer Nature
The registered company is Springer International Publishing AG
The registered company address is: Gewerbestrasse 11, 6330 Cham, Switzerland

Preface and Acknowledgments

This book is a result of the 25th Conference on Postal and Delivery Economics, which was held on May 24–27, 2017, in Barcelona, Spain. The conference was a joint effort of the Florence School of Regulation – Communications and Media (FSR C&M) at the European University Institute (EUI) and the Center for Research in Regulated Industries (CRRI) at the Rutgers Business School.

The conference and book are dedicated to Prof. Michael A. Crew. This 25th conference was the first held without him since he and the late Paul Kleindorfer organized the first conference, held in July 1990 in Rugby, England. Since then, hundreds of participants have come together to discuss and share research on evolving trends in postal and delivery economics. The community of economics, business, law, and policy researchers studying the postal sector that the conferences have fostered in the last three decades would not exist without Michael's effort, intellect, humor, and indomitable spirit. That community will be forever in his debt.

The Conferences on Postal and Delivery Economics that Michael created are a testament to the evolution in the postal and delivery sector over the last 25 years: from high letter volumes to a progressive increase of parcel delivery, from the start of the liberalization process to the disruptive impact of digitalization and the Internet, and from sector-specific activities to new business differentiation. At the same time, the universal service obligation was and still is a central element of the regulatory, policy, and economic debate.

The conference was made possible by the contribution of generous supporters. We would like to thank them not only for financial support but also for the helpful advice they provided in their role on the organizing committee as well as, along with others, intellectual contributions and encouragement: Mohammad Adra, Bruno Basalisco, Geoff Bickerton, Claire Borsenberger, Stephen Brogan, Fabio Camerano, Isabelle Carslake, Margaret Cigno, Peter Dunn, Cristina Falcone, Colm Farrelly, Charles Fattore, Beatriz Galván Santiago, Stefano Gori, Juan Gradolph, Annegret Groebel, Robert Hammond, John Hearn, Paul Hodgson, Adam Houck, George Houpis, Christian Jaag, Denis Joram, Keith Kellison, Caroline Longman, Leonardo Mautino, Hendrik Okholm, Ted Pearsall, Paola Piscioneri, Michela Raco,

Frank Rodríguez, Chris Rowsell, Michael Scanlon, Soterios Soteri, Katherine Steinhoff, David Stubbs, Mark van der Horst, and Tim Walsh.

This year's conference benefited greatly from the efforts of the Conference Unit of the Robert Schuman Centre for Advanced Studies and of the team of the FSR C&M, who were incredibly helpful during the conference, enabling it to operate very smoothly, with special thanks to Paula Gori and Elisabetta Spagnoli. They and colleagues provided both advice and assistance on numerous occasions and contributed greatly to the success of the event.

We would like to thank our distinguished dinner speaker, the President of CNMC (the Spanish National Regulatory Authority), José María Marín Quemada.

Last but not least, we thank all authors and participants of the conference. Without their contributions, the conference and this book would not have been possible. The usual disclaimers are applicable. In particular, the views expressed reflect the views of the authors and are not necessarily those of the editors or supporters.

Florence, Italy — Pier Luigi Parcu
Baltimore, MD, USA — Timothy Brennan
Newark, NJ, USA — Victor Glass

The Conference was kindly supported by

Royal Mail
RR Donnelley Logistics
United Parcel Service
Ofcom
Citizen Advice
Pitney Bowes
Poste Italiane
Le Groupe La Poste
CNMC
Copenhagen Economics
Correos y Telégrafos
IBM Global Business Services
Oxera
ComReg
Frontier Economics
Cullen International
K&L Gates LLP
An Post
New Zealand Post Limited
BNetzA
Swiss Economics

Contents

Academic Hubs and the Intellectual Infrastructure of Economic Regulation

William E. Kovacic

1 Introduction

Michael Crew was one of the most important academics in the past half-century of economic regulation. He wrote books and articles that shaped the way we think about the substance, process, and institutions of regulation. In the classroom, he provided powerful analytical tools and valuable practical guidance to thousands upon thousands of students. He was a much-demanded lecturer to audiences around the globe. He gave astute advice to public bodies and private firms as a consultant. He generously provided invaluable support and guidance to junior academics. In all of these endeavors, he displayed true mastery of the technical details and broad policy considerations of regulation, and he revealed an unsurpassed capacity to identify important connections across the individual domains of regulatory policy.

In no area was Michael's influence more profound than in postal and delivery services. In his own work and in collaboration with other researchers (most notably, his long-time academic colleague and dear friend, Paul Kleindorfer), Michael helped set essential foundations for what we know as postal and delivery economics (Brennan 2017). He created and convened the world's most important annual conference on postal and delivery economics, taking a neglected area of policymaking and providing a forum that linked academics, business managers, government officials, and practitioners (Parcu and Comandini 2017). Starting with

The views expressed here are the author's alone.

W.E. Kovacic (✉)
George Washington University Law School, Washington, DC, USA

Dickson Poon School of Law, King's College London, London, UK

Competition and Markets Authority, London, UK
e-mail: wkovacic@law.gwu.edu

P.L. Parcu et al. (eds.), *The Contribution of the Postal and Delivery Sector*, Topics in Regulatory Economics and Policy, https://doi.org/10.1007/978-3-319-70672-6_1

a small gathering of specialists at Rugby in the United Kingdom in 1992, Michael constructed what became a must-attend annual event. The proceedings of these programs provided the basis for edited volumes that contain some of the most significant papers on postal and delivery services. Michael was not alone in giving due attention to a crucial element of the information services economy, but his role in developing postal and delivery services as a focus of intellectual inquiry, scholarship, and policy discourse was unmatched.

The central vehicle for Michael's work in regulatory policy was the Center for Research in Regulatory Industries (CRRI) at the Rutgers University Graduate School of Management (GSM) in Newark, New Jersey.[1] Michael founded CRRI in the early 1980s, and it served as the chief home for varied programs concerning postal services and other domains of regulatory policy. CRRI became an exemplar of the academic hub—a platform that helps create the intellectual infrastructure of regulatory policy and transmits its insights to the stakeholders in the field. CRRI supported the teaching of Michael and his colleagues at GSM, housed the Journal of Regulatory Economics (which Michael formed in the late 1980s), and convened a wide variety of conferences, seminars, and workshops. Michael's conscious aim in designing these events was to integrate theory with practice—to join up conceptual insights from the academy and inject them into current debates about policy and to alter the course of policy itself.

This paper seeks to do two things. First, it celebrates Michael Crew's remarkable role in building an academic hub that greatly enriched our understanding of postal and delivery economics and the field of economic regulation generally. The motivation for the tribute is deeply personal. In all that I have done as an academic and public official since meeting Michael 30 years ago, every day I have used something I learned from Michael and the academic hub he created. I am most grateful.

The paper's second aim is to highlight the importance of academic hubs as elements of the regulatory ecosystem that supports the development of sensible regulatory policy. CRRI exemplifies the vital support that an academic hub gives to a system of economic regulation. By generating and publishing research, by teaching students who will enter field of regulation, and by making practitioners and regulators aware of relevant theoretical and empirical developments, CRRI has helped build the base of knowledge on which good regulation depends. In convening conferences, seminars, and workshops, CRRI provided settings in which all participants in the policymaking and enforcement process—academics, practitioners, and regulators—could build common understandings about developments in industry and in government and, over time, form a consensus about the design and implementation of public policy.

By appreciating how academic hubs can improve the quality of regulation, we can see how regulatory systems can nurture and engage these institutions to their

[1]This institution now is known as the Rutgers Business School. This paper refers to the Graduate School of Management, or GSM, as this was the name of the school for most of Michael Crew's tenure at Rutgers.

great benefit. Seen this way, academic hubs are striking examples of what Allan Fels, a leading scholar in the fields of economic regulation and public administration and the former chair of the Australian Competition and Consumer Commission, has called "co-producers"—institutions external to the regulatory agency on which regulators can draw to increase their own capability and achieve better regulatory results. Academic hubs should be viewed as vital—perhaps, indispensable—ingredients of the intellectual infrastructure over which good regulatory policy travels.

The paper approaches the topic in two parts. It begins by describing several major problems associated with the development and transmission of knowledge that a regulatory system must overcome to function effectively. This section also suggests how academic hubs can help a regulatory system to overcome otherwise crippling knowledge problems. The second part concludes by suggesting how the existing role of academic hubs might be expanded to play this supporting role more fully. The paper draws heavily upon illustrations from the CRRI's work in postal and delivery economics, but its observations apply more broadly to other systems of economic regulation.

2 Knowledge Requirements and the Contribution of Academic Hubs to Regulatory Policy R&D

Knowledge is a crucial input into the development of good regulatory programs. Successful regulatory regimes require regular investments—by regulatory bodies and by collateral external groups—in regulatory policy research and development (R&D) (Kovacic 2005). Just as many commercial enterprises thrive by reason of R&D investments, so too do regulatory agencies require outlays that build knowledge.

Five conditions relating to the accumulation, assimilation, and transmission of knowledge provide valuable foundations for effective regulation. Each of these is a potential focal point for regulatory R&D. These conditions and the obstacles to their creation are described below.

2.1 Sound Comprehension of Commercial Developments

The regulator stands very much in the position of a physician in the treatment of patents. A vital step in medical practice is the diagnosis of observed phenomena. Good medical practice begins with a careful assessment of the patient's present condition and medical history. This assessment enables the physician to make an accurate diagnosis, which in turn informs the decision of whether and how to intervene.

To approach any assigned task, the regulator must first ask itself if it fully understands the industry it oversees. Does it know how the industry has evolved to its current state, and does it correctly foresee where the sector is going? Does the regulator have access to data that documents trends in performance and supplies an informative view of how the sector will progress in the future?

A central assumption supporting the creation of regulatory bodies is that they would provide a superior means to assemble and apply the expertise suggested above. In theory, a skillful regulator recruits and retains knowledgeable specialists, forms teams which become proficient in addressing specific commercial phenomena, and applies tools that permit the agency to understand how the sector is changing.

Several problems confront a regulator as it seeks to create and sustain a needed base of knowledge about sectors and firms subject to its jurisdiction. Because governments usually resist paying market rates for top talent, it can be very difficult to recruit high quality analysts and retain their skills. Rapid technological change and other forms of intense commercial dynamism place continuous and extreme pressure on the agency's knowledge base. For example, the future configuration of postal and delivery services is a function of rapid change regarding the expansion of electronic commerce, the electronic collection and transmission of data (e.g., the introduction, since the 1980s of the fax machine and email) and in methods for delivering physical objects (e.g., drones). The abrupt displacement of existing business models can simply overwhelm existing regulatory controls, unless the regulator is able to learn and adapt quickly.

The knowledge problem becomes more acute as the range of regulatory tasks or sectors overseen increases (Hyman and Kovacic 2014). Legislators often assign regulators more than one regulatory task—for example, by giving a regulator a portfolio that includes responsibility for competition issues, consumer protection matters, and data protection. Agencies which have succeeded in overseeing a single commercial sector may experience extensions of authority that bring more industries within their purview. As the number of sectors to be overseen or the number of substantive regulatory duties grows, so too does the need to build an even broader base of knowledge.

The discussion so far has spoken in terms of building knowledge through the agency's own recruitment. Of course, an agency may contract externally to obtain the requisite knowledge. It is common practice for regulators to hire consultants to guide the analysis of specific sectors or particular forms of behavior. However, recourse to outsourcing ultimately is constrained by budget limits, which legislative appropriators rarely set in a generous fashion. Legislators usually impose regulatory duties that outrun the ability of the agency, whatever mix of internal expertise development or contracting out it uses, to fulfill its commitments. As discussed more fully below, academic hubs can help fill this gap by performing functions—such as research that studies developments in dynamic sectors—that supplement what the agency can do by itself.

2.2 Improving Theory and Joining it to Practice

Improvements in knowledge relevant to economic regulation often take the form of enhancements to the theoretical state of the art. For example, the identification of price caps as alternatives to traditional rate of return regulation has reshaped policy in a number of regulated sectors. A well-performing regulatory system will engage in a continuous effort to improve theory and use such improvements to increase the quality of regulation. The latter step requires mechanisms that translate the conceptual insights of theoretical refinements into practical operational techniques.

A regulatory system can use various approaches to the twin tasks of advancing theory and joining it successfully to regulatory practice. The vertical integration or disaggregation of these tasks varies considerably across agencies. Virtually every economic regulator has an internal unit assigned to promote improvements in theory and to facilitate applications to practice. In its most austere manifestation, this takes the form of a policy office that conducts research on behalf of the entire institution and works with operating units to incorporate theoretical insights into regulatory programs. A smaller office, however, is unlikely to do much theoretical work of its own and is likely to look to outsiders for ideas to be taken on board.

Other agencies have more complete forms of integration. The US Federal Trade Commission (FTC), for example, has a Bureau of Economics with roughly 70 economists with doctorates in the field. The bureau conducts theoretical and applied work. Several FTC policy offices provide a means for distributing this work into the routine handling of cases and rules. The actual realization of the possibilities for integration of theory into practice presented by this model depends heavily on how strongly the agency's leadership—notably, the FTC chair—presses both the Bureau of Economics and the FTC's main law enforcement units (the Bureau of Consumer Protection and the Bureau of Competition) to cooperate in developing a conceptual research program that is relevant to enforcement practice and to encourage case handlers to embrace what is learned in the agency's R&D shops.

Academic hubs in universities can facilitate improvements in the advancement of theory and the integration of theory into practice in at least two ways. One is to serve as a major source for theoretical research. Compared to most regulatory authorities, an academic department in economics will have a superior ability to do theoretical work. The second is to develop mechanisms for converting theoretical insights into practice. This requires a willingness on the part of academic researchers to devote some of their time to working with regulators and other members of the regulatory community to develop applications for their work. Theorists do not automatically regard this as a good use of their time. One function, emblematic of the work of CRRI in postal and delivery services, is to convene events in which economists describe the implications of theoretical advances to practitioners and regulators and suggest practical applications of these insights.

2.3 Evaluating Processes and Outcomes

Economic regulation, to a major extent, is inherently experimental. When legislators enact regulatory commands, and when regulatory agencies implementing them, they often are performing experiments. Is this the right approach to correcting a specific market failure? Will this regulatory technique improve economic performance and societal welfare?. As experience with a specific legal command or implementation method increases, the uncertainty surrounding the effects of such measures ought to decline. Yet, even the application of much-tried and well-tested regulatory methods in highly dynamic industry environments can involve significant uncertainty: Is a method that has served the regulatory process in the past well-suited for a quickly evolving novel commercial environment?

In science, evaluation routinely follows experimentation. How did the rule or the case affect economic performance? How closely did actual experience match the expectations that accompanied the experiment? Were prior assumptions about the responses of consumers and business operators correct? The development of a sound regulatory program over time would seem to dictate that regulators follow a cycle of experimentation, evaluation, and refinement.

In practice, regulators might be reluctant to do engage in an optimal level of evaluation. Because evaluation sometimes yields the conclusion that a regulatory initiative had no effect or, worse, retarded economic performance or other objectives, there might be an institutional inclination to forego ex post assessments in favor of periodic declarations that the program is working well. Expenditures on evaluation as one species of policy R&D also might be seen as a luxury the agency cannot afford amid pressures to deliver the next case or complete the next rule. The inclination to favor expenditures for new cases and rules might be accentuated by the impulse that some agency leaders feel to generate a maximum number of visible events for which they can claim credit and to minimize disclosure of past mistakes. More than this there is the risk to discover mistakes and the political and mediatic cost to render public these type of discoveries. Measured by this test, allocating resources to new cases and rules may be more appealing that making investments in ex post assessments. Finally, the methodological challenges in doing reliable ex post analysis may seem daunting to regulators, especially more thinly resourced bodies.

Academic hubs can help a regulatory system overcome some of these difficulties. Their research capabilities can provide means for evaluation that some agencies believe to be beyond their reach. In addition, though an agency's self-assessment can be valuable, evaluation by an academic hub may increase confidence in its findings by bringing an outside body to the task. One can envision cooperative programs in which agencies open their doors to academic researchers, provide access to agency records, and allow the publication of the researchers' studies, subject to restrictions on the disclosure of confidential business data.

2.4 Mastering the "Regulatory Craft"

The discussion above has discussed knowledge mainly in terms of the understanding of commercial developments and the development and application of ideas that can be used to determine the substance of economic regulation. This knowledge mainly addresses the question of what the substance of regulation should be. Beyond the question of *what* regulatory systems should do, there is the distinct, significant issue of *how* they should do it. To be effective, a regulatory system must solve the often-vexing problem of policy implementation—to cover the distance between the conception of the policy idea and its successful realization in practice (Allison 1971).

There is a substantial, growing body of knowledge on how agencies can master what Malcolm Sparrow (2011) has called "the regulatory craft." One set of issues involves the design and organization of the regulatory institution itself (Kovacic and Hyman 2012; Kovacic and Lopez-Galdos 2016). Should the institution be governed by a board or a single administrator? How many regulatory functions should an agency perform, and for which sectors? Should the agency's economists be consolidated within a single office, or should they reside within operating units responsible for developing rules and cases? Where should quality control functions be located within the agency, and who should conduct them? Should the regulator be overseen by a specialist tribunal, or by courts of general jurisdiction? By what internal process should an agency set priorities and select projects to achieve them?

An agency can take a number of steps on its own to improve its knowledge about these matters of design, organization, and operations. It can use its evaluation program to measure operational efficiency and use public consultations with external constituencies to identify areas for process improvement. It can benchmark itself with other systems to assess the wisdom of specific approaches and identify superior practices. Diversity across jurisdictions and the accumulation of experience over a substantial number of years affords a useful basis for considering alternatives to a jurisdiction's existing regime.

Here, as well, academic hubs can shed valuable light on a regulatory system's decisions about the regulatory craft. Some academic hubs—such as the Australia and New Zealand School of Government, headquartered at the University of Melbourne—have built educational programs that instruct public officials from the two countries on agency management. Others have created research projects that explore trends in agency design and organization and explore links between specific agency configurations and regulatory outcomes. Another set of universities, in addition to these activities, hosts academic journals dedicated to questions of policy implementation. Nearly all these academic institutions run conferences, workshops, and seminars on implementation topics for practitioners and public officials.

2.5 Understanding Policy Choices in Context

Part of an agency's knowledge consists of its understanding of the larger context in which it operates. A successful agency understands its political environment and uses this understanding to build political support for its programs and to appreciate how changing political conditions could affect its programs.

An agency's proficiency can benefit significantly from a deeper knowledge of history (Kovacic 2007). Successful public institutions progress by learning over time—using past experience as a way to design current initiatives. Ex post evaluation, described above, is one method of learning from experience. The historical perspective suggested here goes beyond this to develop an awareness of the forces that brought the regulatory regime into being, and what influences tend to improve, or detract from its performance. The broader historical perspective enables the agency to understand what types of institution-building investments, carried out over a long period of time, improve program development and delivery. A number of academic hubs run research programs and related activities that offer useful resources to regulators seeking to improve their political awareness and historical acumen.

2.6 Building Common Awareness and Policy Consensus

An important step in regulatory policy improvements is the development of mechanisms to build consensus on the appropriate way forward. This can be difficult to achieve where different participants in the regulatory process hold vastly different views about what should be done. The challenge is to create a setting in which parties open their minds to other ways of thinking and build personal relationships that enhance trust and understanding.

To some extent, regulators can perform this function by serving as "conveners" of events that bring different groups together for discussions (Kovacic 2015). Academic hubs, however, have an advantage in performing the convener function, as regulators might be viewed as a less neutral organizer and more prone, if only unconsciously, to imbue an agenda with its own preferences. An important feature of the CRRI postal conferences since the early 1990s has been their capacity to create a community of interest among disparate elements of the community of those interested in postal services regulation. The events are hardly free of friction, but they take place in settings in which opportunities for extensive interaction within small groups help to separate myth from reality and foster agreement upon certain principles. The smaller group setting is necessary to give individual participants comfort in setting aside views grounded in their institutional or representation affiliations and to entertain other ways of looking at the world.

In performing the function of conveners, academic hubs supplement and enrich the work of public and private multinational institutions that, to a considerable extent, seek to promote the adoption of global standards for economic regulatory policy. These include organizations such the International Competition Network, the Organization for Economic Cooperation and Development, and the United Nations Conference on Trade and Development. These bodies provide mechanisms to create a sense of common cause among the world's regulators and to encourage discussion and consensus building within a community of academics, public officials, and practitioners. Academic hubs not only provide valuable assistance directly to that regulatory community, but they also assist these and other multinational bodies in carrying out their own work as conveners.

3 Conclusions

Economic regulators confront a variety of daunting knowledge problems when seeking to fulfill their mandates. Among other challenges, regulators must strive to comprehend the significance of developments in complex, fast-changing commercial sectors; integrate advances in the theory of regulatory economics into routine operations; assess the consequences of regulatory initiatives; understand current regulatory initiatives in a larger historical and political context; pursue an institutional framework that is well-suited to performing regulatory duties; and assist in building a larger consensus about the correct path for policy. All of these activities place a premium on the regulator's capacity to recruit and retain skilled personnel, to create mechanisms to stay abreast of adjustments in the commercial environment, and to engage with external constituencies with an interest in the regulator's work.

Regulators cannot perform these tasks successfully working alone, if for no other reason that legislators rarely provide resources that match the commitments stated or implied in statutes that establish regulatory regimes. In most countries, there is an inevitable, substantial gap between what regulatory statutes promise and what nations, through their elected officials, are willing to pay to deliver upon the promises.

To cure the mismatch between commitments and capabilities, regulators must enlist the assistance of "co-producers"—institutions that stand outside the agency and have means to supplement the regulator's own resources and increase its effectiveness. Academic hubs are one species of the co-producer that provides this important complement to the agency's own efforts. In forming the Center for Research in Regulatory Industries and, with Paul Kleindorfer, developing its program in postal and delivery economics, Michael Crew supplied a valuable foundation for policy making by postal regulatory systems around the world. It is a relatively small number of postal regulatory regimes that have not benefitted, directly or indirectly, from the Crew-Kleindorfer as scholars, teachers, and conveners. Together, they supplied ideas and nurtured relationships that have supported good policymaking for postal and delivery services and in other areas of economic regulatory policy.

There are various ways in which economic regulatory systems can make better use of the contributions of academic hubs. The first step is for regulators to recognize academic hubs as structures that can support the development of effective regulatory regimes. This involves identifying, as set out in this paper, the contributions that academic hubs can make toward improvements in regulatory performance, and to enlist their cooperation as co-producers of good economic regulation. To put it another way, the contributions of academic hubs might be seen as indispensable for an economic regulatory regime to achieve the fullest beneficial expression of the possibilities inherent in the legislative framework that established the regulatory process.

A second, related step is for universities and related institutions to understand and embrace the role that they can play as regulatory policy co-producers. The Crew-Kleindorfer contributions to policy development in postal and delivery services and the CRRI postal conferences are worthy of close study by university departments in business, economics, law, and public administration because they should how a university's resources and distinctive traits (e.g., its ability to serve as a trusted, neutral forum for policy discussion) can be harnessed to strengthen the quality of public policy. There are many examples beyond the CRRI that one can examine—including impressive programs run by ANSZOG at the University of Melbourne, the European University Institute and its Robert Schumann Center for Advanced Studies, the Toulouse School of Economics, and the University of Paris-Dauphine and its "club of regulators" project—to see how this can be done with considerable skill and positive effect.

A third step, and consequence of the stocktaking implied by the two suggestions offered above, is the attainment of a deeper awareness of what types of investments, by economic regulators and their co-producers, support the development of high quality public policy. This awareness can yield a more focused understanding of the intellectual and institutional infrastructure that supports the regulatory process—the importance, for example, of continuing, substantial investments in policy research and development as vital inputs into the formulation and implementation of economic regulation (Kovacic and Hyman 2016).

To see more clearly where good regulatory programs come from can build a consensus, within the community of academics, government officials, and practitioners, of what a regulatory system needs to prosper, and what regulators and the legislative bodies that established them must do to realize good results in the design and operation of regulatory institutions. Michael Crew and Paul Kleindorfer devoted much of their professional lives to creating this awareness. They were major architects of the intellectual and institutional infrastructure that supports high quality policymaking. The good work that takes place in regulatory policy for postal and delivery services travels on that path every day.

References

Allison, Graham T. The Essence of Decision (Little Brown 1971)

Brennan, Timothy. 2017. Michael Crew's (and Paul Kleindorfer's) Scholarly Contributions to the CRRI Postal Conferences, 1992-2012. In this volume.

Hyman, David A., and William E. Kovacic. 2014. Why Who Does What Matters: Governmental Design and Agency Performance. George Washington University Law Review. 82: 1446-1516.

Kovacic, William E. 2005. Measuring What Matters: The Federal Trade Commission and Investments in Competition Policy Research and Development. Antitrust Law Journal. 72: 861-69.

Kovacic, William E. 2007. The Importance of History to the Design of Competition Policy Strategy: The Federal Trade Commission and Intellectual Property. Seattle University Law Review. 30: 319-47.

Kovacic, William E. 2015. The Federal Trade Commission as Convenor: Developing Regulatory Policy Norms without Litigation or Rulemaking. 13: 17-30.

Kovacic, William E., and David A. Hyman. 2012. Competition Agency Design: What's on the Menu? European Competition Journal. 8: 527-41.

Kovacic, William E., and David A. Hyman. 2016. Consume or Invest? What Do/Should Regulatory Agency Leaders Maximize? Washington Law Review. 91: 295-324.

Kovacic, William E., and Marianela Lopez-Galdos. 2016. Lifecycles of Competition Systems: Explaining Variation in the Implementation of New Regimes. Law & Contemporary Problems. 79: 85-122.

Parcu, Pier Luigi, and Vincenzo Visco Comandini, 2017. On Some Historical Contributions of the Postal and Delivery Conferences. In this volume.

Sparrow, Malcolm K. 2011. The Regulatory Craft – Controlling Risks, Solving Problems, and Managing Compliance. The Brookings Institution.

On Some Historical Contributions of the Postal and Delivery Conference

Pier Luigi Parcu and Vincenzo Visco Comandini

1 Introduction

This paper explores market and regulatory themes developed and debated at CRRI (now EUI-CRRI) Conferences on Postal and Delivery Economics.[1] These include efficiency of postal operators, universal service and financing, third-party access to postal networks, and full market opening (FMO). Thematic development has relied on the cross-fertilizing mixture of participants that includes academics, national postal providers, mail competitors, express courier services, regulators, law scholars, consultants, technology experts and unions.

Since the first Conference in 1990, postal scholars have noted similarities between postal services and telecommunications. Both industries provide connection to consumers through local networks with increasing returns and constant returns to scale for non-delivery functions. However, unlike fixed telecommunication services (TLC), entry into local postal delivery arises because facilities are mainly not fixed, nor are their costs sunk. In addition, legacy national postal operators, called universal service providers (USPs), are always under a universal service obligation (USO) across the country, often at a uniform price.

These characteristics of postal services have led to a debate regarding whether they are natural monopolies, since competition with a natural monopoly need not generate efficient outcomes. Panzar (2001) argued that, where the USP is the only

[1]All works cited in this paper are published in the books produced after each of the 25 Conferences: the year identifies the book and the chapter's author(s).

P.L. Parcu (✉)
European University Institute, RSCAS, Florence School of Regulation, Communications & Media, Florence, Italy
e-mail: pierluigi.parcu@eui.eu

V. Visco Comandini
Department of Management and Law, University of Rome "Tor Vergata", Rome, Italy

P.L. Parcu et al. (eds.), *The Contribution of the Postal and Delivery Sector*, Topics in Regulatory Economics and Policy, https://doi.org/10.1007/978-3-319-70672-6_2

service provider, it is presumptively efficient as a supplier since there are no comparable alternatives. Several empirical studies presented at the Conference examined USP efficiency. Debate at the Conference often focused on whether prices of inputs, particularly labor, are exogenous, since USP employees usually enjoy some sort of wage premium. Other studies presented at the Conference found misallocation of inputs. Presently, in European countries, end-to-end competition tends to align prices to costs, thus pushing USPs toward greater efficiency in order to defend market shares. However, USPs' search for efficiency is made more difficult by letter mail volume declines, since it requires to continuously adjust delivery networks and to discuss it with employees, unions and citizens, unwilling to accept dramatic changes. Also the traditional demand analysis of the sector, primarily focused on price setting, has been affected by e-substitution and, over the years, shifted to much more complex strategies for USPs competing with digital media.

FMO has been implemented in the European Union. The US (and, to some extent, the UK and New Zealand) have allowed competition for partial mail products while delivery remains a monopoly, *de jure* as in the US, or *de facto* as in the UK. Michael Crew and Paul Kleindorfer (2011) stress the need for its gradual and controlled implementation. They said that while FMO seems to produce only modest benefits, the risks of either destructive competition, or USO provision being underfinanced, are very high. Unbundling postal services delivery may facilitate competition under non-discriminatory access conditions and access prices corresponding to the efficient component pricing rule (ECPR). However, both theory and market reality show that the implied regulatory tasks required to implement competition through access are far from trivial.

Section 2 summarizes the main findings relating to the USP efficiency, while Sect. 3 focuses on demand. Section 4 analyzes issues relating to USOs, Sect. 5 investigates network access and its replicability, and Sect. 6 discusses FMO. As usual, the conclusions follow.

2 Natural Monopoly, Returns to Scale and Efficiency in Postal Services

Are postal services a natural monopoly? Estrin and De Meza (1991) defined postal services as an "*unnatural*" and unsustainable monopoly. Final delivery may be a natural monopoly but not other services in the value chain (Panzar 1991). Moreover, competitors may provide delivery in densely populated areas, leaving the USP unprofitable rural delivery and threatening the financial sustainability of USO provision. However, for Lenard (1993), even if the cost of postal services is sub-additive over the relevant output range, entry need not be restricted. He mentions the case of unregulated third class mail in the US, where competitors have lower costs compared to USPS. Campbell (1997) questioned USP's postal monopoly by observing successful market openings in airlines and similar industries.

Economies of scale are very important in relation to postal services (Rogerson and Takis 1993; Bradley and Colvin 1995; Cazals et al. 1997). Rogerson and Takis were the first to estimate cost elasticities by function in the US, showing that final delivery costs are rather inelastic in relation to volumes (elasticity of around 0.35), thus supporting the natural monopoly hypothesis for this crucial function. Conversely, parameter estimations of elasticities for sorting and transport resulted in values close to 1. Cohen et al. (1993) and Roy (1999) shows that unit costs fall as the percentage of a postman's drop points receiving at least one item each day increases. Roy also found that the number of items delivered to each drop point affects delivery costs more than the population density.

These findings may explain why end-to-end competitors in Italy and Spain hold a higher market share than in other member States. These countries have significant densely populated urban areas with tall buildings and relatively few single homes. In such areas competition is fierce because scale economies are low. This allows a competitor to provide services in all of the densely-populated areas, despite low per-capita volumes. In Italy, two main private competitors provide national delivery to almost 70–75% of final recipients, allowing them to jointly hold 20–25% of non-urgent presorted business mail (Visco Comandini and Mazzarella 2011).

Roy's approach gave rise to other papers such as d'Alcantara and Amerlynk (2006) that showed the importance of scale economies on a USP's financial vulnerability following market liberalization. Using data from different countries on volume, unit costs, cost shares and elasticities by function, Cohen et al. (2002) found that higher per capita volumes in a country imply a higher cost elasticity for delivery. Countries facing low per capita volumes provide services at higher unit costs. Thus, their USPs are more vulnerable to competition and at higher risk of a "graveyard spiral" (higher costs – higher prices – lower volumes). Cohen et al. (2010) found that 78% of USO net costs in the US are fixed.

Cost elasticities differ when the volumes go up or down. Cazals et al. (2005) showed that, in the UK, delivery costs rise approximately in line with delivery points, and that cost elasticities for delivery in rural areas are lower than in urban areas. Delivery costs thus crucially depend on the volume per delivery point, implying that delivery costs decline less rapidly than volumes. Bradley et al. (2012) found that the short-run elasticity of delivery time with respect to volume is nearly one third less (0.07 vs. 0.11) when volume declines than when it rises. This asymmetry may be explained by the need to avoid harm to postal workers and unions (Sauber 2002).

Today, the main challenge for USPs is the ability to adjust their delivery networks to falling volumes. For a USP, a more flexible delivery network results in greater efficiency and financial health. The success of the Express Courier industry is largely due to the providers' ability to daily reshape their delivery routes, a strategy that USPs cannot normally apply equally well because of both USO and Political economy issues, in particular, union power. Nevertheless, several European USPs (Royal Mail, La Poste, PostNL, Deutsche Post/DHL) regularly update the postman's delivery rounds, on average four times a year.

Other USPs do not respond as quickly to volume drops. Unions are often able to restrict the USP in workforce adjustments to reduced volume (Harman et al. 2010).

Cross-country efficiency benchmarking has been improved over the years. Cohen et al. (1997) measured the productivity for 21 USPs; Meschi et al. (2015) discussed parametric and semi-parametric methods for measuring the efficiency of postal operators. Gori and Pierleoni (2013) compared the efficiency of some USPs across the Atlantic. USPS ranked second in efficiency after Deutsche Post by applying the maximum likelihood parametric estimate with exogenous variables, for the authors the most reliable technique.

Internal benchmarking can also measure USP efficiency. The Conference has provided many econometric studies (among them Christensen et al. 1993; Pimenta et al. 2000; Maruyama and Takanobu 2002; Moriarty et al. 2006; Horncastle et al. 2006; Cazals et al. 2012), showing evidence of local inefficiencies. Harman et al. (2010) showed that stochastic frontier estimates can be erroneous if union constraints are not properly considered, especially at the local level. Regulators are very interested in this measurement, since it helps in giving advice on the most appropriate productivity factor (X) to apply to price caps; Treworgy et al. (1999) provide an international comparison. Rodriguez (2013) observed that PostComm fixed Royal Mail's X at 3% based on Moriarty et al.'s (2006) internal efficiency estimates.

Crew and Kleindorfer (2001) called for a more realistic approach towards X-efficiency. They introduced an institutional constraint in their model (2002), where both the regulator and the regulated firms can achieve a mutually sustainable commitment. However, this is not a trivial task (Toledano 2010). She observed that in theoretical models of regulation, the incumbent typically keeps secret as much information as possible in order to preserve its informational rents. Her experience on both sides of the regulator-regulated firm game suggests that cooperation with the regulator may be the best strategy for the incumbent, especially if the regulator has alternative sources of information. Hearn (2008) lists many types of accounting data and procedures that postal regulator needs to assess a USP's efficiency and create a level competitive playing field.

3 Demand

Demand is the key driver for keeping USOs viable. In almost all countries, mail volumes grew following GDP trends until around the end of the 1990s, but began to drop after the mid-2000s. Several time series and cross sectional demand models were presented at the Conferences (among them Nankervis et al. 1999; Cazals and Florens 2002; Cazals et al. 2011; Fève et al. 2012; Jarosik et al. 2013; Bzhilyanskaya et al. 2015). Some models included recipients demographic and the economic characteristics (Wolak 1997; Plum 1997; Colin and Davis 1999; Berthélémy and Toledano 2000; DeRycke et al. 2001; Koppe and Bosch 2006), or the economic downturn (Martin et al. 2013). Results may differ for total traffic or specific letter segments such as transactional mail (De Donder et al. 2015). Rodriguez (2013) found that aggregating products into large classes risks biasing coefficient estimates, since each postal product has its own demand function, which includes substitution with others and that anyway quality of service exhibits very little effect.

Own price elasticities are generally low (0.2–0.5); cross sectional estimates are slightly higher. Visco Comandini et al.'s (2009) review of prior studies found that, despite market liberalization, price elasticities tend to decline over time or at least remain stable. This evidence contrasts with standard economic intuition, but is consistent with Brennan and Crew's (2014) finding that if high elasticity users adopt electronic substitutes, remaining postal customers will have less elastic demand.

Nikali (1995, 1999, 2008, 2011) first investigated e-substitution. Adding logistic diffusion curves of competing media (such as telefax or broadband) to his demand models, he showed that e-substitution cannot be captured by a single proxy variable. Other studies (Trinkner and Grossman 2006; Meschi et al. 2011; Elkela and Nikali 2013; Elkela et al. 2015) observed that e-substitution, being correlated to the other traditional explanatory variables, requires a much more sophisticated treatment in demand models. Jimenez et al. (2006a, b) found that US households with an older head receive much more mail than younger households do, the latter being more willing to use electronic substitutes. As B2C is the largest part of mail traffic and the population in industrialized countries is aging, he concluded that e-substitution will reduce mail volumes on average 3% until 2025. Cazals et al. (2008) used a Monte Carlo simulation to show that structural breaks in econometric models to capture step changes in e-substitution increase forecast error. To overcome this problem, Fève et al. (2012) adopted a Bayesian forecast model that combined time series with other source of information on changes in the recipient's preferences and ability to use new technologies.

4 USO Extent and Financing

Free mail delivery for final recipients was adopted worldwide after Rowland Hill's postal reform in 1840 (Crew and Kleindorfer 1991). This allowed booming growth of postal service from both a dramatic reduction in transaction costs and the exploitation of substantial network externalities. Felisberto et al. (2006) proposed a controversial recipient's delivery charge to realign USO's costs and benefits. There are concerns with this policy option, since it risks destroying network externalities, thus lowering senders' willingness to pay.

Postal researchers have long stressed the need to reshape the USO under liberalized markets. Haldi and Merewitz (1997) and Cohen et al. (2000) were among the first to discuss the benefits of relaxing service standards for priority mail, since such a measure could significantly lower (fixed) costs in high cost routes. Robinson et al. (2015) analyzed the effect discontinuing Saturday delivery. Brennan and Crew (2014) showed that falling demand reduces the ability of a USP to fund the USO, suggesting either government support or making USO less demanding.

Governments, in times of severe public deficit constraints, are unwilling to finance the USO through subsidies. In Europe, public transfers to firms under FMO are always carefully scrutinized by the European Commission, since they constitute State aid (Fratini and Filpo 2006; Eccles 2011). Consequently, lowering quality or reducing the number of delivery days per week appears necessary to deal with the volume drop due to competition and e-substitution. However, politics matters, since Post offices, in particular, are a network that plays an implicit institutional role in connecting rural areas with the main towns.[2] National and European legislators are charged with defining the most appropriate USOs in the interest of consumers and citizens, but these interests often conflict directly with enhancing USP efficiency (Cigno et al. 2010). Some countries set minimum geographical density for post offices or require a political decision when the USP wants to close financially unsustainable rural facilities.

Campbell (2010), analyzing the history of the USO in the U.S., showed that political actors are reluctant to enter into any serious reform. Cohen et al. (2008) showed that post office mail distribution in the US and in Italy, in contrast to pharmacies or bank counters, can hardly be considered rational. In rural areas it follows neither income nor population, but instead is adjusted to local government's boundaries.

The Conference provided important contributions on the relation between USO breadth and efficiency, some of them attempting to measure the USO's net welfare effect (Crew and Kleindorfer 2009; De Donder et al. 2010; Jaag et al. 2014). Pearsall and Trozzo (2011), evaluated demand effects when some quality characteristics of the USO (like speed) are reduced. As this body of work found that USO's specification changes affect their costs more than demand, those changes become the main policy for allowing a USP to break even. For customers, reliability has increasingly become more important than speed, which today is supplied by USPs through USO priority mail products. High speed USO regulated products require high-cost dedicated networks, and the exploitation of economies of scale, which are at risk due to e-substitution.

To ascertain whether FMO may endanger USO financing. European and National Regulators have prescribed the measurement of the economic burden due to USO (Crew and Kleindorfer 2001). Many papers have contributed to the debate on the most appropriate methods for this kind of evaluation (among them Rodriguez et al. 1999; Cremer et al. 2000; Panzar 2001; Jaag et al. 2009; Cohen et al. 2010; Bradley et al. 2009; Carlslake et al. 2014). This led to consensus on the profitability approach, calculating the USO net cost as the difference in a USP's profits when charged with a USOs and its profits were it freed from the USO. This method was adopted by the third European directive.

[2] "The Postal Service shall have as its basic function the obligation to provide postal services to bind the Nation together through the personal, educational, literary, and business correspondence of the people" (39 U.S. C. §101(a)).

These contributions did not consider the compensation fund envisaged by the third European Directive as a possible tool for USO financing. The compensation fund, so far put in place only in Poland, does not seem to be viable in other member States (Fratini 2016). Serious implementation difficulties include defining its tax base (who should pay for it), and its tax rate (which should neither distort competition nor push competitors out of the market). The third Directive defined the tax base those non-USO services viewed from the customer's perspective as interchangeable with USO services (Eccles 2011). It defined USOs as "dynamically evolving", but this could lead the USO product boundary, if widely defined, to inevitably overlap with almost all existing and future non-USO deregulated postal products.

Finally, one important issue concerning the USO has been discussed in depth by the Conference participants: International cross-border mail, which is subject to UPU rules. A long list of contributions criticized the present institutional framework for its capability to distort prices (among them, Walsh 2000; Campbell 1993, 2001, 2016; Harford and Eitan 2004; Campbell et al. 2012) but a commonly accepted solution appears far from being easy to find.

5 Network Access and Replicability

A main contribution at the Conferences was a series of papers by Crew and Kleindorfer on access to the postal network (1995, 2000, 2002, 2010, 2011, 2012). They called for prudence in transferring findings about other regulated sectors to the postal industry, as postal entry and access problems are idiosyncratic. Okholm et al. (2015) and Parcu and Silvestri (2017) reached a similar conclusion with respect to comparisons with telecoms.

In the US, upstream competition has been adopted since the '80s through worksharing discounts and regulatory schemes based on the ECPR. Postal scholars (Panzar 1993; Cohen et al. 2006; Billette de Villemeur et al. 2004, 2006; De Donder et al. 2006) generally favored, with *caveats*, this regulatory framework. Crew and Kleindorfer (2002) argued that the standard approach to ECPR assumes a single-product world, which is implausible in postal services, because every delivery area constitutes a different product with different cost characteristics. They proposed, instead, an ECPR where access prices are set for specific delivery zones. This solution eliminated subsidies that would otherwise promote inefficient entry, including use of the USP's facilities for downstream access at rates that do not cover the marginal cost. In their view, zonal pricing was a necessary tool for a USP to compete with end-to-end competitors applying selective by-pass strategies.

The ECPR is intended to limit access to postal networks to only efficient entrants, i.e., those able to operate at a costs not higher than the USP. Market experience shows that this goal is quite hard to reach. In the UK, upstream and first level (i.e., incoming sorting centers) downstream access prices make end-to-end competition virtually nonexistent (Dudley et al. 2009), while access traffic accounts for nearly half of the volumes delivered by the USP (Rodriguez 2013).

This evidence suggest that once end-to-end competition is in place, a full access regime is unfeasible and, *vice versa*, when the latter is adopted, the former becomes uneconomic, as shown by the British experience. Crew and Kleindorfer (2010) explained that if the discount on full price is higher than avoided cost, a potential end-to-end entrant will instead purchase access because it is subsidized by the excessive discount. In Crew and Kleindorfer (2011), they presented a theorem on the superiority of access, showing that it is preferable compared to end-to-end competition.

Considering that postal facilities are almost certainly not economically sunk, network replicability has been discussed at the Conference. In contrast to the last mile wired connection in telecoms, final postal delivery networks are technically, but not necessarily economically, replicable. However, under FMO, regulators have scrutinized other elements of the postal infrastructure, since some ancillary services run by the USP may be needed by alternative operators to compete for delivery. These services include access to a PO Box, a postcode database, changes of address, and 'return to sender'. For such services, the public interest relies more on ensuring interoperability than overcoming a bottleneck. Suggestions provided by papers at the Conference move towards a mixture of ex-ante soft regulation, creating incentives for commercial agreements in which the regulator intervenes only if there are disputes.

Panzar (2002) was the first to identify PO Boxes as being a major problem for competition. Customers who receive their mail at PO Boxes are unwilling to duplicate it in order to get competitor's mail at another PO Box. Under such circumstances, an efficient access charge, equal to the end-to-end service price less the per unit USP's cost savings (i.e., the per unit PO Box service USP's contribution to its overhead costs) may be the solution.

Fratini et al. (2010), analyzing experiences in Sweden and France, noted that the problem is organizational. A USP can insert its mail into the customer's PO Box located within the PO before opening hours, but competitors willing to reach the same PO Box need to inject their mail outside the PO. This requires a commercial agreement since the mixture of avoided and additional activities are not the same in all localities. The authors favored a reciprocal, de-averaged two-part tariff as implemented in France and Germany, where the fixed part reflects billing and the cost of acceptance, and the variable part the costs of conveying mail from the point of acceptance to the PO and its deposition in the PO Box.

The USP manages postcode database and can change codes unilaterally. The problem arises when changes in codes occur, which are unilaterally decided by the incumbent who is willing to change their delivery units. This imposes costs on competitors who are willing to print and sort their mail to obtain worksharing discounts (Dieke and Scholermann 2008). The recipients' address database is another valuable information tool. The USP can regularly enter changes of address, while competitors can do the same only partially. The Swedish experience shows that a consortium maintaining the database and providing access for its members (all postal providers), may solve this technical problem as long as it doesn't become an instrument of collusion.

An additional access problem arises with undelivered registered mail in countries, like Italy, where registered mail represents a significant share of revenues (almost 20–30% for both USP and competitors). Once the first or the second delivery attempt fails, the mail is sent back to either a PO (if the service is run by the USP), or to a facility where the addressee can collect it. While competing facilities for obtaining registered mail can coexist in urban areas, duplication of such facilities in rural areas is likely to be uneconomic. In Italy, competitors are presently discussing with the regulator AGCOM (n. 651/16/CONS consultation document) whether they could access USP's POs for customer pickup of undelivered registered mail. As this mainly relates to rural POs with low mail traffic, availability through a cost plus criterion seems reasonable. Such access, by adding activities that are otherwise not performed, may (marginally) increase the USP's revenues for financing the USO.

6 Market Liberalization

In Europe the decision to liberalize the market was taken in the late 1990s, when postal volumes were growing. However, it was implemented only in 2011 in a different market environment. Harmonization of efficiency, commercialization, and healthy provision of the USO became nearly impossible (Toledano 2013). In some member States, end-to-end competition increased choices for customers and lowered prices for large bulk mailers, but retail consumers of USO products faced higher prices. While competition aligns prices to costs, it can have redistributive consequences: in the example, large customers were better off, but single-piece retail customers worse off.

However, the main difficulty was that FMO was to be applied to a rapidly declining market. With lower volumes, it increased the difference between markets (non-urgent bulk mail) where competition is fierce, and markets (single-piece USO products) where the USP is the only, often loss making, provider. After FMO, some member States (Germany, the Netherlands, Poland, UK, the Scandinavian countries, and others, France for parcels only) have restricted USO products to single piece items being accepted at POs or put into the mailbox, but excluded items accepted at sorting centers. Conversely, France and Italy preferred to maintain a larger USO area for mail that includes some bulk products.

The lack of harmonized rules on bulk mail USO products across member States inevitably affects competitive conditions in both national and cross-border markets. Some problems include asymmetric VAT exemptions (Dietl et al. 2011; Walsh 2011), relevant market definitions (Plum and Schwarz-Schilling 2000; Wojtek and Zauner 2012), and customers' choices in multisided postal markets (Boldron et al. 2009).

Rodriguez (2013) pointed out that FMO implies a shift from ex ante price regulation to ex-post regulation through competition law, in particular ascertaining whether USPs abuse their dominant position by contravening Article 102 of the

TFEU. The three key parameters in the postal sector are stand-alone costs, average avoidable costs, and long-run average incremental costs (LRIC), which are needed to verify whether the incumbent abuses in pricing. This is a difficult exercise to implement, since there are no clear and unambiguous methods for determining whether postal costs are fixed, partially fixed or fully variable. In several competition law cases, the USP claims that delivery costs are almost entirely fixed (thus, LRIC are low), while competitors and antitrust authorities try to challenge this view. Especially for USO products, cross-subsidies between products are, at least partially, inevitable.

Crew and Kleindorfer (2011) called FMO in Europe a train that has left the station, since member States are often puzzled in their attempt to cope simultaneously with end-to-end delivery and access price regimes. They insisted that access should be enlarged from just worksharing discounts to services that are provided at POs, implying a revision of make-or-buy decisions for both the USP and competitors. A USP might use its market power to keep competitors out by restricting access, but this behavior counter-productively reduces volumes. Smith and Vogel (2010) and Wojtek (2015) showed that, in the US and to a lesser extent in Europe, pure competition is increasingly evolving into new hybrid forms, where USPs outsource some logistical activities or cooperate with express courier companies to sell or deliver (in rural areas) their products.

7 Conclusions

In the postal industry fundamental economic and social themes, like the origin and extent of the monopoly, boundaries of universal service obligations, conditions of access to the legacy network, and the process of liberalization, are linked to policy and regulatory choices. The series of Conferences organized, and the books edited, by Michael Crew and Paul Kleindorfer, have explored all these themes with open minds and intellectual independence, significantly contributing to the shaping of the policies and, ultimately, to the evolution of the industry.

To introduce or strengthen competition, the postal industry has to find a new path. The industry may turn towards a more complicated facility sharing framework. The question of whether end-to-end competition is viable or if the postal sector will be brought back to monopoly of the delivery network, looms larger. At the same time, new forms of intermodal competition are developing rapidly, not just between mail and other communication media, but also between different delivery options such as parcel lockers (for parcels) and PO Boxes (for mail).

In today's postal sector, e-substitution is the Mozart's Don Giovanni *guest of stone*, relentlessly changing incentives for all of the industry's players. Market experience shows that, historically, incumbents reacted vigorously to competition, but traditional denial of access should probably be reconsidered. This change of direction could have deep consequences in the near future for both the regulatory structure of the postal sector and its specific antitrust dimension. These are all good topics for future Conferences.

References

Berthélémy, F., Toledano, J. (2000) *In France, mail goes where the money and business are*. In: M. Crew and P. Kleindorfer (Eds) **Current directions in Postal Reform**, Kluwer Academic Publishers: New York

Billette de Villemeur, E., Cremer, H., Roy, B., Toledano, J. (2004) *Access and (non-) uniform pricing in the postal sector*. In: M. Crew and P. Kleindorfer (Eds) **Competitive transformation of the Postal and Delivery Sector**, Kluwer Academic Publishers: New York

Billette de Villemeur, E., Cremer, H., Boldron, F., Roy, B. (2006) *Nonlinear pricing and worksharing in the postal market*. In: M. Crew and P. Kleindorfer (Eds) **Liberalization of the Postal and Delivery Sector**, Edward Elgar: Cheltenham

Boldron, F., Cremer, H., De Donder, P., Joram, D., Roy, B. (2009) *Network externalities and the USO: a two-sided market approach*. In: M. Crew and P. Kleindorfer (Eds) **Progress in the Competitive Agenda in the Postal and Delivery Sector**, Edward Elgar: Cheltenham

Bradley, M., Colvin, J. (1995) *An econometric model of postal delivery*. In: M. Crew and P. Kleindorfer (Eds) **Commercialization of Postal and Delivery Services: National and International Perspectives**, Kluwer Academic Publishers: New York

Bradley, R., Burns, P., Houpis, G. (2009) *Costing elements of the universal service*. In: M. Crew and P. Kleindorfer (Eds) **Progress in the Competitive Agenda in the Postal and Delivery Sector**, Edward Elgar: Cheltenham

Bradley, M., Colvin, J., Perkins, M. (2012) *Do volume increases and decreases have the same effect on labor hours?* In: M. Crew and P. Kleindorfer (Eds) **Multi-modal Competition and the Future of Mail**, Edward Elgar: Cheltenham

Brennan, T., Crew, M. (2014) *Gross substitutes versus marginal substitutes: implications for market definition in the postal sector*. In: M. Crew and T. Brennan (Eds) **The Role of the Postal and Delivery Sector in a Digital Age**, Edward Elgar: Cheltenham

Bzhilyanskaya, L., Cigno, M., Pearsall, E. (2015) *A branching AIDS model for estimating U.S. postal price elasticities*. In: M. Crew and T. Brennan (Eds) **Postal and Delivery Innovation in the Digital Economy**, Springer Verlag: New York

Campbell, J. (1993) *The future of the Universal Postal Union*. In: M. Crew and P. Kleindorfer (Eds) **Regulation and the Nature of Postal and Delivery Services**, Kluwer Academic Publishers: New York

Campbell, J. (1997) *The Roots of Deregulation: Why Aviation and Telecommunications But Not the Post Office?* In: M. Crew and P. Kleindorfer (Eds) **Managing Change in the Postal and Delivery Industries**, Kluwer Academic Publishers: New York

Campbell, J. (2001) *Reforming the Universal Postal Union*. In: M. Crew and P. Kleindorfer (Eds) **Future Directions in Postal Reform**, Kluwer Academic Publishers: New York

Campbell, J. (2010) *Historical development of a universal service obligation in the United States*. In: M. Crew and P. Kleindorfer (Eds) **Heightening Competition in the Postal and Delivery Sector**, Edward Elgar: Cheltenham

Campbell, J. (2016) *Quantifying the Distortive Effects of UPU Terminal Dues*. In: M. Crew and T. Brennan (Eds) **The Future of the Postal Sector in a Digital World**, Springer Verlag: New York

Campbell, J., Dieke, A., Zauner, M. (2012) *UPU terminal dues: losers and winners*. In: M. Crew and P. Kleindorfer (Eds) **Multi-modal Competition and the Future of Mail**, Edward Elgar: Cheltenham

Carlslake, I., Houpis, G., Strobel, C. (2014) *The net cost of the USO under the profitability cost approach: implications of the labor market condition for the net cost calculation*. In: M. Crew and T. Brennan (Eds) **The Role of the Postal and Delivery Sector in a Digital Age**, Edward Elgar: Cheltenham

Cazals, C., Florens, J.P. (2002) *Econometrics of Mail Demand: A Comparison between Cross-Section and Dynamic data*. In: M. Crew and P. Kleindorfer (Eds) **Postal and Delivery Services. Delivering on Competition**, Kluwer Academic Publishers: New York

Cazals, C., de Rycke, M., Florens, J.P., Rouzaud, S. (1997) *Scale economies and natural monopoly in the postal delivery: comparisons between parametric and non-parametric specifications*. In: M. Crew and P. Kleindorfer (Eds) **Managing Change in the Postal and Delivery Industries**, Kluwer Academic Publishers: New York

Cazals, C., Florens, J.P., Soteri, S. (2005) *Delivery costs for postal services in the UK: some results on scale economies with panel data*. In: M. Crew and P. Kleindorfer (Eds) **Regulatory and Economic Challenges in the Postal and Delivery Sector**, Kluwer Academic Publishers: New York

Cazals, C., Florens, J.P., Rodriguez, F., Soteri, S. (2008) *Forecast uncertainty in dynamic models: an application to the demand for mail*. In: M. Crew and P. Kleindorfer (Eds) **Competition and Regulation in the Postal and Delivery Sector**, Edward Elgar: Cheltenham

Cazals, C., Florens, J., Veruete-McKay, L., Rodriguez, F., Soteri, S. (2011) *UK letter mail demand: a content-based time-series analysis using overlapping market survey statistical techniques*. In: M. Crew and P. Kleindorfer (Eds) **Reinventing the Postal Sector in an Electronic Age**, Edward Elgar: Cheltenham

Cazals, C., Dudley, P., Florens, J.P., Jones, M. (2012) *A panel data analysis of inefficiency and heterogeneity in the postal sector*. In: M. Crew and P. Kleindorfer (Eds) **Multi-modal Competition and the Future of Mail**, Edward Elgar: Cheltenham

Christensen, D., Christensen, L., Guy, C., O'Hara, D. (1993) *US Postal Service Productivity: Measurement and Performance*. In: M. Crew and P. Kleindorfer (Eds) **Regulation and the Nature of Postal and Delivery Services**, Kluwer Academic Publishers: New York

Cigno, M., Monaco, D., Pearsall, E. (2010) *An operational measure of the cost of the universal service as cross-subsidy*. In: M. Crew and P. Kleindorfer (Eds) **Heightening Competition in the Postal and Delivery Sector**, Edward Elgar: Cheltenham

Cohen, R., Ferguson, W., Xenakis, S. (1993) *Rural Delivery and Universal Service Obligation: A Quantitative Investigation*. In: M. Crew and P. Kleindorfer (Eds) **Regulation and the Nature of Postal and Delivery Services**, Kluwer Academic Publishers: New York

Cohen, R., Chu, E., Ferguson, W., Xenakis, S. (1997) *A cross sectional comparison and analysis of productivity for 21 national postal administrations*. In: M. Crew and P. Kleindorfer (Eds) **Managing Change in the Postal and Delivery Industries**, Kluwer Academic Publishers: New York

Cohen, R., Ferguson, W., Waller, J., Xenakis, S. (2000) *Universal service without monopoly*. In: M. Crew and P. Kleindorfer (Eds) **Current directions in Postal Reform**, Kluwer Academic Publishers: New York

Cohen, R., Pace, C., Robinson, M., Scarfiglieri, G., Scocchera, R., Visco Comandini, V., Waller, J., Xenakis, S. (2002) *A Comparison of the Burden of Universal Service in Italy and the United States*. In: M. Crew and P. Kleindorfer (Eds) **Postal and Delivery Services. Pricing, Productivity, Regulation and Strategy**, Kluwer Academic Publishers: New York

Cohen, R., Robinson, M., Waller, J., Xenakis, S. (2006) *Worksharing: how much productive efficiency? At what cost? At what price?* In: M. Crew and P. Kleindorfer (Eds) **Progress Toward Liberalization of the Postal and Delivery Sector**, Springer: New York

Cohen, R., Di Paola, L., Sheehy, R., Visco Comandini, V. (2008) *The distribution of Post Offices in Italy and the United States*. In: M. Crew and P. Kleindorfer (Eds) **Competition and Regulation in the Postal and Delivery Sector**, Edward Elgar: Cheltenham

Cohen, R., McBride, C., Panzar, J. (2010) *The cost of the USO in the United States*. In: M. Crew and P. Kleindorfer (Eds) **Heightening Competition in the Postal and Delivery Sector**, Edward Elgar: Cheltenham

Colin, M., Davis, E. (1999) *Mail goes where the money is: a study of rural mail delivery in the U.S.* In: M. Crew and P. Kleindorfer (Eds) **Emerging Competition in Postal and Delivery Services**, Kluwer Academic Publishers: New York

Cremer, H., Grimaud, A., Laffont, J. (2000) *The cost of universal service in the postal sector*. In: M. Crew and P. Kleindorfer (Eds) **Current directions in Postal Reform**, Kluwer Academic Publishers: New York

Crew, M., Kleindorfer, P. (1991) *Rowland Hill's contribution as an economist*. In: M. Crew and P. Kleindorfer (Eds) **Competition and innovation in postal services**, Springer Science: New York

Crew, M., Kleindorfer, P. (1995) *Pricing in Postal Services under Competitive Entry*. In: M. Crew and P. Kleindorfer (Eds) **Commercialization of Postal and Delivery Services: National and International Perspectives**, Kluwer Academic Publishers: New York

Crew, M., Kleindorfer, P. (2000) *Liberalization and the Universal Service Obligation in Postal Service*. In: M. Crew and P. Kleindorfer (Eds) **Current directions in Postal Reform**, Kluwer Academic Publishers: New York

Crew, M., Kleindorfer, P. (2001) *A critique of the Theory of Incentive Regulation: Implications for the Design of Performance Based Regulation for Postal Service*. In: M. Crew and P. Kleindorfer (Eds) **Future Directions in Postal Reform**, Kluwer Academic Publishers: New York

Crew, M., Kleindorfer, P. (2002) *Balancing Access and the Universal Service Obligation*. In: M. Crew and P. Kleindorfer (Eds) **Postal and Delivery Services. Delivering on Competition**, Kluwer Academic Publishers: New York

Crew, M., Kleindorfer, P. (2009) *Service quality, price caps, and the USO under entry*. In: M. Crew and P. Kleindorfer (Eds) **Progress in the Competitive Agenda in the Postal and Delivery Sector**, Edward Elgar: Cheltenham

Crew, M., Kleindorfer, P. (2010) *Access and the USO under full market opening*. In: M. Crew and P. Kleindorfer (Eds) **Heightening Competition in the Postal and Delivery Sector**, Edward Elgar: Cheltenham

Crew, M., Kleindorfer, P. (2011) *Competitive strategies under FMO and intermodal competition*. In: M. Crew and P. Kleindorfer (Eds) **Reinventing the Postal Sector in an Electronic Age**, Edward Elgar: Cheltenham

Crew, M., Kleindorfer, P. (2012) *Non-linear pricing, volume discounts and the USO under entry*. In: M. Crew and P. Kleindorfer (Eds) **Multi-modal Competition and the Future of Mail**, Edward Elgar: Cheltenham

d'Alcantara, G., Amerlyink, B. (2006) *Profitability of the universal service postal provider under entry with economies of scale in collection and delivery*. In: M. Crew and P. Kleindorfer (Eds) **Progress Toward Liberalization of the Postal and Delivery Sector**, Springer: New York

De Donder, P., Cremer H, Dudley, P., Rodriguez, F. (2006) *A welfare analysis of price controls with end-to-end and access services*. In: M. Crew and P. Kleindorfer (Eds) **Liberalization of the Postal and Delivery Sector**, Edward Elgar: Cheltenham

De Donder, P., Cremer, H., Dudley, P., Rodriguez, F. (2010) *Welfare and profit implications for changes in service specification within the universal service*. In: M. Crew and P. Kleindorfer (Eds) **Heightening Competition in the Postal and Delivery Sector**, Edward Elgar: Cheltenham

De Donder, P., Cremer, H., Rodriguez, F., Soteri, S., Tobias, S. (2015) *Analyzing the prospect for transactional mail using a sender-recipient framework*. In: M. Crew and T. Brennan (Eds) **Postal and Delivery Innovation in the Digital Economy**, Springer Verlag: New York

DeRycke, M., Marcy, S., Florens, J. (2001) *Mail Use by Firms*. In: M. Crew and P. Kleindorfer (Eds) **Future Directions in Postal Reform**, Kluwer Academic Publishers: New York

Diecke, A., Scholermann, S. (2008) *Postcodes in competitive postal markets: is there a case for regulation?* In: M. Crew and P. Kleindorfer (Eds) **Competition and Regulation in the Postal and Delivery Sector**, Edward Elgar: Cheltenham

Dietl, H., Jaag, C., Lang, M., Lutzenberger, M., Trinkner, U. (2011) *Impact of VAT exemptions in the postal sector on competition and welfare*. In: M. Crew and P. Kleindorfer (Eds) **Reinventing the Postal Sector in an Electronic Age**, Edward Elgar: Cheltenham

Dudley, P., Agar, S., Mautino, L., Duncan, F.F. (2009) *Competition through downstream access in the UK postal sector: the first four years*. In: M. Crew and P. Kleindorfer (Eds) **Progress in the Competitive Agenda in the Postal and Delivery Sector**, Edward Elgar: Cheltenham

Eccles, R. (2011) *State funding and cost sharing of the USO under the 2008 EU postal services directive*. In: M. Crew and P. Kleindorfer (Eds) **Reinventing the Postal Sector in an Electronic Age**, Edward Elgar: Cheltenham

Elkela, K., Nikali, H. (2013) *Social media challenges the entire postal industry*. In: M. Crew and P. Kleindorfer (Eds) **Reforming the Postal Sector in the Face of Electronic Competition**, Edward Elgar: Cheltenham

Elkela, K., Nikali, H., Rokkanen, P. (2015) *Proactive surveys and calculations for meeting declining mail volumes*. In: M. Crew and T. Brennan (Eds) **Postal and Delivery Innovation in the Digital Economy**, Springer Verlag: New York

Estrin, S., De Meza, D. (1991) *Delivering Letter: Should it be Decriminalized?* In: M. Crew and P. Kleindorfer (Eds) **Competition and innovation in postal services**, Springer Science: New York

Felisberto, C., Finger, M., Friedli, B., Krähenbühl, D., Trinkner, U. (2006) *Pricing the last mile in the postal sector*. In: M. Crew and P. Kleindorfer (Eds) **Progress Toward Liberalization of the Postal and Delivery Sector**, Springer: New York

Fève, F., Florens, J.P., Veruete-McKay L., Soteri, S., Rodriguez, F. (2012) *Uncertainty and projections of the demand for mail*. In: M. Crew and P. Kleindorfer (Eds) **Multi-modal Competition and the Future of Mail**, Edward Elgar: Cheltenham

Fratini, A., (2016) *Compensation Fund Under EU Law: A Suitable Solution for the Postal Market?* In: M. Crew and T. Brennan (Eds) **The Future of the Postal Sector in a Digital World**, Springer Verlag: New York

Fratini, A., Filpo, F. (2006) *The new EC framework for state aid to public service and the postal sector: where we do stand now?* In: M. Crew and P. Kleindorfer (Eds) **Progress Toward Liberalization of the Postal and Delivery Sector**, Springer: New York

Fratini, A., Roy, B., Vantomme, J. (2010) *Access to infrastructure and service elements in the postal service*. In: M. Crew and P. Kleindorfer (Eds) **Heightening Competition in the Postal and Delivery Sector**, Edward Elgar: Cheltenham

Friedli, B., Jaag, C., Krähenbühl, D., Nielsen, O., Pihl, S., Trinckner, U. (2006) *Consumer preferences and last mile pricing in the postal sector*. In: M. Crew and P. Kleindorfer (Eds) **Liberalization of the Postal and Delivery Sector**, Edward Elgar: Cheltenham

Gori, S., Pierleoni, M. (2013) *Efficiency analysis postal operators: comparison between the United States and Europe*. In: M. Crew and P. Kleindorfer (Eds) **Reforming the Postal Sector in the Face of Electronic Competition**, Edward Elgar: Cheltenham

Haldi, J., Merewitz, L. (1997) *Cost and returns from delivery to sparsely settled rural areas*. In: M. Crew and P. Kleindorfer (Eds) **Managing Change in the Postal and Delivery Industries**, Kluwer Academic Publishers: New York

Harford, G., Eitan, W. (2004) *International postal arrangement, trade, and competition law*. In: M. Crew and P. Kleindorfer (Eds) **Competitive transformation of the Postal and Delivery Sector**, Kluwer Academic Publishers: New York

Harman, G., Koevoets, W., Requeio, A., van der Merwe, E., Waghe, N. (2010) *The effect of falling volumes on traditional efficiency analysis*. In: M. Crew and P. Kleindorfer (Eds) **Heightening Competition in the Postal and Delivery Sector**, Edward Elgar: Cheltenham

Hearn, J. (2008) *The accounting implications of the EU's third postal directive*. In: M. Crew and P. Kleindorfer (Eds) **Competition and Regulation in the Postal and Delivery Sector**, Edward Elgar: Cheltenham

Horncastle A., Jevons, D., Dudley, P., Thanassoulis, E. (2006) *Efficiency analysis of delivery offices in the postal sector using stochastic frontier and data envelopment analysis*. In: M. Crew and P. Kleindorfer (Eds) **Liberalization of the Postal and Delivery Sector**, Edward Elgar: Cheltenham

Jaag, C., Koller, M., Trinkner, U. (2009) *Calculating the cost of the universal service obligation: the need for a global approach*. In: M. Crew and P. Kleindorfer (Eds) **Progress in the Competitive Agenda in the Postal and Delivery Sector**, Edward Elgar: Cheltenham

Jaag, C., Trinkner, U., Uotila, P. (2014) *Regulation and the burden of the net cost resulting from the Universal Service Obligation*. In: M. Crew and T. Brennan (Eds) **The Role of the Postal and Delivery Sector in a Digital Age**, Edward Elgar: Cheltenham

Jarosik, M., Nankervis, J., Pope, J., Soteri, S., Veruete-McKay, L. (2013) *Letter demand in the UK: some new evidences and review of econometric analysis over the past decade*. In: M. Crew and P. Kleindorfer (Eds) **Reforming the Postal Sector in the Face of Electronic Competition**, Edward Elgar: Cheltenham

Jimenez, L., Diakova, E., Szeto, C. (2006a) *Generational analysis of mail users*. In: M. Crew and P. Kleindorfer (Eds) **Progress Toward Liberalization of the Postal and Delivery Sector**, Springer: New York

Jimenez, L., Owsiany, A., Szelo, C. (2006b) *Scenarios of mail receipt patterns across generations*. In: M. Crew and P. Kleindorfer (Eds) **Liberalization of the Postal and Delivery Sector**, Edward Elgar: Cheltenham

Koppe, P., Bosch, C. (2006) *Microanalyses of mail demand drivers for large business customers*. In: M. Crew and P. Kleindorfer (Eds) **Liberalization of the Postal and Delivery Sector**, Edward Elgar: Cheltenham

Lenard, T. (1993) *Comments on C. Rogerson and W. Takis Economies of Scale and Scope and Competition in Postal Services*. In: M. Crew and P. Kleindorfer (Eds) **Regulation and the Nature of Postal and Delivery Services**, Kluwer Academic Publishers: New York

Martin, V., Paterson, C., Nikali, H., Li, Q. (2013) *Dynamic letter volume models: how does an economic downturn affect substitution propensities?* In: M. Crew and P. Kleindorfer (Eds) **Reforming the Postal Sector in the Face of Electronic Competition**, Edward Elgar: Cheltenham

Maruyama, S., Takanobu, N. (2002) *The Productivity Analysis of Postal Services: A Global Comparison of Technical Efficiency and Total Factor Productivity*. In: M. Crew and P. Kleindorfer (Eds) **Postal and Delivery Services. Delivering on Competition**, Kluwer Academic Publishers: New York

Meschi, M., Cherry, M., Pace, C., Petrova, M. (2011) *Understanding the impact of e-substitution on letter mail volumes: a multicountry panel study*. In: M. Crew and P. Kleindorfer (Eds) **Reinventing the Postal Sector in an Electronic Age**, Edward Elgar: Cheltenham

Meschi, M., Pierleoni, M., Gori, S. (2015) *Advanced semi-parametric and parametric methods to assess efficiency in the postal sector*. In: M. Crew and T. Brennan (Eds) **Postal and Delivery Innovation in the Digital Economy**, Springer Verlag: New York

Moriarty, R., Yorke, S., Harman, G., Cubbin, J., Meschi, M., Smith, P. (2006) *Economic Analysis of the Efficiency of Royal Mail Units and the Implications for Regulatory Policies*. In: M. Crew and P. Kleindorfer (Eds) **Liberalization of the Postal and Delivery Sector**, Edward Elgar: Cheltenham

Nankervis, J., Carlslake, I., Rodriguez, F. (1999) *How important have price and quality of services been to mail volume growth?* In: M. Crew and P. Kleindorfer (Eds) **Emerging Competition in Postal and Delivery Services**, Kluwer Academic Publishers: New York

Nikali, H. (1995) *Replacement of Letter Mail by Electronic Communications by the year 2010*. In: M. Crew and P. Kleindorfer (Eds) **Commercialization of Postal and Delivery Services: National and International Perspectives**, Kluwer Academic Publishers: New York

Nikali, H. (1999) *The Future of Targeted Communication in Finland*. In: M. Crew and P. Kleindorfer (Eds) **Emerging Competition in Postal and Delivery Services**, Kluwer Academic Publishers: New York

Nikali, H. (2008) *Substitution of letter mail*. In: M. Crew and P. Kleindorfer (Eds) **Competition and Regulation in the Postal and Delivery Sector**, Edward Elgar: Cheltenham

Nikali, H. (2011) *Does the level of price elasticity change with the progression of substitution?* In: M. Crew and P. Kleindorfer (Eds) **Reinventing the Postal Sector in an Electronic Age**, Edward Elgar: Cheltenham

Okholm, H., Moeller, A., Basilisco, B. (2015) *Regulatory developments in post and telecommunications: a tale of two industries*. In: M. Crew and T. Brennan (Eds) **Postal and Delivery Innovation in the Digital Economy**, Springer Verlag: New York

Panzar, J. (1991) *Is Postal Service a Natural Monopoly?* In: M. Crew and P. Kleindorfer (Eds) **Competition and innovation in postal services**, Springer Science: New York

Panzar, J. (1993) *Competition, Efficiency, and the Vertical Structure of Postal Services*. In: M. Crew and P. Kleindorfer (Eds) **Regulation and the Nature of Postal and Delivery Services**, Kluwer Academic Publishers: New York

Panzar, J. (2001) *Funding universal service obligations: the cost of liberalization*. In: M. Crew and P. Kleindorfer (Eds) **Future Directions in Postal Reform**, Kluwer Academic Publishers: New York

Panzar, J. (2002) *Reconciling Competition, Downstream Access, and Universal Service in Postal Markets*. In: M. Crew and P. Kleindorfer (Eds) **Postal and Delivery Services. Delivering on Competition**, Kluwer Academic Publishers: New York

Parcu, P.L., Silvestri, V. (2017) *Lessons from the Postal Sector to Telecommunications and Vice Versa*. In: M. Crew, P. L. Parcu and T. Brennan (Eds) **The Changing Postal and Delivery Sector**, Springer Verlag: New York

Pearsall, E., Trozzo, C. (2011) *Evaluating the demand effects of reductions in the frequency of delivery service*. In: M. Crew and P. Kleindorfer (Eds) **Reinventing the Postal Sector in an Electronic Age**, Edward Elgar: Cheltenham

Pimenta, A., Santos, R., Lagoa, S. (2000) *Technical Efficiency in CCT-Correios de Portugal*. In: M. Crew and P. Kleindorfer (Eds) **Current directions in Postal Reform**, Kluwer Academic Publishers: New York

Plum, M. (1997) *The challenge of electronic competition: empirical analysis of substitution effects on the demand for letter services*. In: M. Crew and P. Kleindorfer (Eds) **Managing Change in the Postal and Delivery Industries**, Kluwer Academic Publishers: New York

Plum, M., Schwarz-Schilling, C. (2000) *Defining postal markets: an antitrust perspective*. In: M. Crew and P. Kleindorfer (Eds) **Current directions in Postal Reform**, Kluwer Academic Publishers: New York

Robinson, M., Klingenberg, J., Haller, A., Trinkner, U. (2015) *Estimating the financial impact on discontinuing Saturday delivery of letter and flats in the U.S.* In: M. Crew and T. Brennan (Eds) **Postal and Delivery Innovation in the Digital Economy**, Springer Verlag: New York

Rodriguez, F. (2013) *The postal economy in the UK and Rutgers CRRI conferences since 1990: a review of developments and economic themes*. In: M. Crew and P. Kleindorfer (Eds) **Reforming the Postal Sector in the Face of Electronic Competition**, Edward Elgar: Cheltenham

Rodriguez, F., Smith, S., Storer, D. (1999) *Estimating the cost of the universal service obligation in postal services*. In: M. Crew and P. Kleindorfer (Eds) **Emerging Competition in Postal and Delivery Services**, Kluwer Academic Publishers: New York

Rogerson, C., Takis, W. (1993) *Economies of scale and scope and competition in postal services*. In: M. Crew and P. Kleindorfer (Eds) **Regulation and the Nature of Postal and Delivery Services**, Kluwer Academic Publishers: New York

Roy, B. (1999) *Techno-Economic Analysis of the Costs of Outside Work in Postal Delivery*. In: M. Crew and P. Kleindorfer (Eds) **Emerging Competition in Postal and Delivery Services**, Kluwer Academic Publishers: New York

Sauber, J. (2002) *U.S. Postal Service Collective Bargaining: Is the Grass Greener on the Other Side of Interest Arbitration?* In: M. Crew and P. Kleindorfer (Eds) **Postal and Delivery Services. Delivering on Competition**, Kluwer Academic Publishers: New York

Smith, P. Vogel, P. (2010) *A team of rivals: collaboration between United States Postal Service and UPS*. In: M. Crew and P. Kleindorfer (Eds) **Heightening Competition in the Postal and Delivery Sector**, Edward Elgar: Cheltenham

Toledano, J. (2010) *Foreword: Enduring questions and some lessons from practice*. In: M. Crew and P. Kleindorfer (Eds) **Heightening Competition in the Postal and Delivery Sector**, Edward Elgar: Cheltenham

Toledano, J. (2013) *Status of the postal service twenty years after the Green Paper: a Franco--European perspective*. In: M. Crew and P. Kleindorfer (Eds) **Reforming the Postal Sector in the Face of Electronic Competition**, Edward Elgar: Cheltenham

Treworgy, D., Sharkey, T., Fronk, D., Kehoe, M. (1999) *Price-Cap Regulation in the Postal Sector. An International Comparison and Assessment*. In: M. Crew and P. Kleindorfer (Eds) **Emerging Competition in Postal and Delivery Services**, Kluwer Academic Publishers: New York

Trinkner, U., Grossman, M. (2006) *Forecasting Swiss mail demand*. In: M. Crew and P. Kleindorfer (Eds) **Progress Toward Liberalization of the Postal and Delivery Sector**, Springer: New York

Visco Comandini, V., Mazzarella, F. (2011) *Competition and regulation in the Italian postal market*. In: M. Crew and P. Kleindorfer (Eds) **Reinventing the Postal Sector in an Electronic Age**, Edward Elgar: Cheltenham

Visco Comandini, V., Lintell, M., Gori, S., Pierleoni, M., Tisdahl, B. (2009) *Postal price elasticities and intermedia competition: a multisided market approach*. In: M. Crew and P. Kleindorfer (Eds) **Progress in the Competitive Agenda in the Postal and Delivery Sector**, Edward Elgar: Cheltenham

Walsh, T. (2000) *Globalization, posts, and the Universal Postal Union*. In: M. Crew and P. Kleindorfer (Eds) **Current directions in Postal Reform**, Kluwer Academic Publishers: New York

Walsh, T., (2011) *The economics of postal payment channels and EU postal VAT*. In: M. Crew and P. Kleindorfer (Eds) **Reinventing the Postal Sector in an Electronic Age**, Edward Elgar: Cheltenham

Wojtek, R. (2015) *E-commerce and the return of unwanted goods: a case of cooperation among providers of postal and non-postal parcel services*. In: M. Crew and T. Brennan (Eds) **Postal and Delivery Innovation in the Digital Economy**, Springer Verlag: New York

Wojtek, R., Zauner, M. (2012) *Postal price regulation in a competitive environment*. In: M. Crew and P. Kleindorfer (Eds) **Multi-modal Competition and the Future of Mail**, Edward Elgar: Cheltenham

Wolak., F. (1997) *Changes in the household-level demand for postal delivery services from 1986 to 1994*. In: M. Crew and P. Kleindorfer (Eds) **Managing Change in the Postal and Delivery Industries**, Kluwer Academic Publishers: New York

Michael Crew's (and Paul Kleindorfer's) Scholarly Contributions to the CRRI Postal Conferences, 1990–2012

Timothy J. Brennan

1 Introduction

Michael Crew held the first Rutgers University Center for Research in Regulated Industries (CRRI) Conference on Postal and Delivery Economics on July 22, 1990 in Rugby, England. Since that first conference, he organized 23 more, the last of them with Pier Luigi Parcu and the Florence School of Regulation (FSR). This 25th was the first organized in his absence.

Michael's contributions to organizing an international community of practitioners drawn from traditional postal operators, regulators, and academics that share an interest in postal economics are as enormous as they are obvious. This community has produced 24 collections of proceedings that Michael and others co-edited as well as other research papers and presentations. This article summarizes papers Michael and Paul Kleindorfer contributed to and presented at these conferences. The focus here is on their joint contributions to the first 20 of them. Their collaboration ended with Paul's untimely death. With one exception (Crew and Geddes 2014) I was the co-author with Michael of his contributions to subsequent conferences, and those are summarized in our contribution to the 24th conference (Crew and Brennan 2017).

The books for the first 20 conferences include 22 papers Michael co-authored with Paul[1]; one also included Marc Smith as a co-author (see box below). A few of

[1] Paul was also co-editor of the books of all of the postal conferences through 2012. After Paul died in August of 2012, Michael asked me to join him as co-organizer of the conference, co-editor of the book, and co-author of papers presented at the 2013–2016 conferences and included in the associated conference volumes.

T.J. Brennan (✉)
School of Public Policy, UMBC, Baltimore, MD, USA
e-mail: brennan@umbc.edu

P.L. Parcu et al. (eds.), *The Contribution of the Postal and Delivery Sector*, Topics in Regulatory Economics and Policy, https://doi.org/10.1007/978-3-319-70672-6_3

the books had two contributions while a few had none. These chapters did not encompass all of their contributions to postal economics. They published a separate book (Crew and Kleindorfer 1992), an article in the *Journal of Regulatory Economics* (Crew and Kleindorfer 1998), and four chapters in a book they edited with James Campbell (Crew et al. 2008).

All chapters except 1997 by Michael Crew and Paul Kleindorfer, and all books edited by Crew and Kleindorfer. References to these in the text are of the form "CK year" or just the year.

1991a. "The Economics of Rowland Hill," in *Competition and Innovation in Postal Services*. Dordrecht, the Netherlands: Kluwer Academic Publishers.

1991b. "Peak-loads and Postal Services," in *Competition and Innovation in Postal Services*. Dordrecht, the Netherlands: Kluwer Academic Publishers.

1994. "Pricing in Postal Service under Competitive Entry," in *Commercialization of Postal and Delivery Services: National and International Perspectives*, Dordrecht, the Netherlands: Kluwer Academic Publishers.

1997 (with Marc Smith). "Peak-loads and Postal Services: Some Implications of Multi-State Production", in *Managing Change in the Postal and Delivery Industries*, Dordrecht, the Netherlands: Kluwer Academic Publishers.

2000a. "Cost Estimation and Economically Efficient Prices: Some Consequences of Error," in *Current Directions in Postal Reform*. Dordrecht, the Netherlands: Kluwer Academic Publishers.

2000b. "Liberalization and the Universal Service Obligation in Postal Service," in *Current Directions in Postal Reform*. Dordrecht, the Netherlands: Kluwer Academic Publishers.

2001a. "A Critique of the Theory of Incentive Regulation," in *Future Directions in Postal Reform*. Dordrecht, the Netherlands: Kluwer Academic Publishers.

2001b. "Whither the USO under Competitive Entry: A Microstructure Approach," in *Future Directions in Postal Reform*. Dordrecht, the Netherlands: Kluwer Academic Publishers.

2002a. "Two-Tier Pricing under Liberalization," in *Postal and Delivery Services: Pricing, Productivity, Regulation and Strategy*. Dordrecht, the Netherlands: Kluwer Academic Publishers.

2002b. "Putty-Putty, Putty-Clay or Humpty-Dumpty? Universal Service under Entry," in *Postal and Delivery Services: Pricing, Productivity, Regulation and Strategy*. Dordrecht, the Netherlands: Kluwer Academic Publishers.

2002c. "Balancing Access and Universal Service Obligations," in *Postal and Delivery Services: Delivering on Competition*. Dordrecht, the Netherlands: Kluwer Academic Publishers.

(continued)

(continued)

2003a. "Access and the USO for Letters and Parcels," in *Competitive Transformation of the Postal and Delivery Sector*. Dordrecht, the Netherlands: Kluwer Academic Publishers.
2003b. "Developing Policies for the Future of the United States Postal Service," in *Competitive Transformation of the Postal and Delivery Sector*. Dordrecht, the Netherlands: Kluwer Academic Publishers.
2005. "Competition, Universal Service and the Graveyard Spiral," in *Regulatory and Economics Changes in the Postal and Delivery Sector*. Dordrecht, the Netherlands: Kluwer Academic Publishers.
2006a. "The Welfare Effects of Entry and Strategies for Maintaining the USO in the Postal Sector," in *Progress toward Liberalization of the Postal and Delivery Sector*. New York: Springer Publishing.
2006b. "Approaches to the USO under Entry," in *Liberalization of the Postal and Delivery Sector*. Cheltenham, UK: Edward Elgar Publishing.
2008. "Regulation and the USO under Entry," in *Competition and Regulation in the Postal and Delivery Sector*. Cheltenham, UK: Edward Elgar Publishing.
2009. "Service Quality, Price Caps and the USO under Entry," in *Progress in the Competitive Agenda in the Postal and Delivery Sector*. Cheltenham, UK: Edward Elgar Publishing.
2010. "Access and the USO under Full Market Opening," in *Heightening Competition in the Postal and Delivery Sector*. Cheltenham, UK: Edward Elgar Publishing.
2011. "Competitive Strategies under FMO and Intermodal Competition," in *Reinventing the Postal Sector in an Electronic Age*. Cheltenham, UK: Edward Elgar Publishing.
2012. "Nonlinear Pricing, Volume Discounts and the USO under Entry," in *MultiModal Competition and the Future of Mail*. Cheltenham, UK: Edward Elgar Publishing.
2013. "Privatization of Postal Operators: Old Arguments and New Realities," in *Reforming the Postal Sector in the Face Electronic Competition*. Cheltenham, UK: Edward Elgar Publishing.

Crew and Kleindorfer's (hereafter CK) first paper (1991a) celebrated Sir Rowland Hill, the creator of the pre-paid stamp system for postal service. However, CK used this discussion of Rowland's nineteenth century contributions to identify themes they would feature in their subsequent research. Among these were the harms from having postal service provided by a state monopoly, where, quoting Hill, its managers "are, therefore, uninfluenced by the ordinary motives to enterprize and good management."

A second theme was that prices should be geographically uniform only for intercity distribution between what we might today call central processing offices—where Hill found that costs were largely insensitive to distance—with differing cost-based rates from these central offices to city, suburban, and rural locations. CK described Hill's adoption of uniform Penny Post pricing as a pragmatic compromise driven by transaction costs in a sender-prepaid system. CK found that Hill properly employed economic measures based on consumer surplus and economic efficiency to assess the benefits of his postal reform—and that new ideas from outsiders, particularly with regard to opening markets to competition, merit consideration.

CK's contributions followed those themes. Section 2 provides a short overview of the methods CK used in these papers. Section 3 surveys CK's applications, generally in their earlier papers, of theories from regulatory economics to postal system practices in general, focusing on peak-load pricing, responses to competition, and the relevance of price cap regulation.[2]

Most of CK's other contributions are tied to the analysis of whether the universal service obligation (USO) can be sustained when POs face competition. Section 4 presents this work in a number of categories: liberalization generally, pricing responses, access by entrants to PO services less amenable to competition, and regulatory responses to entry in light of the USO. Section 5 summarizes two papers on policies going forward for the United States Postal Service (USPS), the still-partial monopoly state-owned US PO, and the merits of privatization—the latter a major theme of Michael's work until his untimely death. Section 6 offers concluding remarks.

2 Methods

As all of Michael's contributions to these conferences were written with Paul, one would be tempted to speculate as to which methods were more likely to be primarily Michael's contributions and which are predominantly Paul's. In light of how close they were as colleagues and friends, it makes no sense to do anything other to attribute all of the content of all of the papers to both Michael and Paul.

Three of the 22 contributions here are largely textual in nature: the aforementioned appreciation of Sir Rowland Hill's contributions and two later discussions (CK 2003b, CK 2013) on the future of the USPS facing entry and advocating privatization. Most of their papers, however, mixed textural description of a regulatory or business issue with a mathematical model to provide rigorous insight and support of their conclusions. Models were included in the text; or relegated to an appendix—with the appendix sometimes as long as the main paper.

In some papers, CK added numerical examples to illustrate possibilities, for example of the "graveyard spiral" (CK 2000b), where following entry a PO has to raise rates to maintain the USO, inviting more entry, leading to higher PO rates, and

[2]Classifying CK's contributions into categories likely risks understating overlapping perspectives.

eventually driving the PO out of business. These examples were not calibrated to match real-world conditions. CK never included econometrics to estimate parameters or to test hypotheses. Whether the absence of econometrics was because of data inadequacy or a methodological aversion, I do not know.[3]

3 Regulatory Theory and Postal Operations

3.1 (Nominally) Peak-Load Pricing

One of CK's most important contributions to regulatory economics, prior to the first postal conference, was their analysis of peak-load pricing (Crew and Kleindorfer 1986). CK's showed how pricing should be set when one technology is profitable only when used all the time and the other used only at peak. In CK 1991b, a precursor to their 1997 contribution with Marc Smith, CK argued that the problem of charging for first class mail, which requires expensive night staffing to meet delivery time expectations relative to second class mail, was formally equivalent to the peak-load pricing problem, which entails using higher average cost facilities to meet demand at peak periods. CK applied this framework to show that prices for different classes of mail, whether defined by more rapid delivery or demand fluctuations over time, will differ based on the different costs of the technologies used to provide services at normal volumes and for the added peak volumes. They concluded by examining how prices would vary among mail classes when a competitive sorting service is available.

CK returned to this theme in CKS 1997 (S for co-author Marc Smith). This chapter clarified characterizing the choice between first class and second class mail as a peak-load pricing problem. The difference between first and second class mail is not that the demand for one or the other varies over time. Rather, the difference is one of quality—one gets delivered faster than the other and requires more expensive overtime night services to do so.

CKS 1997 focused on how increased automation of different stages of postal processing, such as barcode sorting and sequencing of mail for delivery, changes marginal cost and thus the appropriate differential pricing of first and second class mail. CKS found, as did CK 1991b, that the volume of one service can affect the marginal cost of providing the other service because at various times they are processed together due to limits on the ability to sort mail at low cost times. This is why first class mail requires night processing, which occurs when processing has to be shifted from low cost daytime to high cost nighttime.

[3]I share this apparent aversion but most of the economics profession have the opposite view.

3.2 *Postal Pricing, Without and With Entry*

CK 1994 examined pricing when POs face competition through worksharing—having others provide stages in the process of delivering mail, such as sorting or bulk transporting that the PO might normally do—all the way to "downstream access", in which the PO provides only local delivery. The common theme was that the PO faces competition in upstream stages, but retains a monopoly over local delivery.

One could regard the price a PO charges mailers who use worksharing as either a direct fee or a discount from its full service price. CK 1994 employed the "discount" interpretation, endorsing (with a qualification below) a discount equal to the PO's long run marginal cost (LRMC) of providing the sorting or other service that mailers obtain through worksharing. As they point out, this is equivalent to an "efficient component pricing rule" (ECPR), a price that preserves the PO's profits were it to workshare. This has the benefit of deterring entry by worksharing firms who have higher costs than the PO for their services.

On the other hand, ECPR is equivalent to the PO pricing its worksharing service at LRMC and selling the bundle of its other services at the full markup over marginal cost, which may not be efficient if a regulator allows a high markup. Moreover, inefficient entrants can be socially beneficial, in that competition from them can reduce prices below monopoly levels (Economides and White 1995). While CK seemed to suggest that a workshare discount above ECPR subsidizes competitive worksharing, they acknowledged ECPR does not lead to efficient prices subject to covering the PO's cost ("Ramsey pricing;" see Baumol and Bradford 1970). The worksharing discount and the PO's price of other services should reflect markups based on demand elasticities. CK 2002a provided further elaboration of this theme.

CK 2000 differed from CK's other contributions in that it concerned measurement. Optimal pricing requires that the regulator setting price have accurate information on marginal cost and demand elasticity; CK 2000 were concerned with the former. They found that USPS's method then used to determine marginal cost was based on estimates of elasticities of how a mail service affects a cost "driver" (think "input") and the elasticity of cost with respect to that "driver." CK then discussed how to calculate "incremental cost" from product-specific fixed cost and total variable cost. The Ramsey price of a service based on marginal cost might not cover its average incremental cost, inviting accusations of cross-subsidization.

3.3 *Incentive Regulation: Price Caps*

CK 2001a focused on price cap regulation (PCR). Under PCR, a regulated firm's price is divorced from actual cost and profit. The cap is allowed to increase with inflation but required it to decrease over time due to a prescribed productivity factor based on the premise that PCR will lead to productive efficiency and higher profits (Brennan 1989). However, a regulator cannot commit to PCR over the long term because of political pressure if profits are high and, if profits are low, legal requirements that a regulated firm be given a fair opportunity to earn a just reasonable return.[4]

CK modeled a regulator's inability to commit and how a regulated firm might manipulate it. If the regulator can commit to a profit or loss sharing rule in the event of a rate hearing, a firm making high profits may wastefully incur costs to avoid a subsequent rate hearing. Notably, this chapter was published 5 years before the U.S. enacted a law requiring USPS to adopt PCR for its market dominant services.[5]

4 Competition and Sustainability of the USO

Reviewing the titles of the CK contributions shows that the dominant theme is how and whether to sustain the postal universal service obligation as markets are opened to entry. Justifications for a USO may include a civic right to communicate, including for those with little income or who cost a great deal to serve, access to emergency and educational communication, and the network externality that occurs when the value of a communications medium, such as mail, to any user increases when that medium has more users. The importance of a USO forces attention on sustaining it, especially when a PO's revenues shrink because of competition and diversion to electronic alternatives.

4.1 General Effects of Liberalization and the "Graveyard Spiral"

CK 2000b, their earliest contribution on USO issues at the postal conferences, examined the tension between competition and sustaining the USO, a theme they elaborated on in 12 subsequent articles. Entrants would focus on low cost areas, competing away the PO's profits that support the USO in high cost areas.[6] CK defended a USO not by invoking network externalities or the civic value of communication, but by claiming that high transaction costs preclude destination-dependent prices in a sender-pays environment that would require a PO to sort

[4]*Bluefield Water Works v. West Virginia Public Service Commission*, 262 U.S. 679, 683 (1923).
[5]Postal Accountability and Enhancement Act (PAEA), P.L. 109-435 (2006).
[6]CK referred to this here and in CK 2001b as an adverse selection problem, but there is no asymmetric information—both the incumbent and entrant know prices, costs, and their difference. However, the effect is the same, as the inability to charge cost-based prices is akin to having no knowledge about costs.

letters by who they serve and who they do not. Presorting can facilitate entry by reducing these costs, making credible a threat to take away customers from the PO's most profitable routes.

CK applied a model from an earlier article (Crew and Kleindorfer 1998) to analyze situations when entry makes it impossible for the PO to continue funding the USO.[7] They analyzed two other ways to fund the USO after entry beside the status quo. The first, using general revenues, would make entry less of a funding threat. The welfare gains from increased entry have to be weighed against the welfare loss from increasing taxes to provide these revenues. CK found that although having entrants contribute to the USO could makes entry less of a threat to the USO, it also discourages and reduces the benefits of competition from entry.

They then discussed what they called the "graveyard spiral": how entry would force a PO to raise price, inviting more entry, leading to more price increases and eventual unsustainability of the USO. CK 2005 numerically simulated this possibility, where the PO offers entrants access to its delivery network under a variety of rates, customers have different levels of brand loyalty to the PO, and with separate business and residential mail customers. CK 2000b introduced the possibility of responding to entry by reducing the scope of the USO, but they did not analyze that in detail. CK 2001b provided numerical simulations with a continuum of consumer types to illustrate cases where the graveyard spiral would occur.

4.2 Strategic Responses to Entry

CK 2001b concluded with a recommendation that the incumbent PO be given pricing flexibility to respond to entry. CK did not elaborate on whether this is feasible, given the transaction costs mentioned in CK 2000b that preclude region or customer-specific pricing. CK expressed the concern, especially for a state-owned or regulated PO, that cutting price following entry by cutting price can, has and would be construed as predatory pricing funded by cross-subsidization from a PO's captive markets. Such a reaction is predictable despite the optimality of setting margins lower for product or regions as demand becomes more elastic. Entry typically increases elasticity of demand because consumers can turn to entrants if the PO increases its price.

CK 2002b examined this with a model of the USO akin to a requirement in a number of regulated sectors (telecommunications, electricity) that the PO is the default provider of service to small customers that entrants choose not to serve. They noted that while flexible pricing is better for sustaining the incumbent and for entry than uniform pricing, regulators may not allow it. If not, and even if so, the risk of a graveyard spiral and the absence of likely significant innovations from

[7] CK 2000b call this "unsustainable entry," but funding of the USO is what becomes unsustainable.

entrants led CK here to recommend that one should "proceed with deliberation in deregulating this sector".

More recently, CK 2011 took on the entry issue, now called "full market opening" (FMO)—the elimination of any reserved areas (that is, services) under which the incumbent PO would retain a monopoly—while recognizing electronic diversion.[8] They modeled the threat from entry as a loss of scale economies, as distinct from a loss of service to low-cost customers. The focus on scale economies followed from the possibility that an entrant would provide end-to-end service, bypassing the PO's delivery network, not just upstream services through worksharing. Because of scale economies in delivery, bypass would never be economical, but could occur if the PO does not or cannot adjust its access charge to prevent bypass.

A similar result does not apply when either upstream markets lack similar scale economies or where entrants can differentiate themselves. CK recommended that a PO focus on offering upstream entrants access to its delivery network. CK also recommended that a PO consider outsourcing retailing postal services through independent franchises. Reducing quality, e.g., frequency of delivery, could encourage entry. Although CK did not use the phrase here, one could imagine a "graveyard spiral" driven by reducing quality as much as having to raise price to cover USO costs.

CK 2012 examined quantity discounts as a responses to entry. They concluded that quantity discounts can keep high volume users as customers, rather than losing them to entrants. Using numerical examples, they illustrated potential benefits from using quantity discounts to respond to entry, intermodal competition, and the threat of inefficient bypass. CK proposed the regulators may want to employ a "hands-off approach" and allow quantity discounts below the regulated price. These recommendations have been politically unpopular because high volume users would pay a lower average price than low volume users. But as entry and electronic diversion threaten the sustainability of USO funding, the influence of these objections to quantity discounts may fall.

4.3 Welfare, Entry and the USO

At the 2005 and 2006 postal conferences, CK presented papers analyzing welfare effects of entry with special attention to the USO. In the first of these (2006a), they began by observing that entry and electronic diversion that reduce a PO's scale economies, and shrinkage of the reserved area, threaten a PO's ability to fund the

[8]For the PO, the phrase "intermodal competition" may overstate the degree to which diversion to electronic communication depends on the relative prices of using broadband and using mail. If that diversion does not depend on relative prices, a PO may still possess market power, in that it would not lose much business to electronic communications only because it raises its price. But the PO still has a lower pool of potential profit to draw upon to fund its USO (Brennan and Crew 2014).

USO. Ruling out support from general revenues creates a complex tradeoff between liberalization and supporting the USO as currently constructed. POs could cut costs, but CK claimed that unions would object. They also posited that regulators are subject to political influence that precludes forcing regulated firms from acting efficiently.

Nonetheless, CK advocated pricing flexibility along with adding product lines. CK recognized that adding downstream access may not help with revenues if regulators restrict the PO's access prices.[9] CK also suggested relaxing USO service quality in high cost areas. CK employed a numerical simulation where entrants can set their own prices while the PO is required to maintain uniform prices, with demands for each influenced by a parameter reflecting brand loyalty. CK also modeled POs as having higher fixed costs than entrants because of the USO, and higher variable costs because of union contracts. Numerical simulations indicated that welfare is typically higher (a) the lower the entrant's markup over costs, (b) when bypass is not allowed, (c) if the PO has pricing flexibility, (d) the better the PO's information about entrants' costs, and (e) with reductions in USO delivery frequency in high cost regions when entrants can bypass the POs network in low cost areas.

CK 2006b examined the funding problem created when large mailers (outside the scope of the USO, or what CK called here the "social USO" or SUSO) take advantage of below-cost USO mailing rates in high-cost areas. CK rejected the possibility that technologies could feasibly allow charging large mailers higher rates to mail to or from high cost areas, because they could just buy stamps. Assuming a uniform price, they looked at designing a USO under entry with competition for large (business) customers. CK defined the USO (apart from uniform price) as proportional to the number of post offices per letter volume, reducing the costs of using a post office. The optimal USO just balances the marginal reduction in cost of using post offices with the fixed cost of adding them. If households are given more weight in the welfare calculation, one gets more post offices, and the markup to business customers and the price of stamps have to increase to pay for them.

4.4 Access and the USO

CK 2002c, CK 2003a, and CK 2010 directed attention to policies for POs to sell access to their local distribution networks to independent mail service providers. Access is important to entrants not just for those who want to participate in only

[9]Adding a product line in a competitive market will increase a POs ability to support the USO only if the PO has lower costs or competitive advantages in that new market. Entry into competitive markets by a regulated firm also creates risks of discrimination and cross-subsidization that distort competition in that market (Brennan 1987; Crew and Brennan 2015).

upstream sectors, but also for those who want to offer service to all but have distribution facilities in areas with low delivery costs per customer. In CK 2002c, they noted that but for monopoly, firms typically do not grant access to competitors.[10]

CK (2002c) discussed terms of access for letter mail. Preserving a PO's ability to maintain the USO would be promoted best with allowing access tariffs to vary by origin and destination zones, as delivery costs also vary across zones. Where the PO's delivery cost is less than the price of a stamp, the entrant should get a discount from the stamp price to pay for access, based upon ECPR. In high cost areas, there should be no discount at all, and thus no compensation for worksharing, because the stamp price is already too low relative to delivery costs and the required contribution to the USO.

CK 2003a extended the analysis to a PO delivering both mail and parcels. Unlike letter mail, the value of parcel shipping justifies location-specific pricing and thus provides more flexibility. CK foresaw the large growth in parcel delivery from electronic commerce. A USO for parcels, in CK's view, would require universal delivery but not uniform pricing. The uniform pricing constraint in the letters' USO, particularly for regions where the cost of delivery exceeds the PO's price, allows both final and access prices to move closer to the theoretical optimum.[11] CK discounted the possibility that a PO would discriminate against worksharing competitors in the quality of access service it supplies, although this appears to be because the price competitors pay for access is high enough to preserve the PO's profits were it to do the worksharing services itself.[12] PCR is worthwhile, but as an intermediate step toward liberalization and, presumably, deregulation.

CK 2010 returned to this topic 7 years later with full market opening (FMO). CK reiterated here a view expressed earlier that the PO was vulnerable to competition because, unlike telecommunications, postal delivery requires little sunk investment. By 2010, however, the primary threat to PO funding of the USO was not FMO but the Internet. CK modeled mail-based entrants rather than Internet users, with the assumption that there is some set of customers for whom entrants could not beat the PO's end-to-end stamp price. As in earlier papers, CK rejected giving a fixed discount to mailers who provide their own worksharing, and instead would offer a fixed markup over costs only as long as that does not lead to prices in excess of the cost of a stamp. Using a model similar to CK 2006b, CK calculated rates that maximize overall welfare with entry and rates that maximize welfare subject to the

---

[10]A US Supreme Court decision two years after this paper was published, *Verizon v. Trinko*, 540 U.S. 398 (2004), upheld this principle for regulated monopolies. This decision specifically declined to uphold an "essential facilities" doctrine that CK 2002c discussed.

[11]CK distinguished a "Delivery-Area Pricing" (DAP) rule from ECPR in that the former allows non-uniform pricing, which they claim the ECPR does not allow. This distinction is not clear, as ECPR rates would be non-uniform if the PO's LRMC of providing delivery-only varies by location.

[12]The incentive to discriminate arises when the regulated firm can charge a price above cost in the upstream market (Brennan 1987).

PO covering its costs, including USO costs. The technical appendix to CK 2010 warrants their conclusion that "the complexities of access pricing are so significant that the ability and benefits of regulators of intervening constructively in this process under competition are limited."

4.5 Regulatory Responses

CK 2008 and CK 2009 addressed regulatory approaches to sustain the USO following entry. CK 2008 began with three justification regulators could consider in maintaining USO funding: a PO's scale economies, scope economies, or brand loyalty. CK believed that these were somewhat true and would limit entry and render minimal the competitive threat to USO funding, but noted that USPS has lost parcel business to FedEx and UPS. Two more active regulatory policies would be to increase mail rates or reduce the USO. Both may be politically difficult, and the former may lead to the graveyard spiral. CK then mentioned increased operational efficiency and pricing flexibility. To the extent the greater PO efficiency comes about only because entry forces POs to reduce their prices, any potential gain in profits to support a USO may be dissipated. This leaves pricing flexibility, the benefits of which CK presented in CK 2001b, 2003a and 2006a.

With regard to how regulators would respond, CK argued that PCR is unlikely to be effective with a state-owned PO because of the absence of parties who profit from greater efficiency, that is, "residual claimants". This differed from CK 2001a, where they took issue with PCR because regulators lack the ability to commit not to revert to profit-based regulation. CK supported this assertion by modeling a state-owned firm as motivated by a weighted average of sales, wages (to please unions), and overall welfare, as long as costs are covered. In this setting, the firm may not act efficiently. Consequently, CK recommended that regulators adopt FMO, as competition will lead to efficiency, and that the PO be "commercialized" if not privatized, with executive compensation providing incentives to make profits and, therefore, to control cost.

In the following year, CK 2009 turned to the question of service quality—closeness of retail outlets, delivery times—under price caps. The multidimensional and stochastic nature of service quality makes it hard to regulate directly. Moreover, the stricter is a price cap, the lower is a regulated firm's return on investing in quality. CK described quality regulation as a three-stage cycle: (1) identify attributes setting standards and providing incentives, (2) monitoring compliance, penalize underperformance and reward performance above the standards based on the incentives set in (1), and (3) adjust standards and incentives based on the PO's performance.

CK 2009 applied the model in CK 2006b for determining optimal USO price, business customer markup and USO scope, adding in quality that is costly to supply but boosts demand as if price were reduced by a constant times the quality level. This does not reflect multidimensionality or the stochastic nature of quality (e.g., randomness in delivery times) or different consumer tastes for quality. Nevertheless, CK found it difficult to characterize optimal quality, not surprising as the basic model of monopoly does not say whether a monopolist will set quality above or below the welfare-maximizing level. CK then looked at integrating quality into PCR by allowing the firm to increase overall prices if it provides higher quality, recognizing that tying that increase to the gains in consumer surplus from higher quality would not be easy to do.

5 The Future of USPS

CK's assessed, 10 years apart (2003b, 2013), future prospects of and policies toward the postal sector. CK 2003b took aim at a "flawed business model" for USPS. USPS lacked flexibility to respond to entry, particularly regarding labor use. But even if it had that flexibility, CK asserted that the USPS lacked the organizational incentive to respond to entry because, as a state-owned enterprise (SOE) no one got the profits from better performance. Moreover, it could not go out of business, having a last-resort claim on taxpayer bailouts.[13] Specific problems CK identified were salary caps that inhibited hiring high quality managers, inability to offer new products and services, unavoidable labor costs, and funding the USO. Needed reforms included a commercial organization (ultimately privatization) with a board of directors, motivation to maximize profits, ability to control labor cost, and greater flexibility in pricing and product offerings, as well as alternative funding for the USO.

Little had changed when they revisited this issue in CK 2013, the last of their joint contributions to the postal conferences. CK advocated strongly for privatization so a PO can compete effectively in a sector increasingly featuring alternative means of communication. CK acknowledged that separation of corporate ownership from management limits efficiency incentives in private firms, public ownership can lead a PO to pursue social welfare, and both privately-owned and SOEs engage in wasteful rent-seeking. However, looking dynamically, an SOE is not only limited in its incentives but inevitably subject to political influence, not the least of which would involve complaints from competitors that the SOE is cross-subsidizing or underpricing competitive offerings.

CK inferred from this competition will push privatization. A first step, taken in New Zealand and elsewhere, would begin by setting up a corporate structure to be "judged on its profitability". Full privatization may be resisted because public ownership conveys rents that governments can use for assorted political ends, but electronic diversion reduces those rents (Brennan and Crew 2014). CK stated that

[13]Presciently, CK noted that USPS's major liability going forward was deferred retiree health care expenses, which at the time were an "off-balance-sheet item"—a situation that would change with PAEA, *supra* n. 5.

USPS will be in "disastrous shape" without the ability to respond with innovative prices and products that privatization uniquely affords. They admit that getting to privatization will not be easy, and the debate over privatization remains as intense as it was when CK 2013 was published.

6 Conclusion

Had Michael Crew, along with Paul Kleindorfer, done nothing on postal and delivery economics other than organize the first 20 of the postal conferences held by the Rutgers Center for Research in Regulated Industries, which Michael founded, their place in the Postal Economics Hall of Fame would be ensured. However, they went far beyond that. They were among the leading contributors—if not *the* leading contributors—to the theoretical analysis of postal pricing, regulation, entry, and the sustainability of the USO. The community of academics and practitioners they fostered will continue to learn from and build upon their work, with gratitude and astonishment at its breadth, depth, insight, and foresight.

Acknowledgments I am particularly grateful to Victor Glass, Jeremy Guenther and Menahem Spiegel at CRRI for their assistance in this project and to Pier Luigi Parcu, Marc Smith, Paula Gori, and participants in the 25th Conference. All errors remain my responsibility; we all wish that Michael Crew and Paul Kleindorfer were here to correct any errors and challenge my interpretations.

References

Baumol, William and David F. Bradford. 1970. "Optimal Departures from Marginal Cost Pricing." *American Economic Review* 60: 265-283.

Brennan, Timothy. 1987. "Why Regulated Firms Should Be Kept Out Of Unregulated Markets: Understanding the Divestiture in *U.S. v. AT&T*." *Antitrust Bulletin* 32: 741-93.

Brennan, Timothy. 1989. "Regulating by 'Capping' Prices," *Journal of Regulatory Economics* 1: 133-47.

Brennan, Timothy and Michael Crew. 2014. "Gross Substitutes vs. Marginal Substitutes: Implications for Market Definition in the Postal Sector." In Crew, Michael and Timothy Brennan (eds.), *The Role of the Postal and Delivery Sector in a Digital Age*. Cheltenham, UK: Edward Elgar: 1-15

Crew, Michael and Timothy Brennan. 2015. "Business Models: Some Implications for USPS." In Crew, Michael and Timothy Brennan (eds.), *Postal and Delivery Innovation in the Digital Economy*. New York: Springer: 1-15.

Crew, Michael and Timothy Brennan. 2017. "The Postal Accountability and Enhancement Act After 10 Years: Some Proposals for Reform." In Brennan, Timothy, Michael Crew and Pier Luigi Parcu (eds.), *The Changing Postal and Delivery Sector: Towards a Renaissance*. New York: Springer: 1-15.

Crew, Michael and R. Richard Geddes. 2014. "A Business Model for USPS." In Crew, Michael and Timothy Brennan (eds.), *The Role of the Postal and Delivery Sector in a Digital Age*. Cheltenham, UK: Edward Elgar: 16-27.

Crew, Michael and Paul Kleindorfer. 1986. *Economics of Public Utility Regulation*. Cambridge, MA: MIT Press.
Crew, Michael and Paul Kleindorfer. 1992. *The Economics of Postal Service*. Dordrecht, the Netherlands: Kluwer Academic Publishers.
Crew, Michael and Paul Kleindorfer. 1998. "Efficient Entry, Monopoly and the Universal Service Obligation in Postal Service." *Journal of Regulatory Economics* 14: 103-25.
Crew, Michael, James Campbell, and Paul Kleindorfer (Ed.). 2008. *Handbook of Worldwide Postal Reform*. Cheltenham, UK: Edward Elgar.
Economides, Nicholas and Lawrence J. White. 1995. "Access and Interconnection Pricing: How Efficient is the 'Efficient Component Pricing Rule'?" *Antitrust Bulletin* 40: 557-79.

DHL Express (Austria): Towards Legal Certainty on Article 9 and Applicable Obligations for Postal Service Providers

Alessandra Fratini

1 Introduction

This paper looks at the complex and disputed provision of the Postal Services Directive[1] dealing with authorizations in the postal sector (Article 9) and obligations that may be imposed on postal service providers against the recent and pending judgments of the Court of Justice, which are progressively clarifying its wording, context and objectives. In particular, it will assess the implications of the most recent *DHL Express (Austria)* judgment[2] for the other two cases that are pending in this field.

Time after time, postal service providers—specifically providers outside the scope of universal postal services—have challenged the requirements imposed or attached to their authorization at the national level, typically on the ground that obligations under the Postal Services Directive shall only apply to services falling within the scope of the universal service. These obligations may include requirements concerning the quality, availability and performance of the relevant services, financial contributions to the operational costs of the national regulatory authorities (NRAs) and to a compensation fund to help cover costs of the universal service obligation (USO), and complying with national labor conditions.

[1]Directive 97/67/EC of 15 December 1997 on common rules for the development of the internal market of Community postal services and the improvement of quality of service, OJ L 15, 21.1.1998, p. 14, as last amended by Directive 2008/6/EC of 20 February 2008 amending Directive 97/67/EC with regard to the full accomplishment of the internal market of Community postal services, OJ L 52, 27.2.2008, p. 3.

[2]Judgment of 16 November 2016, Case C-2/15, DHL Express (Austria) GmbH v Post-Control-Kommission and Bundesminister für Verkehr, Innovation und Technologie, EU:C:2016:880.

A. Fratini (✉)
FratiniVergano – European Lawyers, Brussels, Belgium
e-mail: a.fratini@fratinivergano.eu

P.L. Parcu et al. (eds.), *The Contribution of the Postal and Delivery Sector*, Topics in Regulatory Economics and Policy, https://doi.org/10.1007/978-3-319-70672-6_4

In *DHL International*,[3] the Court had already concluded that Member States may impose mandatory external procedures for the resolution of disputes between providers and users of all postal services, whether universal or not, irrespective of whether the provider of those services is the universal service provider or the holder of an authorization. In *DHL Express (Austria)* the Court has taken a further step and clarified that all postal operators ("including those which do not provide postal services falling within the scope of the universal service",[4] such as express delivery services) may be subject to the obligation to contribute to the financing of the NRAs. What is more relevant, the Court has provided a key interpretation of Article 9, which is likely to shape the outcome of the *Ilves Jakelu Oy*[5] and *Confetra*[6] cases concerning, respectively, requirements on the quality, availability and performance of services and the obligation to contribute to the compensation fund.

After an overview of the provision of Article 9 (Sect. 2), the paper will study the legal reasoning of the Court in *DHL Express (Austria)* and review the *DHL International* precedent (Sects. 3 and 4). It will then draw the relevant conclusions for the two pending cases and the resulting implications for the notion of "postal services provider" (Sects. 5 and 6).

2 The Provision of Article 9

Article 9 sets out the conditions governing the provision of postal services. At the outset, it has to be acknowledged that Article 9, as "willingly concede[d]" by Advocate General Mengozzi in his Opinion in the *DHL Express (Austria)* case, "is a provision of poor drafting quality and the interpretation of which, focusing on its wording, gives rise to confusion".[7] The wording of Article 9 "is not—by any stretch of the imagination—drafted in such a manner as to facilitate its immediate comprehension".[8]

The current text results from amendments brought to the original text over time. In the 1997 Directive (the "first Postal Services Directive"),[9] the provision was

[3]Judgment of 13 October 2011, Case C-148/10, DHL International NV, formerly Express Line NV v Belgisch Instituut voor Postdiensten en Telecommunicatie, EU:C:2011:654.

[4]Judgment, cit., § 32.

[5]Judgment of 15 June 2017, Case C-368/15, Ilves Jakelu Oy v Ministry of Transport and Communications, EU:C:2017:462. The judgment was issued following the presentation of this paper.

[6]Joined Cases C-259/16 and C-260/16, Confetra and others.

[7]Opinion delivered on 16 March 2016, Case C-2/15, DHL Express (Austria), ECLI:EU:C:2016:168.

[8]*Ibidem.*

[9]Directive 97/67/EC of the European Parliament and of the Council of 15 December 1997 on common rules for the development of the internal market of Community postal services and the improvement of quality of service, OJ L 15, 21.1.1998.

aimed at setting out conditions governing the commercial provision to the public of non-reserved services.[10] It allowed Member States to introduce general authorization schemes for non-reserved services falling outside the scope of the universal service, and authorization procedures, including individual licenses, for non-reserved services falling within the scope of the universal service. In the original wording of Article 9, there were only three kinds of requirements the granting of authorizations could be made conditional upon: (1) where appropriate, universal service obligations; (2) if necessary, requirements concerning quality, availability and performance of the relevant services; and (3) with no limitations, the obligation not to infringe the exclusive or special rights granted to the universal service provider(s) for the reserved postal services. Article 9(4) left it to the Member States whether to establish a compensation fund in the event that their universal service obligations represented an unfair financial burden for the entrusted provider. In that case, the granting of authorizations could be subject to the obligation to make a financial contribution to that fund. While the 2002 Directive (the "second Postal Services Directive")[11] left Article 9 unchanged, the 2008 Directive (the "third Postal Services Directive")[12] carried out substantial changes to its provisions.

Before looking further at Article 9, it is appropriate to recall that Article 2 provides the following definitions:

"authorizations": any permission setting out rights and obligations specific to the postal sector and allowing undertakings to provide postal services and, where applicable, to establish and/or operate their networks for the provision of such services, in the form of a general authorizations or individual license as defined below:

"general authorizations": an authorization, regardless of whether it is regulated by a 'class license' or under general law and regardless of whether such regulation requires registration or declaration procedures, which does not require the postal service provider concerned to obtain an explicit decision by the national regulatory authority before exercising the rights stemming from the authorizations.

"individual license": an authorization which is granted by a national regulatory authority and which gives a postal service provider specific rights, or which subjects that undertaking's operations to specific obligations supplementing the general authorization where applicable, where the postal service provider is not entitled to exercise the rights concerned until it has received the decision by the national regulatory authority.

[10] Recital 24.

[11] Directive 2002/39/EC of the European Parliament and of the Council of 10 June 2002 amending Directive 97/67/EC with regard to the further opening to competition of Community postal services, OJ L 176, 05.07.2002.

[12] Directive 2008/6/EC of the European Parliament and of the Council of 20 February 2008 amending Directive 97/67/EC with regard to the full accomplishment of the internal market of Community postal services, OJ L 52, 27.02.2008.

As noted by AG Mengozzi,[13] it is clear from a reading of Article 2 that "authorization" is a generic term for "any permission setting out rights and obligations specific to the postal sector and allowing undertakings to provide postal services", which includes both general authorizations and individual licenses. It is, in other words, in a *genus-species* relationship with both general authorizations and individual licenses.

Article 9, as amended by the third Postal Services Directive, is instead less clear. It is divided into three paragraphs: Article 9(1) states that, for services which fall outside the scope of the universal service, Member States may introduce "general authorizations". Article 9(2), first subparagraph, provides that, for services that fall within the scope of the universal service, Member States may introduce "authorization procedures including individual licenses". The second subparagraph of that provision provides that the granting of "authorizations" may be made subject to compliance with various conditions, which are listed in the five separate indents within that subparagraph. Article 9(3) provides that Member States shall ensure that authorization procedures be transparent, accessible, non-discriminatory, proportionate, precise and unambiguous, made public in advance and based on objective criteria.

The provision reads as follows (emphasis added):

1. *For services which fall <u>outside the scope of the universal service</u>, Member States may introduce general authorizations to the extent necessary to guarantee compliance with the essential requirements.*
2. *For services which fall <u>within the scope of the universal service</u>, Member States may introduce authorization procedures, including individual licenses, to the extent necessary in order to guarantee compliance with the essential requirements and to ensure the provision of the universal service.*

   The granting of authorizations may:

   - *be made subject to universal service obligations,*
   - *if necessary and justified, impose requirements concerning the quality, availability and performance of the relevant services,*
   - *where appropriate, be subject to an obligation to make a financial contribution to the sharing mechanisms referred to in Article 7, if the provision of the universal service entails a net cost and represents an unfair burden on the universal service provider(s), designated in accordance with Article 4,*

(continued)

[13]Opinion of Advocate General Mengozzi, § 28.

(continued)

- *where appropriate, be subject to an obligation to make a financial contribution to the national regulatory authority's operational costs referred to in Article 22,*
- *where appropriate, be made subject to or impose an obligation to respect working conditions laid down by national legislation.*

Obligations and requirements referred to in the first indent and in Article 3 may only be imposed on designated universal service providers.

Except in the case of undertakings that have been designated as universal service providers in accordance with Article 4, authorizations may not:

- *be limited in number,*
- *for the same elements of the universal service or parts of the national territory, impose universal service obligations and, at the same time, financial contributions to a sharing mechanism,*
- *duplicate conditions which are applicable to undertakings by virtue of other, non-sector-specific national legislation,*
- *impose technical or operational conditions other than those necessary to fulfil the obligations of this Directive.*

3. *The procedures, obligations and requirements referred to in paragraphs 1 and 2 shall be transparent, accessible, non-discriminatory, proportionate, precise and unambiguous, made public in advance and based on objective criteria. Member States shall ensure that the reasons for refusing or withdrawing an authorization in whole or in part are communicated to the applicant and shall establish an appeal procedure".*

"On a first view",[14] because the list of the different conditions which the granting of "authorizations" may be subject to is contained in Article 9(2), and because that paragraph, in its first subparagraph, refers to "services which fall within the scope of the universal service", it could be inferred that those conditions may be imposed only on the providers of services falling within the scope of the universal service. That was indeed what was argued in the context of the national proceedings that triggered the request for preliminary ruling in *DHL Express (Austria)*, in connection with one of the conditions listed in Article 9(2), second subparagraph, namely in its fourth indent.

[14]Opinion of Advocate General Mengozzi, §27.

3 The *DHL Express (Austria)* Judgment

In *DHL Express (Austria)* the Court of Justice (the "Court") was asked by the Verwaltungsgerichtshof (Higher Administrative Court, Austria) to rule on the scope of Article 9 of the Postal Services Directive, after DHL challenged its obligation to make a financial contribution to the operational costs of the Rundfunk und Telekom Regulierungs-GmbH ("RTR"), the NRA for the postal sector, on the ground that, according to the letter of the provision, such an obligation could be only imposed on those undertakings providing universal services. The national court referred a question for preliminary ruling to the Court, by which it asked, in a nutshell, whether Article 9 must be interpreted as precluding national legislation from making it mandatory for all postal service providers to contribute to the financing of the NRA, regardless of whether the operators provide universal services.[15]

The case offered the Court a welcome opportunity to clarify the content and scope of Article 9. The Court moved from the fact that the provision requires an analysis which does not confine itself to the mere, albeit sufficient in some cases, literal interpretation but needs to consider also the context in which the provision was adopted, as well as the objectives pursued by the rules of which it is part.[16] As the Court noted, the background to a provision of EU law may also contain elements relevant to its interpretation.[17]

The Court meant that the provision cannot be read in isolation from the Directive of which it forms part, and not even from the historical context which led to the adoption of the text. While linguistic conflict or ambiguity is not a pre-condition for the application of the schematic and historical approach, which now constitutes a consolidated practice in the Court's interpretation, that method is necessary in cases such as this, where a mere textual analysis would lead to a very restrictive interpretation of the norm that would not fit with the objectives the provision intends to achieve.[18]

---

[15]For completeness, the referring court also asked the following questions, were the first question to be answered in the affirmative:

"(a) Is it sufficient for a financing obligation to exist that the provider concerned provides postal services which are to be classified under the national rules as universal services, but which go beyond the mandatory minimum range of universal services under the directive?

(b) When determining an undertaking's share of the financial contributions, is one to proceed in the same way as when determining the financial contributions to the compensation fund under Article 7(4) of the directive?

(c) Do the requirement to respect the principles of non-discrimination and proportionality within the meaning of Article 7(5) of the directive and the "taking account of inter-changeability with the universal service" within the meaning of recital 27 of Directive 2008/6 . . . then mean that shares of turnover which are attributed to value-added services, hence postal services not assignable to the universal service but which are connected with the universal service, are excluded and are not taken into account when determining the share?".

[16]Opinion, §22.

[17]Judgment, §19.

[18]See Opinion, §§21-22-29; Judgment, §§26-27.

Having set out the interpretative approach it would use in its assessment, the Court engaged in a step-by-step analysis of Article 9(2), by looking first at its overall structure and then at its various elements both separately and in conjunction with the others. While admitting that the provision, at first sight, seems to allow Member States to impose the obligations listed thereunder only on operators providing universal services, the Court acknowledged that its wording, in itself, does not actually make it possible to exclude its application to all service providers. By generally stating that "the granting of authorizations may be subject" to a set of conditions, the provision makes no express reference to the regime referred to in Article 9(1) ("general authorizations for services falling outside the scope of the universal service") or to the regime referred to in Article 9(2), first subparagraph ("authorizations procedures for services falling within the scope of the universal service").[19] This interpretation is also confirmed by Article 9(2), third subparagraph, according to which "obligations and requirements referred to in the first indent and in Article 3 may only be imposed on designated universal service providers". Thus, *a contrario*, obligations and requirements referred to in the indents other than the first may be imposed on undertakings that are not the universal service providers.

The Court, then, went on to examine the conditions listed in the various indents of Article 9(2), second subparagraph, to assess whether they may be imposed solely on operators providing universal services or rather on all service providers.

The obligations laid down in the first indent ("be made subject to universal service obligations") are not controversial, as they clearly refer to designated universal service providers alone, as expressly confirmed by Article 9(2), third subparagraph, seen above.

The second indent, which mentions compliance with requirements concerning the quality, availability and performance of the relevant services, required a more systematic analysis. Given the lack of precision as to which services the obligation may be applied to, the Court turned for support to the *travaux preparatoires* of the third Postal Services Directive, as observed by the Advocate General in his Opinion at §42. From those preparatory works, it emerges that the objective underlining that Directive was the removal not only of the remaining obstacles to full market opening for some universal service providers,[20] but also of all other obstacles to the provision of postal services.[21] In the absence of any indication to the contrary, taking into account the nature of the obligation at issue (certain standards in terms of quality, availability and performance of the services, might help to safeguard the "essential requirements", which the general authorizations shall guarantee

[19]Judgement, §22.

[20]Durviaux, Ann L., "Le marché intérieur des services postaux (Bréve présentation de la directive 2008/Ce du Parlement et du Conseil du 20 février 2008 modifiant la directive 97/67/CE en ce qui concerne l'achévement du marché intérieur des services postaux de la Communauté)", European Journal of Consumer 3/2007–2008: 386–400.

[21]*Ibidem*, §26.

compliance with, such as confidentiality of correspondence or network security), the Court concluded, in line with AG Mengozzi's view,[22] that all postal service providers may be required to fulfil the obligation at stake.

When it comes to the third indent, which concerns the obligation to make a financial contribution to the compensation fund, the establishment of which is provided for in Article 7(4) of the Postal Services Directive, the Court admitted that, as drafted, that provision "does not expressly relate to universal service providers".[23] Yet, it is clear from Article 7(3) of the Directive that the Member States' right to establish such a fund is linked to their right to introduce a mechanism for the sharing of the net cost of universal service obligations, when and where those costs represent an unfair financial burden for the providers. "Above all", it added, recital 27 of the third Postal Services Directive explains that, in order to determine which undertakings may be required to contribute to that fund, Member States should consider whether the services provided may, from a user's perspective, be regarded as falling within the scope of the universal service.[24]

On the fifth indent, which subjects the granting of authorizations to an obligation to respect the working conditions laid down by national legislation, the Court more unambiguously stated that a restrictive interpretation of the provision—as applying to universal service providers alone—is not admissible, insofar the obligation to comply with the terms and conditions of employment is listed among the "essential requirements" as per Article 2(19), whose observance may condition the granting of both general and individual authorizations.[25]

Finally, as regards the specific obligation to contribute to the financing of the NRAs (fourth indent), which was the subject matter of the request from the Austrian judge, the Court pointed out that the activities carried out by the NRAs relate to, and are to the benefit of, all postal operators, not only the universal service providers.[26] The role of these authorities was in fact conceived by the EU legislator as extended to the whole postal sector: under Article 22(2) of the Postal Services Directive, NRAs' tasks vary from establishing monitoring and regulatory procedures to ensure the provision of the universal service to the monitoring of compliance with competition rules and the gathering of information for auditing or statistical purposes. Especially with regard to the latter duty, the provision of information to the NRAs for auditing and statistical purposes is clearly not limited to the universal service providers but reasonably expected from all postal operators.[27] In fact, even this

---

[22]Opinion of Advocate General Mengozzi, §33.

[23]Judgment, §25.

[24]For an example of interchangeable services, see Commission decision No 2016/C 284/01 (*Compensation of Poczta Polska for the net cost of USO 2013–2015*), OJ L 284 of 05/08/2015: these services include "letter items and postal parcels with weight and dimensions defined for universal services and items for the blind, not provided by the operator designated to provide universal services subject to the obligation to provide universal services" (§10).

[25]*Ibidem*, §27.

[26]*Ibidem*, §§29-31.

[27]Opinion of Advocate General Mengozzi, §40.

provision should be placed in the wider context of the full market opening that the third Postal Directive intended to achieve: it would not be logical to consider the NRAs' tasks outside that paradigm shift.[28]

Based on the above, the Court ruled that the provision should be interpreted as meaning that all postal service providers, "including those which do not provide postal services falling within the scope of the universal service", may be required to contribute to the financing of the operations of the NRAs.[29]

Admittedly, the reasoning of the Court is more developed on the obligations under indents 1 (universal service obligations), 4 (financing of the NRAs) and 5 (labor conditions) than it is on the obligations under indents 2 (quality, availability and performance) and 3 (compensation fund). On the latter two, in fact, two other judgments are pending and further fine-tuning is likely to take place in the respective contexts.

4 The Precedent of *DHL International*

That providers of postal services other than universal services, including express delivery, fall within the scope of application of the Postal Services Directive and are not exempted from regulatory obligations was already established by the Court in the *DHL International* case. That case originated in a request submitted by the Brussels Hof van Beroep (Court of Appeal, Belgium) for a preliminary ruling with respect to proceedings between DHL International NV (formerly Express Line NV, "Express Line") and the Belgian Institute for Postal Services and Telecommunications ("BIPT") on, amongst others, the interpretation of Article 19 of the Postal Services Directive.[30] Express Line had denied that it came within the remit of the

---

[28]Friboulet, Amadis "Parlement européen et Conseil: Directive 2008/6/CE du 20 février 2008 modifiant la directive 97/67/CE en ce qui concerne l'achévement du marché intérieur des services postaux de la Communauté", Revue trimestrielle de droit euroéen 2/2009: 381–401.

[29]*Ibidem*, §§ 42-43.

[30]"1. Member States shall ensure that transparent, simple and inexpensive procedures are made available by all postal services providers for dealing with postal users' complaints, particularly in cases involving loss, theft, damage or non-compliance with service quality standards (including procedures for determining where responsibility lies in cases where more than one operator is involved), without prejudice to relevant international and national provisions on compensation schemes. Member States shall adopt measures to ensure that the procedures referred to in the first subparagraph enable disputes to be settled fairly and promptly with provision, where warranted, for a system of reimbursement and/or compensation. Member States shall also encourage the development of independent out-of-court schemes for the resolution of disputes between postal services providers and users.

2. Without prejudice to other possibilities of appeal or means of redress under national and Community legislation, Member States shall ensure that users, acting individually or, where permitted by national law, jointly with organizations representing the interests of users and/or consumers, may bring before the competent national authority cases where users' complaints to undertakings providing postal services within the scope of the universal service have not been

Belgian postal sector ombudsman service by arguing that its express delivery services could not be regarded as postal services but were instead transport and logistics services with added value, designed for businesses.[31] As such, it was not liable for the fee payable for that service. The Court of Appeal of Brussels referred two questions to the Court, the most relevant for the purposes of this paper being whether Article 19, in the light of the amendments made by the second and third Postal Services Directives, must be interpreted as precluding national legislation which imposes on providers of postal services which are outside the scope of the universal service a mandatory external procedure for dealing with complaints from users of those services.

From a general perspective, the judgment is relevant for the clarification given by the Court as to the level of harmonization the Directive aims to achieve: contrary to the view of the referring judge (according to which the text carries out full harmonization as regards complaint procedures), the Court confirmed that the Postal Services Directive is a set of general principles adopted at EU level, the choice of the exact procedures being a matter for the Member States, which should be free to choose the system best adapted to their own circumstances.[32] The Directive provides for minimum harmonization rules, leaving room for the Member States to adjust their application to the national context, by adopting, for example, more protective measures.[33]

At the outset, the Court held that the Postal Services Directive, both in its original version and as subsequently amended, provides for two types of procedures for dealing with complaints by users of postal services: an internal, simple and inexpensive mechanism that shall be made available by all postal service providers and an external, independent, out-of-court scheme that Member States shall encourage for the resolution of this type of disputes.[34] Having reviewed the amendments incorporated into Article 19, the Court noted that the purpose of those amendments was to encourage Member States to extend the internal complaints procedures for the benefit of users of all postal services, whether universal services or not, and "irrespective of whether the provider of those services is the universal service provider or the holder of an authorization". The provision on external out-of-

satisfactorily resolved. In accordance with Article 16, Member States shall ensure that the universal service providers and, wherever appropriate, undertakings providing services within the scope of the universal service, publish, together with the annual report on the monitoring of their performance, information on the number of complaints and the manner in which they have been dealt with".

[31]Judgment of 13 October 2011, Case C-148/10, DHL International NV, formerly Express Line NV v Belgisch Instituut voor Postdiensten en Telecommunicatie, EU:C:2011:654, §§18-22.

[32]Judgment of 11 March 2004, Case C-240/02, Asempre and Asociación Nacional de Empresas de Externalización y Gestión de Envíos y Pequeña Paquetería, ECLI:EU:C:2004:140, § 30.

[33]Judgment of 13 October 2011, Case C-148/10, DHL International NV, formerly Express Line NV v Belgisch Instituut voor Postdiensten en Telecommunicatie, EU:C:2011:654, §36.

[34]Article 19(1), third subparagraph, of the Postal Services Directive, as amended by the third Directive.

court schemes for the resolution of disputes between postal service providers and users, the third subparagraph of Article 19(1), was introduced by the third Postal Services Directive: as it is apparent from recital 42 in the preamble to that Directive, those amendments are intended to extend the application of the minimum principles laid down for dealing with complaints "beyond universal service providers".

Therefore, the Court concluded, a national legislation which imposes on providers of postal services that are outside the scope of the universal service a mandatory external procedure for dealing with complaints from users of those services "not only is not incompatible with the Postal Services Directive, in its original version and in its amended versions, but also complies with the obligation laid down in that Directive, following its last amendment, to encourage the development of independent, out-of-court schemes for the resolution of disputes between postal service providers and users".[35]

Besides the confirmation that external complaints procedure may be imposed on providers of non-universal services, the case is of interest with regard to the recognition of express delivery services as postal services. Express Line had argued that its express delivery business could not constitute postal services within the meaning of Article 2(1) of the Postal Services Directive, as the four activities listed therein (namely, "services involving the clearance, sorting, transport and delivery of postal items") all are necessary for a service to be a postal service. While the Court did not rule on this matter, as the referring judge had rejected that plea and decided that it was not necessary to refer a question on this issue, Advocate General Jääskinen made the point that the wording of Article 2(1) of the Directive gives no indication as to the cumulative nature of the list it contains.[36] In addition, the fact that the third Postal Services Directive has added a new paragraph 1a, which defines "postal services provider" as "an undertaking that provides *one or more* postal services" (emphasis added), supports the view that it is not necessary for the operator concerned to carry out all four of the activities listed.

5 Implications for *Ilves Jakelu Oy* and *Confetra*

Turning back to Article 9(2) of the Postal Services Directive, its scope of application is the subject matter of two further preliminary proceedings, at the time of writing still pending before the Court of Justice, which are likely to be affected by the *DHL Express (Austria)* judgment.

In *Ilves Jakelu Oy*, the Korkein hallinto-oikeus (Supreme Administrative Court, Finland) has asked the Court, amongst others, whether the activity of distribution of

[35]Judgment, §51

[36]Opinion delivered on 26 May 2011, Case C-148/10, DHL International NV, ECLI:EU:C:2011:351, §59.

postal items of contract customers can be made subject to the respect of specific requirements concerning the quality, availability, or performance of the relevant services under Article 9(2), second indent, of the Directive.[37] Ilves Jakelu challenged the possibility to subject the granting of its authorization to those specific requirements, on the ground that its services, which do not fall within the scope of the universal service, may be required to comply only with obligations related to the necessity of safeguarding the essential requirements.

As seen above, in *DHL Express (Austria)* the Court has drawn a clear line on this point. The requirements under the second indent of Article 9(2) are applicable to both general authorizations and individual licenses. In line with AG Mengozzi's view, in fact, compliance with standards in terms of quality, availability and performance of services might help safeguard the essential requirements, which are applicable to all postal services, regardless of whether they are universal or not.[38]

Against that background, it is not reasonable to foresee that the Court will depart from its recent ruling. It has decided to turn down both the opinion of the Advocate General and the oral hearing for this case, which paves the way towards a consistent conclusion on the application of those obligations to providers of non-universal services. Probably, some additional fine-tuning is to be expected in connection with

---

[37] According to the notice (OJ C311, 21.09.2015, p. 34), the Finnish judge referred the following four questions:

"1. In interpreting Article 9 of Postal Directive 97/67/EC, as amended by Directives 2002/39/EC and 2008/6/EC, is the distribution of postal items of contract customers to be considered a service outside the scope of the universal service under Article 9(1) or a service within the scope of the universal service under Article 9(2), where the postal undertaking agrees with its customers on the conditions governing delivery and charges them an individually agreed fee?

2. If the aforementioned distribution of postal items of contract customers involves a service outside the scope of the universal service, are Article 9(1) and Article 2(14) to be interpreted in such a way that the provision of such postal services, under circumstances such as those in the main proceedings, can be made subject to an individual license, as provided for in the Postal Act?

3. If the aforementioned distribution of postal items of contract customers involves a service outside the scope of the universal service, is Article 9(1) to be interpreted in such a way that an authorization concerning such services can be made subject only to terms intended to guarantee compliance with the essential requirements under Article 2(19) of the Postal Directive and that authorizations concerning such services cannot be made subject to any terms with respect to the quality, availability, or performance of the relevant services under Article 9(2) of the Directive?

4. If authorizations concerning the aforementioned distribution of postal items of contract customers can be made subject only to terms intended to guarantee compliance with the essential requirements, can terms such as those at issue in the main proceedings—which relate to the postal service's conditions governing delivery, the frequency of distribution of items, change-of-address and delivery-suspension service, the labelling of items, and clearance locations—be considered consistent with the essential requirements under Article 2(19) and necessary in order to guarantee compliance with the essential requirements under Article 9(1)?".

[38] Opinion of Advocate General Mengozzi delivered on 16 March 2016, Case C-2/15, DHL Express (Austria) GmbH v Post-Control-Kommission and Bundesminister für Verkehr, Innovation und Technologie EU:C:2016:168, §33.

the specific elements of the case, namely on the notion of "essential requirements".[39]

In *Confetra*, the Regional Administrative Court of Lazio (Italy) has referred four questions to the Court. The most relevant for the purposes of this analysis is whether Article 9 should be interpreted as precluding national provisions that impose on all postal operators, including express service providers and freight forwarders, the obligation to contribute to support the USO, without defining different application modalities according to the specific situation of the operator and of the market.

In *DHL Express (Austria)*, the Court acknowledged that, as drafted, the provision at issue "does not expressly relate to universal service providers".[40] The intention of the third Postal Services Directive was to remove all the remaining obstacles to full market opening to ensure a level playing field for all postal operators, irrespective of the type of services they provide.[41] Article 9 in its original version included the possibility for Member States to establish a compensation fund and to subject the granting of "authorizations" to the obligation to make a financial contribution to that fund in a separate provision, the then paragraph 4. The provision did not distinguish between general and individual authorizations, with the consequence that both could incorporate the obligation to contribute to the compensation fund. Following the Court's line of argument, a restrictive interpretation of the applicability of the obligation to contribute to the compensation fund would be therefore against the spirit and the objectives of the third Postal Services Directive.

Having said that, the Court also recalled that "[a]bove all", recital 27 of the third Postal Services Directive provides that, in order to determine which undertakings may be required to contribute to that fund, Member States should consider whether the services provided may, from a user's perspective, be regarded as falling within the scope of the universal service. It did not go further than recalling the provision in *DHL Express (Austria)*. It is reasonable to expect that the Court will expand on the interpretation of recital 27 in the forthcoming *Confetra* judgment and provide the awaited fine-tuning on the providers that can be subject to the obligation to contribute to the compensation fund.

[39]As expected, the Court confirmed its recent case-law in *Ilves Jakelu Oy* (Judgment of 15 June 2017), by ruling that Article 9(1) of Directive 97/67, as amended, must be interpreted to the effect that the provision of postal services not falling within the scope of the universal service may be made subject to compliance with requirements concerning the quality, availability and performance of the relevant services pursuant to Article 9(2), second subparagraph, second indent, of that directive.

[40]Judgment, § 25.

[41]Hatzopoulos, Vassilis "Authorizations under EU internal market rules", Research Papers in Law, 424 College of Europe 5/2013.

6 Conclusions

As the litigation referred to above shows, Article 9 is not a clear-cut provision. Admittedly, the obligations listed in Article 9(2), second subparagraph, would have been better placed in a separate paragraph, rather than in a paragraph whose first subparagraph only concerns the universal service.

However, *DHL Express (Austria)* confirmed that this drafting choice, as tortuous as it is, does not allow excluding general authorizations from the applicability of those obligations. The term "authorization", as used in Article 9(2), second subparagraph, of the Postal Services Directive applies both to the authorizations for services falling within the scope of the universal service and to the authorizations for services that fall outside it. Accordingly, the obligations laid down in the second subparagraph may be imposed, depending on the obligation, either solely on providers of universal services, or of services considered as such, or on all postal service providers. The Court already gave its interpretation of the scope of each of the obligations listed in the five indents of Article 9(2), second subparagraph, based on their respective wording, context and objective, providing a much welcome legal certainty.

Yet, the replies to the preliminary questions raised in *Jakelu Oy* and in *Confetra* will most likely deliver a further fine-tuning of the scope of application of Article 9 (2), possibly putting a definite end to the claims that the postal sector does not go further than the traditional, universal, postal services.

Quantity Rebate Scheme: Applicability of "per sender" Reasoning for Corporate Groups

Til Rozman

1 Introduction

Article 12 of the Postal Services Directive (hereinafter "PSD")[1] stipulates that (special) tariffs for each of the services forming part of the universal service (hereinafter "US") shall be, *inter alia*, non-discriminatory, while Article 102 of the Treaty on the Functioning of the European Union (hereinafter "TFEU")[2] prohibits the abuse of a dominant position. Building on this legal context, the aim of this chapter is to answer the following hypothetical question: Is a universal service provider (hereinafter "USP") with a dominant position entitled to introduce, for services forming part of the US, a quantity rebate scheme that considers a group of companies as a single sender, where the quantity rebate is based on the total quantity of the group, and not as a group of separate senders?

This chapter is organized as follows. Section 2 identifies the relevant EU legal framework to assess this hypothetical. It distinguishes postal legislation (with special focus on non-discrimination) from competition law (with special focus on distinctions between quantity and exclusionary rebates). Section 3 defines the concept of corporate group, explains why corporate groups matter and applies relevant law to the hypothetical. Section 4 concludes that there is no link between mere corporate affiliation and stimulating the demand for postal services. Therefore, granting different rebates solely on the ground of different ownership structure infringes the principle of non-discrimination as stipulated by the Article 12 PSD. In addition, this section questions the compliance of the hypothetical with the EU

[1]OJ L 15, 21.1.1998, p14, OJ L 176, 5.7.2002, p21, and OJ L 52, 27.2.2008, p3.

[2]OJ C 326, 26/10/2012, p1–390.

T. Rozman (✉)
Agency for Communication Networks and Services of the Republic of Slovenia, Ljubljana, Slovenia
e-mail: til.rozman@akos-rs.si

P.L. Parcu et al. (eds.), *The Contribution of the Postal and Delivery Sector*, Topics in Regulatory Economics and Policy, https://doi.org/10.1007/978-3-319-70672-6_5

competition law and therefore proposes further studies. Section 4 provides the conclusion.

2 Relevant Legal Framework

For assessing quantity discounts over corporate groups, the relevant EU postal legislation comprises PSD (2.1.). Since judgments of the Court of Justice of the European Union (hereinafter the "Court") develop the EU law and are, consequently, sources of the EU law (Von Danwitz 2008, p165), leading judgments of the Court as regards the issues of discrimination and quantity rebates in the postal sector (Sect. 2.2) also apply. EU competition law rules are relevant only as far as they deal with rebates (Sect. 2.3).

2.1 Postal Services Directive

From the perspective of this chapter, the key tariff principle is non-discrimination. According to Article 12 PSD, Member States are obliged to ensure that tariffs for each of the services forming part of the US are, *inter alia*, non-discriminatory. If a USP applies special tariffs, *e.g.* contractual tariffs resulting from an individual agreement between the USP and the sender, they shall also be available to other users, including individual users and SMEs, when they are in a comparable situation, *i.e.* when they post under similar conditions.[3]

---

[3]Article 12 PSD: »Member States shall take steps to ensure that the tariffs for each of the services forming part of the universal service comply with the following principles:

- prices shall be affordable and must be such that all users, independent of geographical location, and, in the light of specific national conditions, have access to the services provided. Member States may maintain or introduce the provision of a free postal service for the use of blind and partially-sighted persons,
- prices shall be cost-oriented and give incentives for an efficient universal service provision. Whenever necessary for reasons relating to the public interest, Member States may decide that a uniform tariff shall be applied, throughout their national territory and/or cross-border, to services provided at single piece tariff and to other postal items,
- the application of a uniform tariff shall not exclude the right of the universal service provider (s) to conclude individual agreements on prices with users,
- tariffs shall be transparent and non-discriminatory,
- whenever universal service providers apply special tariffs, for example for services for businesses, bulk mailers or consolidators of mail from different users, they shall apply the principles of transparency and non-discrimination with regard both to the tariffs and to the associated conditions. The tariffs, together with the associated conditions, shall apply equally both as between different third parties and as between third parties and universal service providers supplying equivalent services. Any such tariffs shall also be available to users, in particular individual users and small and medium-sized enterprises, who post under similar conditions.

The meaning of non-discrimination has been elaborated in many judgments and has become settled not only in the jurisprudence but also as a general principle of the EU law.[4] The principle of non-discrimination prohibits different treatment of comparable situations unless such treatment is objectively justified.[5] The former is significantly important for application of "per sender reasoning" (see Sect. 2.2) to the corporate groups.

2.2 Court's Judgments

In *bpost SA v IBPT*[6] (hereinafter "*bpost* case"), the Court confirmed that the principle of non-discrimination in postal tariffs laid down in the PSD is not breached by a USP introducing a "per sender" quantity discounts rebate. Different treatment of senders and consolidators[7] does not constitute prohibited discrimination since senders and consolidators are not in a similar situation regarding stimulating demand for postal services even when they handle the same volume of mail.[8] Consolidators, compared with the senders, do not contribute to an increase in the mail handed on to the *bpost* and, accordingly, in the turnover of the latter.[9]

The judgment in the *bpost* case is one of the most important and influential recent judgments that directly refer to the postal sector.[10] The judgment was a preliminary ruling under Article 267 TFEU and concerned the interpretation of Article 12 PSD. It was not in dispute that at the same volume of postal items, bpost granted different rebates to the consolidators (which hand on to *bpost* volumes of

[4]Case C-356/12 *Wolfgang Glatzel v Freistaat Bayern*, paragraph 43; see also Cases C-441/12 *Almer Beheer BV, Daedalus Holding BV v Van den Dungen Vastgoed BV, Oosterhout II BVBA*, paragraph 47; joined Cases 117/76 *Albert Ruckdeschel & Co., Kulmbach, Hansa-Lagerhaus Stroh & Co ., Hamburg, and Hauptzollamt Hamburg-St . Annen* and 16/77 *Diamalt AG, Munich and Hauptzollamt Itzenhoe*, paragraph 7; Case C-144/04 *Werner Mangold v Rüdiger Helm*, paragraphs 74–77. Although the last case applied to discrimination on the grounds of age, the same reasoning is *mutatis mutandis* applicable also to other areas where non-discrimination is particularly relevant and stipulated by the EU legislation. For a detailed analysis of this case see Craig and de Burca (2011, p212–213).

[5]See Case C-550/07 P *Akzo Nobel Chemicals and Akcros Chemicals* v *Commission*, paragraph 55; Case C-356/12 *Wolfgang Glatzel v Freistaat Bayern*, paragraph 43; see also case C-340/13 *bpost SA v IBPT*, paragraph 27.

[6]Case C-340/13 *bpost SA v IBPT*.

[7]Consolidators are providers of routing services (routing to the distribution center).

[8]*Bpost* case, paragraphs 31 and 33.

[9]*Ibidem*, paragraph 48.

[10]For thorough competition-law based analysis of relevant EU and EFTA courts decisions in the postal sector prior to the *bpost* case, see Geradin and Malamataris (2014).

mail after grouping it from different undertakings or administrations) when compared to the senders (which hand on volumes directly).[11] Quantity discounts were calculated on the basis of the volume of each individual sender and not on the basis of the total volume of mail from different senders (which used services of the consolidator). IBPT held that bpost's rebate discriminated against consolidators and, therefore, infringed the principle of non-discrimination as stipulated by Article 12 PSD.

The Court did not share this view but, conversely, ruled that:

> The principle of non-discrimination in postal tariffs laid down in Article 12 of . . .[PSD]. . . must be interpreted as not precluding a system of quantity discounts per sender, such as that at issue in the main proceedings.

The reasoning of the Court in the *bpost* case derived from the finding that, on one hand, rebates to senders increase the demand in the relevant market since senders originate the postal items. On the other hand, consolidators do not contribute to the increase in the volume of mailings (handed on to *bpost*) since they hand on the mail which they have already collected from different senders.[12] Rebates were different for senders and for consolidators but such different treatment did not constitute prohibited discrimination. Discrimination under Article 12 PSD is prohibited only if subjects (in case at hand, senders and consolidators) are in a similar situation on the postal distribution market and there is no objective justification for different treatment.[13]

As discussed below in Sect. 2.3.2, simple quantity rebates are presumptively lawful because price reductions resulting from economies of scale are economically justified. Therefore, the objective of quantity rebates is to stimulate demand and to generate more volume. The Court explained that activities carried out by the consolidators do not contribute to that objective.[14] If the volume is not raised, average costs for the supplier (*bpost*) do not fall and, consequently, cost reductions are not economically justified.[15] If a sender does not generate enough mail to receive a quantity rebate, such sender is motivated to increase volume to qualify for a quantity rebate. On the other hand, if the sender, at the same quantity of postal items, indirectly receives a quantity rebate solely because it uses services of the consolidator, the Court found that the sender is not encouraged to generate more mail in the future.[16] In other words, receiving a rebate (indirectly) without an

---

[11]*Bpost* case, paragraph 31.

[12]*Ibidem*, paragraph 38.

[13]*Ibidem*, paragraph 33.

[14]Paragraph 38 of the *bpost* case: "However, when the consolidators hand on to bpost the mail which they have already collected from different senders, that does not have the effect of increasing the overall volume of mail in bpost's favour. It follows therefrom that, except to the limited extent that those consolidators are themselves senders, their activity does not, of itself, contribute to the increase in the volume of mailings handed on to bpost."

[15]*Ibidem*, paragraph 47.

[16]*Ibidem*, paragraphs 40 and 41.

increased volume does not stimulate senders to generate more volume in the future.[17]

Accordingly, the Court concluded that senders and consolidators:

> /.../ are not in comparable situations as regards the objective pursued by the system of quantity discounts per sender, which is to stimulate demand in the area of postal services, since only ...[senders] ... are in a position to be encouraged, by the effect of that system, to increase the volume of their mail handed on to bpost and, accordingly, the turnover of that operator.[18,19]

The issue of justification for different treatment, the second step in the assessment of the possible prohibited discriminatory practice, was not relevant for the decision of the Court since it concluded that senders and consolidators are not in a similar situation with regard to postal distribution.

2.3 *Rebates in EU Competition Law*

2.3.1 Rebates in General

Businesses use rebates to compete for market share. For the vast majority of companies, granting rebates is not constrained by competition law. Restrictions apply only to undertakings holding a dominant position. Article 102 TFEU prohibits abuse of a dominant position and is applicable to the rebate schemes used by dominant undertakings (Jones and Surfin 2016, p434). Empirical studies find that competition increases quality in markets where prices are regulated (Pisarkiewicz and West 2013, p34), consequently, efficient competition is *a fortiori* important for postal services. EU law under Article 102 TFEU indicates that rebate schemes by dominant undertakings may reduce competition.

According to the Guidance on the Commission's enforcement priorities in applying Article 82 of the EC Treaty to abusive exclusionary conduct by dominant undertakings (hereinafter "Guidance"),[20] conditional rebates and exclusive purchasing obligations are considered as a form of exclusive dealing.[21] The Guidance defines conditional rebates as "rebates granted to customers to reward them for a particular form of purchasing behavior".[22] Conditional rebates are price deductions targeting specific purchasing behavior, *e.g.* buying a certain quantity of goods/services. Price deductions are either retroactive (*i.e.* the rebate is granted on all quantities within a specified time period) or incremental (*i.e.* the rebate is granted

[17] *Ibidem*, paragraph 41.

[18] *Ibidem*, paragraph 48.

[19] This reasoning was clearly elaborated in the theory before the judgment (Geradin 2011).

[20] OJ C 45, 24.2.2009, p7–20.

[21] Guidance, paragraph 32.

[22] Guidance, paragraph 37.

only for purchases exceeding the threshold). The legitimate rationale for rebates is to attract and stimulate demand with a view to making a profit.

Interestingly, while some argues that exclusive dealing does not necessarily "/ . . ./ entail limits on competition. . ." and has procompetitive benefits (Marvel 1982, p1), the Court unequivocally stated in Hoffmann-La Roche & Co. AG v Commission of the European Communities[23] (hereinafter "*Hoffmann-La Roche* case") that exclusive dealing by the dominant company constitutes *prima facie* abuse of a dominant position.[24] On the same tune, when a dominant undertaking sets a rebate scheme in a manner that the costs of switching from the dominant undertaking to its competitors are very high, and, consequently makes it difficult for customers to switch to an alternative operator, an anti-competitive foreclosing effect is very likely.

2.3.2 Rationale for Quantity Rebates

In general, rebates are divided into two main categories, namely quantity rebates (Sect. 2.3.2) and loyalty/fidelity/exclusivity rebates (Sect. 2.3.3). In the Intel Corp. v European Commission[25] (hereinafter "*INTEL* case"), the Court differentiated between three rebate schemes. In addition to the quantity and loyalty/fidelity/exclusivity rebates, the Court recognized "rebates falling within a third category",[26] *i.e.* rebates that are neither simple quantity rebates nor directly linked to a condition of exclusivity.[27]

The main characteristic of simple quantity rebates is that they are granted solely on the basis of the volume of purchases. Since they are based on the volume of sales only, they do not have the foreclosure effect prohibited by Article 102 TFEU (Colomo 2016, p720, 726, 733–734). The rationale for a quantity rebate is achieving economies of scale and, consequently, lowering costs. Therefore, the supplier has—within the scope of the lowered costs resulted from the increased quantity

[23]Case 85/76 *Hoffmann-La Roche & Co. AG v Commission of the European Communities.*

[24]*Ibidem*, paragraph 89: "An undertaking which is in a dominant position on a market and ties purchasers—even if it does so at their request—by an obligation or promise on their part to obtain all or most of their requirements exclusively from the said undertaking abuses its dominant position within the meaning of Article 86 of the Treaty, whether the obligation in question is stipulated without further qualification or whether it is undertaken in consideration of the grant of a rebate. The same applies if the said undertaking, without tying the purchasers by a formal obligation, applies, either under the terms of agreements concluded with these purchasers or unilaterally, a system of fidelity rebates, that is to say discounts conditional on the customer's obtaining all or most of its requirements—whether the quantity of its purchases be large or small—from the undertaking in a dominant position."

[25]Case T-286/09 *Intel Corp. v European Commission.*

[26]*Ibidem*, paragraphs 76–78.

[27]At the moment of preparing this chapter, the *INTEL* case is still under appeal (Judgment C-413/14 P). However, the Advocate General's Opinion in Case C-413/14 P is clear; the case should be referred back to the General Court for a fresh review.

supplied to the demand side—the economic rationale to pass the cost savings to the demand side by granting a price deduction. As explained by the Court in *Manufacture française des pneumatiques Michelin v Commission of the European Communities*,[28] "Quantity rebates are therefore deemed to reflect gains in efficiency and economies of scale made by the undertaking in a dominant position".[29]

A rebate scheme cannot be subsumed under the simple quantity rebate if the fulfillment of other not purely volume-orientated conditions is required in order to receive the rebate. A typical example is the loyalty-inducing nature of the "quantity" rebate model. If rebates "... are not granted in respect of each individual order, thus corresponding to the cost savings made by the supplier, but on the basis of the aggregate orders placed over a given period"[30] and retroactively "... in the sense that, if the threshold initially set at the beginning of the year in respect of the quantities of mail was exceeded, the rebate rate applied at the end of the year applied to all mailings presented over the reference period and not only to mailings exceeding the threshold initially estimated",[31] the rebate scheme cannot be understood as a simple quantity model.[32]

2.3.3 Exclusivity Rebates

As for the second category of rebates (loyalty/fidelity/exclusivity rebates), the main characteristic is that they make the price deduction conditional upon the purchaser buying all or a significant part of its requirements from the dominant undertaking. As stated in the *Hoffmann-La Roche* case: "... the effect of fidelity rebates is to apply dissimilar conditions to equivalent transactions with other trading parties in that two purchasers pay a different price for the same quantity of the same product depending on whether they obtain their supplies exclusively from the undertaking in a dominant position or have several sources of supply."[33]

Rasmusen, Ramseyer and Wiley (1991, p1144) showed that exclusionary dealings can, but not necessary would, enable a monopolist to exclude rivals by taking "...advantage of its unity and the customers' disunity." They identified situations in which each customer would sign the exclusionary agreement even when all customers are worse off by doing so. On the other hand, they find that exclusionary agreements could also be used by a new entrant and not only as a practice of the dominant undertaking to extend the existing market power.

---

[28]Case T-203/01 *Manufacture française des pneumatiques Michelin v Commission of the European Communities*.

[29]*Ibidem*, paragraph 58.

[30]CaseC-23/14 *Post Danmark A/S v Konkurrencerådet* (hereinafter: "*Post Danmark II case*"), paragraph 28.

[31]*Ibidem*, paragraph 32.

[32]*Ibidem*, paragraph 28.

[33]*Hoffmann-La Roche* case, paragraph 90.

Brennan (2008) examined the question when bundled rebates are exclusionary and points out the importance of coverage of complement markets. He said that the question "...whether bundled rebates are something that should be regarded as presumptively good, like cutting price, or not, like exclusionary contracting that forecloses access to a complement market...cannot be answered ...unless the role of complement market monopolization is appropriately appreciated" (Brennan 2008, p40). Furthermore, Brennan (2008, p39) explains that exclusionary conduct is anticompetitive only when it creates new market power in the complement market. In the absence of monopoly, there is more additional market power to be gained and more profits to be taken when compared with the monopoly market. Therefore, anti-competitive harm is most significant when (anticompetitive) exclusionary rebates are applied by the non-dominant undertaking and when this practice crates the monopoly "...and not when it is imposed by the monopolist" (Brennan 2008, p34).

However, under EU competition law, an loyalty rebate introduced by a dominant company is incompatible with the objective of undistorted competition and constitutes *prima facie* infringement of Article 102 TFEU (Colomo 2016, p715). If special prices are available only to customers that commit to buy all or a significant part of supplies exclusively from the dominant undertaking, such a pricing strategy deters customers from obtaining their supplies from competitors. The costs to the customer who would contemplate using another provider are very high not economically reasonable. The objective of this pricing strategy is to incentivize the purchaser to obtain his supplies exclusively from the undertaking in a dominant position and to deprive the purchaser of other possible choices of sources of supply.[34] Consequently, the pricing strategy aims at excluding or preventing competitors from entering the market.

2.3.4 Differentiating Between Quantity and Exclusivity Rebates

A key question is how to differentiate between presumptively lawful (simple) quantity rebate schemes and unlawful loyalty/fidelity/exclusivity rebates. Interestingly, the absence of a requirement to buy all or a significant part of the supplies from the dominant company does not guarantee a safe harbor for the latter.[35] On the one hand, the category of presumptively lawful rebates is very narrow since it includes only simple quantity rebates without any discrimination and entirely justified on cost savings.[36] On the other hand, the law regarding *per se* unlawful loyalty/fidelity/exclusivity rebates is extensive and includes, *inter alia*, target rebates. In practice, rebate schemes do not fit into one or another clear-cut category.

[34] *Hoffmann-La Roche* case, paragraph 91.

[35] *Post Danmark II case*, paragraph 28.

[36] Even simple quantity rebate may constitute an abuse of a dominant, *e.g.* when the pricing strategy is predatory.

A cautious and case by case approach needs to be taken in the analysis of a specific rebate model.[37] All relevant facts and circumstances must be carefully identified and thoroughly considered. Only if a rebate scheme is nondiscriminatory and applies to all similar purchases, it is safe to conclude that it falls within the category of a simple quantity rebate. For differentiating lawful and unlawful rebates, numerous criteria are to be considered. For instance, in the *Post Danmark II case*, the Court did not follow the European Commission's "more economic approach". Instead of using the as-efficient-competitor test, the Court relied on other factors, esp. length of the reference period (the longer the relevant period, the stronger the fidelity-inducing character) and "suction" effect (Rummel 2016). In the assessment of a specific practice, the role of the "intent" of the dominant company could also be duly considered (Parcu and Stasi 2017, p12–33).

3 Corporate Groups and the Principle of Non-discrimination

This chapter's hypothetical is based on the premise that corporate groups are understood in the sense of corporate (and not merely contractual) affiliation of a leading company that can control the other companies in the group (see 3.1.). In this case, the reasoning from the *bpost* case applies for assessing the quantity rebate scheme in our hypothetical (3.2.).

3.1 The Concept of a Corporate Group and Why It Matters?

Cooperation between companies has become necessary to compete in both the EU internal market and globally. Such cooperation has frequently led to the formation of groups of companies that are legally independent entities but are economically affiliated. Despite several attempts, the EU company law has not codified and harmonized corporate group law.[38] At national levels, many different approaches

[37]For the OECD Competition Committee, the U.S. antitrust agencies, the Department of Justice and the Federal Trade Commission prepared note where they explain that loyalty rebates can have the potential to be exclusionary, but they also have the potential to promote competition. Since they did not adopt particular test for assessment of potentially anticompetitive elements of loyalty rebates, detailed and case-by-case assessment of all relevant facts and circumstances is necessary. [https://www.ftc.gov/system/files/attachments/us-submissions-oecd-other-international-competition-fora/1606fidelity_rebates-us.pdf].

[38]All attempts to codify and harmonize European corporate group law have failed. The first attempts at the EU level were made in 1972, 1974 and 1975, in the Proposal for a Fifth Directive on Company Law and the preliminary draft Ninth Directive (Böhlhoff and Budde 1984, p163–197). The proposals were considered too rigid and too similar to the German *Konzernrecht*

are observed.[39] To avoid different interpretations of the concept of corporate group and to put interpretations on equal footing, this chapter understands corporate group in the sense of the German *Konzernrecht* model. The German model provides the most comprehensive and influential regulation of corporate groups in the EU. This model has been followed by many EU[40] and non-EU countries.[41] In this model, the main distinction is between actual, *de facto* corporate groups (Germ. "faktischer Konzern"), and contractual corporate groups (Germ. "Vertragskonzern").[42]

In both types, affiliated companies are legally independent and can make their own decisions. One of the key differences is that in contractual corporate groups, one company has the right to give mandatory instructions concerning business conduct to the other companies, whereas in the actual corporate group no company has such a right.[43] In practice, there are more actual corporate groups than contractual corporate groups (Conac 2013, p199). Therefore, this chapter deals only with the former type of corporate group. In the *Konzernrecht* model, the contractual corporate group is only theoretical concept, but an actual corporate group is indeed relevant in economic reality.

This is important for our hypothetical question because in the prevailing type of corporate groups the leading company does not have legal right to directly influence the business decisions of other companies in the group, *e.g.* to give instructions to the dependent company regarding the use of postal services. On the other hand, nothing prevents, for instance, organizing joint procurement for all companies that are part of the group or choosing any other ways to optimize business operations. This leads to the finding that existence of corporate affiliation is neither a necessary nor sufficient condition for optimizing business operations. Nothing prevents companies from optimizing their business, regardless of whether companies are part of

approach, and were therefore not successful. Since then, this issue has been raised several times, including in the Report of the High Level Group of Company Law Experts on a Modern Regulatory Framework for Company Law in Europe (Winter et al. 2002), by the Reflection Group on the Future of EU Company Law (Antunes et al. 2011) and its successor, the Informal Company Law Expert Group (Conac et al. 2016).

[39]Germany and countries that adopted German Konzernrecht model, *e.g.* Czech Republic, Slovenia, Croatia, Portugal, Hungary, and some non-European states, *e.g.* Brazil and recently Turkey, developed comprehensive and codified regulation of corporate groups (Emmerich and Habersack 2013, p20). Second approach is partial and codified regulation of corporate groups, *e.g.* Italian Codice Civile, which recognizes the interest of a corporate group (Kousedghi 2007). Third approach is recognition of the specific interests of a corporate group that derives from case law, *e.g.* the so-called Rozenblum decision of the French Court of Cassation, in which, in the context of criminal law, the court stated that if the manager acted in the group's interest, the act cannot be considered as a misuse (Conac et al. 2008, p31). In fourth, last approach there are no specific rules or provisions applicable to corporate groups, *e.g.* the UK model (Antunes et al. 2011).

[40]For instance Czech Republic, Slovenia, Croatia, Portugal and Hungary.

[41]For instance, Brazil, Taiwan and recently Turkey.

[42]German Stock Corporation Act, paragraphs 15–18 and 291.

[43]*Ibidem*, paragraph 308.

a group or not. In other words, mere existence of a corporate group tells us nothing regarding a company's business decision regarding how to obtain postal services.

3.2 *Application to Corporate Groups*

In the hypothetical, the quantity rebate rate depends solely on the existence of the corporate affiliation and not, for instance, on the existence of joint procurement for all companies that are part of the group. Therefore, as in the *bpost* case, the decisive question is whether there is an objective justification for a difference in treatment in a rebate between companies depositing the same volumes of mail. Supposing that company A is a dependent company in which company C holds a 60% share (and the remaining 40% is dispersed among other shareholders), whereas company B is not a dependent company, *e.g.*, its shares are dispersed among many shareholders. In this regard, it has to be highlighted that ownership and, consequently, the existence of a corporate group, has nothing to do with the company size. In economic reality, many large companies, for instance family-run companies, are not part of corporate groups and, *vice versa*, many companies that are part of corporate groups are small companies, sometimes only "letter-box" companies.

In this context, granting different quantity rebate rates to A and B is discriminatory, assuming, firstly, that A and B deposit the same volume of mail and, secondly, that neither A nor B is involved in organized demand or in any other cooperation with other senders/companies that enables cost savings for the postal services supplier—in case at hand, the USP. Mere corporate affiliation of the companies does not *ceteris paribus* stimulate demand in the area of postal services and does not constitute objective justification for different treatment of companies A and B. Both companies post under similar conditions and are therefore in similar situations; consequently, different treatment constitutes discrimination prohibited by Article 12 PSD. This finding is built on the reasoning that has been elaborated in the *bpost* case but from the opposite perspective, that is to say, since senders are in a comparable situation as regards stimulating demand, a dominant USP should treat them equally and not differently. Customers depositing the same quantity of postal items should not be entitled to different quantity rebate rates based on whether or not they are part of a group of companies and, if they are, how many postal items have been deposited by other members of the group.

Building on the above example, the opposite view would imply the following conclusion: If company C acquires majority shareholding in company B, the latter company would be—solely because of the change in ownership—*ceteris paribus* entitled to a higher quantity rebate (corresponding to the total quantity of postal items sent by companies in which company C holds majority stake). Such a conclusion would be legally unjustified and contravene the principle of non-discrimination.

4 Conclusions

This chapter builds on the provisions of corporate group law, as is in force in German model and German-like models, which stipulates that the dominant company does not have the legal right to give mandatory instruction to the dependent company as regards business operations of the latter, including decisions regarding the use of postal services. The main finding of this chapter is that corporate affiliation *ipso facto* does not stimulate demand or lead to cost savings for a dominant postal services supplier exist. On the other hand, corporate affiliation can lead to cooperation between companies that are part of a group. If such cooperation results in cost savings for the postal services supplier (in the case at hand to the USP), quantity rebates are objectively justified. Still, the justified reason for granting quantity rebates is specific cooperation between companies (for instance organizing joint procurement) and not corporate affiliation.

When a quantity rebate granted by a USP with a dominant position depends upon the existence of a corporate group, that is, a different rebate is granted *ceteris paribus* to a company that has a majority shareholder than to a company with dispersed ownership, such a rebate constitutes prohibited discrimination under Article 12 PSD. Furthermore, compliance with EU competition law is called into question. Since postal regulation applies *ex ante*, whereas competition law (except for the merger control procedures) applies *ex post*, one may assume that EU regulators for postal services would deal with this hypothetical case prior to competition authorities. This chapter provides relevant legal assessment aiming to assist them.

From the perspective of competition law, this chapter cannot provide the final answer but only opens some of the relevant questions to consider and provides a starting point for further studies. Three preliminary conclusions can be drawn. Firstly, the rebate model at hand is—in the terminology of the Court—not a simple quantity model since it is not based on only the volume of sales, but requires fulfilment of a different condition (*i.e.* the existence of a corporate group). Therefore, this rebate model is not presumptively lawful. Secondly, allowing the existence of the corporate group as a condition for receiving higher rebate rate is questionable because the link between the existence of a corporate group and quantity of items sent by the companies forming the group need not to exist. If companies cooperate and thus generate more mail or provide other sources for cost savings of the postal services provider, the rationale for quantity rebate are activities generating cost savings and not existence of the group. Thirdly, if different quantity rebates are granted to companies (in the above example companies A and B) that compete on the same market, the price they pay for postal service can raise competition law issues not only with regard to postal services market but also to the market in which they compete.

References

Antunes, J. E., *et al* (2011). Report of the Reflection Group on the Future of EU Company Law, Brussels.

Böhlhoff, K., & Budde, J. (1984). Company Groups – the EEC Proposal for a Ninth Directive in the Light of the Legal Situation in the Federal Republic of Germany, Journal of Comparative Business and Capital Market Law 2.

Brennan, T. (2008). Bundled rebates as exclusion rather than predation. Journal of Competition Law and Economics, 00 (0). Oxford University Press.

Colomo, P. I. (2016). Beyond the "more economic-based approach": A legal perspective on article 102 TFEU case law. Common Market Law Review 53, Kluwer Law International.

Conac, P. H., & Enriques, L., & Gelter, M. (2008). Constraining Dominant Shareholders' Self Dealing: The Legal Framework in France, Germany and Italy. Harvard Law School, Discussion Paper, number 18/2008.

Conac, P. H. (2013). Boards of directors in European companies – reshaping and harmonizing their organization and duties. Birkmose, H., & Neville M., & Sørensen K. E. (eds.). Kluwer Law International.

Conac, P. H., *et al* (2016). Report on the recognition of the interest of the group, Brussels.

Craig, P., & de Burca, G. (2011). EU Law, Oxford University Press, Oxford.

Emmerich, V., & Habersack, M. (2013). Konzernrecht, Verlag C.H. Beck, München.

Geradin, D. (2011). Price discrimination in the postal sector and competition law. Reinventing the Postal Sector in an Electronic Age, Crew and Kleindorfer (eds.), Edward Elgar Publishing.

Geradin, D., & Malamataris, C. (2014). Application of EU competition law in the postal sector: overview of recent cases. The Role of the Postal and Delivery Sector in a Digital Age, Edward Elgar Publishing.

Jones, A., & Sufrin, B. (2016). EU Competition Law, Oxford University Press.

Kousedghi, S. (2007). Protection of Minority Shareholders and Creditors in Italian Corporate Group Law, European Company Law, 4(5).

Marvel, H. (1982). Exclusive Dealing. Journal of Law and Economics, The University of Chicago, Vol. 25.

Parcu, P. L., & Stasi, M. L. (2017). The role of intent in the assessment of conduct under Article 102 TFEU. Abuse of Dominance in EU Competition Law, Parcu, P. L., & Monti, G., & Botta, M. (eds.), Edward Elgar Publishing.

Pisarkiewicz, A., & West, J. (2013). The Role of Quality in Competition Analysis. OECD, DAF/COMP(2013)8.

Rasmusen, E. B., & Ramseyer, J. M., & Wiley, J. S. (1991). Naked Exclusion. The American Economic Review, Volume 81, Issue 5. American Economic Association.

Rummel, P. (2016). Rebate schemes under Article 102 TFEU: Post Danmark II. Common Market Law Review 53. Kluwer Law International.

Von Danwitz, T. (2008). Europäisches Verwaltungsrecht, Springer, Berlin, Heidelberg.

Winter, J., *et al* (2002). Report of the High Level Group of Company Law Experts on A Modern Regulatory Framework for Company Law in Europe, Brussels.

Regulation. Quo Vadis?

John Hearn

1 Introduction

2017 marks the 20th anniversary of the adoption of the first European Postal Directive.[1] What has been achieved? Is Regulation still needed? The Postal Directive had two objectives. The first objective was to ensure the gradual and controlled liberalization of the European postal services market. The second objective was to address concerns that in a fully liberalized market the services offered on an economic basis would not meet the needs of users or guarantee them fair and non-discriminatory treatment.

The first objective was achieved de jure by January 2013. In practice very little direct competition has emerged and the incumbents have retained a dominant position on the market for physical delivery of correspondence, However new digital forms of communication have emerged and postal companies have been losing market share on the wider communications market—see Sect. 2.

To meet the second objective Member States were required to ensure the provision of a universal postal service at an affordable price and encompassing a

Formerly vice-chair CERP and Project Manager Postal Regulation, ComReg

This paper represents the personal views of the author and should not be taken to represent the policy of ComReg, CERP, or any other organization.

[1]Directive 97/67/EC of the European Parliament and of the Council of 15 December 1997 on common rules for the development of the internal market of Community postal services and the improvement of quality of service; as amended by Directive 2002/39/EC of the European Parliament and of the Council of 10 June 2002 and Directive 2008/6/EC of the European Parliament and of the Council of 20 February 2008.

J. Hearn (✉)
Formerly vice-chair CERP and Project Manager Postal Regulation, ComReg,
Dublin, Ireland
e-mail: john@john-hearn.eu

P.L. Parcu et al. (eds.), *The Contribution of the Postal and Delivery Sector*, Topics in Regulatory Economics and Policy, https://doi.org/10.1007/978-3-319-70672-6_6

minimum range of services of specified quality. The legal features of universal service and the detailed specification of the postal universal service are discussed in Sect. 3.

Section 4 considers changes in the technical, economic and social environment since the Postal Directive was enacted. The last 20 years can best be characterized by the admission of countries with less developed postal markets to the EU and increased competition from new communication media such as mobile phones and the internet, resulting in falling volumes and higher prices for postal services.

On the other hand e-commerce is driving significant increases in the volume of merchandise delivered directly to consumers by postal and other delivery services. However in this area the traditional postal services have never benefited from a monopoly. Since 2012 the European Commission has however proposed a number of initiatives to extend regulation to such postal services. Whether these initiatives are needed and can be effective is considered in Sect. 5.

Quo Vadis? In Sect. 6 it is argued that if sector-specific regulation of postal services did not exist there would be little justification to impose it. Competition Law and Consumer Protection legislation would be sufficient to protect the interests of consumers and other users. But regulation does exist and it will probably experience a protracted winding-down process.

2 The Gradual and Controlled Liberalization of the European Postal Services Market

The 1957 Treaty of Rome was based on the principle that State intervention was to be the exception rather than the rule. Undertakings entrusted with the operation of services of general economic interest (SGEI) were subject to competition law, although in most countries the postal services retained the protection of a monopoly for the next 40 years.

In 1957 postal services were non-commercial State services, but a transition to a more commercial customer focused approach started from the late 1960s onwards. Postal service provision became the responsibility of Public Corporations[2] and State Companies, and there was, structural separation of Post and Electronic Communication.[3] The emergence, during the 1970s and 1980s, of the Courier and Express Industry and the subsequent development of Remail[4] was a significant

[2]As early as 1969 the British Government created a government corporation, "the Post Office", to provide postal services. Today this structure is the norm within the EU, and in 19 of the now 28 EU Member States the government owns or controls the incumbent postal operator, through a State owned company or corporation. In another eight countries the State has ceded control and / or ownership to private sector companies.

[3]E.g. British Telecommunications Act 1981

[4]Domestic mail which is transported, physically or electronically, to another country and then mailed back to the country of origin to obtain a lower price; made possible by below cost terminal dues for cross-border mail.

challenge to the monopoly of the traditional State owned operators. Unsurprisingly it took the intervention of the CJEU (European Court of Justice) to bring the challenge to a successful conclusion.

The defining judgment was in the "Corbeau" case.[5] It was held that the Belgian Post Office had a "*dominant position in a substantial part of the common market within the meaning of Article 86 of the Treaty*" and that:

> *It is contrary to Article 90 of the EEC Treaty for legislation of a Member State which confers on a body such as the* ... [Belgian Post Office] *the exclusive right to collect, carry and distribute mail, to prohibit, under threat of criminal penalties, an economic operator established in that State from offering certain specific services dissociable from the service operated of general interest* ....

In terms of the distinction from the traditional postal service the Court observed that:

> ... *the exclusion of competition is not justified as regards specific services dissociable from the service of general interest which meet special needs of economic operators and which call for certain additional services not offered by the traditional postal service, such as collection from the senders' address, greater speed or reliability of distribution or the possibility of changing the destination in the course of transit, in so far as such specific services, by their nature and the conditions in which they are offered, such as the geographical area in which they are provided, do not compromise the economic equilibrium of the service of general economic interest performed by the holder of the exclusive right.*

In other words the exclusive rights granted to postal service providers were demonstrably inconsistent with the principles of competition laid down in the Treaty of Rome. This intervention meant that the introduction of sector specific regulation was inevitable.

The legal effect of the Postal Directive was to give incumbents derogations from competition law to protect some of their revenues during a transitional period of '*gradual and controlled liberalization of the market*'.[6] Table 1 shows how the scope of these derogations was reduced until competitive entry was possible in all postal markets:

Different countries have responded to the liberalization of postal markets in different ways. Sweden anticipated the Postal Directive and opened its postal market to competition in 1993. Others such as Germany, the Netherlands and Britain planned the opening of their markets based on customer needs and fast tracked the transition to fully liberalized markets. But most countries followed the path set out in the Postal Directive.

Legally, the objective of the 1957 Treaty of Rome was achieved by January 2013, a transition that lasted 56 years! But the level of competition for the physical

[5]Case C-320/91 Paul Corbeau 19 May 1993, [1993] ECR 1–2563

[6]Directive 97/67, Recital 8.

Table 1 Elimination of the postal monopolies

Directive	Effective from:	Maximum reserved area permitted	
		Weight Limit	Price Limit
97/67/EC	**1998**	**350 g**	**Five times** the public tariff for an item of correspondence in the first weight step of the fastest standard category
2002/39/EC	**2003**	**100 g**	**Three times** the public tariff ...
2002/39/EC	**2006**	**50 g**	**Two and a half times** the public tariff ...
2008/6/EC	**2011**[a]	**FULL MARKET OPENING**	

[a]11 Member States—Czech Republic, Greece, Cyprus, Latvia, Lithuania, Luxembourg, Hungary, Malta, Poland, Romania and Slovakia—were granted a derogation until January 2013

delivery of correspondence remains limited, in both domestic and international markets[7] and the former State monopolies have retained a dominant position on this market, although they face intense competition from other communication media and in the delivery of merchandise. This can be explained by changes in the technical, economic and social environment and the needs of users discussed in Sect. 4.

3 Guaranteed Provision of a Universal Postal Service

When the first Postal Directive was adopted postal services were considered "*an essential instrument of communication and trade*".[8] There was concern that in the transition to a fully liberalized market the services offered on an economic basis would not meet the needs of users or guarantee them fair and non-discriminatory treatment. The Directive therefore set out specific provisions for the mandatory provision of a universal postal service at an affordable price and encompassing a minimum range of services of specified quality.

It is worth noting that the concept of universal service is not unique to postal services, rather it applies to all Services of General Economic Interest (SGEI). The concept is set out in a European Commission Communication[9]:

> *Services of general economic interest are different from ordinary services in that public authorities consider that they need to be provided even where the market may not have sufficient incentives to do so. This is not to deny that in many cases the market will be the best mechanism for providing such services. Many basic requirements, such as food, clothing, shelter, are provided exclusively or overwhelmingly by the market. However, if the public authorities consider that certain services are in the general interest and market*

[7]See COM (2015) 568 final *op cit*

[8]Directive 97/67, Recital 2

[9]Communication from the Commission. Services of general interest in Europe (2001/C 17/04), Brussels, 19.0.2001 point 14

forces may not result in a satisfactory provision, they can lay down a number of specific service provisions to meet these needs ....

The characteristics of such services are set out in sector specific or general legislation and in relevant judgments of the European Courts.[10] Taking into account the wider EU *acquis* universal service has the following characteristics: it should meet the essential needs of all users; it should be provided by a licensed undertaking; it should offer the specified services to every user requesting them and contract, on consistent conditions, without being able to reject the other contracting party (i.e. there is an "offer" to the customer rather than an "invitation to treat"); the nature of the services is not prescribed and does not have to be provided through the entire territory or be of use to the whole population; there must be transparency as to tariffs and terms and conditions. Uniform tariffs are the norm (i.e. prices are fixed and not subject to individual negotiation) and rates, conditions and quality standards should be as similar as possible for all users.

The Postal Directive required national governments to guarantee the provision of certain basic postal services.[11] The Directive specified some high level requirements, but gave national governments the flexibility to decide what would best meet domestic circumstances.

Article 3(3) required the universal service to be guaranteed every working day and not less than 5 days a week, save in exceptional circumstances or geographical conditions.[12] Each day there must be at least one collection ("clearance") from access points which meet the needs of users and one delivery to the home or premises of every natural or legal person.

At the time this was not perceived as an onerous obligation. In all EU Member States, with the possible exception of Italy and Greece, the volume of mail per capita was sufficient to sustain the specified level of service. In six countries (Denmark,[13] France, Germany, Italy, The Netherlands, and the UK,) deliveries were being provided 6 days a week—see NERA (1998), and in some countries, e.g. the UK, there was more than one delivery each day in urban areas.

The service had as a minimum to cover postal items (i.e. letter post) up to 2 kg, postal packages (i.e. parcels) up to 10 kg, and registered and insured items. In practice 10 of the 15 EU Members of the time applied a 20 kg limit for domestic parcels and all but one applied a 20 kg limit to incoming cross-border parcels.

---

[10]See in particular case T-289/03 British United Provident Association Ltd. (BUPA), BUPA Insurance Ltd. and BUPA Ireland Ltd. v Commission of the European Communities [2008] ECR II-81.

[11]Directive 97/67, Article 3

[12]WiK (2004) reported exceptional geographical conditions mean that more than three percent of the Greek population were served less than five days per week, and in ten more countries under one percent were affected

[13]Letters only, not parcels

There was also an obligation to lay down quality standards for national mail which had to be compatible with those laid down in the Directive for intra-Community cross-border services.[14]

It should be noted that there were no obligations to provide specific services (e.g. First and Second Class or Priority and Economy) or payment methods (franking meters, accounts, etc.), nor was there any obligation to provide next day delivery. The regulatory framework specifically excluded from its scope new and value added services and services provided under individually negotiated contracts.[15] Many commonly used postal services were not part of it, even where they are offered by the universal service provider, particularly value-added services like track and trace or delivery by a specified day or time. This meant that most postal parcel services fell outside the scope of the universal service.

The specification of the universal service is important from the consumers' point of view not just because of its guaranteed provision but also because of other obligations imposed by the Postal Directive including transparent, cost-oriented and affordable prices, detailed cost accounting, measurable quality of service standards, compliance with the essential requirements such as confidentiality of correspondence and data protection, and transparent, simple and inexpensive complaints procedures. Recital 34 to the Postal Directive also confirmed that Council Directive 93/13/EEC of 5 April 1993 on unfair terms in consumer contracts applies to the postal services. The Postal Directive set out a preference for the provision of the universal service through the designation of one or more universal service providers. The Directive also permitted the authorization or licensing of operators providing postal services outside the reserved area.

4 Changes Since 1997

Changes in the technical, economic and social environment have been dramatic since the Postal Directive was enacted almost 20 years ago.

The number of EU Member States has increased from 15 to 28. Postal markets in the new Member States were not as developed as those in the original Member States. WiK (2004) reported that the average number of letters per capita in EU countries in 2002 was just under 200 items. Of the ten new Members that joined in 2004 only two, Slovenia and Malta, had more than 100 letters per capita. The new Member States could not sustain postal services of the scope and quality specified by the Postal Directive.

---

[14]Directive 97/67, Article 17(1)

[15]See Notice from the Commission on the application of the competition rules to the postal sector and on the assessment of certain State measures relating to postal services (98/C 39/02) 06/02/1998

Table 2 New means of communication

Take up per 100 inhabitants	1997	2005	2007	2016
Mobile phones	18			
Developed countries		90	97	
Europe		91.7	111.7	119.5
Internet users	11			
Developed countries		56	62	
Europe		46.3	56.0	79.1
Households with internet access at home (Europe)		42.0	51.7	84.0

Source: ITU database

New means of communication such as mobile phones and the internet in all its forms have become ubiquitous—see Table 2.

Also OECD (2014) recommended that governments should develop and implement digital strategies to unlock economic and social benefits for society as a whole. The European Commission has published three eGovernment Action Plans 2006–2010, 2011–2015 and 2016–2020.

What is clear is that these developments have stimulated indirect competition and that the traditional postal services are losing the ensuing competitive battle.

There has been a significant reduction in the number of letters being sent since the Postal Directive came into force. The European Commission estimates[16] that the number of letters per head of population in 2013 was about 141 items. This suggests a 30% decline since 2002. In absolute terms it reports the number of letters declined from an estimated 107.6 billion in 2008 to 85.5 billion in 2013. Two of the Member States with highest rates of decline, Denmark and Estonia, are two of the most digitally advanced. In Denmark mail volumes fell by over 60% between 2000 and 2014. In Estonia the number of letters fell by 11.3% per annum between 2007 and 2011.[17]

ITA/WiK (2009) reported that the importance of consumer correspondence (C2B and C2C) has declined in many countries and that, overall, more than 85% of letters were sent by businesses. Given the decline in volumes since then the percentage of private correspondence has almost certainly declined further.

The postal community attributes this decline to "e-substitution", i.e. the use of the new electronic communication services. There is a need for a detailed study to identify all the factors influencing this volume decline, in particular to assess whether postal operators' pricing decisions and economic factors have contributed to, or mitigated the decline.

As volumes have fallen prices have increased.

The Postal Directive requires universal service prices to be affordable, cost-oriented, transparent and non-discriminatory. WiK (2013) reports that 12 countries representing 12% of the EU postal market have chosen to subject universal services

[16]See COM (2015) 568 final *op. cit.*

[17]See WiK (2013)

to ex-ante price approval and nine countries corresponding to 63% of the market to a price cap.

Comparison of the latest (2016) edition of Deutsche Post AG's annual review of "*Letter prices in Europe*" with the 2007 edition reveals the evolution of prices since the Postal Directive. In 14 countries nominal prices[18] for a standard domestic letter have increased by more than 50% in the last 10 years. Over the longer period 1996–2015 in 11 of the 20 countries surveyed[19] the inflation adjusted price increase was more than 24%. Full details are shown in Table 3.

Looking at individual countries, three countries, Austria, Germany and Ireland, had the same price (55c) at 1 January 2007. By 1 March 2016 the price had increased to 70c (Germany and Ireland) or 68c (Austria). However after adjusting for inflation the rate of increase varied between 2.5% (Austria) and 16.2% (Ireland). Recently the price in Ireland has increased to €1.00 following a Government decision to remove the National Regulatory Authority's (NRA) price cap. This means prices have increased by 82% since 2007.

It has to be questioned whether the Postal Directive has been effective in controlling prices. It is difficult to reconcile price increases significantly in excess of the rate of inflation with the affordability requirement. Would prices be materially different if they were only subject to competition law and the influence of competition from other means of communication?

The Postal Directive requires that the universal postal service must evolve in response to the technical, economic and social environment and to the needs of users. It has been amended twice, in 2003 and in 2008, but these amendments have been focused on completing the gradual and controlled liberalization of the European Postal Market, Also consequential provision was made for the selection of universal service providers and for financing the net costs of providing the universal service, should this prove to be an unfair burden on the service provider. The independence of NRAs was strengthened and they were given greater market monitoring and consumer protection powers.

The European Commission's latest report on the regulatory framework published in 2015[20] recognized that significant change had taken place in the market but made no specific proposals for reform. Rather it suggested that further analysis of the overall postal market, and the effects of the regulatory framework, were needed, particularly to ensure the sustainability of the sector.

Some Member States have used the permitted flexibilities to mitigate this lack of reform. Nine countries have confined universal service to single-piece letters only and seven countries to letters only.

[18]In euro. The nominal prices shown will be affected by movements in exchange rates between the national currency and euro.

[19]Some countries are excluded from the report because Deutsche Post did not have all the information needed for the period 1996–2006.

[20]See COM (2015) 568 final *op. cit.*

Table 3 Price increases since 1996

	Nominal price in €			Change in prices–adjusted. For inflation		
	at 1 Jan 2007	at 1 March 2016	Change (%)	1996–2006	2006–2015	1996–2015 est
Italy	0.60	**2.80**[a]	**367**	23.85%	291.40%	360.90%
Denmark	0.64	2.55[a]	298	4.74%	240.10%	251.48%
Romania	**0.14**	0.36	157		106.80%	
Estonia	0.28	0.65	132		60.50%	
Czech Rep.	0.26	0.48	85	77.08%	41.60%	73.67%
Slovenia	0.20	0.36	80	0.00%	44.80%	
UK	0.50	0.88	76	12.58%	47.00%	52.91%
Finland	0.70	1.20	71	28.09%	40.70%	52.13%
Netherlands	0.44	0.73	66	(4.30%)	42.20%	40.39%
Bulgaria	0.28	0.44	57		8.10%	
Lithuania	0.29	0.45	55		10.90%	
Belgium	0.52	0.79	52	9.27%	26.50%	28.96%
Slovakia	0.43	0.65	51	312.30%	(0.30%)	(1.24%)
Spain	0.30	0.45[a]	50	25.04%	24.30%	30.38%
France	0.54	0.80	48	0.37%	28.20%	28.30%
Norway	**0.87**	1.23	41	64.40%	33.20%	54.58%
Luxembourg	0.50	0.70	40	(0.70%)	13.20%	13.11%
Greece	0.52	0.72	38	56.01%	15.70%	24.49%
Malta	0.19	**0.26**	37	0.00%	15.30%	
Hungary	0.36	0.47	31	121.04%	5.50%	12.16%
Latvia	0.44	0.57	30		(12.80%)	
Portugal	0.45	0.58	29	(14.50%)	11.00%	9.41%
Ireland	***0.55***	***0.70***	27	0.23%	16.20%	16.24%
Germany	***0.55***	***0.70***	27	(6.20%)	9.40%	8.82%
Austria	***0.55***	***0.68***	24	8.06%	2.50%	2.70%
Sweden	0.59	0.70	19	23.12%	3.70%	4.56%
Cyprus	0.35	0.41	17	54.05%	0.20%	0.31%
Poland	0.54	0.56	**4**		(11.00%)	
Minimum	**0.14**	**0.26**	4	(14.50%)	(12.80%)	(1.24%)
Maximum	**0.87**	**2.80**	367	312.30%	291.40%	360.90%

[a]In the case of Italy and Denmark this price is for a new D + 1 service similar to Registered Mail. Users are encouraged to use slower services priced at 95c (D + 4) and 8Dkr (D + 5) respectively. Spain has never offered a D + 1 service, but does now offer a fast D + 1services similar to those offered in Italy and Denmark, priced at €3.39

Three countries, Denmark, Finland and the Netherlands, have made changes to the frequency of delivery. There has been a reduction from 6 to 5 days, and restrictions on the delivery of non-priority letters on certain days.

Italy has implemented delivery on alternate days in areas with low density, low volumes and high cost (ultimately 23% of the population) but this policy is being challenged before the CJEU (European Court of Justice).[21]

[21]Case C-275/16, Comune di Balzola et al.

More recently price caps have been modified to reflect the effect of volume decline (e.g. France), confined to "second class service" only (e.g. UK), or all ex-ante controls have been removed (e.g. Ireland).

It should also be noted that in eight countries the State has ceded control and/or ownership of their universal service providers to private sector companies.

5 Extension of Regulation to Parcels Markets

In contrast to the declining demand for traditional postal services, e-commerce is driving significant increases in the volume of merchandise delivered directly to consumers by postal and other delivery services.

However postal companies are not dominant players on this market. According to TPR (2015) their market share, at the European level and according to the number of packages delivered, is only 10%. The European Economic and Social Committee (2016) has observed that the share of universal service providers varies from 10% (Bulgaria, Spain, United Kingdom, Italy) to 25% (Czech Republic, Denmark, France, Estonia), while only a small percentage (5–10%) of these parcels are covered by universal service obligations.

Since 2012 the European Commission has however proposed a number of initiatives to extend regulation to these types of postal services.[22] The failure to achieve any consensus after 5 years of debate raises two questions. Is regulation necessary? And if imposed would it be effective?

Is regulation necessary? The European Commission's proposed Regulation is specifically confined to postal companies:

> "parcel delivery services" means services involving ….. **parcels** ….;
>
> "parcel" means a **postal item** … ;
>
> **Postal item**: an **item addressed** in the final form in which it is to be **carried by a postal service provider**. ….; [emphasis added]

As already mentioned postal companies are not dominant players on the market. It is important therefore to understand the difference between the services offered by postal companies and those offered by other delivery companies.

Hearn (2017) describes how postal services are generally provided on a non-contractual basis under public law, and the service provider acts as an intermediary between sender and receiver. International services are subject to the conditions laid down in the UPU Convention and its Regulations, and in principle there are different service providers in the countries of dispatch and delivery.

[22] See Groves P, "The 2016 European Commission Proposal for a Regulation on Cross-Border Parcels: an assessment of the objectives, background, issues and potential impacts" in this book

By contrast other delivery companies operate under private law on the basis of a contract negotiated between the sender[23] and the company. If cross-border transport is involved it will be subject to the Warsaw Convention (air transport) or the CMR Convention[24] (road transport). The whole process is controlled by the contracting company, even if sub-contractors are involved,

The basis for charging is also different. Postal services distinguish between "packets" and "postal parcels". Statistics published by An Post (Ireland) suggest over 94% are packets, and based on average revenue the average weight of a "postal parcel" is less than 3 kg. The former can weight up to 2 kg and be up to about 0.027 m^3 in size, and charges are normally based on weight. "Postal parcels" are larger (up to about 0.85 m^3) and heavier (up to 20 kg or 30 kg).[25] Prices are usually non-negotiable.

Other delivery companies negotiate prices individually A rate card is simply an "invitation to treat" and is only the starting point for negotiations. Generally weight limits are very high, but consignments to consumers probably differ little from the postal service, i.e. 90% are less than 2 kg and few over 3 kg. Where it is necessary to use a special rate card for consumer or "one off" dispatches,[26] these are normally based solely on size, see for example GLS Parcel Shops or DHL Service Points.

The Consumer Rights Directive[27] provides that consumers contract exclusively with the seller (the e-retailer), and title to the goods purchased only passes when the goods are received by the consumer. Because of these obligations it is advisable for e-retailers to use a delivery company that operates on a contractual basis and which does not grant conflicting rights to the receiver[28] as postal companies do.

There are also differences in the way that the item is delivered to the consumer. Postal companies require that the name and address of the receiver is shown on or attached to the item, and the item is normally delivered to this address. Only if it proves impossible to deliver the item as addressed will the receiver be asked to collect the item from a specified post office. Other delivery companies are more flexible in terms of the delivery options they offer, e.g. packet stations, collection from a local store open 7–11 or 24/7 or delivery on a specified day or time. The delivery details are recorded on the waybill/consignment note rather than on the "parcel" and can be changed by agreement.

---

[23] Or in exceptional circumstances the receiver, but not both.

[24] "The Convention on the Contract for the International Carriage of Goods by Road (CMR)" Geneva, 19th May 1956″.

[25] Some operators now charge for "postal parcels" by size or by dimensional/volumetric weight if applicable.

[26] I.e. where individual negotiation is not feasible.

[27] Directive 2011/83/EU of the European Parliament and of the Council of 25 October 2011 on consumer rights, amending Council Directive 93/13/EEC and Directive 1999/44/EC of the European Parliament and of the Council and repealing Council Directive 85/577/EEC and Directive 97/7/EC of the European Parliament and of the Council

[28] Under the UPU Convention the receiver can normally claim compensation from the postal company which delivered the item.

It is difficult to understand why it is necessary to introduce regulation of the parcel services offered by postal companies given their small share of the overall market, the different legal basis on which they must provide service (one which arguably puts them at a competitive disadvantage in bidding for the business of e-retailers), and the absence of any type of monopoly or dominant position in the past.

Innovation comes from competitive pressures and the desire to make profits. Regulation cannot substitute for this fundamental economic principle. As e-commerce develops and achieves its full potential it is increasingly likely that there will be alliances and partnerships with other communications and distribution networks. The key will be to offer a one stop shopping website: electronic advertising and order taking, physical distribution of advertising and sales material and physical distribution of purchased goods often on a pan-European or Global basis. Regulation of a small part of the market for physical delivery of merchandise to consumers is likely to inhibit these developments.

Assuming that Regulation is eventually imposed on postal companies providing "parcel" services, it is difficult to see how it will be an effective instrument of regulation.

Hearn (2016) questioned whether statistics about international e-commerce tell the whole story. E-retailers trading internationally often create a virtual presence in each targeted country so that the customer's perception is that he is purchasing locally[29] In summary the reasons for this are that EU law requires VAT to be charged at the rate applicable in the consumer's country; it is preferable to use the consumer's native language and (where applicable) the local currency[30]; a local "contact point" for consumer care issues gives greater confidence to the consumer; and the Omni-channel approach used by most e-retailers requires a "bricks and mortar" presence to complement the online presence.

Research on behalf of the EU into pricing also often failed to distinguish between delivery charges raised by e-retailers and those charged by service providers to the e-retailer. For example among the 211 consumers who responded to the Commission's 2015 consultation, the price of delivery was a common issue, but it was the price charged by the retailer not the price charged by the postal or delivery company. Specific issues mentioned were "no free delivery option" (over half of respondents), 'high delivery prices' (just under half); cost of delivery (over one third); and "high costs of return" ('just under one third'). Of the 64 retailers who responded, nearly half stated that they charged consumers more than they pay to delivery operators.

---

[29]See for example http://www.marksandspencer.eu/de_DE. This website is in German, there is a German telephone number and an address in Kelsterbach, Germany for returns. Revocation of an order under the Consumer Rights Directive must be sent to an address in Cologne. The 'small print' reveals that the customer is dealing with Marks and Spencer (Ireland) Limited.

[30]Meaning that the e-retailer bears any exchange rate risk.

The proposal to create a European website listing the tariffs of postal companies for 30 types of postal item might potentially distort the overall market by creating the impression that postal services are the only services available. Because the website will only be updated annually the prices shown may become easily out of date.[31] Even if the prices of non-postal operators were included in the website the different basis of charging, size rather than weight, would probably confuse rather than inform.

6 Quo Vadis?

For many years now the argument has been made that there is no need for sector-specific regulation in the postal industry; existing legal instruments, in particular competition law, can deal with any deficiencies that may arise—see for example Tilburg (2005) and IPC (2007).

Although there is little direct competition in the provision of letter delivery services, it is clear, as noted in Sect. 4, that technological developments have stimulated indirect competition and that the traditional postal services are losing the competitive battle. The European Commission's latest report[32] argues that "*Postal services continue to play a vital role across the European Union ... the ability to send letters ... to all parts of the European Union remains a fundamental contributor to social, economic and territorial cohesion and the development of the single market*." On the other hand the decline in mail volumes, and the paltry proportion sent by private individuals, coupled with the ubiquitous availability of electronic alternatives which are cheaper and faster, makes it hard to argue that letter services are still an essential instrument of communication and trade.

The European Commission's latest report on the regulatory framework[33] recognized that significant change had taken place but made no specific proposals for reform. A new Commission will be appointed in 2019; this means that there will be no reform until 2020 at the earliest. By then it is easy to predict that there will have been further significant changes.

It seems that for the foreseeable future Member States will need to make the maximum use of the flexibilities allowed by the current postal directive. Some countries have made changes to delivery frequency. Adjustments to, or abolition, of price caps in response to declines in business can also be observed. In some countries the next day delivery (D + 1) service is now a premium product but there is a more affordable product with a lower transit time. Further changes in the

[31]In 2017 at least three companies, An Post (Ireland), La Posted (France) and Royal Mail (UK), increased prices in late March or April. These price increases would not be reflected on the website until March 2018.

[32]See COM (2015) 568 final *op. cit.*

[33]See COM (2015) 568 final *op. cit.*

scope of universal service, informed by detailed studies of customer needs, can be envisioned.

The Europeans Commission's proposal to extend regulation to the "postal parcel" services currently excluded from regulation has so far failed to achieve a consensus. As discussed in Sect. 5 anyway it is unlikely to be effective.

In conclusion, if sector-specific regulation of postal services did not exist there would be little justification to impose it today. Competition Law and Consumer Protection legislation would be sufficient to protect users. But regulation does exist and it will probably experience a protracted winding-down process.

References

European Economic and Social Committee (2016), Opinion, Proposal for a Regulation of the European Parliament and of the Council on cross-border parcel delivery services [COM(2016) 285 final—2016/0149 (COD)], INT/799 Parcel delivery, 19 October 2016

Hearn (2016), "Implications of recent developments in e-commerce for Universal Service Providers and the USO" in M. A. Crew and T. Brennan (eds.) The Future of the Postal Sector in a Digital World, Springer 2016

Hearn (2017) "Protecting consumers using postal and e-commerce delivery services in competitive European markets" in Pier Luigi Parcu, Michael Crew, Timothy Brennan (EDS), The Changing Postal and Delivery Sector, Towards a Renaissance, Springer 2017

IPC (2007) How to regulate the postal industry' an economic approach, A study prepared by IPC in cooperation with DIW Berlin the German Institute for Economic Research

ITA/WiK (2009) The Evolution of the European Postal Market since 1997, ITA Consulting and WiK Consult, August 2009

Letter Prices in Europe, Deutsche Post AG, 53250 Bonn, Germany, Editor: Alexander Edenhofer, January 2007

Letter Prices in Europe, Deutsche Post AG, 53250 Bonn, Germany, March 2016

NERA (1998) Costing and financing of universal service obligations in the postal sector in the European union, Final Report for EC DG XIII, National Economic Research Associates, London, 1998

OECD (2014) Non-Commercial Service Obligations and Liberalization, JT00168156 DAFFE/COMP(2004)19, Organisation for Economic Co-operation and Development, 18′ August 2004

Tilburg (2005) 'Light is Right'. Competition and Access Regulation in an Open Postal Sectors, Dr. Paul De Bijl, Professor Dr. Eric Van Damme & Professor Dr. Pierre Larouche, Tilburg Law and Economics Center (TILEC), NL-5000 LE Tilburg, The Netherlands, June 2005

TPR (2015) Cross-Border Parcel Delivery Operations and its Cost Drivers, Department of Transport and Regional Economics, University of Antwerp, for the European Commission.

WiK (2004) Main Developments in the European Postal Sector, WIK-Consult, Study for the European Commission, July 2004

WiK (2013) Main Developments in the Postal Sector (2010–2013), WIK-Consult, Study for the European Commission

PAEA's Take on Regulatory Economics

Edward S. Pearsall

1 Introduction

The primary purpose of the Postal Accountability and Enhancement Act (PAEA 2006) was to stabilize the finances of the United States Postal Service (USPS) by creating a "modern" regulatory system to replace the system established by the Postal Reform Act of 1970 (the 1970 Act). Secondary purposes were to deregulate postal markets wherever USPS confronted direct competition, level the playing field by reducing USPS's governmental advantages, and limit USPS's participation in markets for non-postal products. Congress also expected PAEA to "maximize incentives to reduce costs and improve efficiency".

To do these things PAEA dealt with many topics that are subjects of study in regulatory economics. These subjects are mostly problems with formulations, analyses and solutions that are well understood and accepted by economists. However, in almost every case, PAEA either overlooked the appropriate concepts or employed them in modified, restricted or incorrect forms that sow confusion and sacrifice advantages. In hindsight PAEA mostly missed opportunities to improve the efficiency of the US postal sector under regulation. In addition PAEA's defective regulatory system has contributed to an unexpected fiscal crisis for USPS.

This paper describes features of the regulatory system created by PAEA that could be improved by correctly applying concepts and results from economics. The paper is organized in sections as follows: Sect. 2 is PAEA's take on regulation, Sect. 3 on deregulation, Sect. 4 on liberalization, Sect. 5 on efficient pricing, Sect. 6 on price discrimination, Sect. 7 on price caps, Sect. 8 on pricing flexibility, Sect. 9 on cross-subsidies, Sect. 10 on worksharing discounts, Sect. 11 on quality of service,

The views expressed in this paper are the author's.

E.S. Pearsall (✉)
Independent Consultant, Alexandria, VA, USA
e-mail: espearsall@verizon.net

P.L. Parcu et al. (eds.), *The Contribution of the Postal and Delivery Sector*, Topics in Regulatory Economics and Policy, https://doi.org/10.1007/978-3-319-70672-6_7

Sect. 12 on production efficiency, and Sect. 13 on the Universal Service Obligation (USO) and Reserved Area (RA). The conclusion evaluates PAEA's effects on the US postal sector 10 years after its passage.

2 PAEA's Take on Regulation

PAEA distinguishes between "market-dominant" and "competitive" classes of service based upon USPS's market power. PAEA's initial lists of products mostly followed the convention of designating services as competitive if there was an alternative supplier of a directly competing service. Otherwise, postal products were designated as market-dominant.

PAEA creates different regulatory regimes for the two categories. The predominant feature of the law is a class-level set of price caps that limit the permissible annual increase in each market-dominant product's average price to the rate of increase in the Urban Consumer Price Index (CPI-U). The prices of competitive services are subject only to cross-subsidy prohibitions.

PAEA's separation of postal products into polar categories is fundamental to the regulatory system that the legislation creates. But it is a stark distinction without much support in economic theory. Economics recognizes a wide range of possible market organizations ranging from monopoly, through various kinds of oligopolies, to contestable and competitive markets. Whether or not a postal market needs price regulation at all depends upon how it will self-organize without the regulation. And to be effective, the controls of any regulatory system require an understanding of how postal markets will respond. PAEA's un-nuanced division does not permit much tailoring of the regulatory system to diverse markets.

PAEA tries to isolate the accounting for market-dominant and competitive services by instructing the PRC to allocate "institutional" costs among PAEA's classes. Institutional costs are costs that cannot be linked to specific postal products and services. They are composed of a mix of non-product-specific fixed costs and the accumulated effects of decreasing marginal costs up to current volumes. USPS's cost function is not separable by PAEA's classes so there is no generally-accepted economic basis for assigning all of USPS's costs to products.

The idea behind the separated accounting is to treat competitive products as being produced and sold by an independent enterprise. However, the arbitrary division of costs turns this into an empty accounting exercise. PAEA also instructs the Treasury to assess USPS for a tax on its income from competitive products. This provision requires a further arbitrary division of assets and liabilities insofar as they are relevant for applying the tax code.

PAEA created an asymmetry with respect to information on market-dominant and competitive products by permitting USPS to place data and analyses pertaining to competitive products under seal. PAEA allowed the PRC to exercise discretion over what information must be sealed in response to a USPS request. In practice, however, the PRC lets USPS aggressively limit public access to information on competitive services. For example, when USPS submits econometric demand models and forecasts as part of its Annual Compliance Report (ACR), the PRC seals all of the data and analyses pertaining to competitive services.

Revenue, pieces and weight reports (RPWs), billing determinants, cost and revenue analyses (CRAs), quality of service reports, etc. are all in two forms. Non-public files contain all of the information that USPS must regularly report to the PRC; public files exclude most of the information that relates to competitive products. Of course, the PRC relies on the non-public files which are kept under seal for 9 years. Nine years! Pre-PAEA much of the redacted information was made public without complaint from USPS.

Asymmetries in information between buyers and sellers impair the performance of markets. Similar problems arise under postal regulation whenever the PRC depends upon adversarial proceedings. Parties without access to non-public files are disadvantaged versus USPS. For example, USPS's competitors cannot determine if parcel services are cross-subsidized because they cannot obtain the data from the public files that are needed for the appropriate tests.

3 PAEA's Take on De-regulation

The regulatory regime established by the 1970 Act was unusual because it was a system for regulating a public rather than a private enterprise. Its purpose was to relieve Congress of the responsibility for defining services and setting postal rates by creating a rate Commission with powers that roughly matched those of a utility commission.

The Commission conducted public hearings and issued decisions recommending rates and making service classifications. The Commission's procedures followed an adversarial model giving rights of due process to all interested parties. The rate recommendations specified in detail every element of the postal tariff. They were based upon USPS's cost of service and included a breakeven condition. USPS had only very limited powers to amend or reject the recommendations.

In other respects, the 1970 Act gave the Commission very little power. In particular, the Commission could not set standards of service, did not initiate proceedings, had little ability to command USPS to produce data and analyses, and found it awkward to apply its own expertise to the matters it considered.

By 2006 this regulatory arrangement was decidedly old fashioned. During the 1980s several Federal regulatory agencies with similar powers such as the CAB and FCC had seen their powers reduced by deregulation. PAEA brought deregulation to the postal sector by substantially altering the role of the renamed PRC.

PAEA terminated the PRC's authority to set rates. The PRC's role in rate-making today is advisory. The PRC reviews USPS's tariff for compliance with the price caps and discount rules 45 days before being placed in effect (*ex ante* price regulation). The PRC also conducts a backwards-looking Annual Compliance Determination (ACD) reviewing the tariff for compliance with PAEA's rules during the previous fiscal year (*ex post* price regulation). But the PRC is empowered to do no more than inform USPS of violations and demand explanations or adjustments. In recent years the PRC's compliance reviews have revealed many violations of PAEA's rules limiting worksharing discounts. Often, USPS has simply ignored the PRC's demands for explanations or adjustments.

The only vestige of the PRC's former rate authority is PAEA's provision for revising the tariff under "extraordinary and exceptional" circumstances. An aggressive reading of this provision would allow USPS to revise its rates periodically outside the constraints of PAEA's price caps. However, there has been only one "exigent" rate proceeding since 2006. The PRC took a conservative view of the provision and only allowed USPS to collect a temporary 4.3% surcharge on market-dominant services to recoup revenues lost in the Great Recession. This ended periodic reconsideration of the rates under the extraordinary and exceptional provision.

PAEA significantly increased the PRC's powers to collect information. Notably, the PRC was given the subpoena power it lacked under the 1970 Act. PAEA also greatly enlarged the scope of the PRC's collection efforts, particularly with respect to USPS's operations and quality of service.

PAEA tasked the PRC to make many reports to Congress. These include periodic reports such as the ACD and various special reports such as a report on the USO and RA. None of this reporting is found in the 1970 Act which expected the Congress to take a "hands off" approach to postal affairs. In contrast, PAEA's reporting tasks converted the PRC into an agent of the Congress. There is no decision of consequence that can be made by USPS's board and management that will not be preceded by some kind of advance notice to the PRC and delayed as necessary to allow time for Congressional action. This overreach has been critically analyzed by Campbell (2013).

PAEA did not create a postal regulatory system that was familiar at the time to economists. The system does not conform to any model of regulation found in economics. Nor does it correspond to postal regulatory practice abroad or to non-postal regulatory practice within the US. That is not to say that the system is completely unrecognizable. It is essentially the same system in disguise that Congress employs to oversee agencies of the Federal government.

4 PAEA's Take on Liberalization

Full liberalization of a price-regulated market entails two steps. First, the market is opened to entry by competitors to the incumbent monopolist, and second, the incumbent is freed to set its own price. The general idea behind liberalization is to establish price discipline by competition, both actual and potential, to supplant direct price regulation. In a successful liberalization the regulator's role is reduced to enforcing freedom-of-entry, prohibiting cross-subsidies, and preventing other anti-competitive behavior.

There are both advantages and disadvantages to liberalization, even when successful. The advantage for the US postal sector is relaxed regulation. The major disadvantage is that it is less costly to let USPS deliver all of the mail than to have multiple delivery services each with declining average costs.

Not all price-regulated markets can be successfully liberalized. It is possible that liberalized markets will fail to attract entrants. When this happens delivery of the mail is a natural monopoly and the incumbent monopolist cannot be freed from price regulation.

Full liberalizations are commonplace abroad. PAEA's partial liberalizations of US postal markets are almost trivial in comparison. In fact PAEA did little more than recognize the parcel market liberalization that had occurred under the 1970 Act.

The PRC is empowered to change the pre-established lists of market-dominant and competitive products. But there is a catch-22; a service must be classified as market-dominant if USPS is a monopoly supplier. New liberalizations are mostly impossible with this provision because USPS remains a statutory monopolist in the delivery of all non-parcel mail under PAEA.

5 PAEA's Take on Efficient Pricing

The modern approach to efficient regulatory pricing dates from Baumol and Bradford's (1970) rediscovery of Ramsey/Boiteux pricing. Ramsey/Boiteux prices maximize welfare, defined as the sum of consumers' and producers' surplus, subject to a constraint on net revenue. The prices are second-best efficient prices that obey a generalized inverse elasticity rule. The prices are second-best because, absent the net revenue constraint, welfare would be maximized by setting prices equal to marginal costs.

Ramsey/Boiteux pricing can be made operational with respect to US postal prices but the effort requires estimates of cost and demand functions. This makes it difficult to extend the arithmetic to include the reactions of postal competitors. Nevertheless, efficient prices for just USPS products and services can be calculated using the demand and cost models that USPS routinely submits to the PRC. It is also possible to estimate the welfare losses resulting from the installation of sub-optimal rates.

The PRC does not currently evaluate the efficiency of USPS's rates. Such an analysis would be likely to disclose that PAEA's effective freeze of postal prices relative to the CPU-U commenced a long term decline in the efficiency of the rates with respect to market-dominant services.

PAEA did little to focus the objective of postal rate setting specifically on efficiency. Instead, PAEA repeats the treatment found in the 1970 Act by listing 9 "objectives" and 14 "factors" to be taken into account when setting rates for market-dominant services. PAEA does not indicate which objective is paramount and which factors are to be taken as constraints. Nor does it resolve any of the obvious conflicts between the various objectives and factors. Altogether, PAEA cannot be read as an authorization to apply the concepts and results associated with Ramsey/Boiteux pricing.

Instead, PAEA simply recreates the *carte blanche* given to US rate-setters by the 1970 Act. Prior to PAEA, USPS requested, the Commission recommended, and USPS installed revised rates for domestic mail and services about every 3 years. The explanations offered for the revised rates may be found in the hearings testimony of USPS rates witnesses and the recommended decisions of the Commission. One cannot read these explanations and detect any transcending economic principle. Typically, changes in rates are simply explained mechanically as responses to changes in postal cost and institutional cost coverage.

6 PAEA's Take on Price Discrimination

When USPS charges different categories of customers different prices for the same service we have third degree price discrimination. The necessary conditions for third degree price discrimination are that the customers be separable so that USPS can charge them different prices, and that they cannot resell postal services to each other. Otherwise, the different prices would be unsustainable.

Under these conditions a profit maximizing monopoly can increase its profits by exploiting differences between the aggregate demand elasticities of its customers. However, the third degree price discrimination in US postal rates sacrifices rather than promotes USPS profits. The rates discriminate because it has been the long-standing policy of the Congress to aid favored customers. The price discrimination we observe is mostly an extension of the pricing system inherited from the 1970 Act. The system has been reinforced from time to time by the passage of laws dictating price relationships for favored customers.

US postal rates discriminate in three ways that are unrelated to the cost or quality of service. They discriminate by content, by sender and by recipient. Letters and cards with personal messages are carried at First-Class rates; letters and cards without personal messages are eligible for Periodicals and Standard mail rates. Periodicals rates have different pound-rated rates for advertising and editorial content. Package services rates discriminate if the package contains a declared catalogue, book or media rather than something else. Periodicals and Standard mail rates discriminate between Regular and Non-profit mailers and are lower for periodicals sent to classrooms. The mail is free for the blind and handicapped mailers. Official US government mail receives "Penalty" rates that differ from the rates for the same services offered to the general public.

All of this price discrimination is wasteful because the favored postal customers are receiving a donation in kind that they must consume. The utility from this kind of donation is less than the utility that the recipient would derive from an equivalent increase in income.

PAEA neither condemns nor condones the price discrimination that runs through the postal tariff. The pricing factors for market-dominant mail acknowledge indirectly that USPS engages in third degree price discrimination. Otherwise there is almost nothing in PAEA that explicitly recognizes the existence of third degree price discrimination. PAEA just takes the existing discriminatory product categories and enabling legislation as given.

7 PAEA's Take on Price Caps

One of PAEA's objectives is "to create predictability and stability in rates." Predictable and stable postal prices reduce the business risk of postal customers. This enhances the value of postal service primarily to commercial mailers who benefit because the future returns from their activities may be forecast with less uncertainty. Predictable and stable postal prices similarly benefit USPS by reducing variations in net revenues.

Variations in real prices caused by the effects of inflation can be eliminated by indexing prices to a general measure of inflation such as the CPI-U. However, simple indexing does not address any external cause of change except inflation. Therefore, indexing schemes are usually expanded to account for other effects such as predictable economies of scope and scale, autonomous changes in productivity, changes in input prices, and expected improvements in efficiency. (For example, see Brennan and Crew 2016). "Inflation plus (or minus) X" is the formula that describes these additions. However, no refinements are present in the price caps decreed by PAEA. PAEA completely omits the "X" in the formula.

Economists prefer price cap regulation to traditional cost of service regulation because it preserves a private enterprise's incentive to maximize its profits. However, this advantage is of doubtful relevance because USPS is not a private enterprise.

PAEA's simple price caps are a recipe for failure. The caps eliminate all price risk for a time, but cannot be maintained indefinitely. Ultimately, the system fails because there is no proper mechanism for regularly adjusting postal rates for any good cause except inflation.

Over the long run USPS's unit costs increase more rapidly than the CPI-U because mail delivery is unavoidably more labor intensive than the production of goods and services generally within the US economy. This effect is known to economists as Baumol's cost disease. As the economy grows wages increase relative to the cost of capital. This trend is partially offset in the CPI-U because the labor intensity of the US economy is diminishing over time, but it is not offset as much in USPS's costs because of the static labor intensity of mail delivery.

In the short run USPS's unit costs have increased since 2006 with diminishing demand. Passage of PAEA roughly corresponded with the time peak of electronic diversion of the mail. In addition, the Great Recession, beginning in 2008, seriously depressed postal volumes. Basically, as volumes have declined economies of density have operated in reverse to increase USPS's unit costs.

PAEA's caps have effectively frozen the real prices of market-dominant mail while USPS's unit costs have risen. This is the root cause of USPS's current fiscal emergency.

8 PAEA's Take on Pricing Flexibility

Prices are flexible if they can be adjusted to circumstances quickly and easily. Direct price regulation is inherently inflexible when regulators operate under procedural rules that respect due process. Prior to PAEA postal prices in the US could only be changed after the PRC had received a formal request, collected testimony, conducted public hearings, and issued a written decision. Altogether the process usually consumed about 12 months. Sensibly, USPS only requested new rates about once every 3 years.

Flexibility of prices under regulation can be achieved by ceding back to the regulated enterprise some authority to adjust rates subject to conditions. The modern way to do this is with a global price cap. The global cap is the average revenue per unit that results from applying a set of proposed rates to the volumes predicted if the rates are placed in effect. The regulated enterprise is free to set different rates subject to the restriction that when average revenue is calculated using the different prices and the original predicted demand volumes, it cannot exceed the original average revenue.

A global cap produces a win-win outcome for a profit-seeking enterprise and its customers taken altogether. The enterprise wins if it can find new prices that increase its profit. Its customers win because they can always buy the original forecasted quantities for the same (or a smaller) expenditure. Therefore, any change in their demands must improve the net value they receive from their purchases.

PAEA cites price flexibility for market-dominant products as an objective and in its factors. However, PAEA did not establish a global price cap for USPS's prices. Instead, PAEA instructs USPS to set rates under a separate price cap for each market-dominant class of services. This difference sacrifices most of the desirable properties of a global price cap (Borsenberger et al. 2012). A global cap would allow USPS to trade off the net revenue contributions of different classes to find an efficient balance. But when the tradeoffs are restricted to single classes most of the potential welfare gain disappears.

9 PAEA's Take on Cross-Subsidies

A cross-subsidy occurs when the products sold to one group of customers are partially paid for by other customers or by the enterprise's residual claimants. Then the prices charged are too low to fully cover the added costs of the cross-subsidized products and services. Cross-subsidies can be undesirable for many reasons: they inequitably distribute the total cost of production, they are anti-competitive, they are inefficient, and they are unsustainable under competition.

The correct test for cross-subsidies is the Incremental Cost (IC) test (Faulhaber 1975). The incremental cost of a subset of products is the cost the enterprise avoids by not producing the products in the subset. An enterprise's prices are free of cross-subsidies if revenue equals or exceeds incremental cost for every possible proper subset of products.

Congress probably intended to ban all cross-subsidies for postal products. The revenues derived from postal products are required to cover their "attributable" costs. For competitive products PAEA also prohibits "the subsidization of competitive products by market-dominant products."

PAEA's cross-subsidy provisions can easily conflict with its rate caps for market-dominant classes. When this occurs, the rate caps take precedence. A price cannot be raised above the cap to eliminate a cross-subsidy. This situation is known to have occurred with Periodicals and may also have occurred with some rate categories within the classes.

More generally, the provisions are technically defective as a test for cross-subsidies even if they do not conflict with the caps. They use an incorrect cost definition, "attributable" rather than incremental cost, and they consider postal products only singly.

The language of PAEA adds ambiguities and unnecessarily complicates tests for cross-subsidies of competitive products. To be banned by PAEA, the source of a cross-subsidy must be identified as a surplus derived from market-dominant products. This is unnecessary because it is not part of the IC test. It is ambiguous because the imputation can be made in multiple ways. Some may violate PAEA's provisions and some may not.

A practical and complete IC test exists for multi-product enterprises such as USPS (Pearsall 2009). Although there have been several recent occasions when it would have been useful for the PRC to test rates for cross-subsidies, the complete IC test has not been applied to any recent postal tariff.

Complete IC tests of postal tariffs since FY2006 would probably disclose a pattern of cross-subsidies increasing in number and size over time. This result is likely, first, because USPS's mounting losses have tended to increase the number of product subsets that will fail the IC test, and, second, because the price caps have prevented most of the rate increases that would have reduced cross-subsidies.

10 PAEA's Take on Worksharing Discounts

Worksharing discounts are best viewed as implicit prices. The discounts are the prices for component collection, processing and transportation services when composite services are unbundled. For example, when a bulk mailer presents USPS with mail that is delivery sequenced, the discount the mailer receives is the price for the sorting that would have been done by USPS if the mail had instead been un-sequenced. PAEA requires that discounts be less than the cost USPS avoids by not preforming the workshared service.

All of USPS's tariffs effectively unbundle some component services except delivery. Unbundling increases efficiency because the expanded list of services makes it possible for many mailers to choose for themselves a more efficient mix of the components than that offered by the end-to-end composites (Pearsall 2005).

The economic principles for component pricing following an unbundling are essentially the same as those for welfare maximization. The basic rule, known as Efficient Component Pricing (ECP), is price equals marginal cost. If net revenue is constrained, the second-best efficient prices for component services are Ramsey/Boiteux prices and will lie above marginal costs.

PAEA recognizes the role of worksharing discounts in postal pricing, but alters ECP by specifying "cost avoided" as a discount ceiling. PAEA's rule is asymmetric and fails to designate marginal cost as the cost avoided. Nevertheless, the PRC treats the rule as quasi-ECP and compares worksharing discounts to marginal costs.

PAEA's rule limiting worksharing discounts does not seem to have a recognizable purpose. If the intent is to prevent USPS from overpricing component services then the rule is misdirected. The component that is prone to being overpriced is delivery, for which USPS retains a monopoly for all mail except parcels. But the discounts to which PAEA's rule apply are for non-delivery worksharing activities which are mostly performed by mailers themselves. If the intent is to prevent cross-subsidies, then PAEA has gotten the IC test backwards, and again, used the wrong cost concept and neglected combinations. A cross-subsidy occurs if a discount is less than the incremental cost to USPS of supplying the component services. Discounts that obey PAEA's rule will almost always result in cross-subsidies because incremental cost per unit is usually larger than marginal cost for a component service.

11 PAEA's Take on Quality of Service

Individual pieces of mail have properties modern economics labels "hedonic" (Fenster et al. 2006). These include the shape, the piece-weight, the distance the piece is transported, the speed of delivery, the presort level, and so on. To be effective as intended price-cap regulation must account for changes in these hedonic properties.

Conventional price theory assumes that products have fixed properties; however, modern economics treats the hedonic properties as variable. Equilibrium in markets for such products is described by a hedonic price equation (HPE) which relates the price of a product to its hedonic properties.

PAEA's take on quality of service is thoroughly conventional. PAEA attempts to establish and enforce a system of fixed service standards for market-dominant products. Standards are to be defined, performance is to be reported, and changes in standards are subject to PRC review. The PRC was authorized to set service standards but was given no power to enforce them. USPS has responded by setting its standards independently and with a reporting system that fails to provide all of the data needed to calculate speeds of service for many categories of mail.

PAEA's authors were right to be concerned about the quality of postal service. The speed of service, particularly for First-Class mail, has deteriorated as the result of various operational changes since 2011. This is partly USPS's response to the price cap system. Reductions in the speed of service are equivalent to price increases found by moving along the HPE. PAEA capped increases in the nominal price of mail but failed to cap increases resulting from reductions in service standards. USPS has exploited this loophole to indirectly increase the prices of First-Class and Standard mail by decreasing the speeds of delivery (Pearsall 2018).

There is nothing about the system created by PAEA that promotes efficient choices or that imposes consistency between classes with respect to hedonic properties. A well-designed regulatory system for price and service quality would determine the two simultaneously by trading off one for the other to maximize welfare. PAEA's enforcement approach does not recognize this tradeoff so the balance between price and quality of service is unlikely to be efficient for many categories of mail.

A well-designed system would also be concerned about the global mix of hedonic properties. Does USPS offer a mix of services that is sufficiently varied with respect to hedonic properties to allow mailers good choices?

12 PAEA's Take on Production Efficiency

Production efficiency means that an enterprise minimizes its costs. Profit maximization is the objective that aligns best with production efficiency. But a public enterprise such as USPS may pursue its own alternative objective. Two possibilities from the economics literature are sales maximization and size maximization.

Privatization would install profit maximization as the institutional objective of USPS. Privatization simplifies regulation by reducing (but not entirely eliminating) production efficiency as a concern of the regulator. Privatization is feasible for USPS but would likely mean abandoning aspects of USPS's USO. Basically, a privatized USPS would want to raise the price of or abandon every kind of service that is cross-subsidized. It would also want to end the discriminatory rates now offered to favored mailers.

Privatization has not occurred. Instead, PAEA lists production efficiency as a factor in the pricing of market-dominant services. Yet despite the good intentions, PAEA actually decreased USPS's incentive to produce efficiently. It did this by eliminating the net revenue condition that is a central pillar of cost-of-service regulation.

Under the 1970 Act prices were set to yield a small predicted surplus in net revenue during a future "test" year. If a similar constraint had been included in PAEA, it would have introduced a profit motive into USPS's economic objective.

Without a net revenue condition USPS may pursue an alternative objective without regard for cost. A net revenue condition changes this situation in the same way that a constraint enters into a mathematical optimization. The mathematics forms a modified objective called a Lagrangian that is a weighted average of the alternative objective and profit. It rewards USPS for efficient production by converting profits from more efficient production to the alternative objective at an established rate. With the modified objective USPS has an incentive to produce efficiently and to set rates based upon the minimum cost it would incur as an efficient producer. Without the net revenue condition there is little about PAEA's regulatory system that encourages USPS to produce efficiently and price accordingly.

13 PAEA's Take on the Universal Service Obligation and Reserved Area

Modern economics views the institutional arrangements for a national post broadly as a way to absorb the costs of a USO by generating excess profits from an RA. The USO is a set of products, pricing practices and levels of service the post is obligated to supply. The RA consists of markets in which the national post is the monopoly supplier. The monopolies are enforced by prohibiting competitive entry.

PAEA's view of the USO and RA is modern. PAEA tasked the PRC to produce a wide-ranging study to identify the elements of the USO and RA, evaluate costs and benefits, and recommend changes. The report was needed because the USO and RA are poorly defined for USPS. They are mostly the result of obscure past legislation and USPS practices, not PAEA.

Commercialization, privatization and liberalization are reforms that many economists would recommend for the US postal sector. See, for example Crew and Geddes (2014). Commercialization removes the preferences and penalties that apply to USPS but not to private businesses. Without commercialization USPS would continue to operate inefficiently due to market distortions. Privatization tends to reduce the USO; liberalization reduces the RA. A commercialized, privatized and liberalized USPS would have to find a new balance between a reduced USO and a reduced RA.

PAEA badly upset the balance that had been achieved under the 1970 Act. PAEA installed a set of required annual contributions by USPS of about $5.6 billion to a postal Retiree Health Benefit Fund. These payments far exceed actuarial estimates of the contributions needed to amortize USPS's health benefit commitments to retirees. USPS was unable to generate sufficient net revenues to make these payments almost from the outset. Deferred payments to the fund are now the largest component of USPS's current debt to the US Treasury.

14 Conclusion

The regulatory system created by PAEA is an improvisation that owes little to modern economics. It achieves price stability by freezing class rates relative to the CPI-U at the expense of all other considerations. Administratively, it confers effective control on Congress rather than on USPS's board of governors and management. It has transformed the regulator, the PRC, into an omnipresent observer with little real authority. It perpetuates a wasteful system of discriminatory rates for preferred customers. It leaves USPS with no actual incentive to produce efficiently and price accordingly. It relies on defective controls. And, it has prevented most of the reforms that economists have recommended.

We have now had 10 years to observe the effects on the US postal sector of PAEA's take on regulatory economics. The main Congressional purpose in passing PAEA was to achieve financial stability for USPS. Instead, PAEA has caused a train wreck. PAEA increased USPS's obligations to the Treasury but left USPS without the means to cope effectively with the unanticipated declines in postal volumes that occurred after 2006 and continue today. As a result USPS is now entirely dependent on the forbearance of the US Treasury and Congress to remain in operation.

The US postal landscape is littered with consequences of the legislation that are undesirable, unexpected and, probably, unintended by Congress. Some of the poor results, those related to USPS's large losses, are obvious and have been so almost from the start. Other results, such as the growing inefficiency of the postal tariff, the expanding cross-subsidies, and the deteriorating quality of service are equally important but are harder to observe.

But it is what the law has prevented that may be the most serious consequence of PAEA. Progress towards reform of the US postal sector has been suspended for more than 10 years while Congress has awaited the outcome of its experiment with a novel and poorly designed regulatory system. All the while, in Europe and elsewhere, national posts and their customers have been benefiting from the results of enlightened reforms along lines indicated by modern regulatory economics.

References

Baumol, W. J., and D. F. Bradford (1970), "Optimal Departures from Marginal Cost Pricing", *The American Economic Review*, 60-3, June 1970, pp. 265–83.

Borsenberger, C., S. Breville, H. Cremer, P. De Donder and D. Joram (2012), "Price-cap regulation in the postal sector: single versus multiple baskets", in M. A. Crew and P. R. Kleindorfer (eds), *Multi-modal Competition and the Future of Mail*, Edward Elgar, Northampton, MA.

Brennan, T. J. and M. A. Crew (2016), "Price Cap Regulation and Declining Demand", in M. A. Crew and T. Brennan (eds), *The Future of the Postal Sector in a Digital World*, Springer International Publishing, Switzerland.

Campbell, J. I., Jr., (2013), "A new governance model for US postal services", in M. A. Crew and P. R. Kleindorfer (eds), *Reforming the Postal Sector in the Face of Electronic Competition,* Edward Elgar, Northampton, MA.

Crew, M. A. and R. R. Geddes (2014), "A business model for USPS", in M. A. Crew and T. Brennan (eds), *The Role of the Postal and Delivery Sector in a Digital Age*, Springer International Publishing, Switzerland.

Faulhaber, G. R. (1975), "Cross Subsidization: Pricing in Public Enterprises", *American Economic Review* 65:966–77.

Fenster, L., D. Monaco, E. S. Pearsall, C. Robinson and S. Xenakis (2006), "US Postal Services as Composite Goods with Hedonic Properties", in M. A. Crew and P. R. Kleindorfer (eds), *Liberalization of the Postal and Delivery Sector*, Edward Elgar, Northampton, MA.

Pearsall, E. S. (2018), "Adjusting Rates for Quality of Service: Have Market-Dominant Mail Rates Risen Faster Than the CPI-U?" in T. Brennan, V. Glass and P. L. Parcu (eds), The Contribution of the Postal and Delivery Sector, Chapter 19, Springer International Publishing, Switzerland.

Pearsall, E. S., (2009), "The complete incremental cost test for cross-subsidies with a sub-modular cost function", Journal of Regulatory Economics, 36, February 2009, pp. 274–285.

Pearsall, E. S., (2005), "The Effects of Worksharing and Other Product Innovations on U. S. Postal Volumes and Revenues", in M. A. Crew and P. R. Kleindorfer (eds) *Regulatory and Economic Challenges in the Postal and Delivery Sector*", Klewer Academic Publishers, Boston, MA, Klewer Academic Publishers.

Postal Accountability and Enhancement Act (2006), Public Law 109–435, 120 Statute 3198, December 20, 2006.

Are European Cross-Border Parcel Delivery Services Affordable?

Claire Borsenberger

1 Introduction

The European Commission (EC) believes tariffs for parcel delivery services paid by low-volume senders (small and medium enterprises (SMEs) and individuals) are "too high" and are impeding e-commerce market development between EU Member States. In May, 2016, the EC released a proposal aimed at solving this problem (European Commission 2016). They notably proposed that national regulatory authorities assess the affordability of parcel delivery tariffs offered by national postal operators (NPOs) within their jurisdictions (article 5). This proposal goes further the Postal Directive that requires that NPOs offer at least one affordable cross-border delivery service across the EU for parcels weighing up to 10 kg (up to 20 kg in some Member States).[1] Fifteen domestic and cross-border postal items listed in the

Economist, in charge of the department "Doctrine et Modélisation" in the Direction of Regulation and Institutional and European Affairs, Groupe La Poste and associated professor at the University François Rabelais, Tours, France. The opinions expressed here do not necessarily reflect the position of La Poste. I sincerely thank Anna Möller Boivie, economist at Copenhagen Economics, for her valuable comments.

[1]Article 3(1) of the Directive 97/67/EC requires Member States to "ensure that users enjoy the right to a universal service involving the permanent provision of a postal service of specified quality at all points in their territory at affordable prices for all users" and Article 12 requires Member States to take steps to ensure that the tariffs for each of the services forming part of the universal service comply with a number of principles, including that "prices shall be affordable". The Directive does not specify how affordability is to be measured; this is left to the discretion of Member States.

C. Borsenberger (✉)
Doctrine et Modélisation, Direction of Regulation and Institutional and European Affairs, Groupe La Poste, Paris, France

University François Rabelais, Tours, France
e-mail: claire.borsenberger@laposte.fr

P.L. Parcu et al. (eds.), *The Contribution of the Postal and Delivery Sector*, Topics in Regulatory Economics and Policy, https://doi.org/10.1007/978-3-319-70672-6_8

appendix to the proposal would be affected by the proposed measures. These items do not necessarily belong to the NPO's catalog of universal service products.

The objective of this paper is to analyze the extent to which parcel delivery price affordability stimulates online exchanges between EU Member States. The novelty of this analysis is to view parcel delivery within a broader supply chain. It is interesting to note that a revised EC proposal released by the Council in June 2017 replaces the word "affordability" by the phrase "unreasonably high" when characterizing certain tariffs.

After reviewing the economic literature on the meaning of affordability in Sect. 2, this concept will be applied to parcel delivery services in Sect. 3. In particular, the term "vital" used to justify affordable prices for goods such as water, energy, housing, and medical care will be considered for access to (cross-border) parcel delivery services. An implicit question is, "vital" for whom: for final consumers or for intermediate e-tailers? Afterwards, the European Commission's approach to affordability will be examined. Sect. 4, the conclusion, summarizes the analysis.

2 The General Concept of Tariff Affordability

2.1 Definition

Among others, Whitehead (1991), Milne (2006) and Komives et al. (2005) have said the concept of affordability has no theoretical basis in economics. A household consumes a basket of goods and services that maximizes its utility or surplus (i.e. the benefit derived per euro spent) taking into account its preferences and income (budget constraint). Various preferences lead to different choices of consumption. In these circumstances, what constitutes an "affordable" price varies for each household.

However, beyond its microeconomic dimension, affordability has a "societal" or "public policy" dimension when dealing with access to goods or services that satisfy vital needs such as water, housing, medical care or energy. Access to these goods is considered a fundamental right in some countries and, therefore, should not be constrained by prices considered unaffordable. This is why, for example, the right to an affordable water tariff was enshrined in the Lisbon Treaty (Protocol No. 9/26) despite the absence of consensus on its meaning, as the European Economic and Social Committee's opinion on the affordability of SGEIs (2014) emphasized.

This lack of consensus is largely explained by the fact that meaning of affordability is subjective. Affordability depends on the interplay among many private factors, including bill size, which is affected by the price of the service and the level of consumption,[2] the proportion of household income spent, and alternatives available to satisfy a need. The perception of the affordable character of a good

[2] The quantity that is consumed is notably an important factor in judging whether a good is affordable or not. For example, in the case of water, the water bill would remain affordable if it does not involve an abnormally (or abusively) high volume. Given that the "standard" or "normal" quantity consumed varies with the household composition, it is important to take into account this parameter into the affordability analysis.

or a service also depends on a consumer's perceived quality. Quantity, quality, preferences and income (which together determine the willingness to pay) are all important factors when considering the affordability issue.

Despite the lack of consensus on affordability meaning, everyone agrees that some consumer groups may be more vulnerable than others regarding their capacity to afford some goods within "normal" spending patterns. This is why, for example, Hennessy et al. (2015) restricted the affordability assessment of postal products to consumers in the first decile of disposable income, for whom affordability could be an issue. Examining the whole population including individuals in higher income deciles could, according to Hennessy et al., cloud any conclusions on affordability for the more vulnerable segments of postal users.

2.2 Measurement

The most common approach in the economics literature for assessing affordability consists of looking at the share of income spent to purchase a given good or service. The good is then considered unaffordable when its purchase exceeds a given share of household's revenues. This approach is typically used to assess affordability of gas, electricity, water, medical care and housing in many countries (Deller and Waddams 2015). The difficulty is to define this threshold. In practice, medical bills are often considered by public authorities or experts unaffordable if they exceed 10% of global household expenditure or 40% of non-food expenditures (Niëns et al. 2012). In France, public authorities are considering the price of water affordable if water and sanitation spending do not exceed 3% of household consumption expenditure (Bel Franquesa et al. 2009). In the energy sector, the concept of energy precariousness or fuel poverty meets the notion of affordability. In the UK, fuel-poor households are defined as those who spend more than 10% of their income on all fuel use to heat their home to an adequate standard of warmth (Thomson and Snell 2014). In the housing sector, the affordability rule commonly used is that households should not spend more than 30–35% of their income on housing (Quigley and Raphael 2004).

Ofcom (2013), the British regulator of post and telecommunications, noted that this income method is useful in gauging affordability for an average consumer with an average income level, or for cases where spending on the item in question is high relative to income. But this method may be less useful for providing insight on affordability when spending is low relative to income, as is the case for postal services.[3] Ofcom argued that "some low income consumers spend relatively little

[3] In the UK, postal spend accounted for less than 0.15% of average household expenditure and less than 0.25% of low income household expenditure in 2009. According to the latest data available on the Eurostat website (Eurostat data 2014), postal services represented on average 0.12% of consumption expenditure of European households, this percentage varying between 0.02% in Spain, Poland and Latvia and 0.49% in Bulgaria.

on sending post, but this does not necessarily mean that universal postal services are affordable for those consumers, since they may be suffering detriment either as a result of sending those items or not sending more items" (p. 11–12).

As the Ofcom low-income example suggests, affordability measures are further complicated because they do not identify cases where households do not consume a good or restrict their consumption because it is unaffordable for them. To overcome this drawback, a variant of the income method could be used (Hennessy et al. 2015). This variant links affordability to the overall set of resources a household may need and compares the necessary spending level for the service in question to other necessary household requirements. It consists in verifying if the acquisition of the necessary or socially desirable quantity of the good or service in question at the current price leaves consumers or households with sufficient remaining income or spending power to meet their other requirements (e.g. to buy food).[4]

To supplement these approaches based on income to identify those whose basic needs are unsatisfied, one could ask households directly about their opinion about affordability: "Do you find this good affordable?" "Do you buy as much of this good in quantities your household needs?" The drawback of this direct method is its subjectivity: different consumers may understand 'affordability' in different terms or conflate views about affordability and value for money.

Ofcom (2013) dealt with the issue of affordability of postal services by combining these various approaches. It considered a range of evidence[5] on the behavior and attitudes of different types of consumers, especially those who may be particularly reliant on postal services or have low income, to see if universal postal service prices create significant detriments or if expenditure on post is unduly constrained by income. Universal postal prices were considered unaffordable for a consumer if "he frequently suffers significant adverse consequences as a result of the cost of sending post (e.g., because this means foregoing spending on other items) or, as a result of not sending post and foregoing the value of the communication" (p. 11). Ofcom concluded that universal postal services were affordable for almost all residential consumers, including low income and other vulnerable consumers, and for all UK businesses, including small and medium enterprises (SMEs).

The Commission's method to assess affordability of NPOs' services described in its proposal for a regulation on cross-border delivery services differ greatly from these usual approaches (European Commission 2016). According to article 5(1) of the draft proposal, NRAs should use common criteria such as the domestic tariffs of the universal service providers of origin and destination, the level of terminal rates,

[4] In this approach, a good could be considered as unaffordable if its purchase would pull down the household, initially above the poverty line, below it. But again, no consensus exists on what the necessary level of residual income should be.

[5] Data on consumers' postal send and spend patterns, broken down by consumer type and over time; data that compares expenditure on postal services against expenditure on other 'comparator' items and household total expenditure, broken down by consumer type and over time; and qualitative consumer research to explore whether low income and vulnerable consumers face constraints on their ability to send postal items and, if so, whether they suffer detriment as a result.

specific transportation, handling costs, or bilateral volumes between delivery service providers to assess affordability. In the absence of any reference to consumers' purchasing power or analysis of the impact of the acquisition of such a service on their capacity to satisfy essential needs like to buy food, to warm up and so on, this approach is closer to a price regulation based on a cost-plus principle than an affordability assessment. This is even clearer in the last version of the draft proposal which deals with "unreasonably high tariffs" instead of affordable ones.

3 The Concept of Tariff Affordability Applied to Parcel Delivery Services

3.1 The Households' Perspective

In the case of (cross-border) parcel delivery services associated with online purchases of physical goods, one may question their "vital" character for final consumers. Is access to goods sold on (foreign) e-commerce websites an essential need for European consumers, justifying the implementation of a price regulation via an affordable tariff?

Some may say yes: access to goods sold on foreign markets is "vital" or at least necessary for private consumers when a specific commodity is unavailable on a domestic market.[6]

What about countries where domestic (online or offline—in traditional shops) alternatives to imports exist? Is the promotion of cross-border e-commerce at any price economically justified? If less costly domestic alternatives exist for the consumer, what would be the interest to regulate the prices of cross-border delivery services for goods purchased in other Member States (by capping them)?

Such an intervention could be rather counterproductive. In competitive markets, the free play of supply and demand maximizes social welfare. If the consumer is willing to pay the fair price of the goods sold by a foreign e-merchant (reflecting the total costs of production including delivery), the exchange is socially desirable. If the total price of the transaction exceeds the buyer's willingness to pay, it is not socially desirable because the buyer is unwilling to cover the cost of production. Artificially lowering the cost of cross-border delivery in order to promote the development of intra-EU e-commerce through price regulation would destabilize markets and the competitive level playing field in the postal and retail sectors by distorting relative prices (they would no longer reflect marginal costs which in turn

[6] Notice that cross-border B2C e-commerce is particularly well developed in "small" EU countries (such as Luxembourg, Malta, Cyprus, etc.), where domestic supply may be limited due to the reduced size of the domestic market. More data on the characteristics of e-consumers in these countries would be needed to see if vulnerable consumers are not excluded from cross-border transactions and if access to foreign goods is affordable to them.

would yield an inefficient allocation of resources—see Sect. 3.3). It also may increase negative externalities on the environment notably (due to excessive and inefficient carbon emissions from cross-border transportation), reducing the social welfare.

This leads to the conclusion that the only case where parcel delivery services may eventually be considered as "vital" for final e-consumers and where affordability of these services could be an issue is when the domestic market fails to provide goods deemed "vital". In all other cases, regulating competitive cross-border parcel delivery services under the excuse of affordability would reduce global social welfare.

3.2 *The E-tailers' Perspective*

From the e-tailers' point of view, delivery could be considered as an "essential" input. Delivery to a convenient place (at home, at work, or in any other place) is part of the commercial promise of e-tailers. Delivery is the distinctive feature of e-commerce compared to traditional retail (where consumers themselves collect their purchase by their own means). In other words, parcel delivery services are a critical input to the e-tailers' commercial proposition.

Despite this, as argued below, affordability of parcel delivery services provided by postal operators is not really an issue. According to Ofcom (2013), intermediate goods may be defined as "unaffordable" for producers if input prices jeopardized their commercial viability. This is manifestly not the case for e-tailers and parcel delivery services, for at least three reasons.

Firstly, as noted by Hennessy et al. (2015), "if the consumer can merely substitute away from a good, then affordability must not be an issue" (p. 121).[7] This argument is valid for intermediate goods as well. If e-tailers have access to alternatives to delivery services offered by NPOs which are under the Commission's regulatory scope, then affordability of these inputs is not an issue. This is clearly the case. As underlined by the Commission themselves in the last Report to the European Parliament and the Council on the application of the Postal Services Directive (European Commission 2015), several operators are active on the domestic and the cross-border B2C delivery markets of the EU countries (see Table 1).

Moreover, almost every day, new service providers are entering in this growing market. An increasing number of start-ups, some belonging to the sharing economy

[7] Dealing with final goods, these authors consider that "price rise would be affordable if there is a high cross-price elasticity, indicating strong availability of substitutes. Low budget share and significant cross-price elasticity between substitutes and other goods would indicate that prices are affordable, while a high own-price elasticity and a low cross-price elasticity with substitutes would indicates that prices are unaffordable. Similarly, a low own-price elasticity, a low cross-price elasticity with substitutes, and a high price elasticity with other necessities would indicate that prices are unaffordable."

Table 1 Main alternative operators active in domestic and cross-border B2C delivery

	Number of operators	Main operators active in domestic B2C delivery except USP and integrators	Number of operators	Main operators active in cross-border B2C delivery except USP and integrators
AT	4	DPD, GLS, Hermes, Asendia	3	DPD, GLS, Hermes
BE	5	DPD, GLS, PostNL, Kiala, Mondial Relay	6	PostNL, GLS, G3 Worldwide, Swiss Post, Hermes, DPD
BG	6	DPD, Econt Express OOD, Tip Top Courier AD, M&BM Express OOD, GLS	2	GLS, DPD
CY	1	ASC Courier	1	ASC Courier
CZ	2	DPD, GLS	2	GLS, DPD
DK	3	DPD, GLS, Bring	4	DPD, GLS, Bring, DB Schenker
EE	2	DPD, Itella	2	DPD, Itella
FI	3	DB Schenker, Matkahuolto Oy AB, Posten Åland	3	DPD, DB Schenker, GLS
FR	6	Colis Privé, Kiala, Mondial Relay, Relais Colis, Exapaq, Hermes	3	Kiala, Exapaq, Hermes
DE	5	DPD, GLS, GO! General Overnight Service, Hermes, Pin Mail AG	5	DPD, GLS, GO! General Overnight Service, Hermes
EL	5	ACS S.A., TACHYMETAFO-RES ELTA S.A., GENIKI TACHYDROMIKI, Speedex, ACS Courier	3	World Courier, Speed Air, ACS Courier
HU	3	DPD, SPRINTER Kft., GLS	4	DPD, GLS, SPRINTER Kft., GTR
IE	5	DPD, Nightline, GLS, Citypost, DB Schenker	5	DPD, Nightline, GLS, Citypost, DB Schenker
IT	3	GLS, Hermes, BRT Corriere Espresso	3	GLS, BRT Corriere Espresso, Hermes
LV	3	DPD, Itella, GreenCarrier	2	DPD, Itella
LT	2	DPD, Itella	2	DPD, Itella
LU	4	DPD, Kiala, Hermes, Mondial Relay	3	GLS, DPD, Hermes
MT	3	GLS, Arrow Express, Miles Express	1	GLS
NL	4	DPD, Kiala, GLS, Hermes	3	DPD, GLS, Hermes
PL	3	GLS, Siódemka, InPost, DPD	4	DPD, GLS, Siódemka, Hermes
PT	4	GLS, Nacex, Enviália, MRW, Torrestir	6	Enviália, MRW, Nacex, Chronopost International, Torrestir
RO	7	DPD, Cargus International, GLS, Fan Courier Express, Sprint Curier Expres, Urgent Curier	7	DPD, Cargus International, GLS, Fan Courier Express, Sprint Curier Expres, Urgent Curier S.R.L.

(continued)

Table 1 (continued)

	Number of operators	Main operators active in domestic B2C delivery except USP and integrators	Number of operators	Main operators active in cross-border B2C delivery except USP and integrators
SK	3	DPD, GLS, ReMax	2	DPD, GLS
SI	3	DPD, GLS, Doortodoor	2	DPD, GLS, Doortodoor
ES	5	Kiala, GLS, Enviália, Tourline Express, Mondial Relay	4	GLS, Enviália, Chronopost International, Tourline Express
SE	3	DB Schenker, Bussgods, Bring	2	DB Schenker, Bring
UK	12	DPD, Hermes, HDNL/Yodel, City Link, UK Mail, Interlink, Nightfreight, APC, DX, City Sprint, XDP	9	DPD, HDNL/Yodel, City Link, UK Mail, Nightfreight, DX, City Sprint, XDP, Hermes (to Austria and Germany)

Source: Copenhagen Economics (2013), *E-commerce and delivery—Study on the state of play of EU parcel markets with particular emphasis on e-commerce,* p. 118

(like PimPamPost a new cross-border delivery service launched in April 2017 between Barcelona and Paris), is exploiting the resources provided by the digital economy to develop new last mile delivery business models. E-tailers themselves are entering the delivery segment of the e-commerce value chain, by developing their own delivery network or by concluding partnerships with logistics operators. Amazon, for instance, is actively and rapidly developing its own delivery network in many different EU countries (France, UK, Germany, Italy, Spain and Central Europe), becoming at the same time the major customer and the first competitor of many European NPOs.

Secondly, in competitive markets, e-tailers are expected to pass-through the shipping costs into the final price paid by consumers.[8] The amount paid by final consumers for the delivery services are set by the e-tailer who can make a more or less substantial mark-up on this additional service. The relevance of such a strategy will depend among other factors, on the price elasticity of final consumers for the good and the competitive intensity faced by the e-tailer. Even if "free shipping" is the market standard launched by big e-tailers like Amazon in order to attract consumers and induce them to buy online, in the majority of cases, delivery services are not really offered for free to e-shoppers. The words "free delivery" are actually misleading: when displaying an all-inclusive price on their website, e-tailers actually include both the item price and the fee for delivery services.

Last but not least, NPO's parcel delivery prices are not excessive contrary to the European Commission's opinion.[9] Indeed, as shown by Borsenberger (2015), parcel delivery market is not only contestable but it is effectively contested (see Table 1).

[8] At cost or with a positive or negative ("free delivery") margin.

[9] Relying in particular on the study of Claes and Vergote (2015), the European Commission thinks that.

In this context, the probability of facing supra-competitive prices is low. As stated by Copenhagen Economics (2012), "the concern about unreasonable high profits is only relevant for non-contestable segments, as any unreasonably high profits would be competed away in contestable market segments" (p. 155). This conclusion is in line with the Group of European postal regulators' (ERGP 2014) opinion on European cross-border e-commerce parcels delivery markets and the functioning of competition on these markets. The regulators affirmed that they would "not [be] aware of any factor that would make ex-ante regulation of the markets to which European cross-border e-commerce parcels delivery belongs uniformly necessary at this stage" (p. 32). Moreover, contrary to the findings of Claes and Vergote (2015) that some cross-border parcel delivery tariffs are disconnected to costs, allowing the Commission to claim that postal operators to set excessive margins on cross-border parcel delivery services and making prices unaffordable, Borsenberger and Chever (2016) showed that higher prices charged by a given operator are not necessarily synonymous with unjustified margins.

In summary, (i) e-tailers can easily substitute the delivery services offered by NPOs by the services offered by alternative operators; (ii) they are free to pass-through the shipping costs into the final price paid by consumers and (iii) there is no significant evidence of any affordability problem linked to excessive margins which could be settled, as Glaeser and Gyourko (2003) recommended, by asking providers to reduce their tariffs (through a price regulation) or stimulating competition.

The only "problem" some e-tailers, notably SMEs, may encounter is a competitiveness issue. Selling a good abroad automatically generates additional transport costs—depending on the distance between the origin and the destination country, the level of labor costs, other inputs, taxes, etc.—which increase the cost of exporting and may make the foreign supply uncompetitive compared to the domestic supply. In this context, small e-tailers selling standardized and homogenous goods with little added value are likely to be less competitive than big e-tailers who satisfy identical needs, since e-commerce and parcel delivery markets display increasing returns to scale (the unit cost of production decreases with volumes, up to the capacity constraint).

But this does not constitute a parcel delivery market failure requiring public intervention. This is a problem of cost differentials, of competitive advantages, more generally linked to the competitive structure of markets, labor costs, regulations, taxation and demand.

3.3 *Any Intervention Aiming to Regulate the Price of Cross-Border Parcel Delivery Services Used by E-tailers to Provide Their Services to Final Consumers Would Be Detrimental*

Imposing an affordability constraint on the tariffs offered to SMEs by NPOs would be equivalent to subsidizing parcel delivery services, which are an input entering into the production function of e-tailers. In the absence of any significant known market failure on this intermediate, the drawbacks of a policy aiming to subsidize parcel delivery services tariffs will exceed its potential benefits, if any. As pointed out by Mueller (2003), subsidies are rents and thus attract rent seekers. The logic of rent seeking underlying any subsidization policy usually imposes welfare losses on society, which can be substantial depending on the type of rent-seeking behavior that takes place, as well as the political system it occurs in.

Diamond and Mirrlees (1971a, b) demonstrated that subsidizing an input distorts firms' decisions and undermines productive efficiency. Manipulating the prices of some inputs leads to distortions in the efficient allocation of resources, as prices no longer reflect actual marginal costs of production. Users of these inputs are discouraged from using alternative means of production and suppliers to develop new potentially less expensive production process. The same logic and economic distortions work on the terminal dues system: it distorts competition both between parcel delivery operators and between domestic/foreign, electronic/brick-and-mortar retailers (Copenhagen Economics 2014).

4 Conclusion

Affordability often motivates regulation of end-user tariffs by imposing a celling price for goods considered as essential or vital and for which some consumers have to spend a significant share of their budget. The vital aspect of parcel delivery services for final consumers or e-tailers is not clear and no market failure for the provision of this service has been observed. Current postal directive requires NPOs to offer affordable parcel delivery services that small e-tailers could use to send their products to e-consumers throughout Europe.

Nevertheless, the Commission seems to consider that there exists, at least in some EU countries, an affordability problem related to excessive margins made by NPOs preventing e-tailers from developing their cross-border activity. Again, this view is not clearly proved. The only potential "problems" seem rather to be a competitiveness gap between big and small e-tailers and a poverty issue or purchasing power gap between EU citizens. Even if shipping were free for smaller e-tailers, it is not clear their cost structure would allow them to compete with the giants of e-commerce. In this context, the parcel delivery operators are not the right target. Indeed, artificially reducing postal input price paid by small e-tailers will only distort competitive market functioning, altering NPOs and e-tailers profitability. Such a measure would have adverse effects on the quality of delivery services provided since NPOs' capacity to invest in delivery infrastructure will be reduced, and could even push weaker operators to exit the market, relaxing competitive pressure at the detriment to final consumers. In addition, there is no guarantee that e-tailers would pass-through their lower shipping costs into the final price paid by the e-consumers (this will depend among other factors on the competitive intensity on the market).

Last but not least, such a policy would be unmanageable. Due to the heterogeneity in EU consumers' purchasing power, production costs within Member States and maturity degree of e-commerce markets, establishing a common affordability threshold for the whole EU would make no sense. It would be necessary, at the very least, to differentiate the "affordable" rates regarding the destination country. Thus, for the same service, the affordable tariff would vary according to the recipient, which would undermine the non-discrimination principle.

In summary, regulating parcel delivery rates is not the right way to fix the competitive problem some SMEs could face when they export their goods.

References

Bel Franquesa, Laura, Esther Blanco Garcia, Jean-Rémi Duprat, Maëlle Lepoutre (2009), "Water Affordability in Europe", Working paper, https://eau3e.hypotheses.org/files/2009/11/Water_Affordability_in_Europe.pdf.

Borsenberger Claire (2015), "The European Parcel Delivery Market: A contestable market", paper presented at the 23rd Conference on Postal and Delivery Economics, June 3–6, 2015, Athens.

Borsenberger Claire and Lisa Chever (2016), "The drivers of cross-border parcel delivery prices—An econometric study at the EU level", Working paper.

Claes and Vergote (2015), *Econometric study on parcel list prices*, Final Report.

Copenhagen Economics (2012), *Pricing behaviour of postal operators*, Report for the DG Internal Market and Services, 21st December.

Copenhagen Economics (2013), *E-commerce and delivery—Study on the state of play of EU parcel markets with particular emphasis on e-commerce.*

Copenhagen Economics (2014), *The Economics of Terminal Dues*, A report for U.S. Postal Regulatory Commission, 30 September.

Deller, David and Catherine Waddams (2015), "Affordability of Utilities: Extent, Practice, and Policy", Discussion Paper, 11 May.

Diamond, Peter A. and James A. Mirrlees (1971a), "Optimal Taxation and Public Production I: Production Efficiency", The American Economic Review, Vol. 61, No. 1, March, pp. 8–27.

Diamond, Peter A. and James A. Mirrlees (1971b), "Optimal Taxation and Public Production II: Tax Rules", The American Economic Review, Vol. 61, No. 3, Part 1, June, pp. 261–278.

European Commission (2015), "Commission Staff Working Document accompanying the Report from the Commission to the European Parliament and the Council on the application of the Postal Services Directive", SDW(2015)207 final, 17th November.

European Commission (2016), "Proposal for a regulation of the European Parliament and of the Council on cross-border parcel delivery services", COM (2016) 285 final, 25th May.

European Economic and Social Committee (2014), "Opinion of the European Economic and Social Committee on the affordability of SGEIs: definition, measurement, challenges, European initiatives (own-initiative opinion)", Official Journal of the European Union C 177, 11 June 2014, p. 24–31.

ERGP (2014), "European cross-border e-commerce parcels delivery—2014 ERGP opinion to the European Commission on a better understanding of European cross-border e-commerce parcels delivery markets and the functioning of competition on these markets", ERGP (14) 26.

Glaeser and Gyourko (2003), "The impact of building restrictions on housing affordability", FRBNY Economic Policy Review, June, pp. 21–39.

Hennessy, Hugh, Graeme O'Meara and Gregory Swinand (2015), "A Demand System Approach to Affordability", M.A. Crew, T.J. Brennan (eds.), *Postal and Delivery Innovation in the Digital Economy*, pp. 115–129.

Quigley, John, M., and Steven Raphael. 2004. "Is Housing Unaffordable? Why Isn't It More Affordable?", Journal of Economic Perspectives, 18(1), pp. 191–214.

Komives K., Foster V., Halpern J. and Wodon Q. (2005), "Water, electricity, and the poor: Who benefits from utility subsidies?", Washington: World Bank.

Milne Claire (2006), "Telecoms demand: measures for improving demand in developing countries: a toolkit for action", Main report, Lyngby: World Dialogue on Regulation for Network Economies.

Mueller, D. (2003), *Public Choice III*, Cambridge University Press, New York.

Niëns L.M., E. Van de Poel, A. Cameron, M. Ewen, R. Laing and W.B.F. Brouwer (2012), "Practical measurement of affordability: an application to medicines", *Bulletin of the World Health Organization*, 90, pp. 219–227.

Ofcom (2013), "The affordability of universal postal services", 19 March 2013.

Thomson, Harriet and Carolyn Snell (2014), "Fuel Poverty Measurement in Europe: a Pilot Study", The University of York, Department of Social Policy and Social Work, May.

Whitehead Christine M.E. (1991), "From need to affordability: an analysis of UK housing objectives", Urban Studies, vol. 28, pp. 871-87.

The 2016 European Commission Proposal for a Regulation on Cross-Border Parcels: An Assessment of the Objectives, Background, Issues and Potential Impacts

Philip Groves

1 Introduction

On 25 May 2016, the European Commission published its proposals for a regulation on intra-EU cross-border parcels which would, if approved, be directly applicable in all EU Member States.[1] The proposals were based on an analysis of the issues facing consumers and e-retailers buying and distributing goods across EU Member State borders. They took account of the Commission's 2013 Green Paper, a subsequent roadmap and public consultation and various Commission studies.

The published proposals identified two key issues where the Commission considered that regulatory action was needed to complement the Postal Services Directive: First cross-border prices were found, on average, to be almost five times above their domestic equivalents. In addition, smaller e-retailers (and individuals) especially in more rural areas were said to lack the volumes and bargaining power to get reasonable prices from large parcel operators and smaller parcels operators were seen to lack the infrastructure to deliver cross-border services. Second, the Commission considered that national regulatory authorities (NRAs) lacked information about these services due to differing information-gathering powers hindering their ability to identify potential market failures and/or competition concerns.

To counter these two issues, on 25 May 2016, the Commission made proposals in four main areas: First, it proposed to require all parcel delivery service providers

This paper was finalized following the reaching of common positions by the Council and Parliament, but before the expected Trilogue discussions and takes into account developments up to 21 July 2017.

[1]https://ec.europa.eu/growth/sectors/postal-services/parcel-delivery_en.

P. Groves (✉)
110 Clenshaw Path, Basildon, Essex SS14 2FP, UK
e-mail: philip.groves@ofcom.org.uk

P.L. Parcu et al. (eds.), *The Contribution of the Postal and Delivery Sector*, Topics in Regulatory Economics and Policy, https://doi.org/10.1007/978-3-319-70672-6_9

(whether domestic or cross-border) which employed 50 persons or more to provide specified information on turnover, volumes and staffing (the first two categories broken down into national, incoming and outgoing cross-border traffic). Second, it proposed to require Universal Service Providers (USPs) to provide their respective NRAs with the public list of tariffs for 15 categories of service and weight steps combined and the relevant terminal rates,[2] which the Commission would publish on a dedicated web site. Third, it proposed to require NRAs to make an annual assessment of the affordability of the notified USP tariffs, taking into account the domestic tariffs in the sending and receiving Member State, the terminal rates information and any uniform tariffs applied to two or more Member States. NRAs would be required to request further information of USPs in relation to any assessment of non-affordability and then to submit their final assessment to the Commission which would publish a non-confidential version, sometimes referred to as "naming and shaming". Fourth, it would require that third parties could obtain reasonable, transparent and non-discriminatory cross-border parcel delivery services at terminal rates as defined in USP multilateral agreements.

Overall, operators, NRAs and consumer bodies welcomed the Commission's aims to increase price transparency and enhance market monitoring. On the other hand, some stakeholders, including incumbent USPs and some Members of the European Parliament expressed reservations concerning the proportionality, practicality and administrative burden of certain elements, in particular the proposed USP affordability assessment, access obligation and disclosure of terminal dues to NRAs.

Since June 2016, the proposals were discussed in the European Council Working Party on postal services. Subsequently, the European Parliament also began its discussions in the lead Transport and Tourism Committee (TRAN), while the Committee for the Internal Market and Consumer Protection (IMCO) advised it. On 9 June 2017, the Council reached a Common Position on the proposal in the guide of a general approach text. However, the Parliament's TRAN committee, meeting on 11 July 2017, was unable to reach agreement on proposed amendments to the text. In light of these developments, at the time of writing (21 July 2017) the TRAN committee was due to meet again at the end of August 2017 to discuss the remaining issues and try again to reach agreement. Following this, intra-institutional Trilogue meetings were due to take place between the Parliament, Council and Commission to seek to reach agreement on the final legal text under the Estonian Council Presidency.

Section 2 analyzes the Commission documents and thinking which led up to its published proposals. Section 3 then examines key findings from associated studies commissioned by DG Growth while Sect. 4 assesses the regulatory findings and advice in this field to the Commission by the European Regulators' Group for Post (ERGP). Section 5 examines the Commission's 2016 proposals and their rationale

[2]Terminal rates are the wholesale payments that USPs make to each other, which are negotiated by the Universal Postal Union (UPU).

and Sect. 6 assesses potential issues with aspects of the proposals. Section 7 assesses stakeholder views and reactions to the Proposals. Section 8 examines the progress to date (14 July 2017) of the draft Regulation given the Council agreed general approach (of 9 June 2017) and the Parliament lack of agreement (on 11 July 2017). Finally, Sect. 9 presents tentative conclusions on certain main issues arising from the Proposals.

2 Commission Documents Leading Up to the Draft Regulation's Publication

The Commission's May 2016 proposals were the culmination of several years' work including various preparatory documents and in-depth industry studies on the e-commerce parcels market. The Commission's Green Paper (2012) highlighted the importance of delivery systems to e-commerce growth and associated economic growth and jobs, and the concerns of consumers and retailers around delivery failures, damaged or lost items and high delivery prices. It noted that technological innovation had heightened consumer expectations of solutions based on real-time information but that smaller retailers had lower bargaining power.

The Green Paper noted that the Postal Service Directive largely did not address non-USO services in a competitive market. It described the role of the 2014 Consumer Rights Directive and sought views on a possible future parcels USO, cost control and interoperability (e.g. tracking of parcels).

In its Communication (2013), the Commission stated that e-commerce promoted a more prosperous and competitive Europe, but that there was a wide disparity in the proportion of internet users who shopped on-line across borders (ranging from 82% in the UK to 11% in Romania). The Commission proposed a "roadmap" to increase transparency and information for all participants in the e-commerce value chain, improve delivery, and better redress consumer complaints. The Commission found price differences up to a factor of 4 for delivery of a 2-kg weight parcel between different Member States that cost factors could not explain. It said that competition might protect competition, as entry costs are high with new entrants needing to grow volumes quickly to be sustainable.

3 Studies Commissioned by DG Growth

Over the past several years, the European Commission also sponsored several major studies into the EU parcels sector. FTI (2011) surveyed retailers and identified three barriers which they face in arranging cross-border e-shipments, namely: higher prices (compared to domestic shipments); fears about poor quality of service; and lack of information concerning addressing standards, contractual procedures and consumer rights provisions. Retailers were also concerned about linguistic, cultural and advertising issues, VAT and tax and the fragmentation of consumer rights. FTI found that the main concerns for consumers lay around redress, including complaints in cases of delay, damage or loss and concern over returns.

FTI argued that the traffic profile of a buyer of parcel services (volume, frequency and reliability) determines the delivery options it has and the price it pays. Smaller companies are often unable to pass on higher cross-border delivery costs due to the competitiveness of e-commerce markets, thus lowering their market participation. On the other hand, FTI found increasing options for small, infrequent senders in the largest countries through offers from online brokers, parcels consolidators and subsidiaries of national postal operators. FTI found high cross-border/domestic price differentials and the exercise of market power in respect of the market for small, infrequent senders creating what it described as a "vicious circle of low demand, low competitive entry and high prices". It explained lack of regulation of cross-border USO products, because of USO differences, inadequate cooperation among NRAs, and a potential lack of data on volumes, quality of service, costs and termination rates.

Copenhagen Economics (2012 and 2013) reviewed the pricing behavior of operators and the state of play of the EU parcel markets. The second study found that e-shoppers valued low delivery prices, delivery to the home address, access to electronic delivery notifications and track and trace and convenient return options. It reported that cross-border delivery prices were often three to five times higher than the equivalent domestic prices. Such price differentials could be only partly explained by extra costs incurred for cross-border delivery (e.g. transport, sortation and labelling). It further found that e-retailers were primarily dissatisfied with high delivery prices as well as (to a lesser extent) return options and delivery speeds.

WIK-Consult (2013) included a section on parcels, which indicated that parcels per capita showed great variations across Europe, with Western European countries showing far greater volumes per capita, particularly the UK, France and Germany. WIK saw this as linked to differences across countries in the development of mail order and distance selling. In assessing competition, WIK identified eight groups of parcel and express operators active in parcels and express markets, either in domestic and/or cross-border. These included the four international integrators (DHL, FedEx, UPS and TNT Express), national USPs with road-based subsidiary networks (such as La Poste and Geopost), USPs with regional networks (such as the Nordic postal operators), freight forwarders, and mail order companies with their own delivery arm (such as Yodel and Hermes). The international integrators and USPS with separate road networks appeared to be the most active.

WIK-Consult Final Report (2014) examined four country case studies and explored six potential policy initiatives to support the growth of e-commerce. These included promoting open data and information platforms, developing an e-commerce scorecard on prices and performance and encouraging greater use of e-commerce "trust marks". It also discussed improving parcels services in rural areas and monitoring interoperability in domestic parcels networks, and increasing use of tracked services.

4 Reports from the European Regulators' Group for Post (ERGP)

The ERGP produced several reports which informed the development of the Commission's proposals. ERGP (2014) confirmed that competition was developing well in these markets with no evidence to justify ex ante regulation. It distinguished between services available to individuals, described as individually sent offers, likely to be sent by SMEs with relatively weak bargaining power, and services for bulk senders of parcels, who enjoyed greater bargaining power and choice.

ERGP (2014) did not see the need for a full market analysis or collection of information based on a full formal definition of markets. It recommended that the Commission investigate the current use of Article 22a, the information gathering article of the Postal Directive, in light of the information gaps observed. It envisaged in the meantime that individual NRAs might wish to carry out studies in their markets focusing on competition issues, information collection, and consumer needs or quality issues (particularly for single piece items sent individually by SMEs).

ERGP (2015a, b, c) examined legal regimes applicable to European domestic or cross-border parcel delivery. Its survey of NRAs indicated that the majority (18 out of 28) believed they had legal powers to oversee all domestic and cross-border e-commerce parcels. Of the remaining 10, 9 said that they regulated only parcels within the scope of the USO. In addition, 12 NRAs reported that other authorities helped them oversee these markets. Fifteen NRAs also reported that they were responsible, either partly or wholly, for the enforcement of consumer rights.

BEREC–ERGP (2015b) examined price transparency and regulatory oversight drawing on possible regulatory insights from the electronic communications sector. The example of international roaming was included in this analysis, where the Commission decided early on that wholesale and retail price regulation, combined with other measures, was needed to reduce prices for these services. It considered that wider cost differences across countries might be expected between parcel delivery than between telecommunications services due to geographic conditions, volumes per capita, labor costs, terminal dues, and costs of collection, delivery and transit. It noted that consumer pressure to reduce prices had been generally low in relation to international roaming, whereas large e-retailers could put significant pressure on parcel delivery providers to obtain lower prices for bulk services. This helped to explain the less interventionist approach of the Commission to cross-border parcels compared to international roaming.

5 European Commission's Proposals and Their Rationale

In May 2016, the Commission published its proposals, which were focused on four areas:

Article 3—Requiring parcels operators who have at least 50 employees to provide NRAs with information on turnover, number of staff employed, number of parcels handled, characteristics of their services, their general terms and conditions and any publicly available price lists.

Article 4—Requiring USPs to provide to their NRAs a public list of tariffs for 15 "single piece" product types (both domestic and intra-EU) and underlying terminal rates originating from other Member States for intra-EU products. These prices would then be published on a Commission web site.

Article 5—Requiring NRAs to undertake an "affordability assessment" of the tariffs provided under Article 4 (for each of the 15 products listed in the Annex), which would also be informed by the USP terminal rates. This assessment would consider the comparable domestic prices in the originating and destination Member State, terminal rates, and any application of a uniform tariff to two or more Member States. Where an NRA concluded that cross-border tariffs were not affordable, it would request further information or justification from the universal service provider concerned. The Commission would publish a non-confidential version.

Article 6—Requiring USPs to provide transparent and non-discriminatory access to any multilateral agreements on terminal rates for intra-EU parcel delivery services to third parties and for USPs to publish a reference offer for such access after clearance by their NRA. Individual offers to parcel providers should be based on the reference offer and, should no agreement be possible, the applicant would be entitled to submit the individual offer to the NRA who would have the power to change it.

To clarify these articles, the Commission proposed that to clarify (Article 1) that the Regulation is complementary to the Postal Services Directive and that certain definitions remained the same as in that Directive. However, it proposed (Article 2) new definitions to help determine the scope of the proposals, the most significant of which was to define parcel delivery services as "services involving the clearance, sorting, transport or distribution of postal items other than items of correspondence" excluding transport alone and items over 31.5 kg.[3]

The Commission noted the smaller proportion of consumers who buy on-line from other EU countries, 16% in 2015, compared to the 47% who purchase on-line domestically. The Commission's Impact Assessment defined the problem as high prices for cross-border delivery services for e-retailers and consumers, especially in

[3]That made the definition wider than the definition of a parcel in the Postal Services Directive, but less wide than the Universal Postal Union definition. This weight limit also corresponds to the threshold beyond which a parcel cannot be carried by a single person. In addition, Article 2 defines a "parcel delivery service provider" as "an undertaking that provides one or more parcel delivery services".

remote areas and for SMEs. It identified barriers to market entry, combined with low volumes sent by small senders and the limited mandate for NRAs to monitor this market. The Commission remarked on the lack of information on delivery options for both consumers and smaller e-retailers and noted the differences in universal service scope which prevented a harmonized EU-wide approach to regulating these services.

The Commission believed that its proposals would achieve effective regulatory oversight, enhance service and price transparency and encourage competition, leading to a reduction in prices for sending cross-border parcels, especially in remote areas. It concluded that the different levels of market knowledge and variance in powers to request information among regulators required remedying. The Commission justified imposing access requirements on USPs because it considered access to be essential for new market entrants who lacked the scale and scope to develop nation-wide delivery networks or develop commercial delivery agreements on their own.

6 Potential Issues with the Commission Proposals

The Commission's proposals sought to build on harmonized legislation to a minimum level with scope for Member States to go above and beyond it, for example for universal service standards. This minimum harmonized framework has been introduced through three cumulative Postal Directives. Due to the fast development of the e-commerce parcels market, the Commission chose a different, potentially more speedy legal instrument to introduce its proposed provisions for cross-border parcels, using a draft Regulation which would be directly applicable in Member States and not require transposition. This might risk inconsistencies between the two, although the Commission argued that its regulation was a "*Lex specialis*" which would not contradict but only add to the provisions in the Postal Directive. Nevertheless, the new definitions, combined with potential changes in the final text, raise the question of what legal interpretation would prevail in the event of any conflict between the new Regulation and the specific transposition of the Postal Directive in any member State.

The Commission's impact assessment tried to assess the costs and benefits of the proposals, including whether the desired enhancing of the Digital Single Market justified the burdens created by these proposals however this did not cover potential amendments which extended its scope. Extending provisions designed for USPs to non-USPs, and to change the criteria for the non-USPs caught by the regulation, risked substantially increasing these burdens without a corresponding revision to the impact assessment. In addition, the definition of a cross-border parcel is different from the upper limit for a USO parcel, 20 kg, in the Postal Directive, which might seem odd given the two measures are meant to be complementary and the separation of the delivery of goods from items of correspondence is likely to be hard to police in practice given that the normal safeguarding of the security of the mail prevents an analysis of its contents.

Since many USPs' pricing is organized by multi-country delivery zone, rather than country, both cross-border and domestic tariffs mask extensive cross-subsidies both within a country (for domestic traffic) and between several countries (for cross-border services priced in this way). This issue potentially undermines the tariff comparisons which the Commission sees as a major rationale for the proposals. In addition, at the Public Hearing on the proposals organized by the Parliament on 1 March 2017 to discuss the proposals, the UPS representative raised the question as to whether the information requested of operators would be proportionate. The question also arises as to whether the proposed price comparison web site would be fit for purpose due to the range and complexity of tariff information collected and its form had not been disclosed.

The proposals may not fully consider that e-retailers frequently use delivery as a marketing tool. Consumers would not know, or would have a false perception, of the delivery price charged to the e-retailer. The proposals are mainly designed to help e-retailers since they will use the information most, while their customers will take into account the delivery pricing policy of individual e-retailers rather than the actual delivery costs.

Next, there is evidence that despite the noted differences between domestic and cross-border prices, the price increases for cross-border parcels remain modest, a possible sign of a healthy, developing market. ERGP (2016b) reported that in 2015, the average price for posting an international parcel provided by the USP within Europe was 19.54 euro, representing an overall price increase of only 1.8% since 2013. Moreover, this was lower than the reported 4.1% increase for domestic parcels over the same 2-year period.

In three main areas, the likely impacts of the proposals seem unclear or potentially disparate. One relates to the number of operators with a minimum employee level of 50 or any number that would be subject to the regulation. A low threshold might suit a smaller Member State with less extensive e-commerce volumes, whereas a large Member State with high e-commerce volumes might find that a high number of operators were caught by its provisions.

A second area is the proposed affordability assessment for USPs. The Commission proposal referred to price and cost factors rather than a consumers' ability to pay for cross-border parcel services against the other demands on their income. The assessment of affordability masked an embryonic cost orientation assessment, especially given the need to take account of terminal rates. Yet the way such an assessment was to be carried out was not made clear in the text of the article.

The third area concerns the access to multilateral agreements on terminal rates, which also appears to be unclear in purpose and effect. The Commission presented it, in its presentation to the Council Working Party on 9 June 2016, as stemming from the Commission's decision to extend its exemption of the REIMS 2 agreement on terminal dues from the competition rules of the EC Treaty.[4] The exemption

[4]Case Comp/C-1/38.170, OJ L 56 of 24.2.2004, p.76. This was an agreement on remuneration via terminal rates of the delivery of cross-border mail between 17 USPs (letters and packets up to 2 kg in weight).

decision was based on the benefits to consumers arising from allowing third parties to access in a non-discriminatory manner the same terms and conditions as the parties to the agreement. There was an overlap with the parcels proposals since an important part of parcels traffic, the packets and small parcels up to 2 kg, was covered. Yet only one request appeared to have been forthcoming for such access in the 13 years since the decision.

Furthermore, it seems unclear what criteria an NRA would be expected to apply in the required approval of the envisaged Reference Offer and potential review of individual offers where the applicant was unhappy. On individual offers, the Commission text stated that NRAs can make changes to individual offers referred to them "to give effect to the obligations laid down in this article," yet it was not made clear how the other obligations would be relevant to the NRA's judgment. Given the direct applicability of such a Regulation, there seems to be scope for considerable legal uncertainty and potentially different and even contradictory solutions being applied in different Member States, resulting in unnecessary legal and regulatory fragmentation. However, a Directive would have potentially led to greater fragmentation.

7 Stakeholder Reactions Since the Publication of the Proposals

Stakeholders have had varied reactions to the proposals in line with some of the previous comments made at different stages of the Commission's work and consultations leading up to the May 2016 proposals. Since the proposal was published, many USPs have been critical of the main provisions. For example, PostEurop, which represents the USPs, was critical of the affordability provisions on grounds of the lack of a clear justification and impact assessment, the high costs and the perceived undermining of the posts' pricing strategies in a highly competitive market (PostEurop 2017).

ERGP (2016a) indicated support for the Commission's objectives and welcomed the monitoring of the actors in the market under Article 3 of the Commission's proposals as providing a regulatory overview in Member States where NRAs currently had no powers. It noted that USP tariffs were normally transparent, at least for USO services. It called for clarifying the relationship between the cost orientation principle and the principle of affordability and between Article 5 of the draft Regulation and Article 12 of the Postal Directive.

On 1 March 2017, the European Parliament hosted a Public Hearing on the Commission's proposals. Some expressed a strong skepticism about the rationale behind the proposed access measures and questioned why new measures were needed given the provisions of the Postal Directive and competition law. Other views included support for an affordability assessment to look at how much households could afford to spend on these services and the need to address the key problems faced by consumers shopping on line as exposed in the various Commission studies. Some noted a concern about the fragmentation of the sector especially in employment terms, with competition on costs leading to lowest cost employment models. A last observation was that regulation could help remedy the problems identified to only a modest extent.

8 Progress of the Debate on the Wisdom and Potential Impact of the Proposed Changes

The Council and Parliament have been undertaking separate examinations of the Commission's text. The Council met privately in 2016 and 2017 debating and proposing amendments, with the Slovak and Maltese Presidencies respectively taking the lead in proposing Compromise text proposals which were normally published. In the case of the Parliament the debate took place in public sessions and documents in the first half of 2017. At the time of writing, this process is not complete, as the Parliament did not yet reach a common position, however the lines of debate and potential political agreement at the end of the process are gradually becoming clearer.

The Council started its consideration of the proposals in June 2016. Various compromise texts were produced and debated by the Slovak and Maltese Presidencies (July to December 2016 and January to June 2017 respectively). Four of these texts were published: the Compromise texts of 18 November, 17 February, 18 April and 5 May respectively. The 18 November Presidency text recognized that overall Member States supported the Commission's key objectives, but noted the "large amount of concerns and questions raised by delegations and the limited time available to reach a general agreement". The Presidency further reported concerns about the regulatory burden and proportionality from the proposed regulatory activities and the link with the Postal Directive.

The Presidency proposed a new definition of a parcel as "a postal item other than an item of correspondence and with a weight not exceeding 31,5 kg" to complement the Regulation's definition of a "parcel delivery service". Another proposed addition reflected the view that postal items over 20 mm thick are more likely to contain goods than items of correspondence. The Presidency further expressed concerns about the mix of products designated in the Annex because it contained a mix of letter and parcel items. In addition, since the proposed definition of parcel delivery services would only require sorting, clearance or distribution, it appeared to some Member States to be inconsistent with the definition of postal services in the Directive, which requires sorting, clearance, transport and distribution to all be present.

Turning to Article 3, on provision of information, a new "once-only" principle was proposed by the Presidency that information would be required only if not already provided to the NRA, and that the number of persons working for a provider should include sub-contractors. The Presidency also made the affordability and tariff disclosure requirements of Articles 4 and 5 applicable to all operators beyond the cut off threshold. The affordability assessment in Article 5 would be limited to tariffs which seem unreasonably high based on a formula involving domestic tariffs in the home and destination country.

The subsequent Presidency compromise text of 17 February 2017, proposed limiting provision of terminal rates under Article 4 to the concerned NRA and also restricted the need to provide them to circumstances in which a new threshold for the Article 5 assessment—of prices deemed "unreasonably high" rather than unaffordable—had been reached. The proposed new threshold limited the tariffs to be assessed to any that were greater than 1.5 times the sum of the domestic tariff in the originating and destination Member States. Article 6 was also redrafted to limit access to SMEs so it corresponded better with the Regulation's aims.

The 17 April 2017 Presidency compromise text extended the Article 4 requirement on provision of information to all parcels providers meeting the 50-worker threshold and deleted the Article 6 access requirements. The subsequent 5 May 2017 Presidency compromise text, issued with a view to it forming the basis for an agreed general approach by the Council, included keeping the 50-worker threshold for both Articles 3 and 4 and applying both these articles to all parcel delivery providers; and changing the applicability of Article 5 so that it would apply only to universal services of USPs in the Member State where the assessment is carried out rather than to the same range of services in all Member States.

The last Presidency compromise text of 31 May 2017 included final technical changes to Articles 3 and 4 and associated recitals. It was the text adopted by the Council as its agreed "general approach" on 9 June 2017. Key changes included requiring operators to report on all types of person working for them, e.g. including subcontractors, working in whatever capacity including their associated turnover and volume information. It would enable regulators to require operators to include all forms of worker in the 50-person threshold cut-off, including self-employed people working for their subcontractors. Finally, it would require Article 5 assessment of unreasonably high cross-border tariffs follow the principles in Article 12 of the Postal Directive, regarding affordability, cost transparency and non-discrimination.

In parallel, but starting later than the Council, the European Parliament considered the proposal in the lead Committee, TRAN and in the supporting Committee IMCO both of which produced draft reports (TRAN (2017) and IMCO (2017)) comprising amendments for debate. One key change proposed, in both draft reports, was to reduce the threshold for information provision and affordability to all companies with at least 20 workers, including subcontractors, which would increase the reach of the regulation and the burden for operators and regulators.

TRAN (2017) also redrafted the affordability assessment to remove the parts relating to cost orientation from the initial assessment and only require a cost assessment at a new, subsequent stage after an initial affordability screening. It replaced the list of factors in Article 5 of the Commission proposal by a required NRA "initial assessment" of the affordability of cross-border tariffs the purpose of which would be “to assess whether the cost to individuals and small and medium sized enterprises is affordable and to what extent the uptake of cross-border parcel delivery services is affected by the applicable cross-border tariffs”. TRAN put the focus of the initial assessment on individual users, including those with little disposable income, who are disabled or with reduced mobility and individuals and SMEs in remote areas.

Following this initial assessment, NRAs would be permitted, but not required, to request evidence from operators to justify their tariff levels such as “the specific transportation costs” and the “bilateral volumes between different cross-border parcel delivery service providers”. Several of the other draft TRAN amendments focused on social and employment factors and a new draft requirement for traders to pass on specified information to consumers. TRAN also sought to extend the affordability assessment in Article 5 to all operators, not only USPs and, like the Council, it deleted the Article 6 access requirement.

By contrast IMCO (2017) contained several different—rather than single—alternative amendments which covered topics including definitions, thresholds and more technical changes to the articles and covering some of the same areas and concerns in TRAN (2017) One clear difference with TRAN was that IMCO proposed to delete the affordability assessment because most of the services in the Annex were universal services which the Postal Directive already requires to be affordable. However, the draft report of the Lead Committee, TRAN, which took account of the IMCO deliberations, failed to gain agreement when TRAN met on 11 July 2017 to vote on proposed amendments to the Commission’s proposals.

9 Conclusions

The main Commission objectives on market monitoring and transparency have been broadly welcomed. However, there was extensive debate on the rationale and likely impact of the proposals. Some remain concerned that some provisions may be over-engineered, burdensome (for regulators and operators) and potentially counter-productive for the consumers and SMEs they are designed to help.

The debate in the Council and Parliament has reflected different circumstances in Member States, including different mark-ups and pricing structures of cross-border as compared with domestic parcels. In addition, the link between the Postal Directive and the new Regulation was not made sufficiently clear, in light of the new affordability requirements. The final “general approach” document agreed to by the Council requires the previous affordability assessment to take account of the principles in the Postal Directive which include several unrelated to affordability, potentially creating confusion.

From the debate to date, it would seem possible to find a reasonable and proportionate threshold for market monitoring, submission of information to the Commission and/or for carrying out a potential affordability assessment for USPs or a wider set of operators as applicable (covering Articles 3, 4 and 5). However, given the differences between size and maturity of parcels markets in Member States, using an employee/subcontractor threshold based on an absolute number of persons employed could be problematic. It might be better to consider a threshold based on market share within each Member State. This would ensure that all operators of sufficient scale within their Member State will be covered by the regulation, while avoiding disproportionate effects on small carriers.

Unlike telecommunications roaming regulation, where there was a political appetite to regulate high wholesale and retail roaming prices, there appears to be little or no such appetite for such regulation applying to parcels services, where competition is better established. The parcels market is also more complex given the range of services, standard and express, and the historic role of USPs and the imperfect Universal Postal Union arrangements for remunerating USP delivery costs via terminal dues. It is also significant that the delivery price charged to the e-retailer is frequently different from the delivery price then charged to the end consumer ordering on-line so consumer perceptions of prices depend in large part on the pricing policy and marketing strategies of the e-retailers.

The scope of Articles 4 and 5 and their extension to non-USPs might create a burden disproportionate to the regulatory objectives. The main intended beneficiaries of the regulation e.g. individuals or rural SMEs will typically use only USPs for cross-border parcel delivery. USPs have certain privileges related to their universal service role which makes an affordability assessment arguably more relevant for them than non-USPs. Such an assessment could impose significant regulatory costs and burden on those alternative operators and regulators. Moreover, there is evidence from the ERGP that recent cross-border parcel prices are broadly stable or showing only a slight increase year on year (ERGP 2016a).

Up to now, Article 6 received some of the most critical reaction partly because of the existing access provisions in the Postal Directive and partly because of the lack of applications to date under the provisions relating to third party access to cross-border letters and packets services up to 2 kg under the Commission's Exemption of the REIMS 2 agreement from the competition rules in 2002.

Whatever form of secondary legislation or guidance is adopted, the ERGP is likely to have a key role in providing further technical advice that should help ensure smooth implementation. The clarity of the Regulation's articles, especially in relation to the assessment of prices in Article 5, will be critical to their effectiveness. If the qualifying threshold is reasonable, the affordability assessment clear and the burden on regulators and operators relatively low, the Regulation could help secure greater availability and visibility of cross-border parcels services for e-retailers, SMEs and consumers. Finally, given the lack of agreement in the Parliament in July 2017, it remained to be seen whether the final agreement on the text between Council and Parliament could be reached by the end of 2017 on what may turn out to be only relatively modest steps towards improved transparency and regulatory oversight if the proposals are further limited in the negotiations.

References

Commission (2016), European Commission Staff Working Document, Impact Assessment, Proposal for a Regulation of the European Parliament and of the Council on cross-border parcel delivery services, SWD (2016) 166 final

Copenhagen Economics (2012), Study on the pricing behaviour of postal operators and its effect on postal markets

Copenhagen Economics (2013), E-commerce and delivery, A study of the state of play of EU parcel markets with particular emphasis on e-commerce, European Commission, DG Internal Market and Services

ERGP (2014) Opinion to the European Commission on a better understanding of European cross-border e-commerce parcels delivery markets and the functioning of competition on these markets

ERGP (2015a) Report to the European Commission on Legal regimes applicable to European domestic or cross-border e-commerce parcels delivery

ERGP (2015b) Price transparency and regulatory oversight of cross-border parcels delivery, taking into account possible regulatory insights from the electronic communications sector, Joint BEREC-ERGP Opinion, ERGP PL (15) 32 final

ERGP (2015c) Report on Core Indicators for monitoring the European postal market

ERGP (2016a), Technical input papers on the European Commission Proposal for a Regulation of the European Parliament and the Council on cross-border parcel delivery services

ERGP (2016b) Report on Core Indicators for Monitoring the European postal market

FTI (2011) Study on intra-community cross-border parcel delivery (FTI Consulting, December 2011)

IMCO (2017) Opinion on the proposal for a regulation of the European Parliament and of the Council on cross-border parcel delivery services 30-os-2017, IMCO/8/06777

PostEurop (2017) PostEurop position paper on the Commission's proposal for a Regulation of cross-border parcel delivery (Register ID: 092682012915-24) ERGP (2016) Technical input paper on the European Commission's "Proposal for a Regulation of the European Parliament and the Council on cross-border parcel delivery services"

TRAN (2017) Draft Report on the proposal for a regulation of the European Parliament and of the Council on cross-border parcel delivery services, European Parliament Committee on Transport and Tourism, 2016/0149 (COD)

WIK-Consult (2013) Main Developments in the Postal Sector (2010–2013), Bad Honnef, August 2013.

WIK-Consult Final Report (2014), Design and development of initiatives to support the growth of e-commerce via better functioning parcel delivery systems in Europe, Study for the European Commission DG Internal Market and Services.

E-commerce of Goods: Testing the European Single Market

Paula Gori and Virginia Silvestri

1 Introduction

E-commerce has become a major marketplace that provides businesses and consumers new trade opportunities beyond their traditional geographic markets. In light of the European Digital Single Market (DSM), a relevant concern is the existence of several forms of geographic discrimination. Consumers as well as businesses are often faced with undue impediments to free and efficient cross-border transactions within the European Union (EU).

The paper is organized as follows: Sect. 2, proposes an operational definition of e-commerce, and provides metrics both on the size of e-commerce and the difficulty of making cross-border economic trades. Section 3 examines the inherently competitive structure of e-commerce of goods in the EU, with a focus on the recent sector inquiry of the Directorate General for Competition (DG Comp). Section 4 identifies the most relevant obstacles to the spread of e-commerce, and Sect. 5 focuses on the current regulatory answers aiming at tackling these impediments.

2 Economic Dimensions of E-commerce: The Current Situation and its Potential Impact on GDP

E-commerce: an overview E-commerce can be defined as a technology that exploits the ability to digitize characteristics of a product or service being sold and characteristics of the buyer (Cardona et al. 2015). Seen this way, e-commerce is the process

P. Gori (✉) • V. Silvestri
European University Institute, Fiesole, Italy
e-mail: paula.gori@eui.eu

P.L. Parcu et al. (eds.), *The Contribution of the Postal and Delivery Sector*, Topics in Regulatory Economics and Policy, https://doi.org/10.1007/978-3-319-70672-6_10

by which buyer-seller information is digitized and transferred online, thereby reducing transaction costs. Buyers can save on the costs of acquiring information regarding products and services and no longer need to know the location of items prior to sale. Sellers no longer need to maintain inventories close to customer locations.[1] E-commerce also reduces menu costs, facilitating pricing experiments. A major conclusions of a European Commission (EC)'s sector inquiry is that e-commerce leads to a high degree of price transparency that causes an increase in price competition.[2] Moreover, availability of information on consumers' behavior enables more effective price discrimination and marketing techniques.

European policymakers have recently promoted the DSM as one of a top priority. However, it is difficult to find official comprehensive data regarding e-commerce transactions in the DSM. Part of the reason can be attributed to the difficulty of framing such a fast developing and multifaceted phenomenon in a definition that suits accounting criteria. Measuring the degree to which e-commerce attains the above-mentioned market improvements is key for its success. Such measures depend the type of good or service and other characteristics of how the e-transaction is designed, which vary across different industries. E-commerce is also non-uniformly distributed in the economy and among different countries, depending on their typical industrial specializations, as well as on other factors, including Internet penetration. This is illustrated by the wide variation in the share of enterprises making electronic sales in Europe, ranging from 7% in Romania to 30% in Ireland (Eurostat 2016).

While acknowledging that moving many aspects of the buyer-seller relationship online all are part of e-commerce, measurement is difficult in practice. For example, it is not obvious how one would measure how a buyers' ability to find online product information affects purchases that happen offline. The ability to pay online has reduced use of letters for billing and payment. However, it can be used both in offline purchases and online purchases, so it should not be identified as the main distinctive feature of e-commerce. Online delivery, in turn, applies only to services and products that are digital in nature, therefore is even less a characteristic feature for measuring e-commerce.

Accordingly, the order phase of the buyer-seller transaction seems the most suitable to identify the divide between an e-commerce transaction and a traditional offline one. In most empirical studies, e-commerce transactions are indeed counted as the number of orders made online, regardless of whether search, delivery or payment are also taking place online (E-commerce Foundation 2016; Eurostat 2016). On the other hand, e-commerce also creates new types of trade costs, due to the lack of trust towards remote suppliers, delivery services and payment

[1]One can also identify e-commerce in a broader sense to include transactional activities, such as order, payment and delivery (Nikali et al. 2017). Increasingly, other transactional features are becoming indispensable to satisfy customer needs.

[2]Report from the Commission to the Council and the European Parliament, Final report on the E-commerce Sector Inquiry, Brussels, 10.5.2017 COM (2017) 229 final.

systems. Therefore, there is also, marginally, a negative trade effect that can nonetheless be softened using appropriate policies, adopted by private operators as well as by policymakers, as will be discussed below.

2.1 *Economic Dimension of E-commerce and Its Impact on the EU-28 GDP*

Most publicly available statistics (E-commerce Foundation 2016; Eurostat 2016) focus exclusively on B2C trade, which is the biggest portion of e-commerce transactions.[3] Such aggregate statistics show that e-commerce plays an increasingly relevant role in the European markets, in line with the worldwide trend. Its contribution to the EU28 GDP was 2.8% in 2015, rising from 2.45% in 2014. This places the contribution to GDP of the European B2C e-commerce sector in the fourth place in the world, below that of China (7.05% of GDP), South Korea (4.70% of GDP) and the USA (3.32% of GDP) (E-commerce Foundation 2016).

Of all people with an Internet connection in Europe in 2015, about half were online shoppers and 15% bought goods or services online across national borders (Eurostat 2016). These data can be compared against the US figure, where out of all the population of Internet users (88% in 2015) 76% were online shoppers. The proportion of online shoppers is still limited in Europe. In recent years, the annual growth of e-commerce B2C sales in Europe has decreased from an all-time high of 22% in 2013 to a level of 13.3% in 2015. This decrease in the growth rate can attributed to a more mature phase of market development. Another possibility is that increased incomes following the recovery of the European economy led consumers to expend less effort to buy cheaper products online.[4] Indeed, the same slow-down in the growth of B2C e-commerce sales has been observed globally since 2013 (E-commerce Foundation 2016).

E-commerce purchases may be digital or physical goods and services. In Europe, 52% of B2C e-commerce transactions in 2015 involved goods (digital and physical) (E-commerce Foundation 2016). For physical goods, delivery is central to consumers' choices about whether to place an order online and to sellers' decisions about whether to exploit the e-commerce channel. In terms of volumes, the share of online sales in goods tends to be limited. B2C e-commerce sales amounted to 8% of the total of retail sales in Europe in 2015 (E-commerce Foundation 2016). The share of online sales can reach much higher levels in services. The sector most affected by far has been the travel and tourism, where the share of online sales is about 40%

[3]Although the area that most naturally accrues to e-commerce is that of Business-to-Consumer transactions (B2C), there are other types of trade that are generated through it: Business-to-Business (B2B), Customer-to-Customer (C2C), Customer-to-Business (C2B) and Business-to-Government (B2G).

[4]Nikali et al. (2017) found evidence for this in Finland.

(Duch-Brown and Martens 2015). In part, this is also related to the amount of substitution that happens between online and offline sales. The advent of e-commerce has the power of expanding markets, but it may also just be a new distribution channel that moves otherwise offline sales online. It seems that in sectors where the substitution effect is more relevant, like the tourism sector, the share of online sales on total sales is higher, having eroded more rapidly the offline channel role (Duch-Brown and Martens 2015).

Dependence upon a cheap, trustworthy and interactive delivery service becomes more evident in case of cross-border sales and delivery. Just about one third of European online shoppers bought products that involve cross-border delivery, and only 42% of all enterprises making online sales sell cross-border (Eurostat 2016). In the Flash Eurobarometer survey (2015), both sellers and consumers claim that the delivery and return aspect—price, trustworthiness, speed—is among the main reasons to avoid cross-border operations in the sale of goods. Retailers claim that high delivery and return costs make them unable to compete, along with difficulties in complying with different regulations and the connected risks.

The data made available by Eurostat show that 20% of enterprises made electronic sales and the turnover generated by the e-channel was 16% of their total turnover in 2015. In the period 2008–2015, the number of enterprises making e-sales increased by 7%, while the e-turnover increased by 4%. Interestingly it is possible to disentangle the value of e-sales based on the size of the enterprise. There seems to be a positive relationship between the size of the enterprise, the presence of electronic sales and the portion of turnover generated by electronic sales: in 2015, 42% of larger enterprises engaged in e-sales activities, earning 23% of their turnover from it, while the percentages are respectively 28% and 12% for medium size enterprises and 18% and 6% for small size enterprises.

The available European data do not clearly show the difference between volume and value of B2C e-commerce sales in goods. Such information would be interesting to understand the average value of goods purchased online. Although European cross-border B2C online sales have risen by 25% since 2013, that level that is still considered unsatisfactory by the European Commission.[5] They have recently published several *ad-hoc* studies and are in the process of adopting measures to remove obstacles to cross-border e-commerce in Europe, as will be discussed below.

[5]This dissatisfaction is the main engine behind the European Commission Communication "A comprehensive approach to stimulating cross-border e-Commerce for Europe's citizens and businesses", COM (2016) 320 final.

3 Competitive Bottlenecks for a Pan-European E-commerce Market

3.1 *On the E-commerce Side*

In May 2015, the EC launched an e-commerce inquiry as part of its DSM Strategy, which is one of its three pillars of ensuring consumer access to goods and services via e-commerce in the EU. This inquiry ended in May 2017 and its content is summarized in a document by the Commission (the Report).[6] According to the inquiry, with regard to the B2C trade of goods, there is a high degree of price transparency (thus price competition) and direct retail activities by manufacturers have increased. In addition, selective distribution systems strategies have expanded and there are more contractual sales restrictions (on pricing, marketplace, cross-border sales. The use of price comparison tools); free-riding by consumers that use presale services of brick and mortar shops and then shop online, or vice versa, is a frequent practice.

The relationship between manufacturers and retailers (B2B) is a key part of the debate on competition issues relating to e-commerce. E-commerce is also a way for manufacturers to sell directly and thus compete with retail distributors. The high degree of price transparency gives consumers, retailers and manufacturers the ability to compare and monitor online prices of competitors. The inquiry finds that 53% of the respondent retailers track online prices and seven out of ten use automatic software programs to do so. The availability of real-time pricing information could lead to automatized price coordination and the wide-scale use of such software may in some cases raise competition issues.

The sector inquiry identified several potential threats to EU competition law. It found an increase in the use of selective distribution systems (that are not covered by the Vertical Block Exemption Regulation (VBER). According to the Report, these could in some cases be anti-competitive vertical restraints. According to the feedback received by the respondents, price restrictions/recommendations are the most widespread restriction. Online price transparency (and the concurrent use of price comparison software) might be exploited to detect whether retailers deviate from the recommended price. Moreover, the possibility of direct and instant price monitoring could facilitate collusion between retailers.

Selling restrictions in online marketplaces (*e.g.* Ebay, Amazon and Zalando) is another common feature of the distribution contracts. For example, a company selling luxury clothing may restrict the online sales only to marketplaces selling luxury goods, to avoid being mixed with cheap clothing).[7] The choice of a given marketplace as a sale channel depends on factors such as the type of product,

[6] Report from the Commission to the Council and the European Parliament, Final report on the E-commerce Sector Inquiry, Brussels, 10.5.2017 COM (2017) 229 final.

[7] According to the Final Report on the E-commerce Sector Inquiry, 18% of retailers have reported that agreements with suppliers contain marketplace restrictions.

quality and brand, the size of the retailer and of the manufacturer. The inquiry finds that a seller's absolute refusal to permit online marketplace sales does not constitute a "hardcore restriction" of competition, as defined in Article 4(b) and 4(c) of the VBER, and as such they are not automatic violations of EU competition law. Nevertheless, vigilance is required as there might be specific settings in which these bans do violate EU competition law.

Another factor impeding the development of European e-commerce market is the presence of geo-blocking activities enacted by sellers. A business may use technological tools to identify the location of the consumer and block purchases if not in that business's territory (by, for example, refusing payment with credit/debit cards of other countries). The EC's inquiry found that more than one third of e-retailers surveyed use geo-blocking techniques as part of their commercial strategies. In most cases, the choice to geo-block is not due to additional costs (*e.g.* translating the website; arranging for additional marketing efforts; delivery and other services), but to keep their geographical markets separated. Some territorial restrictions may also raise concerns when they are imposed on the retailer, and could be violating the VBER. The EC will continue to monitor the market and will intervene if individual cases require further scrutiny. In this regard, in February 2017 the EC opened three investigations on suspected anticompetitive practices in e-commerce.[8]

3.2 On the Delivery Side

E-commerce is a marketplace phenomenon that has produced *creative disruption*, as coined by Schumpeter (1942). Many commercial activities were heavily impacted on by e-commerce. Some businesses were nearly or completely forced out of the market (e.g. Blockbusters vs. Netflix). Others gained momentum from the wave of innovation; entire new markets were created (e.g. the sharing economy).

The postal and delivery sector benefitted substantially, thanks to parcel delivery. The impact on the postal and delivery sector is particularly relevant because of the expansion of the B2C (and the related C2B, mainly returns) segments, which by their nature are mostly concerned with the shipping of packets (up to 2 kg), parcels (up to 20 kg), and express packages. Packets are considered for regulatory purposes as bulk mail and are usually carried by national postal operators (POs). In the parcel and express sectors, there is robust competition from private delivery operators, which may have pan-European end-to-end networks (*e.g.* DHL, TNT, FedEx, UPS) or may operate within national borders.[9] Various statistics show that national POs

[8]Respectively in the markets of consumer electronics, video games and hotel accommodation, http://europa.eu/rapid/press-release_IP-17-201_en.htm.

[9]The competitive scenario is much more complex, with a host of different players: express operators, consolidators, brokers, and other minor players.

tend to have a higher market share in the B2C segment than in the B2B segment, where private delivery companies are very competitive and POs only play a minor role. Due to their ubiquitous networks and the tendency of private customers and small enterprises to stick to the national POs' service to send their packages, national POs have a opportunity to benefit from the growth of e-commerce especially in the B2C segment, to (at least partially) compensate the loss of revenues due to e-substitution in the mail segment.

The portion of parcels that is currently delivered by national POs varies greatly between Member States (MSs), from less than 10% to above 25%, (ITA/WIK 2009). This difference may be explained by the reactions of national POs to market liberalization, a process which is still on-going, and the concurrent challenge posed by the drop in mail volumes, which has pushed some POs to diversify their core businesses. Some national POs decided to remain focused on traditional core services. To accommodate rising parcel demand, they are taking advantage of their widespread delivery networks. They are also speeding up delivery activities, particularly cross-border, and offering value-added features, such as track-and-trace options or choice of flexible pick-up locations.[10] Other POs focused more on new activities, such as financial services, sometimes partially leaving the growth of B2C delivery demand aside (Parcu and Silvestri 2017).

Both e-retailers and consumers claim quality and availability of affordable delivery are crucial to deciding whether to use online sales channels (Flash Eurobarometer 397 2015). For small companies in particular, the delivery price can constitute a major barrier or a decisive facilitator to e-commerce because they are unable to obtain volume discounts from postal companies that are available to larger competitors. This disadvantage is more pronounced in cross-border operations where delivery prices are generally substantially higher, which include termination fees from the interconnection point to handle parcels to the delivery address.

Small companies and consumers tend to rely on national POs to send parcels and packages. As a matter of proportions, Eurostat 2015 estimates an approximate percentage of small, medium and large retailers in the European e-commerce market on the order respectively of 18%, 28% and 42%. This might be the result of ignorance about the existence of potentially cheaper offers from private delivery companies or lack of trust toward them. Medium and large e-retailers manage to strike better deals with delivery companies, exploiting the large volume of items shipped. Large e-retailers sometimes resort to their own logistic system for certain parts of the service, organizing transportation of items across national borders and then using local delivery operators (*e.g.* Amazon).

This tiered structure marks an important characteristic of market competition between e-retailers, which face different costs regarding the delivery of items,

[10] See for example the European Parcel Group initiative, composed of different national postal operators, which strives to create an integrated service and offers integrated track-and-trace systems.

depending on volume and frequency of parcels shipping. Entry by small operators for this reason is more viable in more densely populated areas, so they can achieve scale economies. For the sake of the development of a truly pan-European e-commerce market, the level of delivery prices is therefore highly relevant, as it may determine the persistence of separated national e-commerce markets if small companies cannot afford paying the high cross-border delivery prices. All in all, high cross-border delivery prices appear to constitute a competitive bottleneck for the development of a truly pan-European e-commerce market.

4 Main Obstacles to E-commerce in the EU

While the potential impact on the economy of e-commerce appears to be of first order relevance, it still faces serious obstacles to becoming more widespread in Europe. Some of these are socio-educational (*e.g.* lack of digital literacy and skills); some psychological (*e.g.* different emotions when buying online and insufficient trust in the online sellers or the online system in general); some practical (*e.g.* customers living close to shopping centers); some related to prices (be it of the product and/or of the delivery); and, finally, some related to essential features of the offer (*e.g.* not having the possibility of choosing the specific characteristic of a given item or being denied to buy from sellers of other EU MSs).

4.1 On the E-commerce Side

Insufficient Trust—When it comes to the online world, trust appears to be crucial in transactions. In case of e-commerce, consumers are willing to buy online only if they trust both the supplier and the shipper to deliver the purchased product on time, that the quality of the product is as expected, and that consumer protection and contract law will be applied at least equally compared to the offline world (Corbitt et al. 2003). Trust in e-commerce is more difficult to develop than off-line because direct physical links with the product and with the seller are missing. This may be worsened when the consumer buys from a trader located in another country because of language barriers, fear of not being able to get in contact, and uncertainty about applicable consumer protection law. As a consequence, consumers need to find other factors of trust to decide whether or not to buy.

Unjustified geo-blocking—This practice refers to the phenomenon by which certain e-retailers decide to disable sales to customers located in other EU Member States (MSs). Geo-blocking is usually implemented by refusing to deliver or to accept payments cross-border, by blocking access to the website when consumers try to access it from another MS or by re-directing consumers to other websites and/or by asking payment with national credit/debit cards. These restrictions often appear at the final stage of the shopping process, when the consumer already spent a certain amount of time on a website.[11] The geo-blocking issue emerges at different stages of the e-commerce chain. Retailers might decide to geo-block cross-border online sales by their own decision, but they could also be obliged to so because of restrictive clauses imposed by manufacturers in the distribution contracts.

Unjustified geo-blocking is an obstacle for cross-border e-commerce and for DSM strategy.[12] A public consultation launched by the EC in 2015 found that the large majority of consumers experience geographical restrictions when buying online.[13] At the same time the majority of businesses highlight the importance of tailoring their prices to different national markets.

4.2 On the Delivery Side

High tariffs—Within the EU, there are significant price differences when delivering nationally or cross-border. This is true also when cross-border delivery would be equivalent or even shorter from a geographical distance point of view. Cross-border delivery prices are often quoted without a clear relation with the effective cost of the delivery.[14] There are concerns that the high cross-border delivery prices arise because of the level of termination fees charged by national POs from the interconnection point to the delivery address (FTI Consulting 2011). The EC is attempting to shed light on how such termination fees are set to understand whether they are a source of excessively high prices. So far there has been a great degree of opacity regarding them, since they are considered sensitive commercial information by the companies. There is not even clear information yet in the regulatory debate about whether such termination fees are excessively high or excessively low (Marcus and Petropoulos 2016).

Lack of transparency and information—Transparency and information are other key elements both for a competitive market and for consumer protection. The more consumers and businesses are aware of existing services and prices, the more effective is their choice and the tougher is market competition.[15]

However, the EC claims that consumers and businesses are only aware about a small number of alternative delivery services and often use the national PO by

[11]Mystery shopping survey on territorial restrictions and geo-blocking in the European Digital Single Market (2016), conducted by GfK Belgium PS for the European Commission.

[12]European Commission (2015). Communication from the Commission to the European Parliament, the Council, the European Economic and Social Committee and the Committee of the Regions a Digital Single Market Strategy for Europe, COM/2015/0192 final.

[13]Proposal for a Regulation of the European Parliament and of the Council on addressing geo-blocking and other forms of discrimination based on customers' nationality, place of residence or place of establishment within the internal market and amending Regulation (EC) No 2006/2004 and Directive 2009/22/EC.

[14]http://ec.europa.eu/growth/tools-databases/newsroom/cf/itemdetail.cfm?item_id=8610.

[15]Vigilance against potential collusion is needed when competitor prices are easily available.

default.[16] This lack of awareness may create barriers for new operators to enter a market or gain market share. From the perspective of incumbent suppliers, lack of market information relaxes the competitive pressure on them. This in turn means not only higher delivery tariffs, but also possibly distorts the incentives to invest in quality features, such as timing, more flexible options (*e.g.* multiple pick-up locations) and value-added services such as tracking (Spence 1975; Sappington 2005).

5 EU Regulatory Strategy to Foster E-commerce

From a regulatory point of view, the EC decided to foster e-commerce by introducing the so-called "E-commerce package". This consists of three legislative proposals to address unjustified geo-blocking, foster cross-border parcel delivery, and improve the enforcement of consumers' rights and clarify which are to be considered unfair commercial practices.

In the postal sector, the main current regulatory instrument is the Third Postal Services Directive.[17] Although it was amended in 2002 and 2008, the current legal framework is now 20 years old, with different national implementations within the EU. The absence of a harmonized regulatory framework constitutes a significant obstacle to cross-border delivery, particularly because of high administrative costs and legal uncertainty. The proposal for regulation on cross-border parcel delivery is a step towards a more unified approach.

5.1 On the E-commerce Side

Insufficient Trust: As already mentioned, trust is a matter of both cognitive/emotional elements that are under the control of sellers and to aspects such as payment security and data protection, on which is primarily up to regulators to intervene. Eventually, consumer protection issues can emerge as a general unifying theme. Regarding payment security, the second Payment Services Directive (PSD 2), adopted in 2015, aims at making payments across EU Member States as easy, efficient and secure as payments within them.[18] The three key-points of the

[16]Proposal for a Regulation of the European Parliament and of the Council on cross-border parcel delivery services (2016).

[17]Directive 2008/6/EC of the European Parliament and of the Council of 20 February 2008 amending Directive 97/67/EC with regard to the full accomplishment of the internal market of Community postal services.

[18]Directive 2015/2366/EU of the European Parliament and of the Council of 25 November 2015 on payment services in the internal market, amending Directives 2002/65/EC, 2009/110/EC and 2013/36/EU and Regulation (EU) No 1093/2010, and repealing Directive 2007/64/EC. The latter entered into force on 12 January 2016 and rules will apply from 13 January 2018 (deadline for transposition in national systems).

Directive are strict security requirements of e-payments (including protection of financial data and reduction of fraud risk), transparency and information; and rights and obligations for users and providers (including limits to surcharging).

In the field of data protection, enshrined in the EU Charter of Fundamental Rights, a new General Data Protection Regulation (GDPR) will become operational in May 2018.[19] Several consumer data protections were specified: enhanced transparency and information, the right to be forgotten, limits to profiling, the right to rectification and erasure, and the right to data portability, among others. On the processor side, precise and strict obligations are also present, including among others maintaining a record of processing activities, implementing all the technical and organizational measures to ensure an appropriate security level, running impact assessments, and notification of any significant security breach to the EC (and to the data subject if directly impacted on).

Finally, the EC introduced a proposal for the review of the Regulation on Consumer Protection Cooperation.[20] One of the main motivations for the review is strong evidence of a suboptimal enforcement of consumer protection rules. The coordination role of the EC and harmonization within the EU can play a pivotal role.[21]

Unjustified geo-blocking—Tackling unjustified geo-blocking is probably the key pillar of the strategy of the EC to foster e-commerce. In May 2016, the EC published a Proposal for a Regulation on Geo-Blocking.[22] It applies to online sales (except for transactions where goods and services are purchased by a business for resale) and to all traders, European and non-European, operating in the EU. The main objective of the proposal is to forbid any discriminatory behavior adopted on the basis of nationality or country of residence, while calling on traders to ensure any necessary action to guarantee that the connected rights of consumers are respected. Its main aim is to tackle all geographic restrictions that are deemed unjustified by, for example, high delivery costs.[23]

[19]Regulation (EU) 2016/679 of the European Parliament and of the Council of 27 April 2016 on the protection of natural persons with regard to the processing of personal data and on the free movement of such data, and repealing Directive 95/46/EC (General Data Protection Regulation). The latter entered into force on 24 May 2016 and will apply from 25 May 2018.

[20]Proposal for a Regulation of the European Parliament and of the Council on cooperation between national authorities responsible for the enforcement of consumer protection laws.

[21]See paragraph 1.3 of the Proposal.

[22]Proposal for a Regulation of the European Parliament and of the Council on addressing geo-blocking and other forms of discrimination based on customers' nationality, place of residence or place of establishment within the internal market and amending Regulation (EC) No 2006/2004 and Directive 2009/22/EC.

[23]https://ec.europa.eu/digital-single-market/en/geo-blocking-digital-single-market (last access on 09/05/2017).

The proposal tackles different geo-blocking techniques: blocking websites, re-directing the costumer to another interface because he is accessing the website from another MS, imposing different prices, refusing to accept payment transactions, and denying delivery. In cross-border purchases, the trader should still sell the goods, but it is not obliged to organize the delivery to the MSs in which the customer resides, where the seller does not pursue or direct his activities (the buyer should arrange the pick-up).

5.2 On the Delivery Side

High tariffs and lack of transparency and information—The main strategy emerging from the "Proposal for a Regulation on cross-border parcel delivery services" (2016)[24] is to use regulatory action and cooperation within the EU to monitor and assess tariffs of USPs and their transparency. By so doing, high terminal rates might be limited and market competition fostered. In particular, each USP would be required to annually submit its list of tariffs to their National Regulatory Authority (NRA). Other operators may submit their tariffs on a voluntary basis, provided that the underlying services are comparable. Moreover, the USP shall also submit its termination rates, but these data would not be published, because they are considered commercially sensitive information. NRAs would use the information to assess the affordability of the prices of the USP. Should they conclude that the cross-border parcel delivery service prices are not affordable, they shall ask the USP to provide justification.

A joint December 2015 statement by the European Regulators Group for Postal Services (ERGP) and the Body of European Regulators for Electronic Communications (BEREC) of December 2015 outlined the power that national regulators should have to monitor cross-border parcel delivery and to intervene in case of transparency issues for European deliveries. The same statement also highlighted the importance of fostering and developing initiatives to increase consumer and supplier information and awareness.[25] The EC also supports the development of an informative platform for delivery services, which would allow e-retailers to have a wider overview of their delivery possibilities.[26]

Lack of regulatory harmonization—The Regulation of cross-border parcel delivery would be a first strong instrument to tackle this issue. NRAs would have a central and key role in the expected trend of declining tariffs. The implementation

[24]European Parliament and Council, Proposal for a Regulation on cross-border parcel delivery services, 25.5.2016 COM (2016) 285 final.

[25]Joint BEREC-ERGP Opinion (2015), Price transparency and regulatory oversight of cross-border parcels delivery, taking into account possible regulatory insights from the electronic communications sector.

[26]European Parliament and Council, Proposal for a Regulation on cross-border parcel delivery services, 25.5.2016 COM (2016) 285 final.

of the assessment procedure is in fact the instrument that the EC is suggesting to monitor and assess prices of the USPs, with the consequent idea fostering competition that would put pressure on USPs to decrease potentially excessive prices.

6 Conclusion

Citizens are moving from receiving letters to receiving parcels and thus there is a link going in both directions between e-commerce and the parcel delivery market. Compared to other phenomena under the DSM umbrella, e-commerce is characterized by the need for an overall regulatory approach. E-commerce indeed brings novelties such as the change in the relationship between seller and buyer, improved price comparison possibilities, disclosure of information (with more risks of fraud), the need of delivering goods in the last segment of the transaction, and protection of personal data.

Within the Single Market, geo-blocking practices, delivery prices and quality (particularly cross-border), potential anti-competitive behaviors, and trust and security issues, are the most crucial elements to be addressed. The EC has adopted an all-embracing approach aiming at eliminating critical barriers that restrict e-commerce's potential. To maximize the level of harmonization, the EC will employ regulations that are binding on Member States. It is now too early to provide an assessment, but one can already see the merit of this horizontal and harmonized approach. The new 2017 Consumer Conditions Scoreboard reveals that consumers are progressively buying more online (also thanks to specific consumer protection initiatives) and that their trust in e-commerce is increasing, in particular when buying from another EU country. While this demand is growing, the survey shows that retailers do still have concerns about selling cross-border within the EU.[27] It will be most insightful to further analyze the complete regulatory framework once it is set and implemented.

References

BEREC-ERGP Joint Opinion (2015), Price transparency and regulatory oversight of cross-border parcels delivery, taking into account possible regulatory insights from the electronic communications sector.

Cardona M., Duch-Brown N., Francois J., Martens B. and F. Yang (2015). The Macro-economic Impact of e-Commerce in the EU Digital Single Market. Institute For Prospective Technological Studies Digital Economy Working Paper 2015/19.

[27]http://europa.eu/rapid/press-release_IP-17-2109_en.htm and http://ec.europa.eu/newsroom/just/item-detail.cfm?item_id=117250.

Corbitt B. J., Thanasankit T. and Yi H. (2003), *Trust and e-commerce: a study of consumer perceptions*, Electronic Commerce Research and Applications.

Duch-Brown N. and B. Martens (2015). The European Digital Single Market: Its Role in Economic Activity in the EU. JRC Technical Reports. Institute For Prospective Technological Studies Digital Economy Working Paper 2015/17.

E-commerce Foundation (2016). European B2C E-Commerce Report 2016.

European Commission (2012). Green Paper, An integrated parcel delivery market for the growth of e-commerce in the EU, COM (2012) 698 final.

European Commission (2015). Communication from the Commission to the European Parliament, the Council, the European Economic and Social Committee and the Committee of the Regions A Digital Single Market Strategy for Europe, COM/2015/0192 final.

European Commission (2016a). Staff Working Document, Preliminary Report on the E-commerce Sector Inquiry, Brussels, 15.9.2016 SWD (2016) 312 final.

European Commission (2016b). Proposal for a Regulation of the European Parliament and of the Council on cross-border parcel delivery services, Brussels, COM/2016/0285 final - 2016/0149 (COD).

European Commission (2017a), Report from the Commission to the Council and the European Parliament, Final report on the E-commerce Sector Inquiry, Brussels, 10.5.2017 COM (2017) 229 final.

European Commission (2017b). Consumers Condition Scoreboard 2017.

European Parliament and Council, Proposal for a Regulation on addressing geo-blocking and other forms of discrimination based on customers' nationality, place of residence or place of establishment within the internal market and amending Regulation (EC) No 2006/2004 and Directive 2009/22/EC.

European Parliament and Council, Directive 2008/6/EC of 20 February 2008 amending Directive 97/67/EC with regard to the full accomplishment of the internal market of Community postal services.

European Parliament and Council, Directive 2015/2366/EU of 25 November 2015 on payment services in the internal market, amending Directives 2002/65/EC, 2009/110/EC and 2013/36/EU and Regulation (EU) No 1093/2010, and repealing Directive 2007/64/EC.

European Parliament and Council, Regulation (EU) 2016/679 of 27 April 2016 on the protection of natural persons with regard to the processing of personal data and on the free movement of such data, and repealing Directive 95/46/EC (General Data Protection Regulation).

European Parliament and Council, Proposal for a Regulation of the on cooperation between national authorities responsible for the enforcement of consumer protection laws, 25.5.2016 COM (2016) 283 final.

European Parliament and Council, Proposal for a Regulation on cross-border parcel delivery services, 25.5.2016 COM (2016) 285 final.

Eurostat (2016). Survey on ICT usage and e-commerce in enterprises.

Flash Eurobarometer 397 (2015), Consumers' attitude towards cross-border trade and consumer protection.

FTI Consulting (2011). Intra-Community cross-border parcel delivery: A study for the European Commission. London.

GfK Belgium PS for the European Commission, Mystery shopping survey on territorial restrictions and geo-blocking in the European Digital Single Market (2016).

ITA/WIK (2009). The Evolution of the European Postal Market since 1997.

Marcus, S. and Petropoulos, G. (2016). E-commerce in Europe: Parcel Delivery Prices in a Digital Single Market. Bruegel Policy Contribution, Issue 2016/09, May 2016.

Nikali H., Mattila J., Rintanen I., and V. Huuhtanen (2017). Demand and Regulation for e-Commerce in Goods. In: The changing postal and delivery sector: towards a Renaissance, ed. Parcu P.L., Brennan T. and Crew M., Topics in Regulatory Economics and Policy, Springer International Publishing, Switzerland.

Parcu, P.L. and Silvestri, V. (2017). Lessons from the Postal Sector to Telecommunications and Vice Versa, in The Changing Postal and Delivery Sector: towards a Renaissance, ed. Parcu P. L., Brennan T. and Crew M., Topics in Regulatory Economics and Policy, Springer International Publishing, Switzerland.

Sappington, D. (2005). Regulating Service Quality: A Survey. Journal of Regulatory Economics 27, 123–154.

Schumpeter, J. (1942). Capitalism, Socialism and Democracy. Harper & Brothers, New York.

Spence, M. (1975). Monopoly, Quality, and Regulation. Bell Journal of Economics, 6, 417–429.

Summary of Responses to the European Commission's 2015 Public Consultation on Cross-border Parcel Delivery, European Commission.

How E-commerce Is Shaping a New Consumer-Focused Regulatory Framework for the European Parcel Delivery Market

Virginie Alloo

1 Introduction

Changing communication behavior has led postal operators to take advantage of new parcel delivery opportunities stemming from the growing e-commerce market. Until fairly recently, the parcel delivery sector was essentially a Business to Business (B2B) market, unregulated and left largely to pure parcel operators like UPS or Fedex. By contrast, the new e-commerce delivery market is mainly Business to Consumers (B2C) and as a result attracts regulatory attention, in particular the consumer protection rules applying throughout the European Union (EU).

The European Commission's recent initiative to introduce a Regulation on cross-border parcel delivery services[1] has generated a significant reaction in the industry and among consumers' organizations. From the delivery operator side, the response has been largely to question the justification for a new set of rules for a sector which the industry considers to be already competitive and customer focused. Users, on the other hand, seem mainly to welcome the Commission's new focus on what is seen to be a critical barrier to e-commerce, i.e. delivery.

In one way, both sides may be wrong, not so much in their views on the need for and the details of the European Commission's suggested intervention, but with regard to the idea that any proposed regulation of parcels delivery is new. In fact, parcel delivery operators have for many years been subject to (or at least have had to keep a close eye upon) regulations governing both competition and consumer protection issues in the sector.

[1] Proposal for a Regulation of the European Parliament and of the Council on cross-border parcel delivery services, May 25, 2016.

V. Alloo (✉)
Cullen International
e-mail: virginie.alloo@cullen-international.com

P.L. Parcu et al. (eds.), *The Contribution of the Postal and Delivery Sector*, Topics in Regulatory Economics and Policy, https://doi.org/10.1007/978-3-319-70672-6_11

Section 2 of this paper discusses the different reasons behind the adoption of the proposal for a Regulation on cross-border parcel delivery. Sections 3 and 4 focus on the existing forms of regulation affecting the sector, questioning in some cases the lack of clarity on the scope of the postal rules (who is captured and when) and describing the whole set of (new) online consumer protection rules related to delivery. Section 5 reviews the overall impact on the sector of facing a set of rules which come from different sources, and which can be unclear and inconsistent in their application.

2 Why a Regulatory Focus on Parcel Delivery?

According to the European Commission (EC), efficient and transparent delivery services are critical to e-commerce growth, which is being stifled, especially cross-border e-commerce, because of a lack of trust from consumers and businesses.

In 2015, a survey by the EC asked companies which were the main obstacles they encountered when selling to or purchasing from other member States.[2] The most important obstacles were in both cases the **high costs of cross-border delivery** and the **costs of cross-border dispute resolution** (Fig. 1).

According to the EC researchers Nestor Duch-Brown and Bertin Martens, reducing delivery prices could increase the probability of European firms engaging in cross-border e-commerce by 7.5%.[3] Among the current top 100 online retailers, 52% only sell in their home country. While 17% of SMEs in the EU sell online (which is very low), only 7% sell cross-border to other EU countries. In 2013 already, a study[4] by Copenhagen Economics showed that most parcel traffic was domestic, representing 85% of total EU shipments.

2.1 Improving Consumer Trust

Since 2012, the EC has been busy adopting and monitoring various initiatives with a view to improve consumer trust in relation to delivery. First, the EC adopted in 2012 a communication on e-commerce.[5] The objective was to put in place a reliable and efficient delivery process in the whole European Union to remedy delivery problems that were believed to hamper the development of online shopping,

[2] EC Eurobarometer 413: companies engaged in online activities, May 6, 2015.

[3] Duch-Brown and Martens, 'Barriers to firms' cross-border e-commerce in the EU Digital Single Market', JRC/IPTS Digital Economy Working Paper, 2015.

[4] Okholm, H. B. et al., e-Commerce and delivery—A study of the state of play of EU parcel markets with particular emphasis on e-commerce, Copenhagen Economics for the European Commission, 2013.

[5] EC communication on "coherent framework for building trust in the digital single market for e-commerce and online services' adopted"—January 11, 2012.

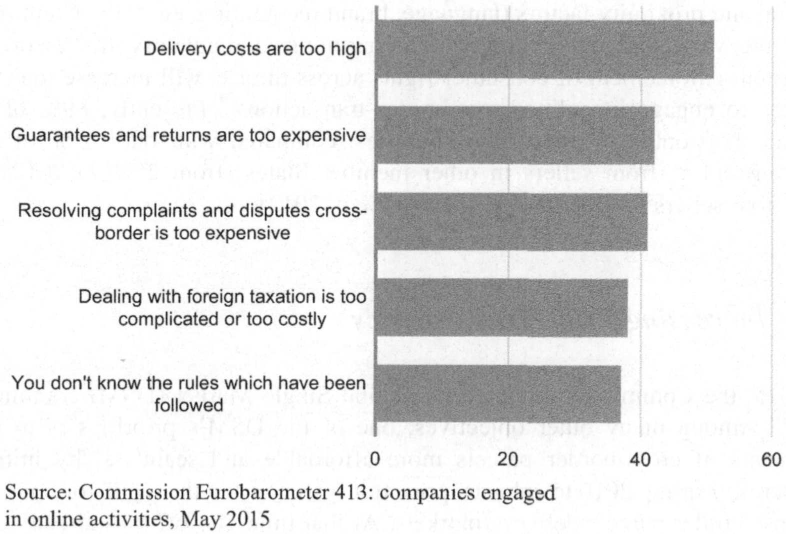

Fig. 1 Most important obstacles to online border sales in %. Source: Commission Eurobarometer 413: companies engaged in online activities, May 2015

especially cross-border. It made a number of recommendations (Sect. 3.3 on Reliable and efficient payment and delivery systems) including that delivery time-scales mentioned during the online ordering process should be respected and that goods should be safely shipped and at an affordable price to rural and remote areas everywhere in the EU. In addition, it called for clarification of the liability for damaged, stolen or lost parcels and that consumers should have access to different delivery options (for example, home delivery at specific times, collection in a partner shop or via automated systems).

Following a green paper[6] specifically dedicated to parcel delivery, the EC adopted in 2013 a roadmap[7] to complete the single market for parcel delivery. The EC's document defined non-legislative actions to be taken by stakeholders to improve transparency and information, delivery solutions, complaint handling, and redress mechanisms. However, the EC did not find it necessary to modify the postal regulatory framework, preferring to give priority to non-legislative options which would be evaluated 18 months later, in 2015.

A Eurobarometer survey conducted in 2014 by the EC showed that European consumers had less trust in cross-border e-commerce than in national online shopping.[8] Even if this home preference could be attributed to some extent to

---

[6] EC green paper on "an integrated parcel delivery market for the growth of e-commerce in the EU"—November 29, 2012.

[7] EC communication for a "roadmap for completing the single market for parcel delivery—build consumer trust in delivery services and encourage online sales"—December 16, 2013.

[8] EC, Flash Eurobarometer 397, 'Consumer attitudes towards cross-border trade and consumer protection', 2014.

cultural and proximity factors (language, brand recognition, etc.), the Commission is of the view that only a strong and harmonized regulatory framework and consistent enforcement of consumer rights across the EU will increase their willingness to engage in online cross-border transactions.[9] Presently, 89% of consumers shop online in their own countries, compared with only 32% of those ordering online from sellers in other member States (from 25% in 2012), and 20% from sellers outside the EU (from 13% in 2012).

2.2 *Increasing Price Transparency*

In 2015, the Commission adopted its Digital Single Market (DSM) communication.[10] Among many other objectives, one of the DSM's priorities is to make shipments of cross-border parcels more affordable and seamless, by initiating measures in spring 2016 to enhance price transparency and the regulatory oversight of cross-border parcels delivery markets. At that time, the EC was already of the view that the parcel delivery market was not transparent enough in terms of pricing and volume information, as well as details of the agreements made between different operators for cross-border delivery. Currently, not all National Regulatory Authorities (NRAs) have the power to require delivery operators to provide information on the evolution of the parcel market (in terms of pricing or volumes). Additionally, the competencies of regulators and the definition of parcel services differ across the EU.

This is in particular due to the Article 9 of the Postal Services Directive which does not clearly define express services or whether such services can be considered to be postal services, which can make it hard for market players to understand which regulatory obligations apply in any particular situation and EU country (see also Sect. 2.1).

2.3 *The Draft Regulation on Cross-Border Parcel Delivery*

In May 2015, the EC launched a consultation, asking for opinions on cross-border delivery within the EU for parcels, packets and express parcels.[11] The results of the consultation showed that the high costs of cross-border parcels delivery discourage consumers and retailers from placing cross-border online orders. Following these findings, in May 2016, the EC took the decision to enable NRAs to gather and

---

[9] Cardona, M., Duch-Brown, N., and Martens, B., 'Consumer perceptions of (cross-border) e-commerce in the EU Digital Single Market', JRC/IPTS Digital Economy Working Paper, 2015.

[10] EC communication for a Digital Single Market strategy for Europe—May 6, 2015.

[11] EC public consultation on cross-border parcel delivery "Initiative to enhance the affordability, quality and convenience of cross-border parcel delivery"—May 5, 2015.

analyze parcel delivery service prices. To achieve this, it introduced a proposal for a Regulation on cross-border parcel delivery services which enables all NRAs to gather and analyze parcel delivery service prices.

The draft Regulation proposes a differentiated approach, with obligations described in Table 1 below imposed on different types of parcel service providers.

Table 1 Summary of the obligations foreseen for different types of operator in the commission's proposed regulation

Obligation	Operators affected	Institution empowered	Deadline/Scope
Provision of general information related to operator—company identification, scope of services provided (art.3.1)	All parcel delivery service providers except national and regional providers employing below 50 persons (art.3.6)	NRAs	Once and within 30 days in case of changes Additional informational obligations may be imposed by NRAs (Art. 3.5)
Information on annual turnover in parcels, number of employees and parcel volumes (Art.3.3)	All parcel delivery service providers	NRAs	By March 31 of each calendar year Data should be broken down into national, incoming and outgoing cross-border traffic
List of tariffs applicable for the delivery of postal items (Art.4.1)	Universal service providers providing parcel delivery services	NRAs (data gathering) EC (publication)	Information to be provided to NRA by January 31 of each calendar year NRAs to submit the lists of tariffs to the Commission by February 28 The Commission to publish them on a dedicated website by April 30
Information on terminal rates applicable to postal items originating from other member States (Art. 4.3)	Universal service providers providing parcel delivery services	NRAs EC	Information to be provided to NRA by January 31 of each calendar year NRAs to submit the information to the Commission and NRAs by February 28 of each calendar year
Accept all reasonable requests from competing operators seeking access to their network for cross-border services (Art. 6) Publish access reference offer	Universal service providers providing parcel delivery services that have concluded agreements on terminal rates	NRAs	NRAs to accept reference offers and to be empowered with dispute resolution powers when no agreement is reached between negotiating operators

Source: Cullen International research

Under the proposed Regulation, postal service providers would have to provide lists of tariffs and information on terminal rates to NRAs. The NRA would assess the affordability of tariffs for cross-border parcel delivery services on the basis of the information gathered. Significant differences between domestic and cross-border tariffs for parcel delivery services would have to be justified by objective criteria, such as additional costs for transport and a reasonable profit margin. Universal service operators providing parcel delivery services may be required by NRAs to provide such justification. Each NRA's final assessment of the affordability of tariffs should be submitted to the EC and to the NRAs of other member States, by March 31 of each calendar year. Additionally, universal service providers would also be obliged to accept all reasonable requests from competing operators seeking access to their network for cross-border parcel delivery services. It would cover parcels with a maximum weight of 31.5 kg (as heavier items cannot be handled without mechanical aid). Small service providers, active only on a national or regional market and which employ fewer than 50 persons, would be partly excluded from the scope of the Regulation.

In April 2017 Lucy Anderson, the rapporteur for the European Parliament's lead Transport and Tourism (TRAN) committee issued her draft report[12] on the proposal. She proposed amendments to widen the scope of the requirements, many of which would now apply to all parcel delivery operators. These also included deleting the proposed obligations relating to the provision of network access and the publication of terminal dues and increasing the range and level of information to be made available for NRAs; and providing more information on delivery options for consumers buying online. The TRAN committee members of the European Parliament rejected the draft report on July 11, 2017. Chair of the TRAN Committee, Karima Delli, called for continuation of work on the report in the autumn. On June 9, 2017, the European Council agreed its position (a 'general approach') on the draft Regulation. The Council believes that Commission proposals for increased price transparency and more effective regulatory oversight should help to lower prices for cross-border parcel delivery services in the EU. However, like the EP rapporteur, the Council also calls for the deletion of some of the Commission's planned measures, such as regulating access and the publication of terminal dues.

3 Existing EU Rules Applying to Delivery

One of the main questions raised by the 2012 green paper and the 2015 consultation was whether, and if so to what extent, the existing regulatory framework was an obstacle to the creation of a truly integrated European parcel delivery market

[12] European Parliament's lead Transport and Tourism (TRAN) committee draft report on the proposed Regulation on cross-border delivery, April 26, 2017.

meeting the needs and expectations of online retailers, consumers and parcel operators. Currently, delivery services are subject to the following EU sector-specific and horizontal rules. First, the postal sector rules broadly define the postal services with their associated essential requirements (see Sect. 3.1). They fail however to define clearly what is an express service and lack provisions related to the flexibility of delivery (which is an important aspect for postal operations when the addressee is not present at home for the delivery).

Second, the general consumer protection rules that are disseminated across five Directives: the Consumer Rights Directive (CRD),[13] the E-commerce Directive[14]; the Services Directive[15]; the Directive on conformity and guarantees[16]; and the Directive for alternative dispute resolution (ADR).[17] The provisions related to delivery apply at each step of the online buying process: before ordering online, when ordering is made, at the time of delivery and in case of return (see Sect. 3.2).

3.1 Existing Postal Rules

The Postal Services Directive[18] provides common rules for the development of the internal market for postal services and the improvement of quality of service. Postal services involve the clearance, sorting, transport and distribution of postal items (Article 2.1). Member States may impose general conditions on the supply of postal services (Article 9.1). These can include rules regarding confidentiality of correspondence and information transmitted or stored, and protection of personal data and privacy. Other issues involve compliance with terms and conditions of employment and social security schemes laid down by law and/or by collective agreement negotiated between national social partners, environmental protection and regional planning, and security of the network as regards the transport of dangerous goods

[13] European Parliament and Council Directive "*on consumer rights*"—October 25, 2011.

[14] European Parliament and Council Directive "*on certain legal aspects of information society services, in particular electronic commerce, in the Internal Market*" (e-Commerce Directive)—June 8, 2000.

[15] European Parliament and Council Directive "*on services in the internal market*"—December 12, 2006.

[16] European Parliament and Council Directive "*on certain aspects of the sale of consumer goods and associated guarantees*"—May 25, 1999.

[17] European Parliament and Council Directive "*on alternative dispute resolution for consumer disputes*" (ADR)—May 21, 2013.

[18] Directive 97/67/EC of the European Parliament and of the Council of December 15, 1997 on "*common rules for the development of the internal market of Community postal services and the improvement of quality of service*" (Postal Service Directive—consolidated version) as amended by Directive 2002/39/EC and Directive 2008/06/EC of February 20, 2008 with regard to "*the full accomplishment of the internal market of Community postal services*".

(Article 2.19). Where appropriate, the granting of authorizations to provide postal services may be subject to obligations to make financial contributions to the sharing mechanism for financing the universal service and the national regulatory authority's operational costs (Article 9.2, third and fourth indents).

3.1.1 No Well-Defined Scope of Postal Rules

Article 9 of the Postal Services Directive does not clearly define express services or whether such services can be considered to be postal services. Even the basic issue whether an authorization is required to provide services cannot always be addressed since in some countries the definition of express services, and whether or not such services are considered to be within the scope of postal services regulatory framework is not clear.

Alessandra Fratini's paper in this volume discusses the 2016 DHL case, in which the Court of Justice of the European Union (CJEU) confirmed that national law can require providers of postal services outside the scope of the universal service also to contribute to the funding of the national regulatory authority (NRA). The Court's decision also included comments on other aspects of article 9 of the Postal Directive and whether certain obligations could be applied only to providers of universal services (or equivalent services) or to all postal providers.

Table 2 below shows that there is no clear definition of "express services" in 16 of the 28 EU countries. In six EU member States, express services are clearly stated to be outside the scope of postal regulations, i.e. there is some legal or regulatory text affirming that express services are not to be included. However, in five of these six countries, there is no clear definition of the term "express services".

Table 3 below shows that in some countries, the NRA's information gathering powers are limited to postal service providers and may not apply to express carriers, where these operators are clearly defined to be outside the scope of postal regulations. However, in Finland and the Netherlands, the NRA's information gathering powers are drafted more widely and could apply effectively to all market players.

Table 2 Express services are often regulated—even if the term is not clearly defined

	Clearly defined	Not clearly defined
Outside scope of regulations	Netherlands	Denmark, Finland, France, Ireland, Sweden
Within scope of regulations	Bulgaria, Cyprus, Czech Republic, Estonia, Greece, Hungary, Latvia, Malta, Portugal, Romania, Slovakia	Austria, Belgium, Croatia, Germany, Italy, Lithuania, Luxembourg, Poland, Slovenia, Spain, UK

Source: Cullen International

Table 3 Express carriers may be required to provide information to NRAs

	Countries where express carriers are within the scope of postal regulations	Countries where express carriers are outside the scope of postal regulations
NRA has generic information gathering powers	Croatia, Cyprus, Czech Republic, Estonia, Germany, Luxembourg, Portugal, Slovenia, Spain, UK	Finland, Netherlands
NRA has specific information gathering powers	Austria, Belgium, Bulgaria, Greece, Hungary, Italy, Latvia, Lithuania, Poland, Romania	
No information requirement on express carriers	Malta, Slovakia	Denmark, France, Ireland, Sweden

Source: Cullen International

3.1.2 No Provision on Delivery Flexibility

In relation to e-commerce parcel delivery, the level of delivery flexibility could be an important aspect for postal operations, particularly in case of larger items where the addressee is not present at home for the delivery. The Postal Directive does not specify whether postal service providers should be permitted to deliver postal items to persons or addresses other than those shown on the respective items.

According to Table 4 below, regulations in many EU countries in practice allow postal service providers some flexibility to deliver postal items to persons or addressees other than those shown on the respective items. However, in 14 countries, there are specific rules which restrict delivery only to other persons residing at the same address, or delivery only to third parties who are legal representatives of the addressee, or only with the explicit agreement of the addressee. For two EU countries (Austria and the United Kingdom), there is flexibility to deliver items to neighbors so long as the addressee has not excluded this possibility (i.e. they use an opt-out approach). In Croatia, delivery to a third party is permitted but with no specific rules governing delivery flexibility. For nine EU member States, flexible delivery practices are essentially unregulated (or simply not mentioned in the regulations). In Estonia and Lithuania, delivery to third parties is expressly forbidden.

3.1.3 The Postal Universal Service

Article 3 of the Directive gives EU consumers the right to a 'universal service', i.e. a basic postal service available at an affordable price, both domestically and cross-border. In relation to parcel delivery, the 'universal service obligation' (USO) includes the clearance, sorting, transport and distribution of basic (without any additional delivery features) postal packages up to 10 kg (Article 3.4). As member States may choose to include packages up to 20 kg within the USO, all member States must ensure that packages up to 20 kg received from other EU countries are delivered within their territory (Article 3.5). According to the EC, packages included within the USO only cover 10% of the total parcel market.

Table 4 Delivery to third parties is permitted to a limited extent (or unregulated) in most EU countries

Flexibility for postal service provider to deliver to third parties	
Permitted (opt-out)	Austria, Croatia, UK
Unregulated	Cyprus, Czech Republic, Finland, Luxembourg, Malta, Netherlands, Portugal, Slovakia, Sweden,
Permitted (but only on a limited basis)	Belgium, Bulgaria, Denmark, France, Germany, Greece, Hungary, Ireland, Italy, Latvia, Poland, Romania, Slovenia, Spain
Forbidden	Estonia, Lithuania

Source: Cullen International

3.2 Existing Consumer Protection Rules

In addition to the specific postal sector rules applying to postal services (outside the scope of the universal service), online shoppers, retailers and deliverers need also to take into account the consumer protection regulatory framework, including the Consumer Rights Directive[19] (CRD), the E-commerce Directive[20]; the Services Directive[21]; the Directive on conformity and guarantees[22]; and the Directive for alternative dispute resolution[23] (ADR). These directives provide rules related to the delivery of physical goods ordered in the context of a B2C transaction at the different steps of the ordering process when buying online.

3.2.1 Before an Order Is Made

According to Articles 5.1 and 5.2 of the E-Commerce Directive, online traders should clearly inform consumers about: the total price of the goods, the taxes and delivery costs. In addition to this general information requirement, Article 6.6 of the Consumer Rights Directive (CRD) specifies that if traders fail to provide information about any additional charges or costs, the online seller will itself have to bear these costs/charges. Traders should also inform consumers on the arrangements for payment, delivery, and the time by which the trader undertakes to deliver the goods (Article 6.1(g) of the CRD). Article 6.1(h) of the CRD requires online traders to

[19] European Parliament and Council Directive "*on consumer rights*"—October 25, 2011.

[20] European Parliament and Council Directive "*on certain legal aspects of information society services, in particular electronic commerce, in the Internal Market*" (e-Commerce Directive)—June 8, 2000.

[21] European Parliament and Council Directive "*on services in the internal market*"—December 12, 2006.

[22] European Parliament and Council Directive "*on certain aspects of the sale of consumer goods and associated guarantees*"—May 25, 1999.

[23] European Parliament and Council Directive "*on alternative dispute resolution for consumer disputes*" (ADR)—May 21, 2013.

mention the existence/absence and conditions of a right of withdrawal of 14 days. If traders fail to do so, consumers get an extended period of 12 months to withdraw from the sale contract (Article 10.1 of the CRD). Consumers should also know the cost of returning goods in case of withdrawal, where applicable—traders have to provide at least an estimate of what the maximum cost of returning bulky goods could amount to (Article 6.1(i) of the CRD). If traders fail to inform consumers, they will have to bear the cost of returning the goods (Article 6.6).

3.2.2 At the Time of Ordering

The trader must indicate clearly, at the latest at the beginning of the ordering process, whether any "delivery restrictions" apply (Article 8.3 of the CRD). According to Article 20 (2) of the Services Directive, member States should ensure that access to services, which are made available to the public at large by a provider, do not contain discriminatory provisions relating to the nationality or place of residence of the recipient. However, it is possible to foresee differences in the conditions of access if these differences are directly justified by objective criteria.

According to a EC implementation report[24] published in 2012, refusing to supply a consumer resident in another member State or in a remote place or making different delivery options available to consumers resident in other member States would be cases of differences in treatment on the grounds of residence. The question of whether such differences are justified or not would have to be assessed on a case-by-case basis. The Commission specified that the lack of a delivery solution can rarely be used by a service provider as an argument to refuse supply to a given member State or place of residence. In any case, for items falling within the universal service (basic postal packages up to at least 10 kg), there should always be a delivery solution available within the EU.

3.2.3 Delivery

According to Article 18.1 of the CRD, goods should be delivered within 30 calendar days everywhere in the EU. In the event of the loss or deterioration of goods during transport, the risk should only pass onto the consumer when he/she or a third party of his/her choice (not the carrier's choice) takes possession of the goods. When it is the consumer that arranges the carriage of the goods, the risk should pass on when the goods are handed over to the consumer's chosen carrier.

[24] European Commission Communication on the implementation of the Services Directive—June 8, 2012.

3.2.4 Right of Withdrawal (Returns)

Consumers may, without any justification, withdraw from a distance sales contract that has been entered into online within 14 days, starting from the day on which the consumer (or a third party other than the carrier and indicated by the consumer) is in possession of the goods ordered (Article 9.2 of the CRD). When the goods are delivered in multiple parcels, the withdrawal period starts only when the consumer is in possession of the last parcel (Article 9.2 (b) (i) of the CRD). The withdrawal period is extended to 12 months if the trader fails to provide information to the consumer on his right of withdrawal (see above). The exercise of the right of withdrawal can either be done in an unequivocal statement drafted by the consumer, or by completing the standard form that is proposed in Annex 1(B) of the CRD.

3.2.5 Right of Return in Case of Lack of Conformity

According to Article 5.1 of the Directive on conformity and guarantees, the seller is liable for any lack of conformity existing when the goods are delivered and apparent within a period of 2 years except if, when the contract was concluded, the consumer knew or could not reasonably be unaware of the lack of conformity. In such a case (i.e. faulty goods or goods that do not match expectations), the consumer has the right to return goods to the seller in case of lack of conformity and the seller should pay for the return of the goods (Article 3.2 of the above mentioned Directive).

3.2.6 When Something Goes Wrong in the Online Buying Process

The Directive for alternative dispute resolution (ADR) establishes a system whereby all EU consumers can solve their problems without going to court, regardless of the kind of product or service (including postal parcel service) purchased in the EU, domestically or cross-border.

4 Additional Rules Stemming from the Development of E-commerce

With the development of (cross-border) e-commerce, postal operators also have to consider new regulations relating to the implementation and rolling-out of the Union Customs Code (UCC).[25] The UCC includes new rules and procedures, in

[25] European Parliament and Council Regulation 952/2013 laying down the Union Customs Code—October 9, 2013.

particular the digitalization of customs paperwork for importing and exporting goods throughout the EU. The UCC legal package entered into force on May 1, 2016. The Code should normally be implemented by December 31, 2020 but the Commission is expected to extend the implementation deadline at EU level until 2023. The new code aims to transform the functioning of the customs operations by implementing electronic customs exchanges and customs controls based on risk analysis using electronic data processing techniques.

In particular, postal operators would have to be able to identify and track every kind of parcel (even a small packet) before its dispatch from the sending country (Articles 6(1) and 9). According to the EC, this new system will reduce the administrative burden and facilitate customs procedures for traders. For postal operators, the implementation of new information technology systems and of the risk analysis entails potentially huge long-term investments in terms of equipment and the labor force.

In December 2016, the EC proposed a new directive to modernize and simplify the Value Added Tax (VAT) rules for cross-border e-commerce.[26] In particular, Recital 9 of the proposal would remove the VAT exemption on small consignments (with a value of less than €22). According to some postal operators, who are responsible for VAT collection, this measure, if adopted, will drastically increase postal operators' labor costs.

5 Are All These (New) Rules Sustainable for the Postal Delivery Market?

In its position paper on the Commission's proposal for a Regulation of cross-border parcel delivery PostEurop's (the association of national postal operators in Europe) is of the view that the parcel delivery market is competitive and does not need to be further regulated.[27] Post Europ also rejects some of the requirements proposed by the EC in its proposal for a Regulation on cross-border delivery, in particular the mandatory submissions by universal service providers (USPs) of information on their terminal rates and the obligations on third party access to USPs' networks. At the Market Force conference in Amsterdam in March 2017, some panelists representing the postal sector queried the relevance and importance of delivery costs when considering the affordability of online cross-border purchases.

Such queries regarding affordability take into account the transaction cost for the purchaser, i.e. the time and effort required to make the purchase, for example,

[26] Proposal for a Council Directive amending Directive 2006/112/EC and Directive 2009/132/EC as regards certain value added tax obligations for supplies of services and distance sales of goods—December 1, 2016.

[27] Post Europ position paper on the EC's proposal for a Regulation of cross-border parcel delivery—January 16, 2017.

bearing in mind potential language issues; the relative cost of the item itself, including price differences between countries, for example, because of different rates of VAT. Other relevant issues include the total price paid for delivery, which could incorporate the actual cost of delivery, any additional cost related to the cross-border element, and the delivery price actually set by the trader (which may or may not reflect the actual costs). Finally, looking at affordability involves assessing behavioral aspects, for example, consumers show a tendency to avoid purchases where there are explicit delivery costs, preferring 'free' delivery (where the cost is hidden within the price of the item itself).

6 Conclusion

Since 2012, the EC has taken a series of regulatory initiatives with a view to make delivery more reliable, seamless and affordable. However, the latest and most concrete initiative, a draft Regulation on cross-border delivery, is not wholly welcomed by the postal industry. Although the EC is of the view that only this binding instrument could achieve a transparent and thus more affordable EU parcel delivery market for online buyers, postal operators are convinced that the market is already competitive and does not need to be further regulated.

In addition to this divergence of views between the European legislator and the delivery operators, the research conducted for this paper reveals some others significant failures and/or gaps in the existing regulatory framework which may add to the negative impact of the predictability and effectiveness of the parcel delivery regulatory framework. Because of the lack of a clear-cut definition of postal services in relation to parcels delivery and, in particular, the differences of treatment between postal and express services, express services are considered to be within the scope of postal services regulation in some countries but not in others. Flexibility to deliver postal items to third parties exists in most countries, but can be very limited in practical scope and, in some countries, is not available at all (and, in many countries, is unregulated and therefore uncertain. NRAs vary in their information gathering powers, and hence the obligations on market players to provide information) across different member States.

The booming e-commerce market has placed delivery at the crossroads between, at least, two different regulatory frameworks: a set of sector-specific postal rules and a series of rules aimed at increasing consumer trust when buying online. Retailers and deliverers need to take into account all these rules deriving from different directives in different market sectors. This complexity creates legal uncertainty which is hardly conducive to the development of the e-commerce or parcels delivery business in a rapidly changing environment.

Consumers and e-retailers want inexpensive, quick and reliable shipment, while postal operators, although willing to embrace the opportunity, have to cope with a range of other business and regulatory uncertainties and new challenges, i.e. the new security and customs rules. It will be a very significant challenge for European and national authorities to establish a clear, predictive and consistent regulatory framework to create a fair level-playing field for every e-commerce parcel operator, taking into account the complex and rapidly changing e-commerce delivery ecosystem.

Bibliography

Cardona, M., Duch-Brown, N., and Martens, B. (2015) "*Consumer perceptions of (cross-border) e-commerce in the EU Digital Single Market*", JRC/IPTS Digital Economy Working Paper.

Duch-Brown, N., and Martens, B. (2015) "*Barriers to firms' cross-border e-commerce in the EU Digital Single Market*", JRC/IPTS Digital Economy Working Paper.

EC Communication (2012) on "*coherent framework for building trust in the digital single market for e-commerce and online services*".

EC communication (2012). on the implementation of the Services Directive.

EC green paper (2012) on "*an integrated parcel delivery market for the growth of e-commerce in the EU*".

European Parliament and Council Directive (2013) "*on alternative dispute resolution for consumer disputes*" (ADR).

EC communication (2013) for a "*roadmap for completing the single market for parcel delivery—build consumer trust in delivery services and encourage online sales*".

EC Eurobarometer 397 (2014) "*Consumer attitudes towards cross-border trade and consumer protection*".

EC Eurobarometer 413 (2015) "*Companies engaged in online activities*".

EC communication (2015) for a Digital Single Market strategy for Europe.

EC staff working document (2015)—A Digital Single Market Strategy for Europe—Analysis and Evidence.

EC public consultation on cross-border parcel delivery (2015) "*Initiative to enhance the affordability, quality and convenience of cross-border parcel delivery*".

EC proposal for a Regulation (2016) on cross-border parcel delivery services (2016).

EC proposal for a Directive (2016) amending Directive 2006/112/EC and Directive 2009/132/EC on "*VAT obligations for supplies of services and distance sales of goods.*

European Parliament and Council Directive (1997) on "*common rules for the development of the internal market of Community postal services and the improvement of quality of services* as amended by Directive 2002/39/EC and Directive 2008/06/EC regarding "*the full accomplishment of the internal market of Community postal services*".

European Parliament and Council Directive (1999) "*on aspects of the sale of consumer goods and associated guarantees*".

European Parliament and Council e-Commerce Directive (2000).

European Parliament and Council Directive (2006) "*on services in the internal market*".

European Parliament and Council Directive (2011) "*on consumer rights*".

European Parliament and Council Regulation 952 (2013) "*laying down the Union Customs Code*".

European Parliament's Transport and Tourism committee draft report (2017) on the draft Regulation on cross-border delivery.

Fratini, Alessandra. (2017). "*DHL Express (Austria)*: Towards Legal Certainty on Article 9 and Applicable Obligations for Postal Service Providers", this volume.

Okholm, H. B. (2013) "*e-Commerce and delivery—A study of the state of play of EU parcel markets with particular emphasis on e-commerce*", Copenhagen Economics.

Post Europ position paper (2017) on the EC's proposal for a Regulation of cross-border parcel delivery.

and national authorities to establish a clear, predictive and consistent regulatory framework to create a fair level playing field for every e-commerce player, taking into account the complex and rapidly changing e-commerce delivery ecosystem.

Bibliography

Life After Volume Declines: Is There a Viable Future for the Postal Sector?

Adam C. Houck

1 Introduction

The current postal sector landscape is an excellent laboratory for examining the effects of a profound market disruption. A critical question is whether the postal services market has reached a tipping point, is it nearing an equilibrium, or is the ride just starting to get bumpy? Evidence clearly suggests the latter.

Much of the discussion on sustainability in the postal sector has focused on declining physical mail volumes, and the ability for postal operators (POs) to remain financially viable in a world where significant amounts of physical communication has shifted to digital communications.

While it is important to continue evaluating the impacts of declining mail volumes, it is perhaps equally important to examine the effects on the postal sector of additional micro- and macro-economic supply side and demand side forces such as nascent last mile collaborative logistics arrangements, evolving customer expectations, changing demographics, entry for parcel delivery in the last mile by firms such as Uber, innovations in key technologies such as the Internet of Things (IoT), and other exogenous factors that are causing tectonic shifts in traditional delivery models and challenging the viability of century-long roles of POs in the social and economic ecosystems.

This paper examines key viability topics beyond declining physical mail volumes that directly apply to the future of POs and how POs could capitalize on opportunities presented by these otherwise disruptive forces. The next section

The views expressed are those of the author and do not necessarily represent those of IBM Global Business Services.

A.C. Houck (✉)
IBM Global Business Services, North Castle, NY, USA
e-mail: ahouck@us.ibm.com

P.L. Parcu et al. (eds.), *The Contribution of the Postal and Delivery Sector*, Topics in Regulatory Economics and Policy, https://doi.org/10.1007/978-3-319-70672-6_12

examines a sample of the most significant and relevant factors shaping the current and future landscape for POs. Section 3 discusses how POs can respond to the disruption and transformation with innovative approaches to capitalize on opportunities and conclusions are presented in Sect. 4.

2 Forces Shaping Current and Future Landscape

The global decline in physical letter volumes over the past decade has been a primary and common element upon which researchers have focused to understand the long-term viability for POs. While indeed critical, declining volumes are only one component in a constellation of forces that will shape the future of the sector. As letter volumes have fallen, e-commerce has fueled a surge in the growth of parcels globally. Since 2011, e-commerce has grown over 20%, three times the rate of in-store sales, offsetting the significant losses from traditional letter products (Howland 2015, online). In the U.S., the United States Postal Service (USPS) delivered over 5.1B parcels in Fiscal Year (FY) 2016, generating $17.4B in revenue, representing a 13.7% increase in volume and a 15.7% increase in revenue compared to FY 2015 (USPS 2016, pp. 24–26). Per a 2016 A.T. Kearney report, global e-commerce sales are set to increase 13–16% annually, even if the annual growth rate may gradually slow (Ben-Shabat et al. 2015). In a previous decade marked by fundamental threats to PO business models worldwide, through economic recession and e-substitution effects, the rise of e-commerce and resulting parcel volumes have buoyed the financial positions of posts and indeed, allowed them to endure in the short-term.

It would be too simple to assert that the growth in parcel volumes will replace the lost letter volumes. First, it takes approximately $3 in new package revenue to make up the contribution to profit of every $1 lost in First-Class Mail revenue for USPS (USPS 2013, online). Second, existing infrastructures were developed to collect, process, transport, and deliver letter mail products, not packages. Very few POs manage separate letter and parcel networks. However, certain historical legacies including ubiquity and trust do position USPS and other POs well to benefit from the growth in e-commerce and may set them on a new path to viability. Nevertheless, varying forces and disruptions make it exceedingly difficult to predict how the future will indeed look for POs and what actions they must take to compete in existing and new markets. Demographics are the first such critical force facing POs.

Urbanization, coupled with aging populations, will present significant challenges for POs in the years ahead. A 2016 McKinsey study reported that the share of the global population living in urban centers will reach 60% by 2030, up from 50% in 2015 (Bouton et al. 2015, online). This density can benefit POs while generating additional threats. The increasing density amplifies advantageous economies of scale and scope and given the ubiquitous networks of POs, positions them to capitalize in the first and last mile. The density, however, creates significant opportunity for new entrants to compete for hyper-local population centers, especially those with higher amounts of wealth and purchasing power. In these small population centers, scale is less important when attempting to cream skim profitable segments. This creates a significant threat for POs, over and above the entry already realized in different market segments. Perhaps most importantly, POs are faced with potential competitors who will increasingly choose to not compete nationally, but only locally. In the U.S., 62.7% of the population lives in cities, but cities comprise only 3.5% of the land area, and roughly 40% of the population is concentrated in 21 metropolitan locations (U.S. Census Bureau 2015, online). Thus, the entry models established POs will face can widely vary by geography, complicating the response needed to counter the cream skimming activities.

Not only are populations moving back to urban areas at an increasing rate; they are becoming older. Globally between 1990 and 2010, the population share of the 60 and older cohort rose from 9.2 to 11.1% (Burnson 2014, online). In the U.S. as the Baby Boomer generation continues to age, the number of people aged 65 and older is projected to nearly double by the year 2050 (Ortman et al. 2014, p. 1). Europe's population as well, is an aging one, with anticipated decreases of 14% of workforce and 7% decrease in consumer populations by 2030 (Hewitt 2007, p. 111). In contrast, less developed countries such as Africa possess a growing share of the working age cohort, where the population growth rate continues to exceed those in the U.S. and Europe. The resulting effects are significant, yet varied for POs. With a globally aging-in-place population that becomes less mobile, the need for delivery of items such as groceries and pharmaceuticals will become increasingly important. The services POs can offer to an aging population could evolve to include more in-home medical checking and monitoring services such as those already seen in Japan Post and Jersey Post. Failure to adjust to these changing demand side forces could quickly marginalize the POs ability to assert first mover advantage, utilizing existing network scale and ubiquity, brand, and trust.

Beyond demographic shifts, changes in customer expectations are disrupting traditional product offerings, fulfillment models, and the role of the PO in ecosystems. Quality, speed, convenience, and transparency are traditional elements that define the expectations of past and current customers. However, new expectations such as an evolving concept of trusted brand in delivery agents as well as environmental sustainability in products and services are forcing POs to respond. For decades, POs enjoyed the effects of being highly trusted brands within their respective countries. This trust was important when, combined with monopoly privilege, the PO was the primary delivery agent whom citizens would see daily to receive letters and parcels. Trust for POs is just as critical today as it was decades ago, yet the growth of startup and alternative delivery agents such as Lasership, Zipments, and Deliv demonstrate how trust can be created more quickly today compared to the past if quality and price meet expectations.

Digital Natives are far more brand savvy than previous generations; they discover, research, and follow brands on various digital platforms and social media at far higher rates than their predecessors (PriceWaterhouseCoopers 2015, p. 25). This points to a future where the average consumer will be less brand-loyal than consumers today. As purchasing power continues to shift to these digitally native generations, differentiation in quality and price will be more important than ever for winning and retaining customers. Indeed, it is possible that even the most trusted brand of POs can be marginalized in a crowded playing field delivering exceptional customer experiences. Following the Uber parcel delivery model where anyone with a smartphone can serve as a delivery agent, POs must be aware of the new threats to existing products and services. For example, currently, USPS serves as the last mile delivery agent for UPS under the Parcel Select product. If trust can be quickly gained and economics support the use of an alternative delivery agent, USPS faces a significant threat to the Parcel Select product. More broadly, if trust in letter and parcel delivery is no longer solely reserved for POs, success will become more dependent on a combination of price and quality irrespective of brand, which poses significant threat to the long-term viability of all POs.

Customer expectations extend well beyond speed, flexibility, and transparency. Today, consumers are more aware of the environmental impacts of delivery, and the growing demand for environmental delivery options could become a further key point of differentiation. Research has shown that many consumers are willing to pay a premium for this service; UPS, FedEx, and DHL all currently provide carbon-free delivery options. Millennials and Digital Natives have shown an increased willingness to pay more for environmentally-friendly logistics services compared to Generation X (Deutsche Post 2010, p. 44). This trend is likely to drive demand for environmentally sustainable options, and logistics providers have already responded. DHL, for example, offers a price premium to offset the environmental impact of a shipment at a cost of under $0.13 more than a standard package (Goldstein 2013, online). Currently, USPS does not offer a green delivery alternative. It is unlikely that customer demand for such products will rise to a level that would affect significant volumes. However, in hyper-local markets the PO could see additional volume divert to new entrants with environmentally conscious brands, products, and services. Whereas the diversion seen in failing to deliver speed, transparency, and flexibility can be extended to all products, these environmentally sensitive products are more niche in nature and driven by different customer expectations and segments of which not every PO or delivery company will choose to compete.

New technology is the great enabler, innovator, creator, disruptor, and destroyer. Changes in digital communication drove much of the e-substitution effects during the last decade that saw global letter volumes collapse. New technology made entry into markets much easier due to the speed, flexibility, and cost advantage it can enable for new competitors such as Deliv and Lasership. It has helped create new digital products that serve new customer segments like Informed Delivery in the U.S.[1] Platform technologies and Application Programming Interfaces (API) have disrupted traditional last mile delivery models, allowing firms to collaborate across digital platforms and allow nearly any person with a smartphone to become a potential

[1]Informed Delivery is a service offered by USPS that allows customers to see a digital preview of their household's incoming daily mail.

delivery agent.[2] Automation and robotics technologies have allowed POs to increase efficiency in collection, mail processing, and delivery, saving significant labor costs in both the short and long term. IoT and blockchain technologies have also helped redefine trust and brand in a digital world, delivering the security needed from both senders and recipients in transactions and exchange.[3] New technology will continue to drive significant change that may threaten the viability of POs into the future.

The last mile of the future will be instrumented, linking vehicles, buildings, postmen, collection receptacles, parcel lockers, and the parcels themselves with POs, local businesses, retailers, governments, and citizens. It will be the choice of the PO to utilize new tools or risk additional volume losses from entrants that effectively deploy innovative technologies. Developments in IoT and blockchain, coupled with dynamic routing algorithms, have the opportunity to improve overall efficiency and security within supply chains and the delivery market, drastically reduce failed delivery attempts, and enhance customer experience. This is critically important, as the cost of failed delivery attempts for both POs and businesses is significant. A survey of businesses in the UK found that the cost of failed delivery was nearly one billion Euros in 2014 (Ecommerce News 2014, online).

Collection receptacles, like parcel lockers today, will require sensors to notify entrants when the boxes are empty, and notify the PO in real-time whether the box can be skipped or a collection needs to be made, helping to optimize daily collection routes. These efficiencies are critical, as current consumers expect free shipping, which is currently subsidized by carrier discounts provided to major retailers. New technologies will also drive improvements in future inventory management. Self-driving ground drones, delivery robots, and autonomous delivery vehicles will help firms deliver the convenience and flexibility customers demand while helping control last mile delivery costs.

New entrants and alternative business models such as ship from store, omnichannel fulfillment, collaborative logistics, and parcel delivery via Uber and other platforms will saturate the landscape in the years ahead, creating significant risk for POs. Borsenberger (2016) concluded: "In the delivery sector, even if the business model of last mile sharing delivery services is in its infancy and not yet always sustainable, it is undeniable that crowdsourced delivery services put pressure on the established courier, express, and POs, pushing them to innovate and to provide even more reliable and fast delivery, to the benefit of customers." Already, bPost is experimenting with collaborative logistics in Antwerp, Uber and Lyft are offering parcel delivery service, and a recent survey from Research System Research and SPS Commerce showed 61% of respondents are providing ship from store capabilities (eMarketer 2016, online). These trends will not cease; in fact, given how nascent these new models are and the advanced maturity of the

---

[2]APIs are communication methods between software components that allow developers to more easily build applications from existing software programs.

[3]Blockchain is an encrypted, decentralized database that allows for the sharing of information where no single party has the authority to tamper with any records.

underlying technologies enabling these approaches, it is likely their creation and adoption will accelerate. These new models require flexibility, transparency, ubiquitous network coverage, and perhaps most importantly, intra-day dynamic pickup and delivery to succeed. While POs possess several of these elements, all are required and entrants likely possess distinct advantages that better position them to capitalize on the opportunity.

While the POs' ubiquitous physical networks provide the de facto coverage, the way the networks must be utilized to compete with these new models is quite different. POs typically visit homes and businesses once per day on set schedules and routes to collect and deliver letters and parcels; often, collection receptacles are checked several times per day. The scale of these networks is massive; in the U.S., the USPS' network of vehicles drive four million miles per day (USPS 2015, online). While this arrangement well serves the paradigm of pickup and delivery from sender to recipient for traditional mail products, it fails to meet the requirements of emerging last mile business models. The role new entrants are playing in ecosystems demands not only ubiquitous coverage, but the ability for the agents within ecosystems to be flexible intra-day to respond to immediate needs from businesses, delivery companies, governments, and other citizens.

A distinct advantage entrants possess that POs must overcome is the flexibility and scalability of the work force needed to meet emerging needs. Unlike POs, entrants can utilize flexible, scalable, non-career personnel such as Uber, Lyft, Deliv, Lasership, and bike courier services have done to serve these intra-day dynamic needs. Independent contractors who can provide this type of ultra-flexible labor can be retail employees delivering products during their lunch breaks and even homebound commutes. In the U.S., Walmart began testing paying employees extra to deliver packages from online orders on their way home from work, noting that 90% of Americans live within 10 miles of a Walmart store (Bhattarai 2017, online). Compared to the fixed labor model of POs, this flexibility puts entrants at a distinct competitive advantage to acquire and shed labor with fluctuations in intra-day demand. Indeed, this is a significant threat to POs, for should the POs seek to hire enough labor to serve peak demand periods, they would be left with significant excess labor capacity at low volume periods, impacting both productivity and bottom line cost. In addition, the PO would have to identify a funding mechanism to pay for this extra labor, whether by increasing postage and fees, or seeking subsidies.

If indeed trust in parcel delivery can be quickly created by new entrants, the growth seen in Business–to–Business (B2B) and Business–to–Consumer (B2C) startups will only accelerate. In the B2C space, DHL has already begun offering alternative models such as MyWays, which connects a crowd-sourced delivery system with DHL's freight network.[4] It allows online retail consumers to choose their mode of delivery and provides a network of last mile deliverers, including

[4]Crowdsourced shipping utilizes technology to communicate with organizations and people, often not employed by the organization, to obtain needed capacity, typically on existing travel routes.

private individuals, that will complete the delivery for DHL's negotiated rate. Crowd sourced applications, especially in the B2C solution area, pose a significant threat to POs and established providers in last mile delivery with low-price options and dynamic, asset-light models. These applications compete against asset-heavy incumbents saddled by high fixed-costs that can lead to comparatively higher delivery costs. In a world where delivery behaves more like a perfectly competitive good, the pricing effects are dire. When alternative delivery agents such as Uber drivers are willing to accept exceedingly low compensation for a given parcel delivery that falls below the stated price of delivery from the PO, there is great risk resulting for the PO that is amplified at scale. One can imagine a reverse auction paradigm will emerge, fueled by online platforms that allow any agent to bid on a given delivery, where the highest quality delivery service could well be the cheapest.

Going forward, urbanization trends will only magnify the effects of alternative models as populations, wealth, demand, and available variable labor supply amplify the density in the last mile. Clearly, the implications for less densely populated areas are quite different, where customers could experience longer fulfillment times just as waiting longer for an Uber to appear after ordering on the app. Even in these rural areas the reverse auction paradigm produces equilibriums of price and quality, with any agent competing against incumbent delivery companies and POs for last mile volume. But even in such areas, Parcel Select volumes for USPS would still be at risk of diversion if entrants can deliver comparable quality at comparatively lower prices.

Lastly, there are several exogenous factors that can impact the business models of POs including regulations, fuel prices, and labor, which if not effectively managed, could threaten their future viability. E-commerce taxes could significantly affect the price of goods in the future. In the U.S., the 1992 Supreme Court ruling in Quill v. North Dakota stipulated that states can only tax e-commerce sales where the retailer has a physical presence within the state. The decision created a loophole allowing e-retailers to strategically place warehouses and distribution centers in states with favorable tax rates such as Texas and Florida, where there is no state income tax. Currently, the definition of physical presence is being challenged in multiple states throughout the U.S. Congressional action was presented in the Marketplace Fairness Act of 2013, however, the proposed bill was highly unpopular and has not been passed for now. Some e-tailers including Amazon believe that taxes should be paid on e-commerce sales. While their position could be interpreted as altruistic, Amazon likely knows it has significant scale advantage over new e-tailers. It likely realizes that it can bear the additional tax burden better than its competition, allowing Amazon to gain market share by driving smaller firms from the marketplace, especially e-tailers who only have a virtual presence. There are likely no direct effects on POs from increased e-commerce taxes as they are neither sellers nor possess any physical inventory. However, if e-commerce taxes are enacted in such a way that in the end leads to a smaller number of large firms having higher levels of concentration, POs could be faced with a smaller number of firms with greater market power which could put downward pressures on delivery prices as e-commerce retailers attempt to keep overall prices unchanged while absorbing the additional tax burden per item.

Changes in the price of oil is another factor that can have significant impacts on PO operational costs, especially long haul transportation. In the U.S., for each $0.01 increase in the price of gasoline, USPS operational costs increase by $8M (AP 2008, online). Between 2004 and 2014 when fuel prices surged, companies and consumers alike sacrificed speed to lower their costs. Since fuel consumption rates rise faster at higher speeds, carriers of all sorts, from ocean-faring container ships to aircraft, reduced their speed to increase fuel efficiency while consumers flocked to smaller and more efficient vehicles. Now, however, fuel prices have fallen sharply and remain comparatively low. Just as expensive fuel had a dilatory effect on carriers, inexpensive fuel can catalyze the opposite trend. If indeed the future sees substantial increases in fuel prices, it is likely transit speeds would again drop and create a need for POs and partners to find innovative ways to preserve the speed and cost of delivery, as customer demands on both immediacy of fulfillment and free shipping will not change.

Various labor factors could also produce significant effects that would threaten PO business models. While labor sustainability initiatives in the delivery market, at least for the present, focus on independent contractors, the labor initiatives in the warehousing space focus on substituting human labor with automated technologies. Per a March 2016 CBRE report, the impact of the minimum wage increase will impact e-commerce more than other retailers because e-commerce supply chains employ a greater number of staff members in warehousing and inventory spaces at a rate of nearly twice those of traditional retailers (Gerrity 2016, online). Minimum wage increases will significantly impact e-commerce companies, and while these additional labor costs could be passed on to the customer, the new cost model could make brick and mortar retailers relatively more affordable than their online counterparts.

Traditional parcel delivery models and operators rely upon more fixed than variable labor staffing. Thus, some have argued that the underlying volatility of the supply of labor that feed the crowd sourced delivery models of Uber, PiggyBee, Friendshippr, and Barnacle will place the viability of these models at risk into the future. However, these shortages have yet to materialize and evidence would suggest that given the composition of labor that operates these models, the shortages are not likely to occur. Indeed, the typical Uber driver is a married male between the age of 30 and 39 with a college or advanced degree, and 70% use their income to support a parent or child living at home (Clifford 2015, online). Nevertheless, the volatility that exists in the last mile delivery market make flexible labor supply models attractive in both densely populated urban areas and in less populated suburban locations. Access to this flexibility, whether by acquisition or by partnering, could become a critical success factor for POs to address the non-uniformity of intra-day pickup and delivery volumes in the last mile.

3 Approaches to Address Forces and Disruption

The question of how POs should respond to the forces discussed in Sect. 2 depends significantly on how they will be able to maintain a brand advantage. The PO must first decide what portfolio of products and services will comprise its brand; it must decide which consumer segments it will serve within the boundaries of current legislation and regulation, which segments it will not serve, with whom it will choose to compete, and with whom will it instead try to collaborate. A choice must be made as to whether to assert first mover advantage, or let the market be defined around the PO in piecemeal fashion by smaller entrants. It must decide whether to offer new value added services to customers or engage in a race to the bottom, driving price to marginal cost, commoditizing delivery, and competing primarily on price. The answer to these questions will inform the future direction of the PO's brand, which will dictate the steps it must take the acquire needed capabilities. Rarely is new technology the limiting factor that prevents firms from pursuing new opportunities. Rather, it is the choice and commitment to strategic direction, even if that strategy involves cannibalizing current products and services, that determines success and failure.

Some POs, such as Austrian Post, bPost, and Singapore Post, have begun to experiment in innovative areas. In a future shaped by the forces explored in Sect. 2 including urbanization, population demographics, technology, new entry, and other exogenous factors, and the strategic decision of the role it wishes to play in local ecosystems of commerce, each PO is faced with a critical decision: maintain current course and speed, pursuing the existing strategic direction which is likely viable in the short-term, or strategically invest to alter its trajectory to combat competition and place itself on a path to long-term viability. The approaches of individual POs will vary across geographies due to customer demands and expectations, as well as regulatory conditions that affect their current operating models. The focus of this paper is the direct response strategies POs can pursue within the core mail and parcel businesses, as well as adjacent areas. While here we do not consider more radical diversification strategies into non-postal business areas that could include banking, financial services, and insurance. POs must acknowledge that the cost of not acting could potentially bring significant volume losses not only in dense urban areas to local courier services, but also in sparsely populated suburban areas until recently believed to be largely invulnerable to efficient competitive entry.

Regardless of the specific strategies selected, POs must continue to acquire and adopt new methods and tools that will drive efficiencies throughout operations to contain costs and increase quality and customer experience such as eliminating inefficient truck routes that waste gasoline and cause pollution. USPS, for example, must make the strategic decision of the role it desires to play, knowing it can continue its current path and likely increase parcel volumes and revenues in-line with overall market increases, or it can make strategic investments to modify its natural trajectory and open new opportunities to compete maintaining for a significantly greater share of marketplace volume, revenue, and profit.

POs must find new ways to utilize the ubiquitous physical networks both to improve core operations and to experiment with alternative business models that increase the relevancy of POs to citizens. This topic has been explored in depth by USPS OIG (2015) regarding the Internet of Postal Things. These delivery networks allow POs to hold substantial market share of parcel deliveries already, however the present situation is not without significant threat as third-party delivery platforms such as Deliv offer comparable price and quality. Indeed, POs must first equip their physical networks with sensors, actuators, and Internet connectivity with an understanding that not every locale must be treated uniformly. This instrumentation can make POs the ideal strategic partner for crowd-sourced deliveries in a collaborative last mile. The solutions offered will clearly be heterogeneous, varying by geography, proposed uses, and customer expectations; other factors including demographics and regulation will also drive differences in approach by location. However, these capabilities are needed to enable ordering, transportation, and delivery intra-day for a single parcel. Clearly, smarter delivery approaches are warranted even if market share gains or partnering approaches are not fully pursued to drive efficiency gains within operations.

One cannot underestimate the pressure the re-urbanization influx has on infrastructures and congestion in cities. People are moving back to cities, they are purchasing more goods online, and yet want deliveries to be made same day, even free of charge, to the location desired, not just to the home. One must consider the externalities these conditions produce, especially vehicle traffic. Many large cities globally are already enacting measures to alleviate gridlock but one risks exacerbating the issue if cities, POs, and other firms cannot solve this last mile congestion issue that not only strains infrastructures but greatly increases vehicle emissions. There is an evident foundation for the need to collaborate in the last mile, to reduce congestion, emissions, and spare capacity from existing vehicle deliveries. This can be done across all delivery agents, not just POs and major players. If anyone can potentially serve as a delivery agent, there must be ways to tap into this delivery potential to alleviate these pressures. Indeed, POs may find it profitable to collaborate within the first and last mile with a focus on growing these ecosystems instead of pursuing traditional siloed strategies.

Instrumenting the networks with IoT sensor and actuator technology is probably only the necessary first step. Beyond instrumentation, POs must explore, acquire, and utilize new technologies that enable the communication, agility, speed, and transparency demanded by not only citizens and customers, but by potential teaming partners. The PO must carefully evaluate potential partners, both established and emerging, to determine strategic fit based upon the role the PO wants to play within the new ecosystem. Partnering with others in ship from store models, collaborative last mile logistics, omnichannel fulfillment, and first mile fulfillment can only occur if the PO joins the technology platforms and communicates in real-time with other participating firms. Even if the PO decides to not serve all market needs, it can still be a significant contributor within ecosystems along with courier services, Deliv, Uber, and others, covering different market segments.

Blockchain technology can deliver the needed trust and security within the instrumented last mile to allow partners to safely collaborate across ecosystems. Here, POs can probably assert a first mover advantage to create the conditions for trust and innovation then contribute and enjoy the resulting network effects downstream. This is still possible, as long as the PO preserves the customer relationship and can build the information and collaboration platforms, invite the participants, lend their trusted brand status to the platforms, then allow the platforms to proliferate and grow. The importance of security cannot be understated within these ecosystems and POs can utilize their trusted brand to establish this foundation in which collaboration can occur. Instrumentation and security are requirements not only for collaboration with partners, but also for the PO to explore more cutting edge technologies and operational models such as autonomous vehicles, delivery robots, and drone delivery. These more cutting edge solutions should be pursued only after primary steps are taken to create trust and partnering within last mile ecosystems.

Repurposing existing assets cannot be ignored because omnichannel fulfillment and same-day delivery consumer expectations have also driven innovations in warehousing. As retailers need smaller warehouses with access to a larger region for same-day delivery, demand for smaller fulfillment centers has increased. POs can seek to utilize already owned physical locations throughout geographic regions and make strategic investments in logistics technologies to become the fulfillment centers for major retailers. They can dedicate space in their facilities for retail warehousing, incorporating omnichannel fulfillment capabilities for retailers, and updating capabilities to include same-day parcel delivery in select locations. This is clearly an easier strategy for POs who possess the required expertise in warehousing and logistics in house. However, for POs who lack these capabilities, they must find partners to assist in such ventures with the required skills to pursue these new offerings. POs such as DHL are already providing comprehensive delivery, logistics, and warehousing solutions. They utilize capabilities and expertise in the delivery space to enhance capabilities in fulfillment, supporting brick and mortar retailers as well as other delivery services for time-sensitive products such as pharmaceuticals. Other POs can seek to replicate DHL's warehousing model concept, creating a shared inventory for its retail partners, providing end-to-end logistics solutions and allowing its partners to focus on operations.

These new alternative models have already been introduced in marketplaces around the globe. Quantium Solutions, a Singapore Post company, provides e-commerce and retail logistics expertise, providing essential services including inventory management, order processing, pick and pack, and after sales support. POs can seek to replicate these services by investing in technological improvements in the areas of inventory management and warehouse automation, utilizing their physical presence to become an essential 3PL for nationwide retailers. Doing so can assist POs in expanding market share in the parcel delivery marketplace and making them more essential to both ecosystem partners and citizens.

4 Conclusion

The decline of physical mail volumes is a critical element in examining the future viability of POs yet there are many other important factors that must be studied. New entry is creating conditions where all areas of the business are susceptible to diversion, even in densely populated areas where POs possess advantages of economies of scale and density. Entry and disruption is also accelerating, especially in the last mile. The challenge lies in Uber parcel delivery, the growth of ship from store models, and by new technology offerings solutions such as delivery robots, driverless vehicles. In a world where anyone with a smartphone and means of transportation can serve as a delivery agent, reverse auction models can proliferate which have the potential to deliver high quality and low price, simultaneously.

One cannot underestimate the pressures that urbanization, wealth concentration, e-commerce, and immediate delivery expectations are placing on POs' infrastructures increasing congestion in cities. The fact that trust in parcel delivery appears quite easily transferrable to alternative delivery agents perhaps presents the most significant threat to POs' future. Given the growth of global parcel volumes and the relatively low share e-commerce possesses within total commerce, new entrants have a significant opportunity to transport and deliver these new volumes in the fastest growing segment of the market.

This analysis suggests POs should utilize their brand to assert first mover advantage and play the role of trusted moderator on collaboration platforms in the last mile. They must not allow smaller entrants to establish leadership positions in markets that could erode the essentiality of POs in these ecosystems of commerce. Research also suggests that collaboration within the last mile ecosystem is perhaps the most promising approach, that the technologies needed to assert this first mover advantage to build collaboration, trust, and security already exist and will not be the complicating factor in implementing such solutions. Lastly, POs must follow the lead of other operators already experimenting with new solutions in core postal and adjacent areas and look to build alternative business models upon the physical infrastructures and assets that will help redefine the role of the PO in the modern commercial ecosystem. The ubiquitous networks that POs possess are their most strategic and important asset that cannot be matched by any entrant. Failure to effectively layer new business models upon this asset could present mortal threats to POs in the years ahead.

References

Associated Press (2008). "Postal Service Pinched by Rising Gas Costs." Web. March 15, 2017. http://www.foxnews.com/story/2008/06/15/postal-service-pinched-by-rising-gas-costs.html

Bhattarai, Abha (2017). "Walmart is Asking Employees to Deliver Packages on Their Way Home from Work." June 1, 2017. Web. June 15, 2017. https://www.washingtonpost.com/news/business/wp/2017/06/01/walmart-is-asking-employees-to-deliver-packages-on-their-way-home-from-work/?utm_term=.67444b68dd80

Ben-Shabat, H., P. Nilforoushan and C. Yuen. "Global Retail E-Commerce Keeps on Clicking." April 1, 2015. Web. March 3, 2017. https://www.atkearney.com/consumer-products-retail/e-commerce-index/full-report/-/asset_publisher/87xbENNHPZ3D/content/global-retail-e-commerce-keeps-on-clicking/10192

Borsenberger, Claire. "The Sharing Economy and the 'Uberization' Phenomenon: What Impacts on the Economy in General and for the Delivery Operators in Particular?" in The Changing Postal and Delivery Sector: Towards a Renaissance, Michael A. Crew and Timothy J. Brennan (eds.), Springer, 2016.

Bouton, S., S. Knupfer, I. Mihov, and S. Swartz. "Urban Mobility at a Tipping Point." September 1, 2015. Web. March 10, 2017. http://www.mckinsey.com/business-functions/sustainability-and-resource-productivity/our-insights/urban-mobility-at-a-tipping-point

Burnson, Patrick. "Global Demographics May Reshape Supply Chains." July 28, 2014. Web. February 8, 2017. http://www.logisticsmgmt.com/article/global_demographics_may_reshape_supply_chains/global_trade

Clifford, Catherine. "Who Exactly Are Uber's Drivers?" January 22, 2015. Web. April 24, 2017. https://www.entrepreneur.com/article/242096

Deutsche Post AG (2010). "Delivering Tomorrow: Towards Sustainable Logistics." Web. February 1, 2017. http://www.dpdhl.com/en/logistics_around_us/future_studies/sustainable_logistics.html

Ecommerce News. "Cost of Failed Deliveries in the UK: 971 Million Euro." August 28, 2014. Web. April 21, 2017. https://ecommercenews.eu/cost-of-failed-deliveries-in-the-uk-e971mn

eMarketer. "Ship to Store is Retailers' Top Fulfillment Option." February 2, 2016. Web. April 3, 2017. https://www.emarketer.com/Article/Ship-Store-Retailers-Top-Fulfillment-Option/1013538

Gerrity, Michael. "Coming Minimum Wage Hikes to Reverberate, Burden Entire U.S. Logistics System." March 22, 2016. Web. April 20, 2017. http://www.worldpropertyjournal.com/real-estate-news/united-states/los-angeles-real-estate-news/coming-minimum-wage-hikes-to-reverberate-burden-entire-us-logistics-ecosystem-9739.php

Goldstein, Allie. "Deutsche Post DHL: Neutral if You Choose." December 17, 2013. Web. April 3, 2017. http://www.ecosystemmarketplace.com/articles/deutsche-post-dhl-neutral-if-you-choose/

Hewitt, Paul S. "Depopulation and Ageing in Europe and Japan: The Hazardous Transition to a Labor Shortage Economy." International Politics and Society. December 27, 2007.

Howland, Daphne. "Report: Online Holiday Sales Growth to Dwarf Overall Retail Lift." November 10, 2015. Web. March 1, 2017. http://www.retaildive.com/news/report-online-holiday-sales-growth-to-dwarf-overall-retail-lift/408926/

Ortman, J., V. Velkoff, and H. Hogan. "An Aging Nation: The Older Population in the United States." May 1, 2014. Web. January 10, 2017. https://www.census.gov/prod/2014pubs/p25-1140.pdf

PriceWaterhouseCoopers (2015). "Total Retail 2015: Retailers and the Age of Disruption." Web. January 7, 2017.

United States Census Bureau. "U.S. Cities are Home to 62.7% of the U.S. Population, but Comprise Just 3.5% of Land Area." March 4, 2015. Web. April 20, 2017. https://www.census.gov/newsroom/press-releases/2015/cb15-33.html

United States Postal Service. "USPS FY2016 Annual Report to Congress." December 8, 2016. Web. April 1, 2017. https://about.usps.com/who-we-are/financials/annual-reports/fy2016.pdf

United States Postal Service (2015). "Postal Facts 2015." Web. April 15, 2017. https://about.usps.com/who-we-are/postal-facts/postalfacts2015.pdf

United States Postal Service. "Five-Year Business Plan." April 16, 2013. Web. April 1, 2017. http://about.usps.com/strategic-planning/fiveyearplan-04162013-final.pdf

USPS Office of Inspector General (2015). "The Internet of Postal Things." https://www.uspsoig.gov/sites/default/files/document-library-files/2015/rarc-wp-15-013_0.pdf

Analysis of the Effect of Management Quality Variables in Delivery Cost Functions

Catherine Cazals, Thierry Magnac, and Soterios Soteri

1 Introduction

Letter volumes in countries with advanced broadband networks have been in decline since the early to mid-2000s while, more recently, parcel volumes have started to grow quite rapidly. The main drivers of these trends, namely the substitution of physical letters with electronic modes of communication and increasing levels of on-line shopping, are expected to continue for some time. This raises two important challenges for postal universal service providers (USPs). The first is to manage operational changes to meet the evolving needs of consumers, such as changes in the quantity, shape, size and weight of mail sent and received. Second, USPs need to reduce costs and increase efficiency as quickly as is practically possible in order to help slow the decline in letters and to compete more effectively with other parcel providers.

The postal economics literature includes numerous papers on different methodologies and techniques to assess USP cost functions and efficiency levels. With regard to econometric applications using parametric methods, they have tended to differ in terms of the type of cost functions used and the choice of external factors to include. For example, Cazals et al. (1997, 2001, 2005) estimated delivery cost functions, in terms of labor hours, that depend on mail volumes and geographic

---

The views expressed in this paper are those of the authors and do not necessarily reflect those of their affiliated organisations. We would like to thank Frank Rodriguez for helpful comments and suggestions.

C. Cazals (✉) • T. Magnac
Toulouse School of Economics and IDEI, Université de Toulouse, Toulouse, France
e-mail: catherine.cazals@tse-fr.eu

S. Soteri
Royal Mail Group, London, UK

P.L. Parcu et al. (eds.), *The Contribution of the Postal and Delivery Sector*, Topics in Regulatory Economics and Policy, https://doi.org/10.1007/978-3-319-70672-6_13

factors. Gori et al. (2006) estimated models for mail operating cost, using alternative functional forms (for example, Cobb-Douglas and Translog forms).

More recently, the motivation for studies estimating cost functions has tended to be stimulated by policy makers and regulators interests in benchmarking postal USP's performance. This helps to inform regulatory reviews and assess the USP's ability to continue to meet universal service obligations via future efficiency gains (for example, see Ferguson et al. 2017). The outputs of this analysis, and in particular the inefficiency rankings of individual units, are intended to provide the USP with useful internal benchmarking information to help reduce costs and raise efficiency in the worse performing units.

An important question that these studies have not tended to directly focus on is the identification of the types of employees and other labor resourcing factors that operational managers could potentially influence to reduce costs. This is a gap in the postal literature that we hope to explore. In particular, we examine the extent to which different delivery offices' mix of part-time staff, overtime rates and employee churn, amongst other factors, influence costs in terms of hours it takes to handle a given level of output (as measured by a weighted volume variable that takes account of differences in handling letter and parcel traffic as well as other factors). To this end we estimate delivery office cost functions in the United Kingdom using a large data set covering 5 years using econometric estimation techniques that take into account the endogeneity effects of management decision variables.

Section 2 of the paper sets out the estimation methodology for modelling delivery cost functions without variables that can be influenced by Royal Mail managers and reports results using OLS pooled regression and random effect panel estimation techniques. Section 3 extends the previous section to include labor resource variables that can be influenced by management actions. In other words, we estimate first the reduced form (in Sect. 2) and then the structural form. Section 4 reports results using estimation techniques that take into account endogeneity effects by applying two-stage least squares methods (2SLS) to pooled data and generalized two-stage least squares (G2SLS) to the random effect panel model. Finally, Sect. 5 provides a summary and conclusions.

2 Postal Delivery Cost Modelling

Postal delivery cost functions are usually estimated as the relation between production costs, denoted by C, in different decision units, each denoted by i, and the level of production denoted by Q, the prices of inputs denoted by P, and environmental (exogenous) variables denoted by X (see for example, Cazals et al. 2005). Where data are available on these variables for n decision units, empirical analysis can be undertaken of the cost function, which can be written as:

$$C_i = f(Q_i, P_i, X_i, u_i) \quad i = 1, \ldots, n \tag{1}$$

where u represents a random error term that captures statistical noise and unobserved heterogeneity.

We estimate cost functions for delivery office (DO) unit hours of activity and the measure of production is weighted mail volumes.[1] Industrial engineering methods are used to weight different types of mail (for example, letters and parcels) in order to better reflect workload or the time taken to process and deliver mail in different locations. If all external factors were perfectly captured by the weights and DO units responded to changes in workload in a timely manner, then the time taken to process mail should, on average, move in line with one another on a one-to-one basis.[2] However, while Royal Mail employed sophisticated techniques to estimate the fixed and variable workload weights associated with movements in traffic, the estimates are unlikely to be perfect. Therefore, environmental variables are also included in the empirical analysis to account for differences in DO hours.

The environmental variables (X) included consist of the following geographical variables: the number of delivery points (DP); types of delivery points, such as business, large users and residential; the area covered by the delivery zone; proportions of urban, suburban, rural areas covered by the delivery zone; a dummy for the London area; and whether a delivery office sorts mail for delivery by other offices, referred to as a mail processing unit (MPU).

The data cover five UK financial year time periods, t, starting in 2010/11 and ending 2014/15, for 1216 delivery offices. This is the same data set informing the study by Ferguson et al. (2017) and more detailed information on the data is contained in Ofcom (2016).

A traditional parametric econometric approach is used to estimate the cost function and a log-linear model is adopted, similar to Cazals et al. (2005), which included mail volumes (Q), the number of delivery points (DP) and environmental factors (X). Furthermore, similar to Ferguson et al. (2017), time variable dummies (T) are also included to capture changes in average efficiency over time.

The data for the n decision units are observed over time during five periods and the cost function takes the following form, for $i = 1, \ldots$ n and $t = 1, \ldots 5$:

$$LnC_{it} = \alpha_0 + \alpha_1 LnDP_{it} + \alpha_2 Ln(Q_{it}) + \sum_{j=1}^{K} \beta_k X_{ik} + \sum_{t=1}^{4} \delta_t T_t + u_{it} \quad (2)$$

where u_{it} is decomposed as the sum of a standard random error term e_{it} and an unobservable individual specific effect a_i such that $u_{it} = a_i + e_{it}$. This model can be estimated by standard OLS or by panel data methods which take into account individual heterogeneity a_i. Typically two panel data approaches can be used for the estimation: fixed effects or random effects. We use the random effect estimator in order to recover the coefficients of the time invariant variables.

[1]Models using financial labour costs were also examined but we obtained quite unstable results that were not robust and due to resource constraints concentrated our efforts on delivery hours.

[2]This point is noted in Ofcom 2016, see page 24.

Table 1 Delivery office hours estimated cost functions

Explanatory variables	Pooled (OLS) regression	Random effects panel GLS regression
Weighted traffic (*Q*)	0.96655***	0.97344***
Delivery points (*DP*)	0.11312***	0.09194***
% of "business" delivery points	−0.00193	−0.00034
% of suburban area	0.00087***	0.00049***
% of rural area	0.00081***	0.00039**
Area	−0.03327***	−0.03324***
London dummy	0.12060***	0.07691***
Mail processing unit dummy	0.02366***	0.01245**
2011/12	−0.00992**	−0.00922***
2012/13	−0.01832***	−0.01749***
2013/14	−0.03593***	−0.03502***
2014/15	−0.05052***	−0.04955***
R^2	0. 9800	0.9798
Sample size	6080	6080

Note: *** denotes statistical significance at 1% level and, similarly, ** at 5% level and *at 10% level. All variables in logarithms except for "%" variables and therefore the latter coefficients need to be multiplied by 100 to estimate the average variation of cost, in percent, for an increase by one point of the corresponding variable

Table 1 reports the estimated coefficients for model (2). The first column of results estimates (2) using standard ordinary least squares (OLS) that pools together data for 1216 delivery offices across all 5 years, providing estimates based on 6080 individual observations. The second column of results in Table 1 provides estimates for (2) using a random effect model estimated by generalized least squares (GLS) which takes into account the panel structure of the data, that is, estimates are based on 1216 independent delivery offices observed over five time periods. Both models are estimated using robust standard errors to prevent effects of potential heteroskedasticity.

The econometric models reported in Table 1 both possess a high level of explanatory power, as denoted by their R^2 values of 0.98, which can be mainly ascribed to the weighted traffic (Q) variable.[3] The estimated coefficients in the two models are directionally broadly similar and, taken at face value, imply a number of important points. In particular, the estimated coefficient for the weighted traffic variable is close to unity and therefore, as this measure attempts to capture changes in potential workload, suggests actual hours broadly move in line with hours required to process and deliver mail over time but there may be further returns to scale that are not fully captured by the workload weights.

[3]Amongst all the explanatory variables in the cost function, the mail volume Q has the strongest explanatory power, with an associated partial R^2 of around 0.7.

The statistical significance of environmental factors can be interpreted in a number of ways: first, they suggest that while the traffic weights used to capture workload movements may be reasonably good they are not perfect and could potentially be improved; and/or second, that DOs with specific characteristics tend, on average, to employ relatively more hours holding all other factors constant than others (for example, London, those with relatively high numbers of delivery points, mail processing units and rural/suburban areas relative to urban areas)) while others use less (for example, those in relatively large areas). The negative coefficients for each of the time dummies suggest efficiency gains relative to the first year (2010/11) of the study of around five percentage points by 2014/15, similar to the findings of Ferguson et al. (2017).

3 Introducing Labor Resource Variables in Delivery Cost Functions

The changing pattern of mail demand, in particular fewer letters and more parcels, raises a number of challenges for USPs, especially if the workload demands of the former are greater than the latter in a competitive market (see De Donder et al. 2018). One important such challenge relates to the need to improve efficiency via the matching of labor hours to continuous changes in mail demand. Operational managers have responded to this challenge in the UK by adopting quite different resourcing requirements. For example, Table 2 below shows that DOs patterns of use of part-time staff, overtime hours and management of employee turnover rates vary substantially. In particular, Table 2 indicates that the distribution of DOs employment of part-time staff and new joiners exhibits a higher degree of variation around the median than the use of overtime hours.

An important question emerging from the statistics reported in Table 2, is whether DOs with higher rates of part-time staff, overtime usage and new joiners are, on average, matching labor hours to meet demand requirements more effectively than those with lower rates. The answer will depend on the extent to which the benefits of better matching actual hours to demand dominates the impact of potentially negative supply side factors, such as replacing full-time staff, who work some overtime hours, with part-time employees and new full-time joiners, who may be less committed or embody a greater proportion of deadweight time.[4] However, new joiners and part-time staff may exhibit greater enthusiasm to do the job and be open to new ways of working which could improve the matching of hours to demand requirements. It is therefore not clear what the direction of impact different DO employee resource strategies could, on average, have on overall delivery unit hours.

[4]For example, people tend to be less productive when starting a new job or at the beginning of their usual day/night shift.

Table 2 Delivery office statistics on staffing numbers, hours and new joiners (for 2014/15)

	No. of operational staff	% of operational staff part-time	% of overtime hours	% new joiners
Mean	70.0	25.1	8.0	4.1
Lower quartile	32.0	15.3	5.9	0.0
Median	50.5	24.5	7.9	3.0
Upper quartile	85.5	33.4	9.9	6.4

The extent to which labor resourcing strategies impact overall delivery unit costs, in terms of hours, can be modelled by modifying (2) to include labor management decisions variables,[5] M_l, such that the cost function becomes:

$$LnC = \alpha_0 + \alpha_1 LnDP + \alpha_2 Ln(Q) + \sum_{j=1}^{K} \beta_k X_k + \sum_{t=1}^{4} \delta_t T_t + \sum_{l=1}^{L} \gamma_l M_l + u \quad (3)$$

where up to L labor resourcing variables are included in the model (that is, $l = 1,..,L$).

An important point to consider with respect to cost functions that include variables that can be influenced by management decisions is that they are highly likely to take account of reactions to the decisions taken and potentially other environmental characteristics and possibly macro economy factors. So we can write, for each management variable M_l (for $l = 1,\ldots, L$):

$$M_l = \mu_0 + \mu_1 LnDP + \mu_2 Ln(Q) + \sum_{j=1}^{K} \theta_k X_k + \sum_{t=1}^{4} \varphi_t T_t + \sum_{r=1}^{R} \rho_r Z_r + v \quad (4)$$

where Z_r, $r = 1,\ldots, R$, represents instrumental variables that affect management variables but that do not affect costs directly. It is important to notice that error terms in (3) and (4), that is u and v, are likely to be correlated, and then there is correlation between management variables M_l, $l = 1,..,L$, and error term u in (3). As a consequence of this endogeneity issue the standard ordinary least squares estimates for (2) (or standard GLS) are likely to be biased. In order to take account of potential endogeneity a two-stage least squares method (2SLS) could be applied to the pooled data and a generalized two-stage least squares method (G2SLS) to the random effect model using the panel structure of the data.

The instruments used in this study to deal with potential endogeneity were real income per capita, Gross Value Added (GVA), unemployment, and labor force in the local neighborhood as those variables reflect the level of tension in the local labor market. Indeed, local labor market conditions in the UK vary significantly across the country and are likely to impact the supply of labor (full- or part-time),

[5]These variables are measured for example by the rates of part-time staff, overtime usage or new joiners used in delivery offices.

employee turnover rates and operational managers hiring strategies and staffing mix.[6]

In order to investigate the presence of endogeneity we used these instruments to test and reject the hypothesis that the employee management variables were exogenous,[7] thereby concluding that they were likely to be endogenous and should apply a 2SLS estimator to pooled data and a G2SLS method to panel data. Second, as we have more instruments than the number of endogenous variables we were able to test the validity of these instruments. The test is rejected when using this set of instruments, suggesting that some instruments should be considered in the main equation (that is, included as exogenous variables in (4)).

On this basis, we estimated our final model with GVA included in equation (4) and the remaining instruments (real income per capita, unemployment and labor force variables) were accepted as valid instruments.[8] Our econometric analysis found the percentage of overtime hours variable to be unstable and possess non robust properties[9] and was dropped from our analysis. The results of our econometric analysis including employee management variables and whether or not all endogeneity issues are taken into account are reported in the following section.

4 Econometric Results

The results of our econometric analysis are reported in Table 3. If we compare the values of estimated coefficients for the two weighted traffic variable in the OLS (pooled) and GLS (panel) models they are similar to those reported in Table 1 and they all round to either 0.9 or 1.0. The estimated coefficients are also of a similar magnitude when 2SLS and G2SLS instrumental variable techniques are used and they round to 0.9. Second, although the estimated coefficients vary, they are of broadly similar magnitude for the number of delivery points and directionally consistent for most other variables. Third, this is not the case for the employee management or London dummy variables, which exhibit substantial differences

---

[6]A complex labor resourcing process is likely to underpin management decisions affecting the composition of labour inputs in DOs across the country that takes into account the relative cost of employing different types of labour, full-and part-time turnover rates, hiring and firing costs and, amongst other factors, their impact on quality of service.

[7]The p-values from a number of tests are reported in Table 3 below. All of these rejected the null hypothesis that these variables were exogenous.

[8]The macro economy variables were informed by local authority district (LAD) data. Since LAD data is only available for 326 different geographies and each district contains one or more DO units the same macro economy data was assigned to multiple DOs.

[9]The statistical properties of the estimated coefficient for the percentage of overtime hours was quite unstable and depended on the mix of variables incorporated. This could be because we do not have particularly good instruments for this management variable. This was therefore excluded from our analysis but we would suggest that this could warrant further investigation at some point in the future.

Table 3 Delivery office hours estimated cost functions including labor resource variables

	Estimation method not accounting for endogeneity		Estimation method accounting for endogeneity	
Explanatory variables	Pooled OLS	Random effects panel GLS	Pooled 2SLS	Random effects Panel G2SLS
Weighted traffic (*Q*)	0.92789***	0.97108***	0.85331***	0.92059***
Delivery points (*DP*)	0.14115***	0.09226***	0.19595***	0.13297***
% business delivery points	−0.00295**	−0.00114	−0.00606***	−0.00887*
% suburban area	0.00085***	0.00047***	0.00058***	0.00042**
% rural area	0.00069***	0.00034*	0.00025*	0.00006
Area	−0.02780***	−0.03115***	−0.01699***	−0.01856**
London	0.07769***	0.06597***	−0.02573	−0.02060
Mail processing unit	0.02626***	0.01335***	0.03511***	0.03101***
2011/12	−0.00808*	−0.00858***	−0.00190	0.00855
2012/13	−0.01515***	−0.01602***	−0.00792	−0.00746
2013/14	−0.03320***	−0.03297***	−0.03075***	−0.03252***
2014/15	−0.04883***	−0.04726***	−0.05774***	−0.06861***
% of part-time staff[1,2]	−0.00245***	−0.00100***	−0.00770***	−0.00708***
% of new joiners[1,2]	−0.00029	0.00024**	−0.00707**	−0.01321
Economic activity (GVA)	–	–	−0.01644***	−0.01493**
R^2	0.9815	0.9807	0.9710	0.9643
Sample size	6080	6080	6080	6080

1. Test of endogeneity (null hypothesis: employee management variables are exogenous)		
	p-value	p-value
Robust score $\chi^2(2)$	0.0000	0.0000
Robust regression (F2,60.63))	0.0000	–

2. Tests of overidentifying restrictions ((null hypothesis: instruments are valid)		
	p-value	p-value
Sargan $\chi^2(1)$	0.8576	0.2270
Basmann $\chi^2(1)$	0.8578	–
Score $\chi^2(1)$	0.8818	–

Note: *** denotes statistical significance at 1% level and, similarly, **5 at 5% level and *at 10% level

when taking account of potential endogeneity effects. Specifically, the magnitude of the employee management variables is substantially bigger and the London dummy changes sign when using instrumental variable estimators.

Fourth, estimates of the average gain in efficiency by the end of the period examined, 2014/15, are a little higher in the models that take endogeneity into account, that is around 6–7% over 4 years versus estimates of around 5% in the pooled OLS and random effects panel GLS estimates reported in Tables 1 and 3. Fifth, the negative coefficient on economic activity (GVA) suggests that periods of stronger economic growth tend to, on average, be associated with lower overall hours, holding all other factors constant. This could suggest that changes to working practices or managing out staff via redundancy programs to achieve efficiency gains may be more easily handled when economic conditions are more favorable.

The estimated coefficients for the employee variables reported in Table 3 are of particular interest from an operational management point of view. For example, the coefficients for the percentage of part-time staff and new joiners in Table 3 appear to be very close to zero when using standard OLS and GLS estimation techniques but are many times higher when using instrumental variable techniques. The substantial difference in the magnitude of the estimated coefficients is likely to be due to endogeneity bias in the OLS and GLS estimators. Therefore, greater emphasis should be placed on the 2SLS and G2SLS estimators reported in Table 3. In particular, these instrumental variable estimators suggest that a one percentage point increase in the rate of new joiners is, on average, associated with a reduction in hours of between 0.7 and 1.3%.[10] Similarly, estimates of the impact of increasing the ratio of part-time employees could, on average, result in a reduction in hours of around 0.7–0.8%.[11]

However, it should be noted that an element of the estimated impact of increasing the part-time employee rate is a mechanical outcome, described in more detail in the Appendix. For example, as "part-time" staff hours, on average, corresponds to around "half of full-time" hours, this mechanical effect would be equal to 0.5 if the number of employees is fixed (see appendix). The extent to which the estimated coefficient is higher in absolute terms than this mechanical effect can be interpreted as an indicator of the degree to which the use of part-time staff has led, on average, to a better matching of hours to varying work requirements. The results reported in Table 3, suggest the absolute size of the estimated coefficient for part-time staff is around 0.2–0.3 percentage points higher than the mechanical effect. We can therefore conclude that variations in mail demand are, on average, met with fewer hours by DOs that have a greater proportion of part-time employees.

A further observation is the extent to which the London dummy variable changes sign and becomes insignificantly different from zero. This suggests that when all the variables reported in Table 3 are taken into account, costs in terms of hours are not significantly higher than in other DOs.

---

[10]Note that the "% of new joiners" estimated coefficients in the pooled 2SLS estimator (−0.00707) and the random effects G2SLS estimator (−0.01321) need to be multiplied by 100 to obtain the impact of a one percentage point increase in the percentage of new joiners.

[11]Similar to the previous footnote, the "% of part-time staff" estimated coefficients (−0.00770 and −0.00708) need to be multiplied by 100 to obtain the impact of a one percentage point increase in the ratio of part-time employees.

5 Conclusions

Letter volumes in the UK are in long term structural decline while parcel volumes are increasing but operate in a highly competitive market. This raises operational challenges in terms of adapting to changing consumer demands and reducing costs in order to continue to profitably provide existing universal service obligations and compete effectively with other parcel operators. Numerous studies have examined postal USPs' delivery costs to assess the extent of economies of scale in delivery and overall levels of relative inefficiency to inform regulatory reviews. However, to the best of our knowledge, no other study has focused on identifying the extent to which management variables directly impact delivery costs and could be used to better inform operational resourcing strategies. This is a gap in the literature that we have explored in this paper. Our analysis provides valuable insights into the econometric challenges facing prospective studies in this area and some preliminary findings into the potential benefits of UK delivery offices adopting different employee resourcing policies.

The econometric results contained in Sect. 4 suggest that differences in delivery office costs after taking into account variations in workload to handle different types of traffic (for example, letters and parcels) and geographic factors, are significantly impacted by resourcing decisions relating to the use of part-time staff and managing labor turnover rates, but these are in turn influenced by external factors such as local labor market conditions. We tested for this circularity effect in terms of cause and effect and concluded that endogeneity bias is likely to be present and could potentially lead to biased estimated. In order to address this issue, instrumental variable (IV) techniques (pooled 2SLS and panel G2SLS) were used to estimate cost functions containing management variables. The estimated coefficients for weighted mail volumes and most environmental variables were found to be broadly similar to those using OLS and random effects panel estimates. However, the absolute magnitude of the coefficients for the proportion of part-time staff employed and percentage of new joiners were found to be many times higher when using IV estimation techniques and suggests that endogeneity issues are likely to be leading to significant levels of downward bias with respect to these variables.

In addition to identifying the overall positive effect that a higher ratio of part-time staff and new leavers have on reducing delivery hours, our econometric findings also indicate that periods of stronger economic growth tend to be associated with lower overall hours. An important operational management question relating to each of these findings is: why is this so? For example, is it the case that periods of higher economic growth help to facilitate reductions in labor demand? Do offices with a higher proportion of new joiners provide managers with more opportunities to implement change or are new joiners more motivated and productive? Do delivery offices with higher ratios of part-time staff use fewer hours to deliver the same level of mail because they can more easily flex the hours of part-time staff to better meet fluctuating levels of demand or are individuals who tend to work part-time generally more productive? These are questions that cannot be answered by econometrics alone, but econometric analysis can provide a first step in identifying which factors are potentially worth investigating from an operational and human resourcing perspective.

This econometric study has explored a number of employee resource factors that can be influenced by operational managers. However it is by no means an exhaustive analysis and future research may wish to extend the scope of the human resource variables examined in this study or, indeed, a range of other factors under management control that could help to inform policies targeting reductions in hours.

Appendix

The estimated coefficient for the percentage of operational staff working part-time in labor cost models expressed in hours has a mathematical tendency, referred to as the mechanical effect in this paper, to equal some specific value. In particular, this can be shown to depend on the proportion of hours part-time employees work relative to full-time employees. In order to examine the mathematical property of this mechanical effect, let us denote by n_{FT} and n_{PT}, the numbers of full-time and part-time employees respectively, and by H_{FT} and H_{PT}, the numbers of full-time hours and part-time hours per employees respectively. The total number of labor hours in a DO can then be specified as $H = n_{FT}H_{FT} + n_{PT}H_{PT}$.

Then, as we consider the logarithm of labor hours in ours models, we can write:

$$\begin{aligned} Ln\, H &= Ln(n_{FT}H_{FT} + n_{PT}H_{PT}) \\ &= Ln[(n_{FT} + n_{PT})H_{FT} + n_{FT}(H_{PT} - H_{FT})] \end{aligned}$$

By using the properties: $Ln(a+b) = Ln\, a + Ln\left(1+\frac{b}{a}\right)$ and $Ln(1 + x) = x$ if x small, we can re-write the previous equation as:

$$Ln\, H = Ln[(n_{FT} + n_{PT})H_{FT}] + \underbrace{\left(\frac{H_{PT} - H_{FT}}{H_{FT}}\right)}_{\alpha} \frac{n_{PT}}{n_{FT} + n_{PT}}$$

Then, if all part-time hours are, say "half-time" full-time hours, the coefficient α of the proportion of part-time employees is equal to -0.5.

References

Cazals C., M. de Rycke, JP. Florens, and S. Rouzaud (1997) "Scale economies and natural monopoly in the postal delivery: comparison between parametric and non parametric specifications", in *Managing Change in the Postal and Delivery Industries*, edited by M.A. Crew and P.R. Kleindorfer, Kluwer Academic Publishers.

Cazals C., P. Duchemin, JP. Florens, B. Roy and O. Vialaneix (2001) "An econometric study of cost elasticity in the activities of post office counters", in *Postal and Delivery Services: Pricing, Productivity, Regulation and Strategy*, edited by M.A. Crew and P.R. Kleindorfer, Kluwer Academic Publishers.

Cazals C., JP. Florens, and S. Soteri (2005): "Delivery costs for postal services in the UK", in *Regulatory and Economic Challenges in the Postal and Delivery Sector*, edited by M.A. Crew and P.R. Kleindorfer, Kluwer Academic Publishers.

De Donder P., F. Rodriguez and S. Soteri (2018), "Pricing and Efficiency Decisions for Letter and Parcel Markets when Industrial Relations Matter", see chapter 17 of this book.

Ferguson H., K. Curry and N. Convery (2017), "Econometric Benchmarking of Delivery and Processing Costs in the UK Postal Sector", in *The Changing Postal and Delivery Sector*, edited by P.L. Parcu, M.A. Crew and T. Brennan. Springer International Publishing, Switzerland.

Gori S., E. Piccinin, S. Romito and G. Scarfiglieri (2006). "On the use of cost functions in the assessment of the impact of liberalization on postal universal Service burden", in *Progress Toward Liberalization of the Postal and Delivery Sector*, edited by M.A. Crew and P. R. Kleindorfer, New York Springer.

Ofcom 2016 Econometric benchmarking in the UK postal sector. Final report Non-confidential version 24 May 2016. https://www.ofcom.org.uk/data/assets/pdf_file /0019/69400/ benchmarking-report.pdf

Postal Users' Needs Regarding Accessibility to the Postal Network

João Confraria, Filipa Silva, Frederico Pereira, and Agostinho Franco

1 Introduction

Under the Postal Services Directive[1] (henceforth, Directive), and in the framework of the universal service obligation (USO), European Union's (EU) Member States (MS) shall ensure that users enjoy the right to a postal service of a specified quality at all points in their territory at affordable prices for all users. To this end, EU MS shall take steps to ensure that the density of the points of contact and of the access points takes into account users' needs. In our view, the Directive gives substantial discretion to EU MS and to National Regulatory Authorities on identifying users' needs and defining the allocation of costs involved. In this paper we discuss an approach under discussion at ANACOM, the Portuguese NRA.

Section 2 reviews literature on postal network density. Section 3 characterizes the distribution of postal outlets in Portugal. Section 4 presents Portuguese residential and businesses' usage of postal outlets, based on surveys promoted by ANACOM to identify the needs of users regarding access to postal outlets. In Sect. 5, the results of estimated logit models on the probability of going to postal

The views in this paper are those of the authors and do not reflect the views of ANACOM, neither UCP.

[1]Directive 97/67/EC, amended by Directive 2002/39/EC and by Directive 2008/6/EC.

J. Confraria
Católica Lisbon School of Business & Economics, Palma de Cima, 1649-023 Lisbon, Portugal

F. Silva
Autoridade Nacional de Comunicações - ANACOM, Área de Estudos - DAC, Avenida José Malhoa, 12 1099-017 Lisbon, Portugal

F. Pereira • A. Franco (✉)
Autoridade Nacional de Comunicações - ANACOM, Núcleo de Serviços Postais - DRM, Avenida José Malhoa, 12 1099-017 Lisbon, Portugal

P.L. Parcu et al. (eds.), *The Contribution of the Postal and Delivery Sector*, Topics in Regulatory Economics and Policy, https://doi.org/10.1007/978-3-319-70672-6_14

outlets and on the willingness to pay (WTP) are presented. Concluding remarks are provided in Sect. 6, highlighting the redistributive nature of current network density arrangements.

2 Literature Review

According to Borsenberger et al. (2011), decisions regarding the configuration of the postal network are complex and multidimensional because, in addition to economic efficiency, they are strongly influenced by the socio-economic and political context. The authors provide cross-country analysis of postal network accessibility relying on demographic and geographic coverage dimensions. The number of working hours of the postal outlets was introduced as an explanatory variable of the degree of access to the postal retail network. The authors considered that accessibility to postal services in a given country may be lower if postal outlets are open less hours per day or per week, even if the country has the same (or higher) density of outlets compared to other countries.

Regulated postal retail networks simultaneously embrace public and business objectives. According to some views, this leads to oversized postal retail networks as compared to the ones that would be sustained in purely commercial basis (Cohen et al. 2008).

Boldron et al. (2008) argued that, broadly speaking, commercial services networks tend to be more concentrated in urban areas and tend to offer a much better accessibility in urban areas than in rural areas. Notwithstanding, they have shown that postal outlets in rural areas create positive spillovers that may enhance social welfare.

It has also been suggested that the role of postal services in local communities' dynamics should be considered when evaluating network density. Bradley (1986), Cloke (1997) or Higgs and White (2000), provided evidence on the influence of public services, particularly when they establish direct interaction with citizens, in the health and well-being of communities.

According to a report produced by the Boston Borough Council (2006), the postal retail network in rural areas gain ascendancy and importance among the population by being decoded as essential service delivery points for everyday life.

A report published by Age Concern (2006), has shown that in the United Kingdom (UK), postal outlets are very important for the older population and are highly relied on. In addition to meeting the needs of postal services, the UK's senior population uses postal outlets to meet needs of a different nature, such as savings, payment or pension withdrawal, as well as social interaction either with employees or with other customers.

Higgs and Langford (2013) conducted an in-depth research with the rural elderly population in Wales to assess the impact of the closure of rural postal outlets on the ability of these populations to meet postal needs and other services usually performed at postal outlets, such as payment of expenses and the execution of financial investments. They have concluded that this age group is very dependent on the postal retail network.

Woods (2009) argued that heterogeneity in the availability of postal services in rural areas contributes to explain the dynamism or decay of specific local communities.

More recently, ERGP (2016) and Zurel (2016) surveyed recent studies on changes in postal users' needs. Zurel (2016) found that, in general, the postal network seems to correspond to the postal users' needs, although there appear to be large differences between EU MS.[2] ERGP (2016) concludes that users are generally satisfied with the current provision of access points, though in some countries there is demand for longer opening hours.

Results in this paper are broadly consistent with some of these views but the relevance of network density for specific residential and business users is highlighted. Moreover, our results suggest that it seems fair to say that users are happy with current network density as long as they are not paying directly or explicitly most of its costs.

3 Distribution of Postal Outlets in Portugal

The distribution of postal outlets in Portugal is disproportionate both in relation to the area covered and to the population. A large proportion of postal outlets (46%) is located in predominantly urban areas, which represent only 18% of the country's land area but a most of the population (72%). At the same time, 35% of postal outlets are located in predominantly rural areas, which represent only 13% of the population but 62% of the land area (Table 1).[3]

Almost all outlets located in predominantly rural areas are postal agencies (postal outlets managed by third entities) and only 1% post offices (postal outlets owned by the USP), these representing also only 1% of the total number of post offices. The majority (76%) of post offices are located in predominantly urban areas and the other 23% in medium urban areas. Compared to post offices, postal agencies are relatively more evenly spread across the country's land area (47% are located in predominantly rural areas, 31% in predominantly urban areas and 22% in medium urban areas).

Postal agencies are also characterized by having more diversified opening hours during the day and week, compared to post offices. While the opening hours of postal agencies ranges from 3 to 168 h per week, postal offices opening hours range between 35 and 45 h a week.

[2]Zurel (2016) came to this conclusion from the analysis of studies in eight countries: Belgium, UK, Ireland, Italy, Poland, Netherlands, Romania and Sweden.

[3]Data are similar when comparing the distribution of postal outlets relatively to business users.

Table 1 Postal outlets, population and land area by level of ruralness in Portugal

Level of ruralness[a]	Number of Postal outlets			Population	Land area (km^2)	Population density	People per Postal outlet
	Post offices	Postal agencies	Total				
Predominantly urban area	469	534	**1003**	7,614,451	16,825	453	7592
Medium urban area	140	379	**519**	1,539,280	18,642	83	2996
Predominantly rural area	6	811	**817**	1,408,447	56,758	25	1724
Total	**615**	**1724**	**2339**	**10,562,178**	**92,225**	**115**	**4516**

Source: Postal outlets (USP—end of 2016); Population, land area and level of ruralness (Statistics Portugal)

[a]According to the classification of the level of ruralness of the parish where the postal outlet is located. The outlet may serve users in areas with different ruralness levels

Postal outlets provide postal and non-postal services, e.g. issuance and payment of postal money order, utility bills payments, financial services and (since 2016) CTT's bank branches.[4]

Globally, mail business represents circa 72% of the revenues of the USP's Group, express and parcels account for 18% of the revenues and financial services for 10%.

4 Usage of Postal Outlets

ANACOM promoted a survey, between February 13 and March 15 of 2017, on users' needs and usage of postal access points, separately for two groups of users of the postal access points: (a) residential users and (b) micro, small and medium-sized enterprise (MSME) users (IMR 2017).[5]

For residential users, results are representative of the level of ruralness, place of residence[6] and vulnerability of the respondent. For MSME users, the sample is representative of the level of ruralness of enterprise's location, number of employees and activity sector.

The survey concluded that 77.5% of residential users and 91.4% of MSME users use postal outlets. While half of the MSME users claim to visit it every week, half of the residential users claim to visit it every month.[7] Residential users generally use

[4]At post offices.

[5]A computer-assisted personal interviewing (CAPI) was used. The sample was composed of 3240 respondents for both residential (15 years old and above) and MSME users.

[6]Predominantly rural, medium urban or predominantly urban areas.

[7]Studies made by Ernst & Young for the Maltese regulator in 2014, cited by ERGP (2016), have shown that 70% of residential users and 72% of business users claimed to have visited the postal outlet in the last 12 months, 43% of the residential users every month and only (when compared to the result in Portugal) 11% of business users every week.

postal outlets to receive postal items (parcels and registered letters) while MSME users mainly use postal outlets to send letters. In terms of user profile, two specific groups of residential users show different patterns: (i) people aged between 15 and 24 use postal outlets to send or receive parcels and (ii) people with more than 74 years use postal outlets mainly to collect their pension funds.

Among residential users of postal outlets (Table 2), 54.8% use them to send postal items of any kind. This is considerably lower (34.5% and 27.8%) among the youngest respondents (15–24 years old) and oldest respondents (more than 74 years old), respectively. When MSME are considered, 75.6% of these users claimed to use postal outlets to send any kind of postal items. MSME situated in urban areas use more frequently postal outlets to send postal items (78.1%).

Concerning the reception of postal items, 62.7% and 58.4% of residential and MSME users, respectively, said that they use postal outlets to receive postal items. Again, the frequency of usage is lower among the youngest and oldest respondents (41.6% and 42.4% respectively). MSME users situated in urban areas use more frequently postal outlets to receive postal items (60%).

Table 2 Usage of postal outlets

		% of users that use outlets			
Residential users		In general	To send	To receive	To use/purchase non-postal services
Urban areas	Rural	73.7%	52.5%	61.7%	31.7%
	Urban	72.2%	55.2%	63.0%	26.6%
Professional situation	Does not work	62.2%	40.9%	52.7%	26.4%
	Works	79.3%	63.9%	69.3%	28.2%
Age	15–24	51.8%	34.5%	41.6%	17.1%
	25–34	79.7%	62.1%	70.8%	24.7%
	35–44	79.1%	66.3%	71.6%	28.6%
	45–54	78.8%	63.2%	68.5%	31.5%
	55–64	75.8%	57.1%	63.6%	31.6%
	65–74	70.9%	45.5%	59.5%	29.9%
	More than 74	50.5%	27.8%	42.4%	27.8%
Education level	Illiterate	63.6%	35.0%	51.2%	36.7%
	Elementary school	68.4%	40.3%	56.9%	34.7%
	Preparatory school	65.3%	44.7%	54.2%	26.8%
	High school	71.9%	56.7%	62.2%	23.6%
	University	81.9%	70.9%	74.4%	27.1%
Total		72.5%	54.8%	62.7%	27.5%
MSME USERS					
Ruralness	Medium urban	75.7%	69.0%	56.0%	13.3%
	Rural	63.3%	57.8%	44.5%	6.9%
	Urban	84.1%	78.1%	60.0%	9.5%
Total		81.6%	75.6%	58.4%	9.8%

The survey concluded that only 27.5% and 9.8% of residential and MSME users, respectively, use postal outlets for non-postal services.[8]

For residential users, proximity to home or work is the main factor when choosing a postal outlet, but proximity to home is more relevant for users in urban areas than for rural areas.[9]

On average, both type of users spend 13 min and 3 km in a round trip to a postal outlet, values very similar to the ones mentioned by the same users as being adequate ones. An increase of 5 km in the distance to travel by car to the postal outlet was viewed negatively by 70.6% of residential users and by 57.0% of MSME. MSME mentioned that they would move to digital solutions or reduce the current level of postal items sent if the distance increases.

Most of the respondents don't have a specific day to use postal outlets and half have no specific period of the day either. The majority of users rejected a scenario of reduction of the opening hours, a result that is in line with ERGP (2016) and Zurel (2016).

Both residential and MSME (more than 80%) reject a reduction of the number of postal outlets. This rejection is stronger among users located in rural areas when compared to users in urban areas.

In general, the majority of respondents (77.5% of residential users and 85.1% of MSME) are satisfied with the current access points in Portugal and consider that there is no need to make any changes (83.8% of residential users and 81.0% of MSME).

Residential and MSME users of postal outlets were asked about the hypothetical payment of an annual rate to maintain the current number of postal outlets.[10] The rate of responses willing to pay an amount zero was very high (around 50% for both users, in all scenarios).

On average,[11] residential respondents admit a value between 3.7 and 4.8 euros, while MSME users admit a value between 9.8 and 10.6 euros (Figs. 1 and 2).

5 Estimated Models

In this section, the results of estimated Logit models are presented. The objectives were to (1) estimate the probability of users using a postal outlet to send, receive postal items (in general and, specifically, correspondence and parcels) or to use non-postal services and to (2) estimate the probability of a user's WTP a fee for

[8]Such as financial services, bill payments (e.g. utilities) and purchase of non-postal products (e.g. books, concert tickets, etc.).

[9]According to a study by Input Consulting (2012) cited by ERGP (2016), 82% of residential users consider a short distance to the closest postal outlet as very or rather important.

[10]Three types of values for the rates were asked: Ideal, admissible and exaggerated value.

[11]Considers the responses above zero euros.

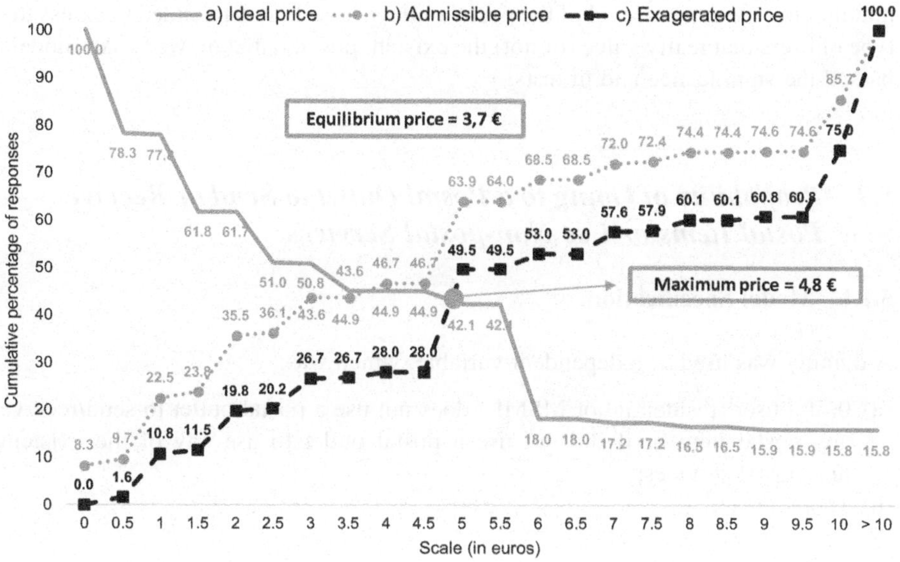

Fig. 1 Predisposition of residential users to pay an annual fee to maintain the number of postal outlets. Source: Adapted from IMR (2017)

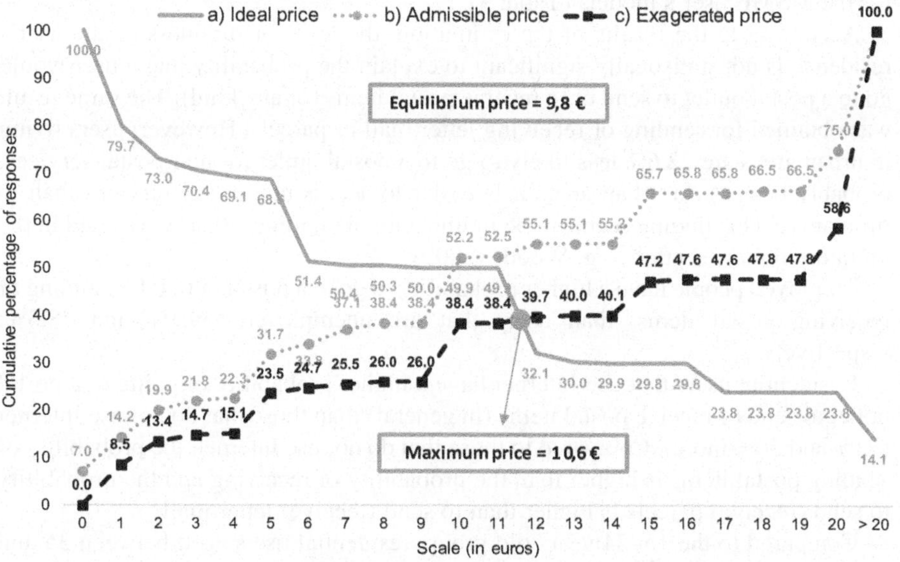

Fig. 2 Predisposition of MSME users to pay an annual fee to maintain the number of postal outlets. Source: Adapted from IMR (2017)

maintaining the current level of the postal outlet network. It is intended to assess the type of users that really value (or not) the existent postal outlet network. All models passed the significance and fit tests.

5.1 Probability of Going to a Postal Outlet to Send or Receive Postal Items or Use Non-postal Services

5.1.1 Model Specification

A dummy was used as a dependent variable, which was:

(a) 0, if a user (residential or MSME) does not use a postal outlet to send/receive any postal item or if did not use a postal outlet to use any of the existent non-postal services;
(b) 1, otherwise.

5.1.2 Estimated Results: Residential

The model correctly predicts between 63.5% and 69.8% (depending on the model) of the real outcomes for the residential users' model and between 59.4% and 90.2% for the MSME user's models (Table 3).

According to the results of the estimation, the level of ruralness of the user's residence is not statistically significant to explain the probability that a user would go to a postal outlet to send or to receive postal items (of any kind). The same result was obtained for sending or receiving letter mail or parcels. However, users living in urban areas are 22.6% less likely to go to a postal outlet for non-postal services, probably because in urban areas it is easier to access non-postal services than in rural areas. This finding seems to be in line with the findings of surveys cited in the literature review section, e.g. Woods (2009).

Employed people have a higher probability to go to a postal outlet, for sending or receiving postal items, than users that are unemployed (59.1% and 38.3%, respectively).

Residential users that use Internet have a higher probability of going to a postal outlet to send or receive postal items (in general) than those that do not use Internet (92% and 36% more). Compared to those that do not use Internet, the probability of sending postal items is higher than the probability of receiving and the probability to send (receive) parcels is higher than to send (receive) letter mail.

Compared to the 15–24 years old group, residential users aged between 35 and 44 years old have a higher probability of using a postal outlet to send or receive parcels (133% and 118% more, respectively) and people between 45 and 54 have a higher probability to use postal outlets to send or receive correspondence (332% and 390%, respectively). The group of age between 15 and 24 years is the one less likely to use a postal outlet to send or receive postal items (in general). People aged

Table 3 Odds ratio of the models estimation: residential users

	Went to postal outlet to send (odd ratios)			Went to postal outlet to receive (odd ratios)			
	Any postal item	Correspondence	Parcels	Any postal item	Correspondence	Parcels	Went to postal outlet for non-postal services
Urban area (dummy)	NS	NS	NS	NS	NS	NS	−22.6%
Professional situation (base = employed)	59.1%	49.9%	38.5%	38.3%	43.1%	59.8%	NS
Internet usage (dummy)	92.3%	74.9%	139.7%	35.8%	51.6%	75.1%	NS
Gender—male (dummy)	NS	NS	NS	NS	NS	NS	NS
Physical problems (dummy)	NS	NS	NS	−22.7%	−22.4%	NS	NS
Age (base = 15–24)							
25–34	114.0%	172.0%	95.8%	155.0%	233.0%	102.0%	NS
35–44	189.0%	277.0%	133.0%	190.0%	329.0%	118.0%	76.0%
45–54	247.0%	332.0%	94.2%	207.0%	390.0%	78.5%	95.0%
55–64	269.0%	328.0%	111.0%	194.0%	377.0%	NS	85.2%
65–74	246.0%	304.0%	67.6%	216.0%	310.0%	NS	63.5%
More than 74	108.0%	133.0%	NS	77.0%	129.0%	NS	NS
Education level (base = completed university)							
Illiterate	−47.3%	NS	−72.4%	NS	NS	−87.6%	NS
Elementary school	−59.5%	−56.8%	−64.1%	−40.5%	−41.4%	−55.6%	NS
Preparatory school	−67.0%	−65.9%	−65.5%	−59.2%	−45.1%	−67.1%	NS
High school	−43.0%	−43.5%	−30.6%	−38.7%	−33.0%	−30.9%	NS
Wage (base = more than 2350 euros)							
400 euros or less	NS	NS	NS	NS	NS	NS	NS
401 euros to 700 euros	59.3%	37.7%	NS	46.4%	34.8%	NS	NS
701 euros to 1100 euros	70.5%	47.2%	NS	56.9%	57.5%	NS	NS
1101 euros to 1350 euros	NS	NS	NS	NS	NS	NS	NS

(continued)

Table 3 (continued)

	Went to postal outlet to send (odd ratios)			Went to postal outlet to receive (odd ratios)			
	Any postal item	Correspondence	Parcels	Any postal item	Correspondence	Parcels	Went to postal outlet for non-postal services
1351 euros to 1850 euros	50.8%	NS	NS	NS	NS	NS	NS
1851 euros to 2350 euros	NS	NS	NS	NS	NS	NS	NS
Correctly Predicted Results	65.4%	64.9%	69.8%	65.8%	63.5%	67.0%	72.6%

NS Non-significant, p-value was equal or more than 0.05

To facilitate the interpretation of the results, only the odds ratios of predictors as percentages are shown. The percentage odds ratios are the result of the exponentiation of the coefficients of the logit regressions: $(e^{\beta} - 1) \times 100$

between 35 and 74 years old are more likely to go to a postal outlet to use non-postal services, compared to people between 15 and 24 years old.

According to the results of the models, when compared to users with college degrees, any other education level has a lower probability of sending or receiving postal items. The lower the education level, the bigger is the difference, when comparing to college degree users. The education level is not an explanatory factor of using non-postal services.

People who earn between 401 and 1100 euros are more likely to send or receive postal items, when compared to users that earn more than 2350 euros. The models did not produce statistically significant results for the other levels of income and for the relation between the level of income and the usage of postal outlets for sending or receiving parcels and neither for the access to postal outlets for non-postal services.

Vulnerable people are less likely to go to a postal outlet to receive a postal item when compared to someone not physically vulnerable.

Gender is not an explanatory factor for one to use a postal outlet.

5.1.3 Estimated Results: MSME

The percentage of outcomes predicted correctly is higher for the model regarding access to postal outlets for non-postal services (90.2%), while for the model regarding access to postal outlets to send any postal item the percentage is 75.7% and for the model to receive any postal item the percentage is lower (59.4%).

According to the results, number of workers and sales are not explanatory factors of the usage of postal outlets. The activity sector and the ruralness of the geographical localization of the company are explanatory factors. Compared with companies in urban areas, companies in rural areas are less likely to go to postal outlets to send (52.9% less) or receive (46.8% less) postal items and companies in medium urban areas are 65.6% more likely to go to postal outlets for non-postal services, compared to MSME in urban areas (Table 4).

5.2 WTP to Keep the Current Number of the Postal Outlets

5.2.1 Model Specification

In order to explain the WTP for network density a Logit model was estimated, in which the dependent variable was equal to 0, when there was no WTP and 1 if WTP was higher than zero. For that purpose, the answers to the question related to the hypothetical admissible value for the annual rate were used.

Table 4 Odds ratio of the models estimation: MSME users

	Went to a postal outlet to send any postal item	Went to a postal outlet to receive any postal item	Uses postal outlet for non-postal services
Urban tipology			
Medium urban areas	−28.5%	NS	65.6%
Rural areas	−52.9%	−46.8%	NS
Number of employees	NS	NS	NS
Sales volume	NS	NS	NS
Activity sector (Other activities)			
Fisheries and agriculture	NS	46.6%	NS
transforming industries	500.0%	NS	NS
Construction	153.0%	NS	NS
Wholesale and retail trade; repair of motor vehicles and motorcycles	151.0%	59.2%	NS
Accommodation, restoration and similar	82.5%	66.6%	120.0%
Information and communication activities	NS	NS	NS
Real estate activities	474.0%	102.0%	NS
Consulting, scientific, technical and similar	382.0%	51.8%	NS
Administrative activities and support services	167.0%	NS	NS
Education	207.0%	NS	NS
Artistic, spectacular, sports and recreational	78.3%	128.0%	NS
Other sectors	NS	NS	NS
Correctly Predicted Results	75.7%	59.4%	90.2%

NS Non-significant, p-value was equal or more than 0.05

5.2.2 Estimated Results: Residential

The model correctly predicts 67.5% of outcomes. The results are presented in Table 5. The main highlights are as follows:

(a) Compared to people between 15 and 24 years old, people aged 55 years or more are less willing to pay than people younger than 55 years.
(b) Those who use most frequently postal outlets are also those more willing to pay an annual rate to keep the same number of postal outlets. However, those who most frequently use postal agencies are less willing to pay to keep the current level of postal agencies when compared to users that do not use these access points. A possible explanation for this may be that users may prefer post offices to postal agencies.[12]

[12]RARC (2015) found that both consumers and MSME value maintaining postal outlets compared to alternative retail access, such as postal counters and postal kiosks.

Table 5 Odds ratio of the model estimation: residential users

Urban tipology (base = urban)	
Rural areas	NS
Medium urban areas	NS
District (base = Viseu)	
Beja	4170.2%
Braga	113.6%
Castelo Branco	−57.7%
Coimbra	−46.0%
Faro	−53.0%
Guarda	−84.3%
Leiria	124.5%
Other districts	NS
Gender (base = male)	NS
Age (base = 15–24 years old)	
25–54	NS
55–64	−37.6%
65–74	−40.4%
More than 74 years old	−58.0%
Physical problems (dummy)	2.7%
Education level (base = completed university)	
Illiterate/Elementary school	NS
Preparatory school	−27.0%
High school	NS
Wage (base = 400€ or less)	
401€ to 1350€	NS
1351€ to 1850€	94.5%
1851€ to 2350€/More than 2350€	NS
Household size	NS
Internet usage (base = every day)	
3–6 days per week	NS
1–2 days per week	151.3%
Less than 1 day per week	53.4%
Never	43.5%
Frequency of access to post offices (base = never)	
1–3 times month/1 time per quarter	NS
Once a week or more	94.2%
Frequency of access to postal agencies (base = never)	
1–3 times month/1 time per quarter	NS
Once a week or more	−59.1%
Sent non-registered letters (dummy)	43.1%
Sent registered letters (dummy)	−19.9%
Sent parcels (dummy)	NS
Received registered letters (dummy)	NS

(continued)

Table 5 (continued)

Received parcels (dummy)	NS
Time to postal outlet in a round trip (base = more than 20 min)	
Up to 10	NS
11–15	−34.2%
16–20	NS
Would you change something in the current network of access to postal services (dummy)?	NS
Level of satisfaction with the current network of access to postal services (using a scale from 1 to 10, where 1 is Not Satisfied and 10 is Very Satisfied)	17.3%

NS Non-significant, p-value was equal or more than 0.05

(c) Users that send registered letters are less likely (−20%) to pay an annual rate than those who do not use this service. Conversely, users who send non-registered letters seem to be more willing (+43%) to pay an annual rate, when compared to those that do not use this service.
(d) Sending or receiving parcels by residential users seems not to be relevant to the WTP an annual rate to keep the current level of postal outlets. It may also imply that users may use other points of contact (at least to receive parcels) or that they may use other postal service providers.
(e) The higher the level of satisfaction of residential users with the postal network, the higher is the WTP to keep it as it is.
(f) The model did not produce relevant results as to the WTP an annual rate to keep the current level of postal outlets based on ruralness of where people live but showed some differences between districts.

5.2.3 Estimated Results: MSME

The model correctly predicts 67.3% of the outcomes (see Table 6). According to the results:

(a) WTP of MSME users located in rural areas is 65% higher when compared to MSME users located in predominantly urban areas. This finding suggests that postal outlets may still have an important role on the economic inclusion of rural areas.
(b) WTP is 38.5% higher among MSME users employing between 10 and 49 employees compared to MSME with less than ten employees.
(c) The number of non-registered letters seems to be relevant. MSME sending more than 120 letters in 2016 have a higher propensity to pay (50% higher) an annual rate than other MSME.
(d) Compared to the fisheries and agriculture sector, the human health activities and social support sector have 73.6% more chances of paying an annual rate,

Table 6 Odds ratio of the model estimation: MSME users

Urban tipology (base = urban)	
Rural areas	65.7%
Medium urban areas	29.9%
District (base = Viseu)	
Other districts	NS
Beja	240.1%
Bragança	315.4%
Coimbra	−58.3%
Faro	−76.9%
Setubal	151.2%
Activity sector (base = A—Fisheries and agriculture)	
Other sectors	NS
Water collection, treatment and distribution	−59.9%
Real estate activities	−43.7%
Human health activities and social support	73.6%
Other activities	−48.3%
Number of employees (base = less than 10)	
10–49	38.5%
50–249	NS
Number of non-registered letters sent (base = 1–50)	
0–119	NS
120–270	47.8%
271–830	47.2%
Number of registered letters sent (base = 0)	
Up to 5/6 to 12	NS
13–36	65.2%
37–115	67.4%
More than 115	64.1%
Number of non-registered letters received (base = 0)	
Up to150	−27.9%
151–240	NS
241–720	−59.6%
721–1480	−35.6%
More than 1480	−58.4%
Number of registered letters received (base = 0)	
Up to 270/More than 270	NS
Parcels sent (base = 0)	
1–9	NS
10–12	−49.2%
13–45	−43.1%
More than 45	NS
Parcels received (base = 0)	
Up to 36	NS

(continued)

Table 6 (continued)

37–100	46.4%
101–240	88.6%
More than 240	NS
Newspapers and periodicals received	
Up to 300/More than 300	NS
Internal mail treatment (base = expedition managed by administr. serv.)	
Didn't send	−64.0%
Have an own centralized service to deal with posted mail	−35.4%
Each department treatment of e-email issued/ Contract other companies to sort and ship mail	NS
Reception of mail (base = Mail acceptance is managed by administrative services)	
Didn't receive Possess an own and centralized service to treat the received mail Each department receives its own mail Contract other companies to handle the mail received	NS
Delivery to postal offices operators by employees (dummy)	−48.0%
Delivery of parcels to postal operators by employees (dummy)	NS
Frequency of access to postal outlets (base = every day)	
2–3 days a week/Once a week/2–3 times per month	NS
1 Time per month	75.7%
1 Time per quarter	109.0%
2 Times per year or less	293.7%
Less frequently	NS
Period of the day to go to the postal outlets (base = none in particular)	
Does not go	106.3%
Until 10 h	61.7%
10–12 h	NS
12–14 h	45.9%
14–16 h	109.9%
16–18 h/After 18 h	NS
Time, in minutes, to postal offices in a round trip (base = Does not go)	
Up to 20 min/More than 20 min	NS
Would you change something in the current network of access to postal services (dummy)?	NS
Level of satisfaction with the current network of access to postal services (using a scale from 1 to 10, where 1 is Not Satisfied and 10 is Very Satisfied)	NS

NS Non-significant, p-value was equal or more than 0.05

while the Real estate activities sector (−43.7%) and the water collection, treatment and distribution sector (−59.9%) have less chance.

(e) MSME that send more than 12 registered letters per year have a higher propensity to pay (60% more) than MSME that send less registered letters per year.

(f) MSME users that received more than 240 non-registered letters in the last year are less willing to pay.

(g) MSME users that send 10–45 parcels are less willing to pay an annual rate compared to those that do not send or send more than 45 parcels. MSME users that receive 37–240 parcels are more willing to pay than those receiving less than 37 parcels or more than 240.
(h) The WTP of MSME that go to postal outlets on a daily basis, is 76% lower when compared to MSME that go once a month, which is a counterintuitive result. This percentage is 109% for those that use postal outlets quarterly and 294% twice a year.
(i) MSME that have a specific moment of the day to go to postal outlets are more willing to pay for the annual rate than those that do not have a specific moment to go, 62% more for those who go until 10 a.m., 46% for those between 12 and 14 and 110% for those between 14 and 16.
(j) The time spent to travel to a postal outlet was not statistically relevant.
(k) The degree of satisfaction with the postal network is not statistically relevant.

6 Conclusions

The results presented in this paper suggest that network density is important for specific groups of residential and business users, but not for all of them. Network density regulation may be seen as a way to address specific concerns of these users. Arguably, some of these groups may become less important as digitalization of mail increases. Thus, from a strictly postal point of view, network density regulation should aim at trying to make sure that some (traditional) users do not loose, or their losses are reduced, given the changes in the mail business. Therefore, at least for now, it seems a matter of managing the changes going on in postal markets. With the development and increasing use of e-commerce, access to postal outlets will have a different meaning, the problem being to make sure that users are able to receive (and send) parcels at convenient times and locations.

Residential users and MSME, in general, are satisfied with the retail access points they use, but, more often than not, they do not pay for it and (more than half of the respondents to the survey) claim not to be willing to pay for it. Those that are willing to pay for it are willing to pay an amount unlikely to be enough to pay for the current levels of network density.

Considering that the issue is the payment of an annual rate, it is expected that respondents ultimately indicate that they will not pay for a service they already have "for free", even when they rationally consider that it could be worth paying for keeping the current postal network if the alternative was to stop having it (at the same level as today).

This suggests that users are happy with current network density levels. The current level of satisfaction is subject to the underlying financing mechanisms in place. Data on loss making postal outlets is not publically available. The same happens with the contribution of network density to the net costs of the universal service. However, it should be noticed that users do not pay for most of the services demanded in accessing local postal outlets – receiving standard mail, receiving parcels or acquiring some financial services. Actually, mail senders, or in the case of financial services, the State and insurance companies, are the ones paying the services provided at postal outlets. Basically, many users are happy to have convenient locations to access these services, not paying for them. Cohen et al. (2008) argued that under a competitive scenario the network of post offices would largely be paid by single-piece revenue,[13] which would be a heavy burden to place on single piece mailers. The Portuguese USP, and this may be the case for others, has however been able to internalize the costs of the retail network,[14] something that may change in the future with additional decreasing volumes of traffic and if competition emerges. This suggests that, when appraising the appropriate levels of network density, regulators should keep in mind the underlying pricing arrangements.

Any way it should be noted that the model estimates use outputs of a survey that was not specifically designed to study the annual rate users are willing to pay, but a more comprehensive matter, and therefore there might be missing explanatory variables in order to estimate well fit models. This may be the subject of future research.

References

Age Concern (2006). Rural postal outlets are a lifeline and center of community, Age Concern, London.

Boldron, F., Dewulf, K., Joram, D., Panet, C., Roy, B., & Vialaneix, O. (2008). Accessibility of the postal retail network, social cohesion and economic development. In M. A. Crew & P. R. Kleindorfer (Eds.), Competition and regulation in the postal and delivery sector (pp. 47–61). Cheltenham, UK and Northampton, US: Edward Elgar.

Borsenberger, C., Joram, D. & Roy, B. (2011). How many outlets if the USP does not face any USO? A cross-country comparison. In: *Reinventing the Postal Sector in an Electronic Age*, 123–141. Edited by M.A. Crew and P.R. Kleindorfer. Cheltenham, UK and Northampton MA, US: Edward Elgar.

Boston Borough Council (2006). A sustainability Study of the Rural Settlements Consultation of Stage One - The Methodology. http://www.boston.gov.uk/index.php?option = com_docman&task = doc_view&gid =915

Bradley T., (1986) Poverty and dependency in village England in: Lowe, P., Bradley T., Wright, S. (Eds), Deprivation and Welfare in Rural Areas. GeoBooks

Cloke, Paul J., Goodwin, Mark, and Milbourne, Paul. (1997). Rural Wales: Community and Marginalization. University of Wales Press, Cardiff.

Cohen, R., Di Paola, L., Sheehy, R., & Comandini, V. V. (2008). The distribution of postal outlets in Italy and the United States. In: *Competition and Regulation in the Postal and Delivery Sector*, 36–46. Edited by M.A. Crew and P.R. Kleindorfer. Cheltenham, UK and Lyme, US: Edward Elgar.

ERGP (2016). ERGP report Universal Services in light of changing postal end users' needs

[13]Since most mail related retail activities are for singe-piece mail.

[14]Costs have been reduced, by outsourcing a significant part of the retail access points.

Higgs, G. White, S.D., (2000). Alternative indicators of social disadvantage in rural communities: the example of rural Wales. Progress in Planning 53 (1), 1–81

Higgs, G., Langford, M. (2013). Investigating the validity of rural urban distinctions in the impacts of changing service provision.

IMR (2017). Study on the postal users' needs on the accessibility to the retail access points of the Universal Service Provider (USP) in Portugal. https://www.anacom.pt/render.jsp?contentId=1411504

RARC (2015). What postal services do people value the most? A quantitative survey of the postal universal service obligation

Woods, M. 2009. Changing communities: restructuring rural services. In: Woods, M. (Ed.), Rural Geography. Sage, London

Zurel, O. (2016). A Systematic Review of Postal Consumers' Needs Within the USO Framework. Paper presented at the 24th Conference on Postal and Delivery Economics, Florence

Kill Your Darlings: When Does Sacrificing Next-Day Delivery Help USO Sustainability?

Henrik Ballebye Okholm, Mindaugas Cerpickis, Anna Möller Boivie, and Bruno Basalisco

1 Introduction

The financial pressure on universal service providers (USPs) arising from declining letter mail volumes and changing user needs increasingly burdens national universal service obligations (USOs). These dynamics have been recently reviewed by Cape and Groves (2017), who provided an overview of different changes to national USOs, their implications and possible future trends.

The continually declining demand for letter services and increasing demand for parcels forces national postal operators (NPOs) to change their business model insofar as they strive to secure the best possible financial position. In several European countries, we observe a reduction in the network delivery capacity in response to lower demand. In July 2016, the Danish PostNord changed its next-day delivery to an express product, while tripling letter prices from around € 1.3 to € 3.6.[1] In Italy, Poste Italiane withdrew its priority mail product in October 2015 and replaced it by a slower delivery service product (D + 5/7). As in Denmark, the new Italian next-day delivery service has become significantly more expensive, with the price for a 20 g letter increasing from € 0.60 in 2010 to € 2.8 in 2016.[2] Alongside the price increase of next-day delivery service, Poste Italiane is reducing the frequency of delivery from 5 to 2.5 weekdays in rural areas.[3]

[1]Prices for lowest weight categories available: 1.3 EUR price is for 50 g weight category, 3.6 EUR price is for 100 g (in 2016, the lowest weight category was changed from 50 to 100 g).

[2]Poste Italiane, annual reports.

[3]WIK (2016), "Future scenario developments in the Dutch postal market".

H.B. Okholm (✉) • M. Cerpickis • A.M. Boivie • B. Basalisco
Copenhagen Economics, Copenhagen, Denmark
e-mail: hbo@copenhageneconomics.com

P.L. Parcu et al. (eds.), *The Contribution of the Postal and Delivery Sector*, Topics in Regulatory Economics and Policy, https://doi.org/10.1007/978-3-319-70672-6_15

In our chapter we analyze, using case studies of several European countries, the risks and implications of significant price increases of the next-day letter services.

Section 2 introduces main market developments, the response strategies available to incumbent postal operators, as well as a synopsis of country cases where alterations to next-day service have been applied or considered. Sacrificing next-day services is a counterintuitive strategy, since it prima facie challenges key economic principles, which are briefly set out in Sect. 3. Section 4 analyses the key dimensions of the strategy of sacrificing D + 1: significant price increases for next day delivery services with the aim to shift demand to non-priority services. Section 5 provides recommendations to national postal operators as to conditions that justify sacrificing next day delivery service, as well as regulatory and policy implications.

2 Key Market Developments and Strategies Underpinning Revisions to the Next-Day Delivery Service

One of the most important market developments is digitalization and the associated mail volume decline. At the same time, the product mix of postal operators is changing—the relative importance of parcel products is increasing, a development which is driven by e-commerce. According to UPU data, the amount of letters has fallen by around 12% globally since 1990, while the amount of parcels has increased by around 14% over the same period.

The change in product mix demanded forces incumbent postal operators to innovate in order to remain relevant to changing users' needs in the e-commerce area as well as to cut costs and maintain affordable prices for services within the USO. Sacrificing next day delivery service is one of the possible responses to mail volume decline. Why has this been implemented in Denmark and Italy and broadly considered by many other European NPOs? In this chapter we seek to shed light on this by focusing on the rationale and regulatory implications of deliberate substitution from next day delivery service to non-priority service (within or outside the USO).

In this chapter we summarize recent developments in Denmark and Italy, where NPOs went all the way of shifting demand from next day delivery services to slower products. In addition, we discuss developments in several other European countries (Finland, Norway and Sweden) where NPOs and governments are starting to review the future of their mail services in light of continuing mail volume decline, as described in Table 1.

Declining letter volumes decrease economies of scale, which leads to higher unit costs. Higher unit costs effectively put an upward pressure on prices. As a response to this development, two countries, namely Denmark and Italy, have chosen to significantly increase the next day delivery service prices to (gradually) shift postal users' demand from expensive (and costly) priority letter products to non-priority products. In addition, we find that recent developments in Finland, Norway and Sweden have some features of the abovementioned factors and thus suggest that, in

Table 1 Countries included in the case study analysis

USP	Mail volume decline 2011–2014	Share of D + 1 mail	Priority letter price (CPL adjusted)[a]	Slow product	XY/AB delivery	Last change of minimum delivery frequency requirements	E2E competition
Denmark (PostNord)	−31%	From 81% in 2008 to 27% in 2016	3.63 EUR	D + 5, since 2008	Yes	Reduced in 2016[b]	Citymail (only in 2007–2009)
Italy (Poste Italiane)	−25%	41–45%	2.80 EUR	D + 4, since 2015	Yes	Reduced in 2014	E2E competition covering 75% of population
Finland (Posti)	−15%	n/a	1.30 EUR	D + 2	No	Changes proposed in 2016	No[c]
Sweden (PostNord)	−11%	From 50% in 2008[d] to 43% in 2016[e]	0.74 EUR	D + 3	No	Proposed clarifications for exceptions in 2016	Yes, in urban areas (Bring)
Norway (Post Norge)	−14%	n/a	1.40 EUR	D + 2	No	Proposed to relax in 2017	No[c]

Source: Copenhagen Economics based on IPC
[a]Deutsche Post (2017) Letter prices in Europe
[b]The Danish Ministry of Transport (2016), "Agreement concerning the USO 2017-2019 in a liberalized postal market"
[c]ERGP (2014) Report on end-2-end competition
[d]PostNord (2009) Annual report, http://www.postnord.com/globalassets/global/english/document/reports/annual-reports/2009/posten-norden-annual-report-2009.pdf
[e]PostNord (2016) annual report. http://www.postnord.com/contentassets/28039a622d0c4dd0872fc57c7778ecd2/postnord-annual-report.pdf

tandem with public policy decisions, NPOs in these countries may be able to pursue similar strategies as PostNord in Denmark and Poste Italiane in Italy, even if only in a partial way.

2.1 Case Study: Denmark

In 2016, PostNord announced tripling its prices for next day delivery in primo 2016. Following a period of constant prices since the increase in 2011, prices for next day delivery increased from around EUR 1.3 to EUR 3.6 in 2016. Such drastic price increase for next day delivery had a direct impact on further mail volumes development, shifting demand to non-priority letters. Between 2015 and 2016, the priority mail volume dropped to 101 million pieces, corresponding to a decrease of around 50% and almost a tenfold decline in the last 10 years.

Conversely, volumes for non-priority letters have slightly increased during the last 10 years. This is despite an overall decreasing trend in volumes, implying a shift in demand from priority letters following the introduction of the C-letter in 2008 and subsequently price increases for priority mail in 2011 and 2016. Consequently, the share of priority letters has decreased from 81% of total mail volume to 27% during the last 10 years. In 2017, PostNord announced its plans to restructure production process and phase out the separate infrastructure for letters. In other words, by shifting a significant amount of priority mail volume to non-priority, PostNord expects to continue its reduction of operating costs in mail delivery activities.

2.2 Case Study: Italy

In Italy, letter mail volumes have declined more than in Europe on average. For instance, Poste Italiane's priority mail volume declined by 53% in the 2007–2014 period. In response to the overall market trend and end-to-end competition,[4] in 2015 and 2016 Poste Italiane introduced a slow letter mail product in 2015, called Posta4, which is delivered in 4 (90%) to 6 days (98%). They also significantly increased priority letter price from 0.80€ to 2.80€. In 2016, it introduced an alternate-day delivery system where the postman delivers and collects mails on Monday, Wednesday, Friday of 1 week and Tuesday, Thursday the week after. The model is being rolled out in three phases, targeting specific municipalities where the delivery is particularly expensive. The new system should not affect more than 25% of the population. Poste Italiane expects this model to save between 30% and 50% of costs of serving these areas.[5]

[4]In Italy, there are two quasi-national end-to-end competitors, namely, Nexive and Fulmine.

[5]According to what reported in Delibera n. 395/15/CONS, point 23.

2.3 *Case Study: Finland*

In an ongoing review of the Finnish Postal Act, The Ministry of Communications and Transport proposed to reduce delivery frequency to minimum 3 days per week in areas where there are competing delivery networks (morning newspapers) and to keep 5 day delivery in rural areas where this is not the case. In addition, the USP would have the opportunity to subcontract delivery in those areas, in order to ensure that newspapers are delivered 5 days per week.[6] To adapt to changing market conditions, Posti announced a decrease in delivery frequency starting January 2017. It would no longer deliver letters on Tuesdays if all letters on Monday have been delivered in time. Letters sent and stamped on Monday will be delivered on the following Wednesday.

2.4 *Case Study: Sweden*

In 2016, the Swedish Ministry of Enterprise and Innovation (Näringsdepartementet) published a revision of the Postal Services Act in a digital society, in which they make recommendations on changing the USO scope. Following a thorough review of domestic and international developments in the postal sector, the Ministry found that the needs for postal services are no longer compatible with the costs of providing such services. It concluded that the regulatory framework must be as flexible as possible for the postal service to adapt to different needs across user groups.

Further, the Ministry recommended that regulations should allow services in individual cases to be adapted to the overall needs of the users so that these can be met in a cost-effective way. In particular, the Ministry proposed to expand the minimum delivery frequency requirement of the Postal Services Act (2010) to cover exemptions, that is, the requirement of 5-day delivery shall take into account different users' needs.[7] In addition, the Ministry proposed to give the Swedish Post and Telecom Authority the right to issue regulations on when exemptions may be made from 5-day delivery. The Ministry noted that mandatory next day delivery is no longer justified. Instead, the Ministry proposed having a 2 day delivery requirement for basic postal service.

[6]Finnish Ministry of Communications (2016), note on ongoing review of the Finnish Postal Act. Link: https://www.lvm.fi/en/-/requirement-for-competitive-tendering-to-help-guarantee-postal-delivery-five-days-a-week-in-rural-areas-912399

[7]PTS (2016), "The Swedish Postal Services Market 2016", *report from the Swedish Post and Telecom Authority.*

2.5 *Case Study: Norway*

In 2016, Posten Norge has taken measures to reduce delivery costs and has proposed moving away from next day delivery to D + 2 service. One measure has been to cancel Saturday letter deliveries of local newspapers, which was then tendered by the government to a small delivery company. As a result, Posten Norge reported that cancellation of Saturday letter deliveries will lead to a reduction of about 400 full-time equivalents.[8]

Posten Norge also plans to merge priority and non-priority mail into a single mail stream with 2-day delivery. The strategy was, in principle, approved by the Norwegian Parliament in 2016, subject to solving the issues of (i) fast delivery of medicine and (ii) daily delivery of local newspapers to areas at the other end of the country. Posten Norge's ambition is to implement this change during 2017. Currently, Posten Norge's proposal for a single stream mail is subject to discussion in Parliament.

3 Economic Principles Testing the Strategy of Sacrificing Next-Day Delivery

Sacrificing next-day services can at first sight be a counterintuitive strategy, since it cannot solely be explained by key economic principles, which we set out in what follows.

3.1 *Ramsey Pricing*

The first economic concept is Ramsey pricing. It helps us understand pricing in incumbent markets in general and may therefore shed light on the strategy of sacrificing next-day delivery—albeit with some caveats that we will explore. The Ramsey-Boiteux price rule prescribes that it is optimal for a multi-product firm seeking to recover common costs (i.e. second best scenario) to set price-cost margins that reflect the differences in the elasticity of demand for its different services. The usual intuition of Ramsey prices is that higher prices correspond to products for which customers are less price sensitive and vice versa. The economic cost of raising prices is based on the reduction in sales that follow. Putting these together, holding costs constant, price increases for product X should follow when customers of product X become less price elastic, i.e. less price sensitive. Specifically, the Ramsey rule says that price-cost margins—the percentage of price that is

[8]Posten Norge Annual Report 2015, p. 36.

above cost, otherwise known as the Lerner index—should be inversely proportional to the elasticity of demand.[9]

The initial intuition behind Ramsey pricing suggests that significantly raising the price for next-day delivery should reflect a change to lower price sensitivity for these services. However, one may reject this initial intuition if empirical evidence were to show that users of postal services have generally obtained higher elasticity via experiencing a greater range of options (including digital substitutes). It is unclear whether composition effects (a change in demand elasticity due to the migration of former users of postal services to other services) are sufficient to counterbalance the gradual increase in available alternatives to postal services. Therefore price increases in priority mail in these countries need not be explained by a reduction in the price elasticity of demand.

Price increases can also serve as a tool to shift demand from one product to another, but only provided that cross-product elasticities are sufficiently high, i.e. the operator's products are close enough substitutes in the eye of consumers.[10] Slower mail is certainly an alternative to next-day delivery for many users. Thus, a postal operator applying price increases for next-day services is expected to generate a diversion back to another service offered by the operator, i.e. slower mail—although likely not on a one-for-one basis. The more the supplier can benefit from diversion to its other service, the more this provides an incentive for that increase in the first place.

3.2 Multi-product Economies of Scope: E-commerce Packages and Next-Day Mail

The economy of scope that is "traditionally" relevant for next-day letter delivery is that between this service and slower letter mail services, with which it shares several activities (sorting, delivery, acceptance)—even if on a staggered timeframe. The same workers and equipment are used for the provision of both a fast and slow letter, although separate processes and resources are often needed for the next-day letter mail network. This balance of inputs shared by next-day delivery and slower letter services fundamentally defines the economies of scope for this service. The implication is that decreases in volumes supplied of either of the two services will raise the unit cost attributable to each of those services—which, in turn, could alter price incentives.

---

[9] A key caveat is that Ramsey-Boiteux pricing was historically designed for and applied to markets where products are independent. If products are substitute (or complements) the Ramsey pricing implication is that the firm should set price-cost margins that reflect cross-price elasticities. The markup is then proportional to the full set of elasticities, which can be aggregated into "super-elasticities", i.e. a modified Lerner index. See Laffont, J-J. and Tirole, J. (1993), *A Theory of Incentives in Procurement and Regulation*.

[10] Indeed, this intuition is reflected in the modified Lerner index, insofar as the modification accounts for the role of cross-elasticity between the different products and the extent of diversion to competing suppliers.

However, the economic balance between next-day letters and slower letter services is changing. E-commerce is expected to be one of the saviors of the postal market. A share of e-commerce demand requires fast delivery and this can in part be provided via next-day mail delivery (i.e. flats and letterbox-able packages). Consequently, the resources that are specific to next-day letters can now potentially serve a further purpose, i.e. to deliver e-commerce goods that fit the specifications of the mail network. Thus, while some types of parcels require an infrastructure and process with different specifications (i.e. cars/vans instead of bicycles; manual or cell-machine based sorting instead of automated flat/conveyor sorting), the question arises of whether next-day letter mail delivery is a valuable part of the product portfolio in synergy with delivery of next-day e-commerce packages/parcels. The choice of optimal network design and the identification of inputs shared by next-day letter and parcel services (i.e. the level and pattern of economies of scope) can be expected to change as e-commerce traffic and needs evolve.

4 Key Drivers of Migration from Priority to Non-priority Mail

Based on the case study and economic analysis above, recent developments in countries where priority letter prices were significantly increased, were primarily driven by low users' needs for the next day delivery service, significant cost reduction potential due to having less time-critical deliveries, and competition (actual or threatened) in the "slow-end" letter mail market. In the following, we discuss each motivation in more detail. It needs to be noted that in this chapter we are looking at factors consistent with behavior in the selected countries and do not discuss other countries that are not going in this direction.

4.1 First Hypothesis: Demand for Next Day Delivery Service Has Declined Due to Changes in Users' Needs

Based on the cases above, in at least these five countries, the vast majority of users no longer require next day delivery services. This can be explained by the development of electronic means of communication, which is unarguably superior in terms of speed of delivery. This insight is supported by various surveys conducted throughout Europe. Following a review of domestic and international developments in the postal sector, the Swedish the Ministry of Enterprise and Innovation found that mandatory next day delivery was no longer justified.[11] In Denmark, a Voxmeter survey conducted for the Danish Ministry of Transport revealed a very

[11]The Swedish Ministry if Enterprise and Innovation (2016), "A revision of the Postal Act in a digital society".

low demand for next day delivery service.[12] In the ongoing review of the Finnish Postal Act, the Finnish Ministry of Communications and Transport likewise consider loosening the delivery speed regulation following its own assessment of the postal market.[13] However, some segments of users still depend on postal next day delivery services. For instance, a recent users' needs study by ComReg in Ireland have shown that SMEs depend on the next day delivery service.[14]

4.2 Second Hypothesis: Costs of Next Day Delivery Services Have Increased as Economies of Scale and Scope Are Much Lower Than Before

Traditionally, premium products often have higher margins than the basic product, especially in the differentiated product industries like the postal industry. However, due to changes in users' valuation of services discussed above, this may no longer hold for priority letter mail services. In some countries—depending on economies of scale—less expensive non-priority mail services may actually yield higher profit margins.

In practice, postal networks were designed to cater to customers with the most demanding service requirement, i.e. next day delivery. Non-priority services were an add-on to cater to niche client segments. Traditionally the volumes and revenues for next day deliveries were large enough to cover the costs of the network. However, where priority mail volumes and revenues have fallen by a large amount, the cost of having such a network may no longer be justified, as the Swedish government's decision discussed above illustrates.

Economies of scope between priority mail and parcels may change too. Previous studies have provided models showing that joint delivery becomes relatively more important when volumes of letters and parcels are high and balanced.[15] However, one can imagine that when letter volumes decrease and parcel volumes increase, at some point it can be more efficient to deliver letters and parcels separately.

---

[12]CEM Institute (2014), "Analysis of the Danes' usage of postal services", *report for the Danish Ministry of Transport*.

[13]The Finnish Ministry of Communications (2016), note on ongoing review of the Finnish Postal Act.

[14]See ComReg (2016) research on postal users' needs. Link: https://www.comreg.ie/?dlm_download=research-postal-users-needs.

[15]See, for instance, Bender et al. (2016) Economies of scope in delivering parcels and letters together. Link to presentation: http://www.wik.org/uploads/media/AD_2016_05_18_EoScope_Florenz.pdf.

4.2.1 Third Hypothesis: When the First Two Hypotheses Are True, Competition in the Letter Mail Market Is a Catalyst for a NPO to Move from Priority to Non-priority Mail Services

Our third hypothesis is that changes in next day delivery services specifications are also driven by liberalization of the postal markets in Europe and new entries of competitors. Changes in users' needs as well as liberalization of the postal market have opened up new business opportunities for market entrants. In countries with competing alternative postal operators, it is rare to find alternative postal operators offering next day deliveries. Most of them focus on non-priority mail deliveries. This can be explained by the previous two hypotheses: Users may no longer require next day deliveries, so they would chose a cheaper service between the priority and non-priority services. In addition, Existing postal networks embed significant costs that new market entrants can avoid and thus, tap into the margin between market prices (set by the incumbent postal operator) and costs.

New market entries with low cost non-priority mail services may exacerbate the shift from priority services to non-priority services. If such development is significant (or the mere threat of such possibility) it will incentivize an incumbent postal operator to respond.[16] Consequently, in an extreme situation, such adaptation may lead to sacrificing the next day delivery and focusing on non-priority mail services, see Fig. 1 below.

However, competition in the postal market does not necessarily lead to reductions in delivery speeds. For instance, in the Netherlands, where end-to-end competition in postal services is one of the strongest in Europe, next day deliveries comprise a significant share of total letter volumes delivered. We understand that postal users in the Netherlands value faster delivery options (i.e. our first hypothesis is not satisfied), since they are not substituting to cheaper alternatives provided by PostNL and alternative operators (The Ministry of Economic Affairs in The Netherlands (2014), The Dutch Postal Market and the Postal Directive).

5 Implications for NPOs and Policy Makers

5.1 Implications for National Postal Operators

In practice, the next day delivery strategy is about significantly increasing next day delivery prices to (gradually) shift postal users' demand from expensive (and costly) priority letter products to non-priority products. Having less time critical deliveries allows for cost cuts in delivery as they provide the postal operator with more flexibility to optimize sorting and delivery routes.

[16]Equally, in a scenario where competitors were to target rapid mail delivery (provided that users' had high valuation for this service), this may force an equivalent reaction from the NPO, with a focus on rapid delivery.

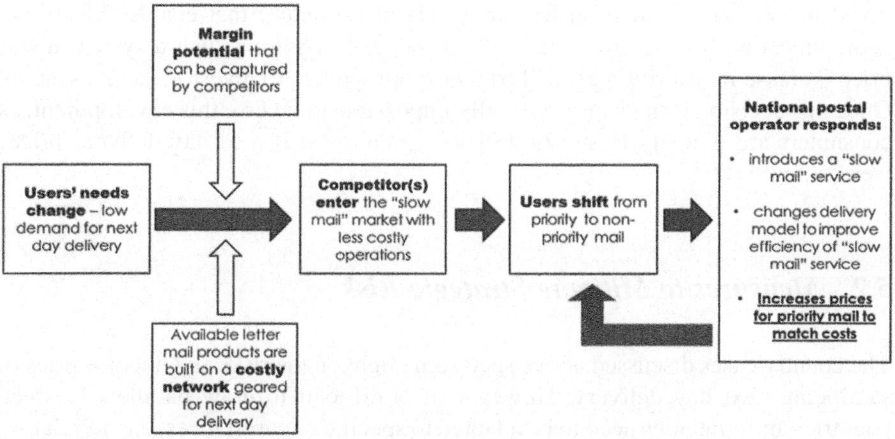

Fig. 1 Competition drives changes in priority mail market

In addition, postal operators may find it profitable to tap into the willingness to pay for next-day delivery of some users, e.g. small individual consignments and e-commerce lightweight shipments. Although large clients require less time-critical mail deliveries, there are still some client segments that are willing to pay more for such services and currently benefit from low prices. Their typical alternative to priority mail service is express delivery service, which is substantially more expensive. Increasing prices of priority mail service to such customers may thus increase revenues for NPOs. Such strategy is about limiting damages caused by e-substitution. The company may still end up being unprofitable in the letter mail business (as is the case in Denmark and Italy).

In some markets, extreme changes to priority mail services may entail high risks. A strategy to sacrifice next-day can only succeed if buyers have options and the strategy is compatible with the incentives of (most) senders. Simply establishing a slower product cannot succeed if its price is comparable to that of the faster service (since buyers would likely stick with the faster). Senders require a price incentive to migrate from priority to non-priority mail service, which can be achieved either via discounts or via price increases. Both options are costly to the company. Discounts to non-priority services will reduce revenue from letter services. Drastic price increases may harm reputation of the postal operator for consumers, business mailers and policy makers. We have seen in the analyzed cases that reputational harm can extend beyond mere dissatisfaction with prices, but also to overall fulfilment of service requirements (even though all requirements are met).

Moreover, drastic cost cuts and changes to delivery may lead to revenue losses from other services that cannot be fulfilled with the new delivery model, e.g. delivery of newspapers, parcels. Raising prices may trigger investments in e-substitution by consumers. That is, the decision for a large sender to take the step from mail to an electronic alternative is a cost-benefit analysis that trade-off the cost saved in the longer run from having an IT-infrastructure that enables electronic communication (of e.g. invoices) against the cost of setting such a system up. A price increase in priority mail will trigger more senders to invest in such a system. Once this decision is made, it is virtually impossible to reverse this development, as consumers are unlikely to substitute back again, even if next day delivery prices were to fall back.

5.2 Measures to Mitigate Strategic Risk

The country cases discussed above shed some light on the risks and opportunities of sacrificing next day delivery. However, it is difficult to draw parallels between countries and strategies need to be adapted to specific circumstances, e.g. regulatory framework, users' needs, competitive landscape, elasticities (cross-product as well as to e-substitution), and postal operator's strategy.

To minimize the abovementioned risks, based on the above analysis, we have identified three recommendations to postal operators that are considering the sacrifice of next day delivery. The purpose of these recommendations is not to answer whether such strategy should be implemented in a specific country, but rather to guide through an important set of challenges pertaining to this particular change:

First, *examine users' needs*. What part of the demand will accept a significantly larger price for next day letter services? What share of the demand will switch to slower speed products or leave the NPO, perhaps turning to electronic substitutes? To answer these questions, one possible source of information would be a users' needs survey, which may include analysis of users' willingness to pay and cross-product elasticities between priority, non-priority, and digital services.

Second, *examine cost savings potential*. Lower volumes of next day letter services may allow NPOs to restructure and rationalize their costs, but reaching a balance between potential cost savings and potential lost revenue may be challenging. Particularly, the largest economic potential is in optimized capacities and delivery routes. For instance, as tested in Denmark, next day letter services can be delivered via express delivery, while the general postal network can be geared to non-priority services.

However, the cost saving potential may vary among countries. Each network has its own economies of scale. If there are fewer next day delivery letters and some competition from other carriers (e.g. express), it might explain why the margin of next day delivery has become smaller than the margin of nonpriority mail (D + 3 and slower). In addition, geographical conditions also play a role such that in densely populated countries with relatively easy access to all households making next day deliveries may have lower costs than in mountainous, scarcely populated areas.

In addition, each network has its own economies of scope. Postal networks are typically utilized by a number of services. To reduce costs, postal operators may be required to change the operational model of other services. Would unaddressed mail delivery fit the new model? How would daily newspapers be handled? Are there any synergies between parcels and priority letters delivery were the mail network to be geared for D + 3,4,5 letters delivery only? Operational changes might not accommodate all services and thus some revenues may be lost.

Third, *manage regulatory risk*. Some of the USPs' changes to next day letter services may test the boundaries of the national postal legislation as well as of the Postal Directive. For instance, one of the apparent regulatory constraints is price caps, i.e. the affordability criterion. Will the national regulatory authorities allow pricing flexibility when multiple studies[17] in a number of countries show that users do not require next day letter services?

In addition, the number of delivery days is another important constraint for USPs to reduce their costs. Some countries' postal acts mandate network access for next day deliveries. This may constrain an NPO's ability to change their D + 1 specification without a change in its national government's law. Given the political sensitivity of USO provision, USPs may find it easier to start with strategies that do not interfere with the boundaries of postal regulations.

5.3 *Policy and Regulatory Implications*

Many of the developments discussed in this chapter were not possible to implement without changes in the policies governing national postal operators. These had to allow increased flexibility of price regulation enabling stronger price differentiation—necessary to induce the desired volume shift from priority to non-priority letter mail services (cf. DK, IT). The governments also had to be willing to decrease USO requirements (e.g., delivery days, geographical scope) according to user needs, necessary to further reduce cost of the postal network (cf. DK, FI, IT, SE).

In the examples analyzed, it is clear that policy makers considered the challenges that postal operators faced. In fact, the drivers forcing postal operators from the next-day delivery market are also relevant for policymaking: users' needs, efficiency, and sustainability of the USO. However, some users that previously benefited from cheap next day deliveries, such as daily newspapers, could be disadvantaged in a new system.

Finally, competition, insofar as it is a catalyst for the demise of next day services as we have come to know them, is a reminder to policymakers of the law of unintended consequences. National and European legislators, if truly committed to the virtue of competition, should also accept that competitive dynamics can lead

[17]The Swedish Ministry if Enterprise and Innovation (2016), "A revision of the Postal Act in a digital society"; CEM Institute (2014), "Analysis of the Danes' usage of postal services", *report for the Danish Ministry of Transport;* The Finnish Ministry of Communications (2016), note on ongoing review of the Finnish Postal Act.

to a change in service standards and product specifications. Incumbents and entrants follow evolving customer preferences (mail senders' and, indirectly, recipients') and catch up with each other in devising strategies that can serve evolving user needs in the most efficient way. This is what we expect of a market subject to competitive pressure, whether from inside or from outside the market.

If policymakers are comfortable with competition, then they should also embrace the dynamics it brings to services. In the case of next-day delivery, this may imply fundamental changes. In order to predict what may happen in each country, we recommend monitoring the key trade-offs identified in this chapter and ultimately understanding how USPs attempt to maximize profits in light of the economies of scale and scope in their networks through evolutionary or radically new business models.

6 Conclusion

This chapter investigates the recent strategies by some NPOs to raise dramatically the price of priority mail services. We note, however, that it can be risky for one NPO to copy the strategies of another. We find that the most plausible explanation for the strategy of raising dramatically the priority mail price includes three factors.

First is changing user needs, with lower demand for next-day letter delivery, a relatively more stable demand for slower mail services, and an increase in parcel demand.

A second factor is the increased cost for next-day delivery due to lower economies of scale and scope.

Third, actual or potential competition in the non-priority letter segment is also part of the explanation—as a catalyst for changes in postal services strategies.

Finally, we acknowledge that the benefits of such strategies may only come under a given regulatory environment. This is because a significant increase in prices of priority mail requires flexible price regulation that permits it. Furthermore, the cost-saving potential may depend on a reduction in the USO requirements (e.g., delivery days, geographical scope). This highlights the ongoing need for policy makers to make a comprehensive review of the rationale for the USO specification. This may be an opportunity but also a challenge for NPOs, insofar as postal policies are not viewed in isolation and the principle of technology neutrality is considered in the provision of services of general economic interest.[18]

[18]Fabra et al. (2014, pp. 40–41) argued that "The European Commission should initiate a discussion on whether USO is still meaningful in mail alone, as there are alternative technologies that allow communications to benefit also more remote areas. The Commission should therefore consider a comprehensive redefinition of the USO concept, towards a more general 'right to communicate'".

References

Bender et al. (2016) Economies of scope in delivering parcels and letters together. Link to presentation: http://www.wik.org/uploads/media/AD_2016_05_18_EoScope_Florenz.pdf.

Cape, Steven & Groves, Philip (2017), Changes to the Universal Service: Influencing Factors, Impacts and Regulatory Implications. In: Crew and Brennan (Eds.) The Changing Postal and Delivery Sector

CEM Institute (2014), Analysis of the Danes' usage of postal services, *report for the Danish Ministry of Transport*

ComReg (2016), Research on postal users' needs

Fabra, N., Çarouche, P., Peitz, M., Valletti T., Waddams, C., and Liebhaberg, B. (2014), Network industries: efficient regulation, affordable and adequate service, CERRE dossier for the European Commission (2014–2018)

Laffont, J-J. and Tirole, J. (1993), *A Theory of Incentives in Procurement and Regulation*

PostNL (2017), European Postal Markets – an overview

PTS (2016), The Swedish Postal Services Market 2016, *report for the Swedish Post and Telecom Authority*

The Finnish Ministry of Communications (2016) Note on ongoing review of the Finnish Postal Act

The Ministry of Economic Affairs in The Netherlands (2014), The Dutch Postal Market and the Postal Directive

The Swedish Ministry if Enterprise and Innovation (2016), A revision of the Postal Act in a digital society

The Swedish Postal Services Act (2010) Chap. 3, Sec. 1

WIK (2016), Future scenario developments in the Dutch Postal Markets

The Pricing of Cross-Border Parcel Delivery Services

Claire Borsenberger, Lisa Chever, Helmuth Cremer, Denis Joram, and Jean-Marie Lozachmeur

1 Introduction

The role of parcel delivery services in cross-border e-commerce is a hotly debated topic within the EU and beyond. While volumes of domestic e-commerce have increased dramatically over the last years in all member States, cross-border purchases remain lower, even though the latest figures released by E-commerce Europe (2016) showed an acceleration of cross-border transactions. This can be explained by a variety of factors including language and cultural barriers and bureaucratic obstacles (in particular the complexity of VAT regimes—see E-commerce Europe last cross-border barometer) but also simply by the fact that

We thank all the conference participants, and in particular our discussants Anna Möller Boivie and Leonardo Mautino for their insightful remarks. Thanks also to Tim Brennan and Pier Luigi Pacu for their detailed comments and suggestions.

C. Borsenberger
Doctrine et Modélisation, Direction of Regulation and Institutional and European Affairs, Groupe La Poste, Paris, France

University François Rabelais, Tours, France

L. Chever
Regulation and Institutional and European Affairs Division, Groupe La Poste, Paris, France

H. Cremer (✉)
Toulouse School of Economics (IDEI), University of Toulouse Capitole, Toulouse, France
e-mail: helmuth.cremer@tse-fr.eu

D. Joram
Regulation and Studies Department, Direction of Regulation and Institutional and European Affairs, Groupe La Poste, Paris, France

J.-M. Lozachmeur
Toulouse School of Economics (IDEI, CNRS), Toulouse, France

P.L. Parcu et al. (eds.), *The Contribution of the Postal and Delivery Sector*, Topics in Regulatory Economics and Policy, https://doi.org/10.1007/978-3-319-70672-6_16

goods are available on the domestic market without any significant price differential. The EU Commission has recently launched a proposal that focuses on parcel delivery services and particularly their pricing as an alleged major impediment for the development of cross-border e-commerce (European Commission 2016).

To enlighten this debate it is essential to clarify its underlying economic foundations. So far the economics literature has paid little or no attention to cross-border delivery markets. While similar issues arise in other sectors, parcel delivery services present many characteristics that render models borrowed from, say, telecommunications, of little relevance.[1]

We take a first but crucial step towards filling this gap. We develop in Sect. 2 a simple model of cross-border e-commerce and delivery services. That model allows us to determine the optimal (efficient) pricing structure. This is a crucial benchmark to assess the observed pricing structure as well as potential reforms. We also study different competitive scenarios in order to identify potential market failures. Finally, we use our setting to study the impact of considered regulatory measures.

We consider a two-country setting. In each country customers may patronize a domestic e-retailer or the one located in the other country. To keep the model manageable, we assume there is a single parcel delivery operator in each country who delivers both domestic and cross-border parcels.[2] Specifically, the retailer in country B who sends a parcel to a customer in country A pays the international rate charged by the delivery operator in country B. This operator processes the parcel within its territory, while processing and delivery in the destination country is then carried out by A's parcel delivery operator against a payment from the first-mile operator set in a negotiated agreement. We use the term "terminal dues" to refer to these rates paid by postal operators for last-mile handling of cross-border parcels. Each of these steps, including the transition from B to A's network involves a specific (marginal) cost. Operators also have to cover a fixed cost to manage a regular delivery network. The relevant prices are the domestic and international (end to end) rates charged by both operators. They contribute to the cost of the e-retailers which ultimately affects the price charged to the final customers.

We first determine, in Sect. 3, the "global Ramsey" solution that is the pricing structure of domestic and cross-border parcel delivery services which maximizes total surplus in both countries subject to the parcel delivery operator's break-even

---

[1]The domestic parcel delivery market and its integration into the e-commerce value chain has received some attention in the recent literature; see for example, Borsenberger et al. (2015), (2016a, b). Another part of the postal economic literature was dedicated to the study of terminal dues, the amount posts pay to compensate one another for international deliveries (see among others, Copenhagen Economics 2014; OIG 2015). For a survey of economic literature on telecommunications regulatory issues including international roaming, see for example Vogelsang (2013).

[2]This is clearly a simplifying assumption: in the majority of European Member States, several parcel service providers are competing to handle domestic and cross-border items. Competition is however, not absent from our model: the two national operators are competing with each other and they also face "competition" from their customers who may use "direct injection".

constraints. To keep the problem tractable we assume that e-retailers set their prices at marginal cost (including delivery charges). Again, this is a simplifying assumption: in the real world, e-retailers could make a positive margin on the delivery services they resell to e-consumers. In Sect. 4, we consider the competitive equilibrium.

Throughout the paper, we assume that e-retailers selling to the other country's customers may both deal with their domestic operator or use direct injection, that is transport the shipments across the border as freight by their own means, before they are injected into the domestic delivery network in the destination country.[3] They then pay either the domestic rate or a specific price charged by the delivery operator in the destination country (instead of the generally more expensive international rate set by the domestic operator).

In this framework, we deal with the issue of which rate should be charged by the operator in the destination country to a e-retailer using direct injection. In particular, should this retailer pay the same terminal dues as the delivery operator?[4] The EU has been considering imposing such a regulation and our model is meant to assess this policy. We calibrate this theoretical model in Sect. 5. Section 6 concludes.

2 Model

2.1 Goods, Customers and Retailers

2.1.1 Retailers

There are two countries indexed by superscript $i = A, B$. In each country there is a representative retailer R^i; R^A sells a good x and R^B good y. Both goods are produced at constant marginal costs denoted c^A and c^B. There is one incumbent postal (delivery) operator I^i in each country. Retailers can "bypass" their domestic operator to deliver their goods abroad by using direct injection. In that case they ship part of their exports directly to the delivery operator in the destination country. Denote by b_x, the endogeneous share of x^B that retailer A directly injects into operator I^B's delivery network and by b_y the endogeneous share of y^A directly injected by retailer B into I^A's delivery network, where b_x, $b_y \in [0, 1]$.

[3]Direct injection is a common business practice used by "big" retailers. For example, in France, this solution is used by Vente privée. For a description of e-retailer's process for cross-border direct injection, see Copenhagen Economics (2016), page 25.

[4]Here, we do not question the relevance of the UPU or European terminal dues systems. To go further on this topic, see among others, Campbell et al. (2011), Geradin (2012), Haller et al. (2013), Sorensen (2014), Okholm et al. (2016), Campbell (2014, 2016).

Retailers face the following delivery rates:

• t_x^A per unit of x^A (domestic demand, D_x^A), t_x^B per unit of $(1-b_x)x^B$ (non bypassed foreign demand, $(1-b_x)D_x^B$) and t_d^B per unit of $b_x x^B$ (bypassed foreign demand $b_x D_x^B$).

• t_y^A per unit of $(1-b_y)y^A$ (not directly injected foreign demand, $(1-b_y)D_y^A$), t_y^B per unit of y^B (domestic demand, D_y^B) and t_d^A per unit of $b_y y^A$ (directly injected foreign demand $b_x D_x^B$).

The total shipping costs incurred by retailer A for x^B is given by

$$Z^A(D_x^B) = t_x^B(1-b_x)D_x^B + t_d^B b_x D_x^B + z(b_x D_x^B),$$

where $z(x) = (\varsigma/2)(x)^2$ is the cost of the direct injection technology as a function of the injected volume x, while t_d^B is the delivery rate charged by the operator in the destination country. We assume that the cost of the direct injection technology increases at an increasing pace with volumes. As volume increases, e-retailer must draw on more and more expensive means to carry parcels to the delivery operator's warehouse in the destination country. Note that a volume of $(1-b_x)x^B$ is processed by operator I^A at the rate t_x^B. Recall that this is an end to end rate which includes delivery by the operator in the destination country. Symmetrically, one has

$$Z^B\left(D_y^A\right) = t_y^A(1-b_y)D_y^A + t_d^A b_y D_y^A + z\left(b_y D_y^A\right).$$

While the operator in the origin country is effectively "bypassed", direct injection is different from bypass as considered in the access pricing literature. Specifically, delivery in the destination country is *not* bypassed here.

Retailers' A and B profits are given by

$$\pi^A = (p_x^A - t_x^A)D_x^A + p_x^B D_x^B - c^A(D_x^A + D_x^B) - Z^A(D_x^B), \tag{1}$$

$$\pi^B = p_y^A D_y^A + \left(p_y^B - t_y^B\right)D_y^B - c^B\left(D_y^A + D_y^B\right) - Z^B\left(D_y^A\right). \tag{2}$$

2.1.2 Customers

There are N_i consumers in country i, whose utility (surplus) is given by

$$u^i(x,y) = S^i(x,y) - p_x^i x - p_y^i y.$$

While goods x and y are imperfect substitutes in our general specification, our subsequent arguments will for simplicity concentrate on the case where $\partial S^i(x,y)/\partial x \partial y = 0$, so that demands are independent. The prices faced by consumers may differ according to their country of residence.

2.1.3 The Delivery Sector

Each operator has its domestic network, which is given. There are two activities: delivery within their own county, d, and t a composite activity including sorting and collection of parcels in their domestic country; we refer to this as processing. We separately identify these costs to justify cross-border costs differences in the domestic delivery that one might not observe with direct injection. The marginal cost to handle domestic mail is $k^i = k_t^i + k_d^i, i = A, B$; it applies to good x shipped to customers in country A and good y shipped to country B.

The marginal cost of processing cross-border exchanges, that is good y in country A's network and good x in country B's network is k. In other words, k is the cost of processing a parcel which emanates from the other country. It is incurred by the operator in the origin country. This cost of processing cross-border exchanges is different from the domestic marginal cost of the upstream (before delivery) processing activity t (k_t). In particular, the sorting process of cross-border items is less advanced than that of domestic parcels.

Delivery cost is the same as for domestic parcels. Terminal dues applied for delivering parcel emanating from the operator in the other country are denoted a^A and a^B. To stick with current industry practice, we assume that postal operators set terminal dues as a percentage of domestic rates, in a negotiated way:

$$a^A = \alpha t_x^A, \tag{3}$$

$$a^B = \alpha t_y^B. \tag{4}$$

The profits of delivery operators are given by

$$\begin{aligned}\Pi^A = {} & (t_x^A - k^A)D_x^A + (t_x^B - a^B - k)(1 - b_x)D_x^B \\ & + (a^A - k_d^A)(1 - b_y)D_y^A + (t_d^A - k_d^A)b_yD_y^A - F^A,\end{aligned} \tag{5}$$

$$\begin{aligned}\Pi^B = {} & \left(t_y^B - k^B\right)D_y^B + \left(t_y^A - a^A - k\right)(1 - b_y)D_y^A \\ & + (a^B - k_d^B)(1 - b_x)D_x^B + (t_d^B - k_d^B)b_xD_x^B - F^B,\end{aligned} \tag{6}$$

where F^A and F^B are the fixed costs.

2.2 *Demands, Retailers' Prices and Direct Injections*

The timing of the game is as follow. In stage 1, postal operator I^A sets the rates t_x^A, t_x^B and t_d^A and operator I^B sets t_y^B, t_y^A and t_d^B in order to maximize their respective profits. In stage 2, the retailers R^i are price takers and choose their level of production x^i and y^i together with the rate of direct injection b_x (for retailer A) and b_y (for retailer B). In stage 3, demand is realized. As usual, we solve the model backward. The next sections consider successively stage 3 to stage 1.

2.2.1 The Demand Levels

Customers in country i choose their levels of domestic and foreign consumptions so as to maximize their utility. The problem is thus to solve:

$$\max_{x,y} u^i(x,y) = S^i(x,y) - p_x^i x - p_y^i y.$$

The first-order conditions with respect to x and y are respectively

$$\frac{\partial S^i(x,y)}{\partial x} = p_x^i, \tag{7}$$

$$\frac{\partial S^i(x,y)}{\partial y} = p_y^i, \tag{8}$$

for $i = A, B$. These equations implicitly define the individual demands for the two goods in country A: $x^A \equiv x^A(p_x^A)$ for the domestic good and $y^A \equiv y^A\left(p_y^A\right)$ for the foreign good. Similarly in country B we have $x^B \equiv x^B(p_x^B)$ and $y^B \equiv y^B\left(p_y^B\right)$. Let ε_x^i and ε_y^i denote the elasticities of x and y with respect to their prices p_x^i and p_y^i.

2.2.2 Retailer's Prices and Direct Injection

Assume that retailers are price-takers. Retailer R^A solves:

$$\max_{p_x^A, p_x^B, b_x} \pi^A = (p_x^A - t_x^A)D_x^A + p_x^B D_x^B - c^A(D_x^A + D_x^B) - Z^A(D_x^B),$$

where $D_x^A = N^A x^A(p_x^A)$ and $D_x^B = N^B x^B(p_x^B)$

while R^B's problem is

$$\max_{p_y^A, p_y^B, b_y} \pi^B = p_y^A D_y^A + \left(p_y^B - t_y^B\right)D_y^B - c^A\left(D_y^A + D_y^B\right) - Z^B\left(D_y^A\right).$$

This implies that prices are respectively:

$$p_x^A = t_x^A + c^A, \tag{9}$$

$$p_x^B = t_x^B + c^A, \tag{10}$$

$$p_y^B = t_y^B + c^B, \tag{11}$$

$$p_y^A = t_y^A + c^B. \tag{12}$$

In words, consumer prices are equal to marginal costs (marginal cost of production plus delivery). The direct injection rates b_x and b_y are implicitly given by:

$$\left(t_x^B - t_d^B\right) - z'\left(N^B b_x x^B\right) = 0, \tag{13}$$

$$\left(t_y^A - t_d^A\right) - z'\left(N^A b_y y^A\right) = 0. \tag{14}$$

The volume of directly injected share of x^B by retailer R^A is determined by equalizing the benefits (rate savings) of exporting the good by the retailers' own means $\Delta t^B = t_x^B - t_d^B$ and its corresponding marginal cost $z'(N^B b_x x^B)$. A similar relationship holds for R^B. With the quadratic formulation of z, this simply yields:

$$N^B b_x x^B = \frac{\Delta t^B}{\varsigma},$$

$$N^A b_y y^A = \frac{\Delta t^A}{\varsigma}.$$

Because of our quadratic cost assumption, we can find a closed form solution for the elasticity of injected volumes with respect to the opportunity benefit of export through direct injection, which is

$$\varepsilon_{b_y y^A} = \frac{\partial\left(N^A b_y y^A\right)}{\partial \Delta t^A} \frac{\Delta t^A}{N^A b_y y^A} = 1,$$

$$\varepsilon_{b_x x^B} = \frac{\partial\left(N^B b_x x^B\right)}{\partial \Delta t^B} \frac{\Delta t^B}{N^B b_x x^B} = 1,$$

so that a 1% increase in t^i increases the volume of direct injection by 1%. Retailers' profits are then given by:

$$\pi^A = N^B b_x x^B \left(t_x^B - t_d^B\right) - z\left(N^B b_x x^B\right) = \frac{1}{2\varsigma}\left(\Delta t^B\right)^2,$$

and

$$\pi^B = N^A b_y x^A \left(t_y^A - t_d^A\right) - z\left(N^A b_y y^A\right) = \frac{1}{2\varsigma}\left(\Delta t^A\right)^2.$$

Retailers realize a positive profit which is equal to the cost savings brought about by direct injection. Since only part of the total foreign demand is shipped via direct injection, marginal costs are determined by their domestic operator's international rates.

3 Ramsey Solutions

3.1 Negotiated Agreement on Terminal Dues Between Postal Operators

In the remainder of the chapter, we assume that the parameter α defining terminal dues is exogenous and determined by an agreement (such as the REIMS/IRAE agreement) which has previously been freely negotiated by postal operators. We start by studying the Ramsey solution that is the rate structure which maximizes total welfare subject to the delivery operators' break even constraints. This outcome would emerge either when rates are regulated by some supra-national authorities or when all rates are set by domestic regulators which cooperate, but face separate budget constraints. The problem is to maximize welfare represented by

$$W = N^A\left\{S^A[x^A, y^A] - p_x^A x^A - p_y^A y^A\right\} + N^B\left\{S^B[x^B, y^B] - p_x^B x^B - p_y^B y^B\right\} \\ +\pi^A + \pi^B + \Pi^A + \Pi^B, \tag{15}$$

which is maximized subject to

$$\Pi^A = 0, \tag{16}$$

$$\Pi^B = 0, \tag{17}$$

with respect to $t_x^A, t_x^B, t_y^A, t_y^B, t_d^A, t_d^B$, anticipating the induced prices, access fees, levels of demand and direct injection. When the two countries are symmetric, the Lagrange multipliers associated with the zero profit conditions (16 and 17) are equal to λ so that the problem of the regulator can be reformulated as

$$\max_{t_x^A, t_x^B, t_y^A, t_y^B, t_d^A, t_d^B} \mathcal{L} = N^A\left\{S^A[x^A, y^A] - p_x^A x^A - p_y^A y^A\right\} \\ + N^B\left\{S^B[x^B, y^A] - p_x^B x^B - p_y^B y^B\right\} + \pi^A + \pi^B \\ + \Pi^A + \Pi^B + \lambda(\Pi^A + \Pi^B). \tag{18}$$

For future reference note that

$$\Pi^A + \Pi^B \\ = N^A(t_x^A - k^A)x^A + N^B x^B(t_x^B - k_d^B - k) - N^B b_x x^B(\Delta t^B - k) - F^A \\ + N^B\left(t_y^B - k^B\right)y^B + N^A y^A\left(t_y^A - k_d^A - k\right) - N^A b_y y^A(\Delta t^A - k) - F^B \tag{19}$$

which does not depend on $a^i, i = A, B$ because in a Ramsey setting terminal dues do not affect consumer prices. Moreover, the total markup realized on exported goods, such as x^B, is equal to the sum of the exporting operator's revenues, net of the delivery cost *in the destination country* $(1 - b_x)\left(t_x^B - k_d^B - k\right)$ and the profit of the importing delivery operator $b_x\left(t_d^B - k_d^B\right)$ from direct injection. The total markup on

x^B is thus given by $(t_x^B - k_d^B - k) - b_x(\Delta t^B - k)$. In other words, the total markup is the one that would be realized without direct injection, minus the foregone net revenue because of direct injection.

Total profits (including the ones of retailers) are given by:

$$\begin{aligned}\Pi^A + \Pi^B + \pi^A + \pi^B \\ &= N^A(t_x^A - k^A)x^A + N^Bx^B(t_x^B - k_d^B - k) + N^Bx^Bb_xk - z(N^Bb_xx^B) - F^A \\ &+ N^B\left(t_y^B - k^B\right)y^B + N^Ay^A\left(t_y^A - k_d^A - k\right) + N^Ay^Ab_yk - z(N^Ab_yy^A) - F^B.\end{aligned} \tag{20}$$

In other words, the total surplus of the retailers and the postal operators is given by the postal operators' profits without direct injection plus the net opportunity gain of direct injection due to lower shipping cost. Since the volumes of direct injection $N^Bb_xx^B$ and $N^Ab_yy^A$ depend solely on the opportunity gain Δt^B and Δt^A, the problem of the regulator in (18) is given by

$$\begin{aligned}\max_{t_x^A,\, t_x^B,\, t_y^A,\, t_y^B,\, \Delta t^B,\, \Delta t^A} \mathcal{L} = & N^A\left\{S^A[x^A, y^A] - p_x^Ax^A - p_y^Ay^A\right\} \\ & + N^B\left\{S^B[x^B, y^A] - p_x^Bx^B - p_y^By^B\right\} \ + N^A(t_x^A - k^A)x^A \\ & + N^Bx^B(t_x^B - k_d^B - k) + N^Bx^Bb_xk - z(N^Bb_xx^B) \\ & - F^A \ + N^B\left(t_y^B - k^B\right)y^B + N^Ay^A\left(t_y^A - k_d^A - k\right) \\ & + N^Ay^Ab_yk - z(N^Ab_yy^A) - F^B \\ & + \lambda\Big[N^A(t_x^A - k^A)x^A + N^Bx^B(t_x^B - k_d^B - k) \\ & - N^Bb_xx^B(\Delta t^B - k) - F^A + N^B\left(t_y^B - k^B\right)y^B \\ & + N^Ay^A\left(t_y^A - k_d^A - k\right) - N^Ab_yy^A(\Delta t^A - k) - F^B\Big]\end{aligned} \tag{21}$$

The optimal Ramsey delivery rates are given by:

$$\frac{t_x^A - k^A}{t_x^A} = \frac{1}{|\varepsilon_x^A|}\frac{\lambda}{1+\lambda}, \tag{22}$$

$$\frac{t_x^B - k_d^B - k}{t_x^B} = \frac{1}{|\varepsilon_x^B|}\frac{\lambda}{1+\lambda}, \tag{23}$$

$$\Delta t^A - k = \frac{\lambda}{(1+\lambda)}, \tag{24}$$

$$\frac{t_y^A - k_d^A - k}{t_y^A} = \frac{1}{|\varepsilon_y^A|}\frac{\lambda}{1+\lambda} \tag{25}$$

$$\frac{t_y^B - k^B}{t_y^B} = \frac{1}{|\varepsilon_y^B|}\frac{\lambda}{1+\lambda}, \tag{26}$$

$$\Delta t^B - k = \frac{\lambda}{(1+\lambda)} \tag{27}$$

These are traditional Ramsey expressions. The numerator in the LHS of these equations measures the markup of the delivery rate over the relevant marginal cost. The relevant delivery rate for direct injection is the opportunity benefit of direct injection as measured by Δt^A net of the crossborder shipping cost k. The expressions show that we have for instance $\Delta t^B \geq k$ i.e. $t_x^B > t_d^B$ so that the level of direct injection is always strictly positive (and does not depend on ς). This result is due to the quadratic cost or more specifically, the property that the marginal cost of bypassing is zero when the volume is zero. When that is true, it is efficient to have some direct injection; the cost savings for the retailer outweigh the (social cost of) the profit loss of the operator, which is always the case.

3.2 *Negotiated Agreement on Terminal Dues Between Postal Operators Extended to Direct Injection Fees Paid by E-retailers*

Assume now that the rate charged for direct injection is required by a third party to be equal to the terminal dues (in other words, e-retailers have access to terminal dues agreement negotiated by postal operators).[5] Such a regulation has indeed been considered in the policy debate within the EU. Analytically, this amounts setting $a^A = t_d^A = \alpha t_x^A$ and $a^B = t_d^B = \alpha t_y^B$. We show in Appendix 2 that

$$\frac{\left(t_x^A - k^A\right)}{t_x^A} = \frac{1}{\left|\varepsilon_x^A\right|}\left[\frac{\lambda\left(1+\alpha\frac{b_y y^A}{x^A}\right)}{(1+\lambda)} + \alpha\frac{b_y y^A}{x^A}\left(\Delta t^A - k\right)\right], \tag{28}$$

$$\frac{\left(t_x^B - k^B\right)}{t_x^B} = \frac{1}{\left|\varepsilon_x^B\right|}\left[\frac{\lambda(1-b_x)}{(1+\lambda)} - b_x\left(\Delta t^B - k\right)\right], \tag{29}$$

$$\frac{\left(t_y^B - k^B\right)}{t_y^B} = \frac{1}{\left|\varepsilon_y^B\right|}\left[\frac{\lambda\left(1+\alpha\frac{b_x x^B}{y^B}\right)}{(1+\lambda)} + \alpha\frac{b_x x^B}{y^B}\left(\Delta t^B - k\right)\right], \tag{30}$$

$$\frac{\left(t_y^A - k^A\right)}{t_y^A} = \frac{1}{\left|\varepsilon_y^A\right|}\left[\frac{\lambda(1-b_y)}{(1+\lambda)} - b_y\left(\Delta t^A - k\right)\right]. \tag{31}$$

[5]The optimal direct injection tariff is higher than the access fee if and only if:

$$\left(k - (1-\alpha)k^A\right) > \frac{\lambda}{(1+\lambda)}\left(1 + \frac{t_x^A}{\varepsilon_x^A}\right)$$

The markup on domestic delivery is now higher than the one without regulation of direct injection. An increase in the domestic rate now decreases the opportunity cost of direct injection Δt^A by a proportion α. This has a direct positive impact on postal operators' and retailers' profits, and it increases the share of direct injection, which in turn increases social welfare by an amount proportional to the cost saving of direct injection $\Delta t^A - k$.[6] Note that these two additional effects increase with the share of injected volumes in total domestic delivery.

Conversely, the optimal markup on export rates is lower when direct injection is regulated. Unlike in the case of domestic delivery, an increase in export rates increases the opportunity cost of direct injection so that the argument just discussed is reversed and pleads in favor of a lower markup.

4 Competitive Solutions

We consider two different scenarios according to the degree of regulation that is involved. In the first setting, negotiated terminal dues given by Eq. (3) and (Campbell James et al. 2011) apply to postal operators only. In the second setting, we consider the competitive solution when the negociated agreement are available to e-retailers: $a^A = t_d^A = \alpha t_x^A$ and $a^B = t_d^B = \alpha t_y^B$.

4.1 Negotiated Agreement on Terminal Dues Between Postal Operators

The problem is given by

$$\max_{t_x^A, t_x^B, t_d^A} \Pi^A = N^A (t_x^A - k^A) x^A + N^B (t_x^B - a^B - k)(1 - b_x) x^B$$
$$+ N^A (1 - b_y)(a^A - k_d^A) y^A + N^A b_y (t_d^A - k_d^A) y^A - F^A,$$
$$\text{s.t.} a^A = \alpha t_x^A,$$

which yields

$$\frac{(t_x^A - k^A)}{t_x^A} = \frac{1 + \frac{\alpha(1-b_y)y^A}{x^A}}{|\varepsilon_x^A|}, \tag{32}$$

[6]Retailers' profits increase with the share of direct injection. Delivery rates are passed on to consumers but direct injection does not affect marginal cost and thus not the consumer price.

$$\frac{\left(t_x^B - a^B - k\right)}{t_x^B} = \frac{1}{\left|\varepsilon_{(1-b_x)x^B}\right|}, \tag{33}$$

$$t_d^A - a^A = 1, \tag{34}$$

Where

$$\begin{aligned}\left|\varepsilon_{(1-b_x)x^B}\right| &= \frac{\partial[(1-b_x)x^B]}{\partial t_x^B}, \\ &= \left|\varepsilon_x^B - \frac{\partial b_x}{t^B}\frac{t_x^B}{(1-b_x)}\right| > \left|\varepsilon_x^B\right|.\end{aligned}$$

Let us compare these markups with their counterparts in the Ramsey case with $\lambda \rightarrow +\infty$ described in Sect. 3. First, the markup on export and direct injection depends directly upon the terminal dues agreement: the competitor's access fee a^B instead of k_d^B is the cost of export of the postal operator while the internal access fee a^A is the opportunity cost of direct injection. Second, postal operators take into account the positive impact of their domestic tariff on their access fee. The markup of the domestic rates is then higher than the ones that would prevail in the Ramsey case. Conversely, the markup on exports is lower since the elasticity of imported volumes is higher (in absolute value) due to the possibility of direct injection.

Symmetrically, one has

$$\frac{\left(t_y^B - k^B\right)}{t_y^B} = \frac{1 + \alpha\frac{(1-b_x)x^B}{y^B}}{\left|\varepsilon_y^B\right|}, \tag{35}$$

$$\frac{\left(t_y^A - a^A - k\right)}{t_x^B} = \frac{1}{\left|\varepsilon_{(1-b_y)y^A}\right|}, \tag{36}$$

$$t_d^B - a^B = 1. \tag{37}$$

for postal operator R^B's rates.

The resulting direct injection rates are always larger than the terminal dues. We now turn to the case where direct injection rates are equal to terminal dues.

4.2 Negotiated Agreement on Terminal Dues Between Postal Operators Extended to Direct Injection Fees Paid by E-retailers

The problem of operator R^A is now:

$$\begin{aligned}\max_{t_x^A, t_x^B, t_d^A} \Pi^A &= N^A(t_x^A - k^A)x^A + N^B(t_x^B - a^B - k)(1 - b_x)x^B \\ &\quad + N^A(1 - b_y)(a^A - k_d^A)y^A + N^A b_y(t_d^A - k_d^A)y^A - F^A \\ \text{s.t. } a^A &= \alpha t_x^A \\ t_d^A &= \alpha t_x^A\end{aligned}$$

which is equivalent to solving

$$\begin{aligned}\max_{t_x^A, t_x^B} \Pi^A &= N^A(t_x^A - k^A)x^A + N^B(t_x^B - a^B - k)(1 - b_x)x^B \\ &\quad + N^A y^A(a^A - k_d^A) - F^A \\ \text{s.t. } a^A &= \alpha t_x^A \\ t_d^A &= \alpha t_x^A\end{aligned}$$

In other words, the markup on imported products is the same for non injected and injected volumes and equal to $a^A - k_d^A$. This yields

$$\frac{(t_x^A - k^A)}{t_x^A} = \frac{1 + \alpha \frac{y^A}{x^A}}{|\varepsilon_x^A|} \tag{38}$$

$$\frac{(t_x^B - a^B - k)}{t_x^B} = \frac{1}{|\varepsilon_{(1-b_x)x^B}|} \tag{39}$$

It is interesting to compare the markups to those obtained when direct injection fees are not equal to the terminal dues negotiated by postal operators. The expressions show that the markup on domestic delivery is larger since it affects both the terminal dues and the direct injection fees. However, the markup rule on export rates is not affected. Recall that the domestic delivery rate now affects both terminal dues and the direct injection rate. The impact of export rates, on the other hand is not affected by this constraint.

5 Numerical Example

We calibrate the model as follow. Utilities are quadratic (so that demands are linear) and defined by

$$S^i(x, y) = u^i(x) + v^i(y)$$

where

$$\begin{aligned}u^A(x) &= \delta x - \gamma x^2 \\ v^A(y) &= \beta^A(\delta y - \gamma y^2) \\ u^B(x) &= \beta^B(\delta x - \gamma x^2) \\ v^B(y) &= \delta y - \gamma y^2\end{aligned}$$

Table 1 Ramsey and competitive solutions under various scenarios

	Ramsey	Ramsey, e-retailers access to terminal dues	Competition with injection	Competition, e-retailers access to terminal dues
a^A	0.57	0.60	0.94	0.98
a^B	0.57	0.60	0.94	0.98
t_x^A	0.86	0.90	1.41	1.47
t_x^B	1.11	0.91	1.65	1.58
t_d^A	0.95	0.60	1.30	0.98
t_y^A	1.11	0.91	1.65	1.58
t_y^B	0.86	0.90	1.41	1.47
t_d^B	0.95	0.60	1.30	0.98
x^A	5.68	5.48	2.9	2.62
x^B	3.33	3.62	2.5	2.21
y^A	3.33	3.62	2.5	2.21
y^B	5.68	5.48	2.9	2.62
b_x	0.1	0.17	0.28	0.46
b_y	0.1	0.17	0.28	0.46
π^A	0.03	0.1	0.06	0.36
π^B	0.03	0.1	0.06	0.36
Π^A	3.21	2.72	4.92	4.39
Π^B	3.21	2.72	4.92	4.39
CS	13.87	14.80	5.88	5.95
SWF	22.27	22.09	18.94	18.11

The elasticity of domestic demand is set equal to -5, with a volume of 10 at a price 10 (which is equal to the marginal production cost of the goods). The elasticity of foreign demand is equal to -3 with a volume of 5 at a price 10. This implies that the γ and the δ differ for domestic and for foreign demands. Costs are given by $k^A = k_t + k_d^A = 0.6$. The domestic cost includes a process cost and the delivery cost with $k_t = 0.2$, and $k_d^A = 0.4$. The export cost is equal to the cost of the first process: $k = k_t = 0.2$, while import cost is equal to the delivery cost $k_d^A = 0.4$. Note that $k_d^A/k^A = 2/3$ so that delivery represents 2/3 of total cost. Consequently, we also assume $\alpha = 2/3$, while the other parameters are given by $c^A = 10$, $c^B = 10$, $n^A = 1$, $n^B = 1$, $\beta_x^A = \beta_x^B = \beta_y^A = \beta_y^B = 1$, $\lambda = 0.3$ and ς is set at 0.5.

Two main results can be drawn from Table 1. The first one is that giving e-retailers access to the terminal dues reduces the global welfare in all cases (under Ramsey or competition): e-retailers benefit from lower than optimal injection tariffs which increases their profits (by boosting exports) but decreases delivery operators' profits. Cross-border consumers benefit from this situation at the expense of consumers of the domestic product. While this is a numerical result, it is in line with the analytical expressions obtained in the previous section which show that when terminal dues agreements are extended to e-retailers, domestic rate are inflated. The second lesson is that the optimal delivery rates paid by e-retailers (that maximize the global welfare) are always larger than the marginal costs incurred by delivery operators.

6 Conclusion

We have studied a simple model of cross-border e-commerce and delivery services. We have determined the optimal (efficient) pricing structure, which is a crucial benchmark to assess the observed pricing structure, as well as potential reforms. We have also examined various competitive scenarios in order to identify potential market failures. Finally, we have used our setting to study the impact of regulatory policies.

The following main lessons emerge from our results. First, the maximization of global welfare requires that delivery rates are obtained by applying a markup to marginal costs. This markup varies across goods, but it is always positive. In particular it is never optimal to set international delivery rates below the corresponding marginal cost. Similarly, applying a uniform delivery rate to domestic and international delivery is not desirable; this would decrease both domestic and global welfare. Second, when direct injection is possible, it is not desirable in our model to make terminal dues negotiated by postal operators also available to retailers using direct injection.

Appendix 1: Proof of Expressions

The first-order conditions of the Lagrangian problem (21) with respect to t_x^A and t_x^B and t_d^A are respectively:

$$-N^A x^A + N^A\left(t_x^A - k^A\right)\frac{\partial x^A}{\partial t_x^A} + (1+\lambda)\left(N^A x^A + N^A\left(t_x^A - k^A\right)\frac{\partial x^A}{\partial t_x^A}\right) = 0,$$

$$-N^B x^B + N^B\frac{\partial x^B}{\partial t_x^B}\left(t_x^B - k_d^B - k\right) + N^B x^B + \lambda\left(N^B x^B + N^B\frac{\partial x^B}{\partial t_x^B}\right)\left(t_x^B - k_d^B - k\right)$$

$$= 0, N^A\frac{\partial\left(b_y y^A\right)}{\partial t^A}\left(k - t^A\right) - \lambda N^A\frac{\partial\left(b_y y^A\right)}{\partial t^A}\left[t^A - k\right] - \lambda N^A b_y y^A(.) = 0.$$

which respectively yield (22)–(24).

Appendix 2: Proof of Expressions (28)–(31)

Setting $a^A = t_d^A = \alpha t_x^A$ and $a^B = t_d^B = \alpha t_y^B$ the first order conditions with respect to t_x^A and t_x^B are:

$$\frac{\partial \mathcal{L}}{\partial t_x^A} = -N^A x^A + (1+\lambda)\left[N^A x^A(.) + N^A\left(t_x^A - k^A\right)\frac{\partial x^A}{t_x^A}\right] +$$
$$(1+\lambda)\alpha N^A \frac{\partial\left(b_y y^A(.)\right)}{t^A}\left[t^A - k\right] + \lambda b_y \alpha N^A y^A(.) = 0$$
$$\frac{\partial \mathcal{L}}{\partial t_x^B} = \lambda N^B x^B + (1+\lambda)N^B\left(t_x^B - k_d^B - k\right)\frac{\partial x^B}{\partial t_x^B} -$$
$$\lambda b_x x^B - (1+\lambda)N^B \frac{\partial b_x(.)x^B(.)}{\partial t^B}\left(t^B - k\right) = 0$$

which can be rewritten as

$$\frac{\partial \mathcal{L}}{\partial t_x^A} = \lambda N^A x^A(.) + (1+\lambda)N^A\left(t_x^A - k^A\right)\frac{\partial x^A}{t_x^A} +$$
$$\lambda b_y \alpha N^A y^A(.) + (1+\lambda)\alpha N^A y^A(.)\frac{\partial b_y}{t^A}\left[t^A - k\right] = 0$$
$$\frac{\partial \mathcal{L}}{\partial t_x^B} = \lambda N^B x^B\left(1 + (1+\lambda)N^B\frac{\left(t_x^B - k_d^B - k\right)}{t_x^B}\frac{\partial x^B}{\partial t_x^B}\frac{t_x^B}{x_B}\right) -$$
$$\lambda b_x N^B x^B\left(1 + \frac{(1+\lambda)}{\lambda}\frac{\left(t^B - k\right)}{t^B}\frac{\partial b_x x^B}{\partial t^B}\frac{t^B}{b_x(.)x^B}\right) = 0$$

This yields:

$$\frac{\partial \mathcal{L}}{\partial t_x^A} = N^A x^A\left(1 - \frac{(1+\lambda)}{\lambda}\frac{\left(t_x^A - k^A\right)}{t_x^A}\left|\varepsilon_x^A\right|\right) + \alpha N^A b_y y^A\left(1 + \frac{(1+\lambda)}{\lambda}\frac{\left(t^A - k\right)}{t^A}\varepsilon_{b_y y^A}\right)$$
$$= N^A x^A\left(1 - \frac{(1+\lambda)}{\lambda}\frac{\left(t_x^A - k^A\right)}{t_x^A}\left|\varepsilon_x^A\right|\right) + \alpha N^A b_y y^A\left(1 + \frac{(1+\lambda)}{\lambda}\right) = 0 \tag{40}$$

$$\frac{\partial \mathcal{L}}{\partial t_x^B} = N^B x^B\left(1 - \frac{(1+\lambda)}{\lambda}\frac{\left(t_x^B - k_d^B - k\right)}{t_x^B}\left|\varepsilon_x^B\right|\right)$$
$$- N^B b_x x^B\left(1 + \frac{(1+\lambda)}{\lambda}\frac{\left(t^B - k\right)}{t^B}\varepsilon_{b_x x^B}\right) = 0 \tag{41}$$

which after some rearrangement yield (28) and (29).

References

Borsenberger Claire, Helmuth Cremer, Philippe De Donder and Denis Joram (2015), " Quality and Pricing of Delivery Services in the E-commerce Sector", in M.A. Crew and T.J. Brennan (eds), Postal and Delivery Innovation in the Digital Economy, Springer International Publishing, 77–90.

Borsenberger Claire, Helmuth Cremer, Philippe De Donder and Denis Joram (2016a), " Differentiated Pricing of Delivery Services in the e-Commerce Sector", in M.A. Crew and T.J. Brennan (eds), The Future of the Postal Sector in a Digital World, Springer International Publishing, 191–212.

Borsenberger Claire, Helmuth Cremer, Denis Joram and Jean-Marie Lozachmeur (2016b), " Pricing of delivery services and the emergence of marketplace platforms", IDEI Working Paper n° 865, August.

Campbell James I, Alex Kalevi Dieke, Martin Zauner (2011), "Terminal dues: winners, losers, and the path to reform", Presentation at the 19th Conference on Postal and Delivery Economics, 1–4 June 2011.

Campbell James I. Jr (2014), "Estimating the effects of UPU terminal dues, 2014–2017", Paper presented at the 8th Bi-annual postal economics conference on e-commerce, digital economy and delivery services, Toulouse.

Campbell James I. Jr. (2016), "Quantifying the Distortive Effects of UPU Terminal Dues", in M.A. Crew and T.J. Brennan (eds), The Future of the Postal Sector in a Digital World, Springer International Publishing, pp. 313–330.

Copenhagen Economics (2014), " The Economics of Terminal Dues", Final Report, 30 September.

Copenhagen Economics (2016), "Principles of e-commerce delivery prices", Final Report, 9 February.

E-commerce Europe (2016), " Cross-border e-commerce barometer – Barriers to Growth", May.

European Commission (2016), " Proposal for a regulation of the European Parliament and of the Council on cross-border parcel delivery service", COM(2016)285 final, 25 May.

Geradin Damien (2012), "Legal opinion on the compatibility of the proposed target system for terminal dues with EU law".

Haller Andreas, Christian Jaag and Urs Trinkner (2013), "Termination charges in the international parcel market", in M.A. Crew and P.R. Kleindorfer (eds), Reforming the postal sector in the face of electronic competition, Edward Elgar, Cheltenham, pp 277–293.

Office of Inspector General USPS (2015), " Terminal Dues in the Age of E-commerce", RARC Report, RARC-WP-16-003, 14 December.

Okholm Henrik Ballebye, Anna Möller Boivie, Bruno Basalisco and Julia Wahl (2016), "An Economist's Perspective on Terminal Dues", in M.A. Crew and T.J. Brennan (eds), The Future of the Postal Sector in a Digital World, Springer International Publishing, pp. 283–294.

Sorensen Janet M. (2014), "International terminal dues white paper", Office of Inspector General, United States Postal Service.

Vogelsang, Ingo (2013), " The Endgame of Telecommunications Policy? A Survey", Review of Economics, 64, pp. 193–270.

Pricing and Efficiency Decisions for Letter and Parcel Markets When Industrial Relations Matter

Philippe De Donder, Frank Rodriguez, and Soterios Soteri

1 Introduction

A key feature of postal markets today is the changing mix of physical mail. While the demand for letters is in decline, predominantly because of e-substitution, parcel volumes are increasing due to the rapid growth of e-commerce.[1] Universal service providers (USPs) in the postal sector serve both markets. In the former, universal service obligations (USOs) are in place and regulators and private shareholders, where the USP is privatized, press for improvements in efficiency. In the latter, markets are highly competitive with parcel companies offering differentiated services. In both markets, USPs are under pressure to lower costs and prices to maintain financial viability. But postal operations are labor intensive and the pressure to lower costs poses a threat of industrial action.

This chapter explores these issues, and extends De Donder et al. (2017)'s analysis in two ways. First, we consider separately the USP's letter and bulk or contract parcel services delivered through its universal service network which allows the analysis to reflect significant differences between the two markets'

The views expressed in this paper are those of the authors and do not necessarily reflect those of their affiliated organizations.

[1]For example, Jaag et al. (2016) illustrate the development of letter mail and parcel volumes for a number of postal providers.

P. De Donder (✉)
Toulouse School of Economics, Toulouse, France
e-mail: philippe.dedonder@tse-fr.eu

F. Rodriguez
Oxera Consulting LLP, Oxford, UK

S. Soteri
Royal Mail Group, London, UK

P.L. Parcu et al. (eds.), *The Contribution of the Postal and Delivery Sector*, Topics in Regulatory Economics and Policy, https://doi.org/10.1007/978-3-319-70672-6_17

growth prospects and cost structures. Second, we expand the model's treatment of the effects of a potential strike on volumes and profitability by allowing for an explicit diversion of traffic from the USP to competitors. Further, a higher USP target to improve efficiency is likely to increase the extent of changes to work practices and reductions in workforce leading to greater resistance by employees to such changes through industrial action. A higher efficiency target is then likely to result in a greater adverse impact on the USP's mail volumes from a strike.

The paper is structured as follows. Section 2 outlines our model. Section 3 illustrates its operation with numerical simulations based on a calibrated version of the model. Section 4 reports results for sensitivities on some key assumptions. Section 5 concludes. An appendix provides more detail on the analytics of the model and its calibration.

2 The Model

2.1 *Operators and Markets*

The model we develop extends that presented in De Donder et al. (2017). For this paper to be self-contained, we outline all the building blocks of the model and further develop the model analytically in Appendix 1.

There are two types of postal operators: a USP, denoted by I, and a set of competitors, denoted by E. There are four postal services: single-piece (SP) mail, bulk letters (BL), an access service for delivery of competitors' BL through the USP's network, and contract parcels (CP). We consider two delivery areas: urban (U) and rural (R).

The USP is subject to a USO to provide SP mail of a given quality, at the same price and delivering to all addresses. The USP enjoys a de facto monopoly on the SP mail market as competitors do not find it profitable to offer an SP service with these features.

The USP faces competition in the BL and CP markets. Competition in the former can be end-to-end (E2E) or through access, with the USP selling both an E2E BL product to final consumers and an access service to competitors. In the case of access, each unit of competitors' BL requires one unit of access to the USP delivery network. The BL products offered by both operators are imperfect substitutes, whether the competitor uses access or bypasses the USP delivery network. Competitors then choose the cheapest way to deliver, offering an E2E product if the access charge is larger than their delivery cost, and access the USP delivery network otherwise. Competitors charge an exogenous mark-up over their marginal cost in both cases whose level reflects the intensity of competition on the market.

Competition on the CP market is E2E only. CP products sold by the USP and competitors are imperfect substitutes and competitors charge an exogenous mark-up over their marginal costs. There is no substitution between SP mail, BL and CP. Both types of operators face constant variable costs but the USO provided by the USP results in this operator incurring also a fixed cost.

2.2 Timing and Decisions

We consider two periods, P_1 and P_2. All firms announce their prices for P_1 at the beginning of P_1. The USP chooses its BL and CP prices in order to maximize profit. The USP faces two regulatory constraints on its prices. First, the SP mail price is capped at $\bar{p}$ by the regulator (constraint C1) so that the USP makes a normal rate of return (that is, it breaks-even achieving zero economic profit and the margin made by selling its services exactly covers its fixed cost). Second, the regulator sets a constraint on the USP's access prices in the BL market. It can either cap the USP's access price at a percentage mark-up over the USP's downstream cost (constraint C2a) or set a margin squeeze constraint, such that the difference between the USP's BL price and access charge cannot be smaller than the USP's BL upstream cost (constraint C2b).[2] The regulator's choice of constraint impacts materially on whether entrants offer a BL service through access or bypass.

The regulator then announces details of the price constraints it will set during the next regulatory cycle, which is assumed to last five years, based on its assessment of prospects for mail demand and efficiency improvements. The regulator assesses the value of e, which is the yearly percentage reduction in (both variable and fixed) costs the USP could be expected to attain, and sets $\bar{p}$ and access price constraint for the second regulatory cycle. Reductions in costs may arise from improvements in productivity or lower wage costs or a mix of both factors. The value of e is assumed to be obtained from a rigorous efficiency review process undertaken in P_1 that yields a challenging yet achievable estimate in P_2.

The USP then announces (in P_1) efficiency targets to be achieved during the next regulatory cycle, but the value of e it chooses need not equal that used by the regulator to set its price constraint $\bar{p}$. The announcement of efficiency targets by the USP is associated with risks of industrial action. P_{1S} (respectively, P_{1NS}) denotes P_1 when a strike does (respectively, does not) occur and it is assumed the regulator does not take a strike into account when assessing its value of e.

If a strike occurs, the USP is assumed not to adapt its prices in P_1.[3] The strike results in a decrease of $\gamma_1^L(e)\%$ in the USP's SP and BL volumes in P_1 and if competitors use access in the BL market, they are similarly affected. If they deliver BL themselves, then a fraction β_1^L of the USP volume decrease diverts to competitors, whose volumes increase by $\beta_1^L\gamma_1^L(e)\%$ of the USP volumes. In the CP market, the USP volumes decrease by $\gamma_1^P(e)\%$, but a fraction β_1^P of this decrease diverts to competitors, whose volumes increase by $\beta_1^P\gamma_1^P(e)\%$ of the USP volumes.

[2]There is a formal statement of these constraints in Appendix 1 where we also consider constraint C3: that the difference between the SP price and the USP's BL price must be greater than the upstream preparation costs of the USP's BL final customers.

[3]As explained at the end of this section, it would not wish to change them anyway.

The functions γ_1^L and γ_1^P are increasing in e, as the announcement of a larger decrease in costs is likely to result in more severe industrial action.[4]

We now move to P_2. The model assumes the USP efficiency targets announced in P_1 are achieved in P_2 whether or not a strike occurred in P_1 and, with a regulatory cycle of five years, USP costs decrease by $5e$ by the end of P_2. For simplicity, competitors' costs are assumed to be the same as in P_1, such that e can be interpreted as the amount by which the USP lowers its costs relative to competitors. At the same time, and independently from the variation in costs, we assume that market volumes of both operators follow the same trend, with volumes varying by the same proportion for any given set of prices. This variation is given by the parameter λ so that, for any given set of prices, mail volumes are $\lambda\%$ higher in P_2 than in P_1. We assume that letter volumes face a negative trend ($\lambda = \lambda_L < 0$, due to e-substitution) while parcel volumes benefit from a positive trend ($\lambda = \lambda_P > 0$, due to e-commerce).

When a strike occurred in P_1, USP SP volumes decrease by $\gamma_2^L(e)\%$ in P_2. We assume that $\gamma_2^L(e) < \gamma_1^L(e)$ since there is likely to be a reduced but continuing effect from the strike in P_1 due, for example, to additional e-substitution. The impact of a strike in P_1 on BL volumes depends on the type of competition. If competitors use access they are affected in the same way as the USP by the strike, with volumes decreasing by $\gamma_2^L(e)\%$ for both in P_2. If competition occurs with bypass, we contrast two scenarios. Under "Full Reversion", traffic lost by the USP to competitors in P_1 following a strike is assumed to revert in full in P_2 to the USP. Under the "Full Retention" scenario, market BL volumes also decrease, but there is also substitution in favor of the competitors and the traffic gained by competitors in P_1 is retained by them in full in P_2.

CP market volumes in P_2 are not affected by whether a strike occurred or not in P_1 but again we contrast the two scenarios of Full Reversion and Full Retention. Under the latter, a fraction $\gamma_2^P(e)$ of USP volumes diverts to competitors. Here also, we assume that $\gamma_2^P(e)$ is increasing in e with $\gamma_2^P(e) < \gamma_1^P(e)$.

P_{2S} and P_{2NS} denote the second-period when a strike did (or did not) occur in P_1. The USP then chooses prices for P_2 to maximize profit in P_2, subject to the price constraints C1 to C3, its costs (given its choice of e) and market demand during P_2. The USP of course knows whether a strike occurred in P_1, and can charge different prices accordingly. Competitors post their prices for P_2 simultaneously.

The USP's profit is denoted by π_{kj} in period $k = \{1, 2\}$ whether a strike occurred in P_1 ($j = S$) or not ($j = NS$). Observe that the same set of USP prices maximize π_{kS} and π_{kNS} in the model because the impact of a strike is to scale down volumes by a given percentage, and prices which maximize a specific function also maximize a fraction of this function. So, prices will not differ between P_{2S} and P_{2NS}, and it does not matter whether first-period prices maximize π_{1S}, π_{1NS} or any linear combination of the two. Appendix 2 explains how the USP weighs the two periods to evaluate overall discounted profit when considering the value of e to set in period 1.

[4]When choosing whether to access or bypass the USP delivery network, competitors do not anticipate that the form of competition they choose will affect the volume of their demand in case of a strike.

3 Results from the Model: Low Access Prices Case

For reasons of space, we illustrate the operation of the model for one of the two cases in De Donder et al. (2017), that of low access prices in the BL market. Here constraint C2a determines the USP's access prices and we assume the regulator sets the value of the mark-up on the USP' downstream cost at 10%, its aim being to encourage competitive entry upstream. The low access prices resulting lead to the difference between the SP mail price and the USP's BL prices being greater than the assumed preparation cost of the USP's BL final customers so that constraint C3 is not binding in the equilibria reported in this section.[5] The regulator also sets constraint C1, the price cap on SP mail, at a level (assuming no strike) that allows the USP to achieve zero economic profit when it sets profit-maximizing prices in the BL and CP markets. Appendix 3 sets out the calibration assumptions applied in deriving the results in this section, which are based on published information or assumptions reflecting broadly the operation of postal markets in Europe.

The first column of Table 1 presents results for P_1 when no strike occurs. In the BL market, entrants price at a mark-up of 2% over their variable costs including the access charge. The USP sets profit-maximizing prices above those offered by entrants with prices for both being higher in the rural area than the urban, reflecting differences in delivery costs. In the CP market competitors offer a higher specification service to senders than the USP and price at a mark-up of 3% over their variable costs. The USP's profit-maximizing prices are then below those of competitors. In the BL and CP markets, competitors gain more than 50% of the market although delivery of all BL is by the USP. At the base case calibration values, the price cap on SP mail by the regulator allows the USP to breakeven at 1.49€ (against a fully allocated cost, FAC, of 1) and is binding at equilibrium.

The second column of Table 1 reports results for P_1 where the USP faces a strike in P_1. As outlined in Sect. 2, prices are unchanged from their no strike values. The effect of the strike on volumes depends on the efficiency target the USP is seeking to achieve in P_2. The column reports outcomes where that target is 2% per annum. From Appendix 3, this results in a 12% loss in letter volume for both the USP and entrants. For parcels, the loss of volume by the USP is higher at 24% as alternative services are on offer from competitors and some 80% of this is assumed to switch to competitors. As a result of these volume losses, at these calibration values the USP makes a loss of economic profit of 335 m€ and there is a drop in the net consumer surplus. The volume losses from a strike increase (decline) as the USP's target for efficiency increases (declines). For example, and although not shown in Table 1, from Appendix 3, if the USP sought an efficiency improvement of 3% per annum in P_2 and a strike were to occur, the reduction in all letter volumes in P_1 would be 16% and, of its parcels traffic, 32%. Its loss of economic profit would increase to 447m€.

[5] In simulations where the regulator constrains access prices using the margin squeeze constraint C2b competitors enter the BL market in the urban area through E2E competition rather than access because the access price the USP would choose to set there exceeds competitors' delivery costs.

Table 1 Prices, volumes and economic profit where entry to bulk letter market through access. Alternative industrial action scenarios

	P_1		P_2 with 2% efficiency Strike: Volume effect scenario		
	No strike	Strike (2% efficiency)	No strike	Full reversion to USP	Full retention by competitors
Prices, euro					
USP, single piece	1.493		⟵	1.414	⟶
USP, bulk letters urban	0.295			0.274	
USP, bulk letters rural	0.456			0.419	
USP, access urban	0.209			0.188	
USP, access rural	0.374			0.337	
USP, contract parcels urban	1.735			1.678	
USP, contract parcels rural	2.236			2.164	
Competitors, bulk letters urban	0.234			0.212	
Competitors, bulk letters rural	0.402			0.364	
Competitors, contract parcels urban	2.060			2.060	
Competitors, contract parcels rural	2.678		⟵	2.678	⟶
Volumes, billions items	12.794	11.519	11.373	11.118	11.118
USP, total	5.657	4.905	4.923	4.800	4.645
USP, single piece	1.803	1.586	1.468	1.424	1.424
USP, bulk letters urban	2.615	2.301	2.135	2.071	2.071
USP, bulk letters rural	0.625	0.55	0.513	0.497	0.497
USP, contract parcels urban	0.487	0.37	0.640	0.640	0.517
USP, contract parcels rural	0.129	0.098	0.168	0.168	0.136
Competitors, total	7.136	6.614	6.450	6.318	6.474
Competitors, bulk letters urban	4.459	3.924	3.634	3.525	3.525
Competitors, bulk letters rural	0.879	0.773	0.739	0.716	0.716
Competitors, contract parcels urban	1.447	1.54	1.672	1.672	1.795
Competitors, contract parcels rural	0.351	0.376	0.405	0.405	0.437
Competitor share, bulk letters (%)	62%	62%	62%	62%	62%
Competitor share, contract parcels (%)	74%	80%	72%	72%	77%
USP economic profit net of fixed costs[a]	0	−0.335	0	−0.048	−0.156
USP Contribution to profit	2.4	2.065	2.160	2.112	2.004
Competitor contribution to profit	0.142	0.146	0.152	0.152	0.162
Net consumer surplus (single piece mail)	4.062	3.575	3.366	3.265	3.265

[a]Billions, euros

Letter volumes are declining by significant amounts in most developed countries while parcel volumes are growing rapidly. In the numerical simulation, in P_2 it is assumed that the SP and BL markets contract by 20% compared with the no strike volume level in P_1 while the CP market expands by 20%. The USP seeks to reduce its costs relative to competitors and sets profit-maximizing prices in the BL and CP markets. Table 1 reports these prices where the USP achieves a 2% per annum reduction in costs (10% in total by P_2) consistent with an assumed value the regulator assesses is a reasonable rate of efficiency improvement. The assumed passing through of lower USP costs in delivery into reduced access prices results in competitor prices declining by almost 10%. It is profit-maximizing for the USP to reduce its BL prices by about 7% (for example, to 0.274 in the urban area from 0.295) rather than 10% but BL's share of contribution in P_2 to the reduced fixed cost of 2.16bn€ still declines marginally compared with P_1.

In the CP market, the USP's profit-maximizing prices are only about 3% below those in P_1 (for example, 1.678 in the urban area from 1.735). This price cut leads the USP to gain market share and with growth in the CP market allows it to increase volumes and contribution to profit in P_2 from parcels traffic. At the model's base case calibration values these effects are sufficient to reduce the required contribution from the SP market to fund the fixed cost of universal service. The regulator can lower the price cap on SP mail by about 5% (to 1.414), less than in USP costs.

The two final columns in Table 1 report results where a strike occurs in P_1. Two cases are reported. In the first, losses in volumes to competitors in the CP market from the strike in P_1 revert fully to the USP in P_2 although there are some continuing losses in letter demand for the USP due to an assumption of increased e-substitution resulting from the strike. In the second, additionally, competitors in the CP market retain proportionately all of the volume they gained during the strike in P_1. In the former, the USP make a loss of 48 m€. There is also a loss of net consumer surplus on SP mail. In the latter, additionally the USP loses market share and contribution from the CP market resulting in a larger loss of 156 m€.

Although it is assumed that the regulator sets the SP price cap for P_2 on the basis that the USP reduces its costs by 2% per annum, the USP may aim for a different rate of efficiency improvement. If it chose to target 3%, its costs and prices in P_2 would be lower but, if a strike were to occur in P_1, its impact on the USP's volumes in both P_1 and P_2 would be greater. The cost reduction effect raises profitability compared with the 2% case while the strike effect lowers it. At a 3% reduction without a strike, the USP's volumes and contribution per unit would increase as would its economic profit in P_2 at 212 m€. With a strike this gain would reduce to 146 m€ in the full reversion case and a loss of 11 m€ under full retention.

The relationship between efficiency, e, and the USP's economic profit at equilibrium prices is examined further in Fig. 1. Profits in P_1 and P_2 in the cases where there is no strike in P_1 (π_{NS}), or a strike in P_1 with full reversion of CP volumes to the USP in P_2 or a strike in P_1 with full retention of CP volumes by competitors in P_2 are discounted to their present value in P_1 using the method outlined in Appendix 2. Figure 1 plots the present value of economic profits for the three cases at each value of e. Table 1 reported these prices and associated volumes for just one value of e, 2%.

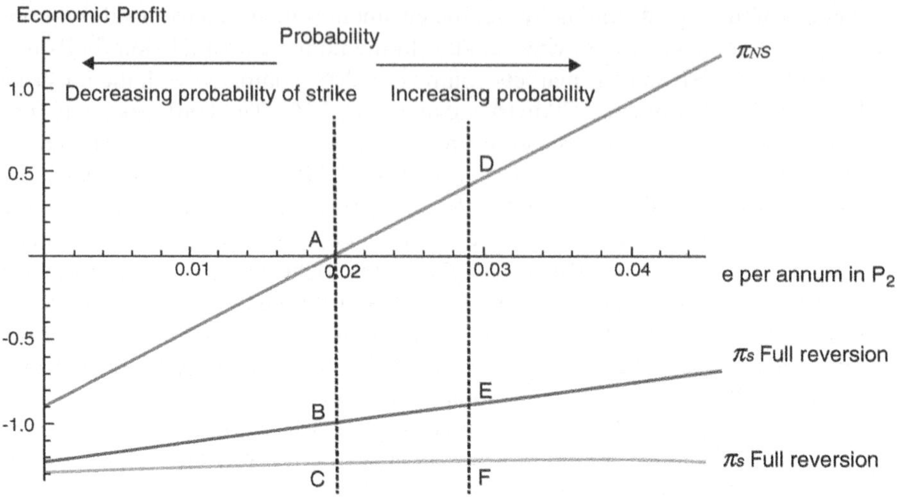

Fig. 1 USP's economic profit: No strike, strike full reversion and full retention scenarios

The schedule for the no strike case (π_{NS}) rises approximately linearly in e. Lowering costs allows the USP to reduce its prices so that it can gain market share and raise contribution per unit. As its costs decline, the USP's economic profit increases being zero at 2% by construction from the price cap on SP mail set by the regulator. Failure to secure an efficiency improvement of at least 2% would lead to the USP making negative economic profits.

The schedules for the two strike cases reflect a trade-off for the USP. A higher efficiency target for P_2, if it leads to a strike in P_1, results in a greater loss of profit in P_1. But in P_2, the USP's costs and prices are lower so that contribution per unit and volumes increase raising profitability. At the base case calibration values the second of these effects is the stronger in the full reversion case and the present value of losses declines as e rises. In the full retention case the two effects roughly cancel and the present value of losses is broadly flat.

4 Sensitivities

This section considers sensitivities to assumptions and their effects on economic profit. The first row of Table 2 records the present value of economic profits in the base case calculated at a discount rate of 10%. In the no strike case the USP achieves breakeven in P_1 and P_2 by construction, from the price cap for SP mail set to facilitate this outcome (point A, Fig. 1). As reported in Table 1, a strike in P_1 in the base case is modelled to result in a loss of 335 m€. Where volume lost reverts

Table 2 Sensitivities to assumptions and USP changes to economic profit relative to the base case, €bns[a]

	Strike volume scenario		
	No strike	Full reversion to USP	Full retention by competitors
Base Case (2% Efficiency in P_2)	0	−0.995	−1.266
Changes in Economic Profit from Base Case:			
Letter volumes lower by 10% in P_2[b]	−0.428	−0.413	−0.415
Parcel volumes lower by 10% in P_2[b]	−0.100	−0.100	−0.081
Strike impact on volumes higher by 25%[b]	0	−0.249	−0.307
Discount rate lowered from 10% to 5%	0	−0.065	−0.103
Base Case with 3% Efficiency in P_2	0.453	0.116	0.012

[a]Calculated as present values in P_1 using the method outlined in Appendix 2. For example, in the sensitivity of "Letter Volumes lower by 10% in P_2" with the strike volume scenario of "Full Reversion to USP", the base case is a loss of economic profit of 0.995bn€ which increases in the sensitivity by 0.413bn€ so that the total loss in this sensitivity is 1.408bn€
[b]Changes affecting volumes approximately symmetric in opposite direction

fully to the USP in P_2 the loss to the USP in P_2 is 48 m€ while full retention of these volume gains by competitors implies a larger loss of 156 m€. The present values of these two scenarios are −0.995bn€ (point B) and −1.266bn€ (point C).

The remaining rows of Table 2 report the impact of each sensitivity as a change in the USP's economic profit from the base case. In the first, letter volumes are assumed to be 10% lower in P_2 (and so 30% below their level in P_1) and lower than expected by the USP or the regulator in setting its price cap on SP mail which it cannot then adjust to compensate for this unexpected shortfall. In present value terms the shortfall in volumes would lead to a loss of a little over 400 m€ whether or not a strike occurred in P_1. Note that if the regulator had expected letter volumes to decline by 30% rather than 20%, then given the highly price inelastic nature of SP mail it would have been necessary to set a higher price cap on such mail to allow the USP to breakeven but, as a result, senders of SP mail would suffer a loss of net consumer surplus due to the higher SP price.

In the second sensitivity, parcel volumes are assumed to outturn at 10% less than expected and increase by only 10% by the end of P_2, the reduced volume of parcels resulting in a lower contribution to the USP's profit. The present value of this shortfall is about 100 m€ and smaller than that from a 10% shortfall in letters as CP mail is a smaller contributor to the USP's profit. The third sensitivity examines the effect of the strike impact on volumes being 25% higher than the base. While the effect in P_1 in the two strike scenarios is the same, the full retention by competitors in P_2 of volumes gained in P_1 has a greater impact on the USP's profit.

Each of the three sensitivities on volumes assumes that these are lower than in the base case. Within the model, if these effects had been in the reverse direction the effects on profitability would have been approximately equal and opposite in sign to those reported in Table 2. The impacts also are approximately additive.

For example, in the strike scenario of full reversion, if both letter and parcel volumes had been 10% lower in P_2 than assumed in the base, the change in economic profit from the base would have been approximately the sum of these effects or about −510 m€.

The two remaining sensitivities in Table 2 are rather different in nature. The discount rate used to calculate present values in the base case is 10% and the sensitivity considers the impact of reducing this to 5% which values losses in P_2 more highly and worsens the loss of economic profit relative to the base case. The final row of Table 2 considers the impact on economic profit of increasing the target rate of efficiency by the USP in P_2 to 3%. These results were also reported graphically in Fig. 1. A higher rate of efficiency improvement by the USP in P_2 results in the USP increasing its profitability if no strike occurs (point D). With a strike the full retention case would negate any gain in profitability from higher efficiency (point F) while in the full reversion case this gain would be modest (point E).

5 Conclusions

This chapter extends the two-period model developed by De Donder et al. (2017) to examine the challenges faced by a USP aiming to deliver efficiency gains in the future but which may lead to costly strike action in advance of these being achieved. Our model structure and assumptions consist of a number of key elements. First, letter volumes are in long term decline due to e-substitution. Second, the USP is required to meet a pre-specified USO but entrants are not required to do so. Third, the USP is subject to price controls set by a regulator. Fourth, fixed costs are inherent in meeting the USO. However, we extend that model in two important ways. First, we separate the letter and parcel services the USP delivers through its universal service network to take account of differences in their growth prospects and impacts on their respective volumes from a strike. Additionally, we link the cost of strike action, which is assumed to occur in the first period (P_1), to the magnitude of targeted efficiency gains that accrue in the second period (P_2).

Our model assumes a high level of competition in the bulk letters (BL) and contract parcels (CP) markets, with the USP competing against other letter and parcel operators, and that the regulator intervenes in the BL market, but only by constraining the access prices the USP can set in delivering BL for competitors. We examine through a simulation of the model the case where these constraints lead to low access prices resulting in competition upstream in the BL market between the USP and competitors in all geographies (rural and urban) and no bypass competition. In both the BL and CP markets, competitors gain more than 50% of the market although, in the former, delivery of all BL is by the USP. Competition in the BL market leads to significant differences in prices between single-piece and BL traffic with competitors offering lower BL prices than the USP. However, as parcel competitors are assumed to offer a higher specification service their prices are higher than those of the USP.

The USP is assumed to operate within a price control structure that requires a specific rate of efficiency to be achieved to maintain a normal rate of return during the next price control period if no strike takes place. In such an environment the USP is assumed to be able to achieve higher/lower efficiency than this specific level but there is an increasing/decreasing risk of industrial action whose costs increase with the scale of targeted efficiency. The paper does not explore explicitly the rising risk of industrial action occurring as the efficiency target rises only that, if it occurs, the impact of a strike on volumes will be higher. In the event of a strike being avoided our results suggest that the USP's profit could increase considerably if it targets higher rates of efficiency. However, our modelling also indicates that if a strike occurs the USP will suffer significant losses that cannot be recouped during the price control period. The main factors underpinning this result are two-fold. First, industrial action results in lost volume during the strike which over the longer term encourages further losses as letter mail switches to electronic alternatives. Second, a significant proportion of parcel traffic is assumed to switch to parcel competitors. With regards to the latter, the extent of the loss suffered by the USP will depend on the quantity of parcels the USP loses during the strike period (that is, switch to competitors or customers decide to not send in P_1) and how much returns when the strike is over as well as efficiency gains achieved (in P_2).

The paper concludes with a number of sensitivities to assess the impact of plausible alternative assumptions. Three points in particular are worth noting. First, the impact of lower than expected letter and parcel volumes could have a substantial negative impact on the USP's finances. Second, the industrial action sensitivity suggests that if the extent of traffic loss associated with strike action differed from the base case, this could impact the results considerably. However, given the high losses assumed under the two base case strike scenarios this suggests the final outcome could be significantly worse or just somewhat less bad. Third, achieving higher efficiency rates can result in considerably higher levels of economic profit but all of this gain and more could be lost if securing these efficiency improvements results in significant industrial action.

Appendix 1: Analytical model

The net utility that consumers in zone $i \in \{U, R\}$ obtain from consuming quantity x of SP mail at unit price p is denoted by $u_i(x) - px$. The demand function for SP mail in zone i is obtained by maximizing utility with respect to x, and is denoted by $x_i(p)$. Utility is quadratic in quantities, so that the demand function is linear and of the form $x(p) = \alpha - \beta p$. The utility function $u_i(x)$ is calibrated (see Appendix 3) and used to obtain the demand function in P_{1NS}. In P_{1S}, demand is given by $(1 - \gamma_1^L(e))x(p)$. In P_{2NS}, volumes are given by $(1 + \lambda_L)x(p)$ while they are given by $(1 + \lambda_L)(1 - \gamma_2^L(e))x(p)$ in P_{2S}.

The unit variable cost for SP mail is denoted by c_i. The contribution to USP profit of SP mail in zone i is then $(p - c_i)x_i(p)$ in P_{1NS}, and is obtained by replacing $x_i(p)$ by the relevant demand function (see above) in P_{1S}, P_{2NS} and P_{2S}.

The net utility obtained by consumers in zone i from consuming BL is $v_i(y_i^I, y_i^E) - q_i^I y_i^I - q_i^E y_i^E$, where q_i^j denotes the consumer price operator $j \in \{I, E\}$ posts in zone i, and y_i^j the quantity consumed of that good. The demand for goods in each zone is obtained by maximizing consumers' utility, and is denoted by $y_i^I(q_i^I, q_i^E)$ and $y_i^E(q_i^I, q_i^E)$. Note that both operators' prices influence demand for both goods, because the function v_i is non separable in y_i^I and y_i^E. The utility function $v_i(.)$ is quadratic in quantities, so that BL demand functions are linear in prices. Appendix 3 details how we calibrate utility and demand functions for BL in P_{1NS}.

As for BL costs, d_i^j denotes operator j's (constant) marginal delivery cost in zone i, and b_i^j operator j's upstream constant unit cost in zone i. If the access charge a_i is smaller than the competitor's delivery cost d_i^E, the competitor chooses to access the USP's delivery network in zone i and charges a price $q_i^E = (1 + m_L^E)(a_i + b_i^E)$. If $a_i > d_i^E$, the competitor prefers to offer an E2E product in zone i, whose price is $q_i^E = (1 + m_L^E)(d_i^E + b_i^E)$.

In P_{1S}, demands are given by $(1 - \gamma_1^L(e))y_i^I(q_i^I, q_i^E)$ for the USP, and, for the competitors, by $(1 - \gamma_1^L(e))y_i^E(q_i^I, q_i^E)$ if access occurs in zone i, and by $y_i^E(q_i^I, q_i^E) + \beta_1^L \gamma_1^L(e) y_i^I(q_i^I, q_i^E)$ if bypass occurs. In P_{2NS}, volumes are given by $(1 + \lambda_L)y_i^I(q_i^I, q_i^E)$ and $(1 + \lambda_L)y_i^E(q_i^I, q_i^E)$, respectively. Volumes in P_{2S} depend on whether access takes place or not. Under access, and bypass with the "Full Reversion" scenario, volumes are given by $(1 + \lambda_L)(1 - \gamma_2^L(e))y_i^I(q_i^I, q_i^E)$ and $(1 + \lambda_L)(1 - \gamma_2^L(e))y_i^E(q_i^I, q_i^E)$. Under bypass and the "Full Retention" scenario, volumes are given by $(1 + \lambda_L)(1 - \gamma_2^{LRet}(e))y_i^I(q_i^I, q_i^E)$ and $(1 + \lambda_L)(y_i^E(q_i^I, q_i^E) + \beta_2^L \gamma_2^{LRet}(e) y_i^I(q_i^I, q_i^E))$.

The contribution to USP's profit of BL in zone i is given by $(q_i^I - b_i^I - d_i^I)y_i^I(q_i^I, q_i^E) + (a_i - d_i^I)y_i^E(q_i^I, q_i^E)$ in P_{1NS}, in the access case, and by $(q_i^I - b_i^I - d_i^I)y_i^I(q_i^I, q_i^E)$ in the bypass case. Contributions to profit are obtained similarly in P_{1S}, P_{2NS} and P_{2S} by modifying adequately the demand functions. The contribution to competitor's profit of BL in zone i is given by $(q_i^E - a_i - b_i^E)y_i^E(q_i^I, q_i^E)$ in P_{1NS} in the access case and by $(q_i^E - d_i^E - b_i^E)y_i^E(q_i^I, q_i^E)$ for bypass. They are obtained similarly in P_{1S}, P_{2NS} and P_{2S} by modifying adequately the demand functions.

The net utility obtained by consumers in zone i from consuming CP is $w_i(z_i^I, z_i^E) - s_i^I z_i^I - s_i^E z_i^E$, where s_i^j denotes the consumer price operator $j \in \{I, E\}$ posts in zone i, and z_i^j the quantity consumed of that good. The demand for goods in each zone is obtained by maximizing the consumers' utility, and is denoted by $z_i^I(s_i^I, s_i^E)$ and $z_i^E(s_i^I, s_i^E)$. Note that both operators' prices influence demand for both goods, because the function w_i is non separable in z_i^I and z_i^E. The utility function $w_i(.)$ is quadratic in quantities, so that CP demand functions are linear in prices. Appendix 3 explains how we calibrate utility and demand functions for CP in P_{1NS}. In P_{1S}, demands are given by $(1 - \gamma_1^P(e))z_i^I(s_i^I, s_i^E)$ and

$z_i^E(s_i^I, s_i^E) + \beta_1\gamma_1^P(e)z_i^I(s_i^I, s_i^E)$, respectively. In P_{2NS}, volumes are given by $(1+\lambda_P)z_i^I(s_i^I, s_i^E)$ and $(1+\lambda_P)z_i^E(s_i^I, s_i^E)$. Volumes in P_{2S} depend on the scenario considered. In the "Full Reversion" scenario, volumes are the same as in P_{2NS}. In the "Full Retention" case, they are given by $(1+\lambda_P)(1-\gamma_2^P(e))z_i^I(s_i^I, s_i^E)$ and $(1+\lambda_P)(z_1^E(s_i^I, s_i^E)+\gamma_2^P(e)z_i^I(s_i^I, s_i^E))$.

The constant unit variable cost for CP for operator j in zone i is denoted by f_i^j. There is no need to distinguish upstream and downstream costs as no access is provided for this good. The competitors' price is $s_i^E = (1+m_P^E)f_i^E$. The USP also faces a fixed cost F in order to meet the USO.

The USP faces three price constraints, the second of which can take either of two forms. The first constraint is a cap on the SP mail price set by the regulator: $p \leq \bar{p}$. (C1)

The second constraint is on the access prices that the USP can charge and is determined by the regulator. It can take either one of two forms: a pre-specified mark-up on the USP's downstream cost $a_i = (1+m_L^I)d_i^I$, (C2a) as applied in the numerical simulations in this paper; or a margin squeeze constraint: the difference between the USP's BL price and access charge, in any zone i, must be at least equal to upstream FAC of the USP in that zone: $q_i^I - a_i \geq b_i^I(1+\phi)$ (C2b) where ϕ is the FAC factor. The third constraint is that the difference between the (higher) SP mail price and the USP's (lower) BL price, in each zone, must be greater than the upstream preparation cost of the USP's BL final customers, $b^p : p - q_i^I > b^p$ (C3), $i \in \{U, R\}$.

Appendix 2: Weighting the Two Periods

P_1 and P_2 are both the last year of a five year regulatory cycle. In the case where a strike occurs in P_1, the USP's profit levels in P_1 and P_2 are, respectively, π_{1S} and π_{2S}. A linear progression is assumed from the final year of P_1 to P_2, and a yearly discount factor of δ where $\delta = 1/(1+r)$ and r is the discount rate. The discounted value of the USP's profit over six years, evaluated in P_1, is given by

$$\pi_{1S} + \sum_{i=1}^{5} \delta^i \left(\pi_{1S} + i\frac{\pi_{2S} - \pi_{1S}}{5}\right) = w_1\pi_{1S} + w_2\pi_{2S}$$

where

$$w_1 = \frac{5 + 4\delta + 3\delta^2 + 2\delta^3 + \delta^4}{5}, \quad w_2 = \frac{1 + 2\delta + 3\delta^2 + 4\delta^3 + 5\delta^4}{5}\delta.$$

We proceed similarly with π_{1NS} and π_{2NS}.

Appendix 3: Calibration for Simulations

(a) **Demand**. For SP mail, BL and CP markets, when the retail price of the good considered is the same in both zones, the urban zone represents 80% of total volumes, and the rural zone 20%. SP mail market: at a price of 1, price elasticity is −0.2 (both zones) and total volume 2bn items. BL market, hypothetical monopoly setting: at a price of 0.4, demand price elasticity of −0.4 (in both zones), and total volume of 7.5 billion items. With competition, displacement ratio $-\left[\partial y_i^I(q_i^I, q_i^E)/\partial q_i^E\right]/\left[\partial y_i^E(q_i^I, q_I^E)/\partial q_i^E\right]$ of 0.9. Market share of 25% for competitors when $q_i^I = q_i^E = 0.4$ and of 50% when $q_i^I = 0.4$ and $q_i^E = 0.36$. In the CP market the USP price in the urban (resp., rural) area is 1.9 (resp., 2.4) and competitors are 10% more expensive than the USP while (i) the displacement ratio is 0.75, (ii) the demand price elasticity is −0.2, (iii) the USP volume is 0.4 (resp., 0.1), (iv) the USP's market share is 35%. For equal USP and competitors' prices, the USP's market share is 10%.

(b) **Costs (in P_1)**. SP mail market: unit variable cost c_i of 0.57 in urban area ($i = U$) and 0.72 in rural area ($i = R$). BL market: same upstream variable cost in both zones for both operators: $b_U^I = b_U^E = b_R^I = b_R^E = 0.02$. Upstream preparation cost of the USP's BL final customers: $b^p = 0.15$. USP's downstream cost: $d_U^I = 0.19$ and $d_R^I = 0.34$. Competitors' downstream cost: $d_U^E = 0.28$ and $d_R^E = 0.74$. CP market: unit variable costs: $f_U^I = 1.14$, $f_R^I = 1.44$, $f_U^E = 2$, $f_R^E = 2.6$. USP: fixed cost of $F = 2.4$; and FAC factor ϕ of 2/3. All (variable and fixed) USP costs decrease by $5e\%$ between P_1 and P_2.

(c) **Mark-ups**. USP mark-up for access charge set by the regulator where constraint C2a applies: $m_L^I = 0.1$. Competitors' mark-up in BL market: $m_L^E = 0.02$; and in CP market: $m_P^E = 0.03$.

(d) **Exogenous variations in volumes.** Exogenous volume trend between P_1 and $P_2 : \lambda_L = -0.2$ and $\lambda_P = 0.2$. Volume loss by the USP in the case of a strike in P_1 as a proportion of the USP's pre-strike volume $\gamma_1^L(e) = 0.04 + 4e$, $\gamma_2^L(e) = 0.01 + e$, $\gamma_1^P(e) = 0.08 + 8e$ and $\gamma_2^P(e) = 0.064 + 6.4e$ where e is expressed as a proportion (for example, $e = 2\%$ as $e = 0.02$). Volume loss by the USP for BL under the "Full Retention" scenario in P_{2S}: $\gamma_2^{LRet}(e) = 0.03 + 3e$. Volume diversion in P_{1S}: $\beta_1^L = 0.5$ and $\beta_1^P = 0.8$; and for BL under the "Full Retention" scenario in $P_{2S} : \beta_2^L = 2/3$.

(e) **Discount factor for present value calculation.** Discount rate of 10%: $\delta = 0.91$; 5% $\delta = 0.95$.

References

De Donder P., Rodriguez F., and Soteri S. (2017). An examination of the links between postal price constraints, efficiency, competition and public welfare. M. Crew, P.L Parcu, T. Brennan (eds.), *The Changing Postal and Delivery Sector*. Springer.

Jaag C., Moyano J.P., and Trinkner U. (2016). Postal Strategies in a Digital Age. M. Crew, T. Brennan (eds.), *The Future of the Postal Sector in a Digital World*. Springer.

The Impact of Competition on Consumer Prices for Cross-Border Parcels

Sonja Thiele and Alex Kalevi Dieke

1 Introduction

Over the last years, all European parcel and express markets have experienced remarkable volume growth. In particular, B2C parcels have grown due to developments in e-commerce. Return parcels and the success of platforms like ebay or dawanda have also increased parcel volumes sent by consumers (C2X parcel). Cross-border e-commerce has experienced a similar growth trend: Although on a relatively low level compared to domestic e-commerce, online shoppers are buying more and more from e-retailers in other countries.

E-commerce growth has attracted new players to enter the B2C delivery market. Operators from the B2B segment with integrated international parcel networks are entering B2C delivery. New actors from others sectors (e.g. logistics, e-commerce) have emerged as well as intermediaries for domestic and international parcel services. Although the competitive landscape is very different across the EU, competition on domestic and cross-border parcel and express markets has intensified overall.

With this market growth, it would be expected, from an economic point of view, that growing volumes, increasing economies of scale, and increased competition lead to lower parcel prices. In the past, prices for cross-border parcels have been accused of being too high. A particular issue of concern are high price differences between national and cross-border parcel prices that seem hard to justify. Lower

This paper presents the personal views of the authors only and should not be interpreted as the views of WIK or of any clients of WIK.

S. Thiele (✉) • A.K. Dieke
Wissenschaftliches Institut für Infrastruktur und Kommunikationsdienste (WIK),
Bad Honnef, Germany
e-mail: s.thiele@wik.org

P.L. Parcu et al. (eds.), *The Contribution of the Postal and Delivery Sector*, Topics in Regulatory Economics and Policy, https://doi.org/10.1007/978-3-319-70672-6_18

parcel prices are one of the objectives of the European Commission's proposed regulation on cross-border parcel delivery services.[1] With this proposal, the European Commission focusses on public list prices for cross-border parcels that are paid by low volume senders such as consumers or very small e-retailers. Other proposed measures, such as access obligations to cross-border parcel delivery or assessing affordability of cross-border tariffs, have been reduced or removed by the Council's General approach published in May 2017.[2]

This paper analyses whether the expected impact of market growth on reducing parcel prices can already be observed. It takes a specific look at (public) prices for consumer parcels as these are of importance to the European Commission. The paper covers ten selected European countries: Austria, Belgium, Czech Republic, Germany, Ireland, the Netherlands, Portugal, Spain, Sweden, and the United Kingdom.

Section 2 of the paper summarises the development of e-commerce in the ten countries. Section 3 analyses competition on parcel and express markets. Section 4 highlights developments of public list prices for cross border parcels and presents some indications for price levels offered to business customers. Section 5 summarizes our findings, and relates them to current political discussions about regulating cross-border parcels in the EU.

2 The State of E-commerce in Ten European Countries

E-commerce is growing in all ten countries. E-commerce revenues have been growing at two-digit rate on average between 2012 and 2015 in nine out of ten countries (except Germany). However, the ten countries are very different in their e-commerce spending per capita.

Figure 1 shows that spending on e-commerce per capita in the UK outstrips online shoppers from other countries in this benchmark by far, followed by Ireland and Sweden. E-commerce spending per capita is lowest in the Southern European countries Spain and Portugal as well as in Czech Republic and Belgium. Consumers in the UK spend more than five times as much on e-commerce than online shoppers in CZ, ES, and PT.[3] Yet these countries may catch up in the future, as e-commerce spend per capita is growing strongly.

Online shopping is most common for consumers in the UK, Germany, Sweden, and the Netherlands. The share of consumers that buy online across borders is much lower than the share of those buying domestically (see Fig. 2). While this is true for

[1]European Commission (2016), Proposal for a Regulation of the European Parliament and of the Council on cross-border parcel delivery services, 25 May 2016 and European Commission SWD (2016), Impact assessment accompanying the document COM (2016) 285 final.

[2]Council of the European Union (2017), Proposal for a Regulation of the European Parliament and of the Council on cross-border parcel delivery services - General approach, 31 May 2017.

[3]Based on E-commerce Europe (2016), European B2C E-commerce Report 2016.

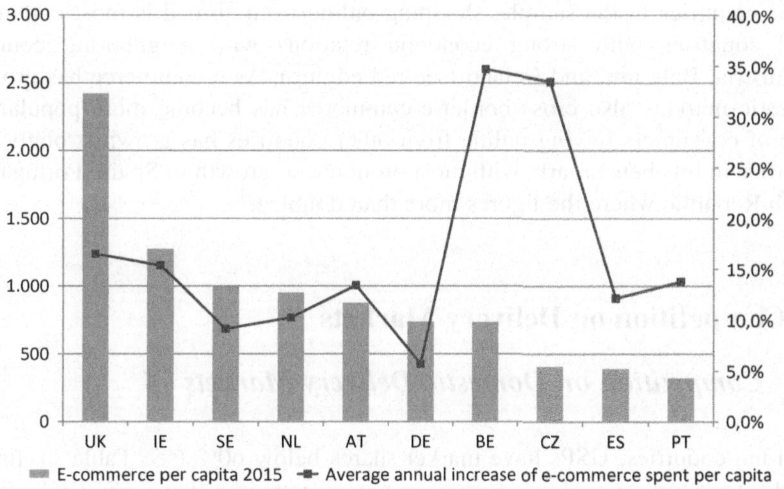

Fig. 1 E-commerce spending per capita. Note: Growth figures show CAGR 2012–2015 except for Belgium and Austria (year-on-year growth 2014–2015). Source: based on e-commerce revenues by E-commerce Europe and population data by Eurostat

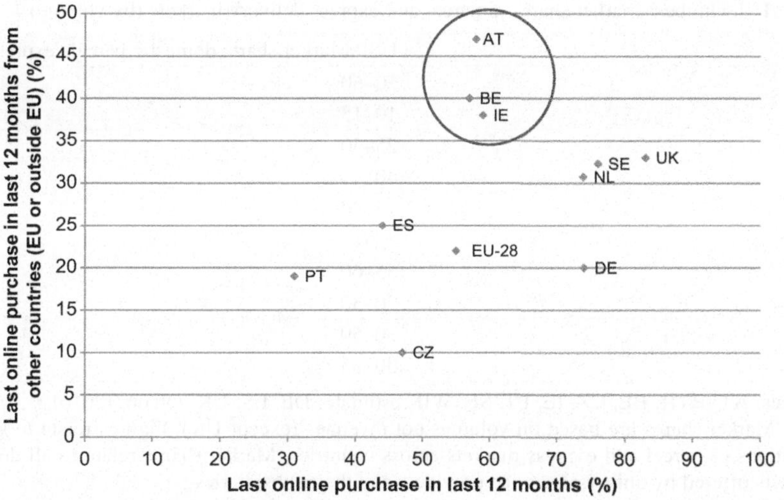

Fig. 2 Online shopping in home countries and from abroad (2016). Source: based on Eurostat. Note: Last online purchase includes physical as well as digital goods and services

all the countries in the sample, shopping online from abroad is most common in small countries with strong economic relations with neighboring countries, i.e. Austria, Belgium, and Ireland (see red edging). As e-commerce has grown in domestic markets also cross border-e-commerce has become more popular. The share of consumers buying online from other countries has grown strongly in all countries in this benchmark, with most pronounced growth in Spain, Portugal, and Czech Republic where the figures more than doubled.[4]

3 Competition on Delivery Markets

3.1 Competition on Domestic Delivery Markets

In all ten countries, USPs have market shares below 60% (see Table 1). International integrators or regional European parcel networks like UPS, DHL, FedEx, DPD, and GLS are present in nearly all ten countries, as well as local parcel and courier operators.

Most competitors of national USPs are active in B2B, and partly in B2C delivery. Due to the growth of e-commerce parcel volumes, many competitors enter the B2C segment which has traditionally been dominated by USPs. To be

Table 1 Incumbent market shares in parcel and express delivery markets (by volume)

	USP Market share, domestic parcels/express (%)
AT	50–60
BE	10–15
CZ	25–30
DE	40
ES	15–20
IE	<20
NL	55–60
PT	20–30
SE	30–50
UK	30–35

Sources: AT: RTR; BE, CZ, IE, PT, SE: WIK estimate; DE, ES, UK: Ofcom (2016)
Note: Market shares are based on volumes not revenues (except UK). Figures relate to varying definitions of parcel and express markets across countries. Market shares relate to all domestic products offered by universal service providers and their subsidiaries

[4]Based on Eurostat data for share of individuals buying online from other countries in 2011 and 2016.

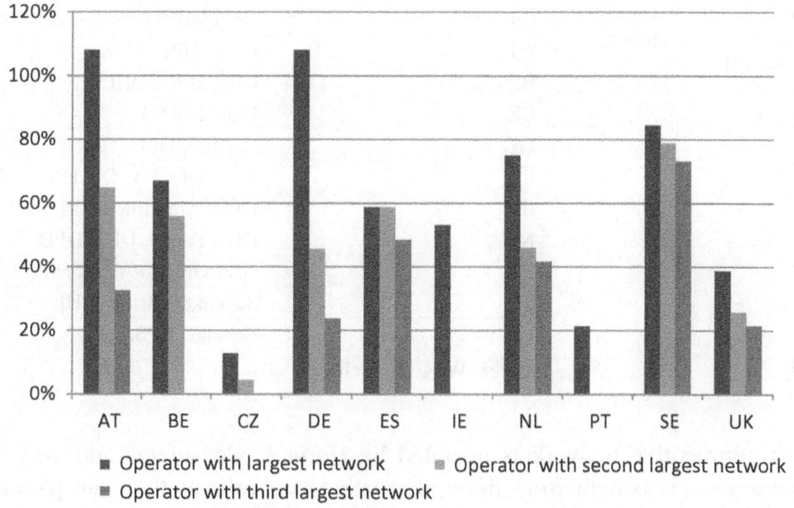

Fig. 3 Parcel shop networks of competitors compared to the USP's public postal network. Source: based on annual reports of USPs and information provided on competitors' websites. Note: Values represent ratio of three operators' parcel shops, compared to the public postal network operated by the USP

successful in B2C delivery, operators need a network of parcel shop to collect e-commerce return parcels. These outlets may as well be used as pick-up points when receivers are not at home, or as a cost-effective place to deliver to.

For each of the ten countries, Fig. 3 shows the size of three competitors' parcel shop networks compared to the access network of the national USP. To facilitate comparison between countries with different sizes, the competitor networks are expressed as a percentage of the incumbent network. The access network of the national USP for each country is 100%. For example, the columns for Austria show the largest competitor network is 108% of the network of Austrian Post (as the competitive network operated by DHL consists of more parcel shops than the Austrian Post's post office network). The second and third largest parcel shop networks are 87 resp. 64% of Austrian Post's network. In seven out of ten countries, competitors have built up extensive networks which are at least half the size of the incumbent's. The networks generally belong to the parcel networks such as DHL, DPD, and UPS. In Sweden, the two largest networks belong to BringCitymail and DB Schenker. In Czech Republic, logistics operator Geis Group runs a network of parcel pick up and return points. Another operator with an extensive network in several countries is Hermes with networks in Germany, Spain, and the UK.

There are especially two countries in which competitors have built up networks which match the incumbent network (or are even larger): Austria and Germany. In Austria, German-based DHL operates the largest network, in Germany the

Table 2 Competing parcel operators with own parcel shop networks

Country	Alternative parcel shop networks
AT	DHL, DPD, GLS
BE	UPS, DPD, DHL
CZ	Geis, DPD
DE	Hermes, DPD, UPS
ES	Mondial relay, DPD/Seur, UPS
IE	DPD, Nightline, GLS
NL	DHL Parcel, UPS, DPD
PT	GLS/Groupo Adicional
SE	Schenker, Bring, DHL
UK	Hermes, UPS, DPD

Source: WIK research

largest competitive network is operated by Hermes. Consumers and very small business senders benefit from these alternative networks as they can pick up or return e-commerce parcels, and post consumer parcels at the shops. The larger the alternative network, the more it is a viable sending option for small volume customers. As most networks are operated by players with international operations (see Table 2), small volume senders also have more options for sending cross-border parcels.

3.2 Competition on Cross-Border Delivery Markets

Traditionally, the vast majority of cross-border parcel volumes are B2B items which have been transported by specialised express operators at high costs and with high quality standards. Services of these providers were normally not targeted at consumers and competition for cross-border B2C was (and still is) lower than in domestic markets. Many national USPs had not been very successful in delivering international B2B shipments but had strong market positions in cross-border delivery of parcels from consumers and other small volume senders. Consumers in most countries had no choice but to send cross-border parcels with their national USP. However, this is beginning to change as B2B operators with international networks such as DPD and UPS migrate into B2C markets.

It is a complex operational change for traditional B2B delivery operators to enter B2C delivery markets. Typical B2B delivery concepts do not work in B2C markets as most private receivers are not at home during the day. In addition, B2B deliveries are typically operated five times a day (and preferably during morning hours) while consumers often also expect deliveries on Saturdays (at least). Finally, parking and related vehicle requirements are more restrictive for deliveries to residential addresses compared to business locations.

Parcel operators have to offer attractive return solutions for international parcels which requires access networks in the destination country. In recent years, in particular DPD, UPS, Hermes and DHL have built up parcel shop networks throughout Europe to enable easy access for consumers to national and international returns.

The case of Austria illustrates how competition has led to more ubiquitous parcel shops: As a small country with German-speaking population, there is a lot of cross-border e-commerce between Germany and Austria. In particular, Austrian consumers order from German webshops and send return parcels to Germany. International inbound parcels account for a quarter of total domestic and international parcels in Austria, and outbound parcels make up 10% of the parcel volumes (RTR 2016). Austrian Post has a strong market position in B2C parcel delivery but this is challenged by several operators.

In 2015, DHL announced plans to build up a parcel shop network in Austria and rapidly scaled up these activities. The company now runs the largest network in Austria. It benefits from its strong market position in Germany and delivers parcels from German e-retailers directly to Austrian consumers through its integrated network. DPD had started integrating its European parcel shop networks also at about the same time (2014). Today, DHL and DPD run competitive parcel shop networks with about 2000 DHL parcel shops (DHL 2017) and about 1200 DPD parcel shops (DPD 2017). Both companies offer domestic as well as international parcel services for private and business customers. In DHL and DPD parcel shops, customers can pick up e-commerce parcels or send domestic and international parcels which are transported to and from other countries through the international parcel networks of the two service providers.

In addition to DHL and DPD, there are other competitors for cross-border parcels.[5] According to RTR, the five biggest players (including Austrian Post) have a combined market share of 78% for cross-border parcels in 2015 (RTR 2016), while no single operator had a market share of more than 23% (volume-based). The situation for cross-border parcel services in Austria is thus very competitive, and not only in the B2B segment but also for B2C and C2X parcels. The strong presence of competitors in Austria is not only a benefit to domestic customers. Parcel operators from other countries, e.g. outside Europe, can easily find delivery partners in Austria.

[5]Hermes, the German-based delivery operator of e-commerce items (owned by retail company Otto Group), has tried market entry in Austria about a decade earlier and had likewise built up an extensive parcel shop network (known as 'Hermes-shops' in Austria). However, Hermes stopped own delivery operations in 2009 and now cooperates with Austrian Post for delivery of Hermes parcels.

4 The Development of Cross-Border Parcel Prices Between 2013 and 2017

Cross-border parcel prices are higher than domestic prices for a number of reasons, including more complex operations, additional sorting, differences in labor costs between the country of origin and the country of destination, and other factors.[6] There are some cases in which cross-border prices of national USPs are several times higher than prices for domestic parcel services. For example, parcels from Czech Republic to Portugal are up to six times higher than domestic Czech parcels. At the same time, parcels from Portugal to Czech Republic are slightly more than three times higher than domestic parcels in Portugal. This section examines whether cross-border prices have decreased between 2013 and 2017.

Figure 4 shows the level of consumer prices of the national USP in 2017 for a 2 kg cross-border parcel to the other nine selected countries in columns 'Min 2kg (2017)' and 'Max 2kg (2017)'. All prices displayed in Fig. 4 relate to parcel products posted at the counter (no express products included). The minimum and maximum columns reflect the fact that most parcel operators apply country-specific prices instead of a uniform price for cross-border parcels to different countries. Where a uniform price is applied, the columns for the minimum and maximum international price have the same length. The figure also displays dark blue columns for each country indicating the average revenues per parcel of the national USP.

Consumer prices for sending cross-border parcels have very different levels in the ten countries. This is not surprising given for example different qualities, different cost structures of operators with low or high parcel volumes or the geographic location.[7] Consumer prices for cross-border parcels range between 16.19€ (sent from Czech Republic) to 44€ (sent from Ireland). There are only two countries where the maximum price for low volume senders is less than 20€ for a cross-border parcel (Austria and Germany).

Figure 5 shows real price changes for single-piece parcels posted at the counter.[8] There is no clear downward trend for consumer parcel prices. Some domestic and/or cross-border parcel prices for consumers have even increased since 2013 (see Fig. 5). However, looking at the details yields a mixed picture: Cross-border prices for a 1 kg letter have increased less than domestic prices in seven out of ten countries. The picture is mixed for 2 kg parcels. Cross-border prices for 2 kg parcel

---

[6]See e.g. Copenhagen Economics (2016).

[7]See research by Claes and Vergote (2015), Econometric study on parcel list prices.

[8]In addition to consumer parcel products, most universal service providers offer discounted parcel prices for large amounts of parcels with specific service features sent by business customers. The regulatory framework for business parcels differs significantly in all Member States. In some Member States, all or part of 'bulk parcels' offered to business customers are considered to be within the scope of the USO while they are outside the scope of USO in other Member States. See WIK-Consult (2013), Main Developments in the Postal Sector (2010–2013), Study for the European Commission, Directorate General for Internal Market and Services, p. 129.

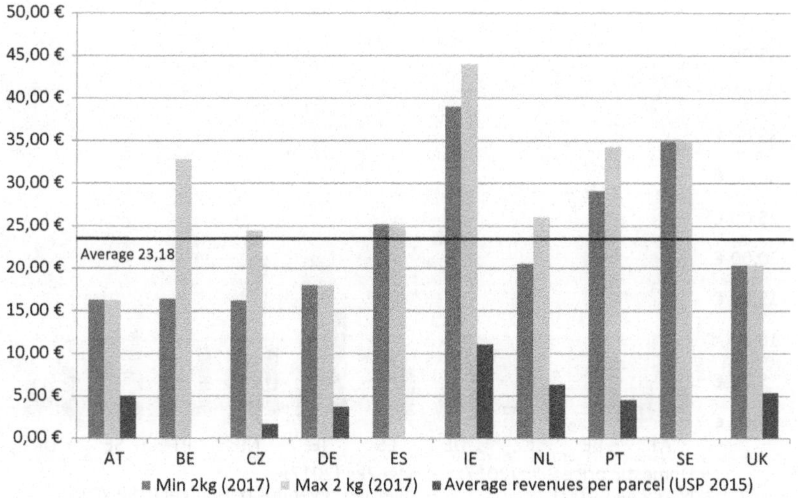

Fig. 4 USP's public prices for international 2 kg parcels compared to average revenues per parcel. Sources: Public price lists of national USPs (2017), WIK analysis of average revenues based on annual reports

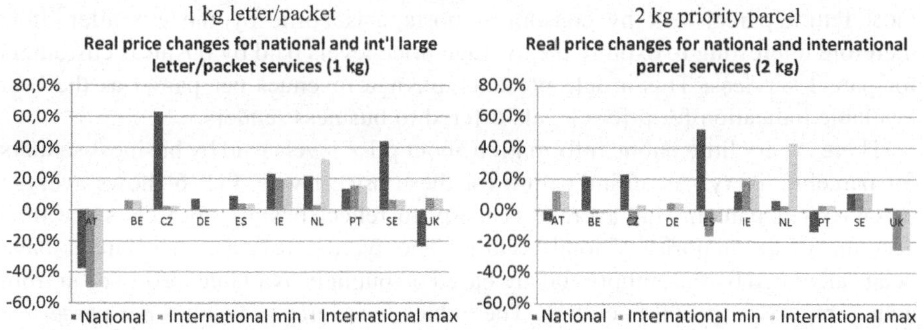

Fig. 5 Real price changes for domestic and cross-border parcels, public tariffs, 2013–2017, USO products. Sources based on public price lists of national USPs in 2013 and 2017 and inflation data by Eurostat

have increased less than domestic prices only in four out of ten countries. But there are a number of USPs that have considerably reduced cross-border prices to all or some destinations for 1 or 2 kg items, i.e. in Austria, Belgium, Czech Republic, Spain, and UK.

Overall, one can observe that international parcel prices for consumers have decreased or increased less than domestic prices in several countries. Yet consumer parcel volumes constitute only a very small part of total parcel volumes-and for

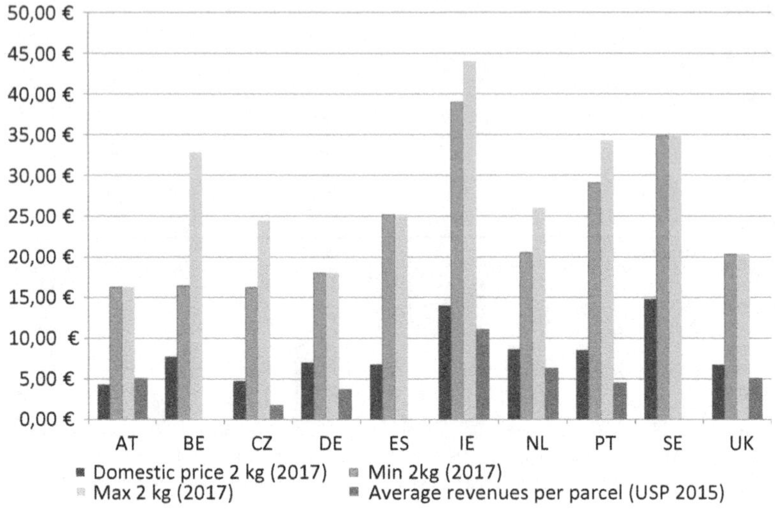

Fig. 6 Consumer prices and average revenues per parcel. Sources: Prices: public price lists of national USPs (2017). Average revenues per parcel: own calculation based on annual reports of national postal regulators and annual reports of postal operators. Note: Average revenues per parcel refer to 2015 data except for CZ (2013)

most return parcel sent by consumers postage is borne by the e-retailer. It is therefore interesting to explore the average price levels paid by business customers for parcel services. This article presents average revenues per parcel as the best available indication for prices levels offered to business senders.

There is very little public information about price levels paid by business senders for parcel delivery. As an indication for these price levels, Fig. 6 shows average revenues per parcel. This average is likely to reflect business parcels since they account for the majority of total volume. The average revenues per parcels have been calculated by the authors and are based on publicly available information from annual reports of postal operators. The values for average revenues per parcel are not specific to international parcels, they rather refer to different parcel definitions and a different product mix. They include parcels of all weight steps, and domestic as well as cross border parcels. Yet they are a useful indicator for comparing business customer price levels between national USPs (though not specifically for cross border prices). In the figure, average revenues per parcel are highest in Ireland and Belgium and lowest in Germany and the Czech Republic. The low level of average parcel revenues in Czech Republic might be explained by a different product mix (e.g. less express items or added value parcels) but also lower labor costs. German parcel prices might be particularly affected by scale and competition in the market.

Average revenues per parcel are much lower than consumer prices for 2 kg cross-border parcels but also substantially lower than prices for 2 kg domestic items (with the exception of Austria[9]). In addition, the average revenues per parcel seem to have decreased in those four out of seven countries for which such data was available (although average revenues might not be directly comparable over time).

5 Conclusions

As e-commerce is growing, consumers are increasingly buying online across borders. This has increased the volumes of international parcels, and changed the competitive landscape for cross-border parcels. While historically there have been either express operators for B2B parcels or national universal service providers in this segment, there are now several operators offering cross-border parcel services. Parcel operators in the ten selected countries have extended their pick-up and delivery office (PUDO) networks to comply with the needs of e-retailers and e-commerce receivers. This indicates that quality has improved for parcel services, and may result from increasing competition in parcel delivery. Primarily though, the level of competition has increased in domestic markets. This does not necessarily affect the prices of cross-border parcels: for the prices of outbound parcels, competition in the destination country, and inter-company prices paid for delivery in the destination country, appear more important explaining factors.

In most countries, operators with international parcel networks (such as DPD, DHL, UPS, Hermes) are active in the domestic parcel delivery markets. In recent years, parcel customers have experienced increased choice between operators and improved quality of service (due to integrated parcel networks). This already is good news to parcel customers, but the story does not end here. In the view of many EU politicians and the European Commission, consumer prices for cross-border parcels within the internal market remain too high. According to basic economic theory, parcel prices should decrease if volumes are growing and competitive pressure increases.

Our analysis concludes that there is a downward trend for (public) cross-border parcel prices in some countries but not overall. There are countries in which consumer prices for parcels have increased, both domestically and for cross-border services. At first sight, this is surprising from an economic perspective. There are, however, a number of reasons why prices might increase even though USPs can

[9]In Austria, the share of heavy parcels (above 10 kg) is about one quarter of all parcels according to market statistics of RTR. Combined with the high share of cross border parcels, this may explain high average revenues per unit in Austria.

realize economies of scale and competition is intense, including situations where prices may have been below cost in the past.[10]

First, B2C parcels are costly to deliver. Many parcel operators struggle with increasing costs on the last mile and introduce alternative delivery options to keep costs under control, and meet customer expectations. The effect of economies of scale might, at least for some operators, simply be offset by costly delivery to consumers. In addition, extending parcel delivery to consumers on a large scale, and meeting expectation of senders and receivers concerning tracking, required significant investments. At this stage, operators may be making different choices regarding depreciation of those investments, and time allowed for pay-off.

Second, although competition has increased, it might not have increased enough to have an impact on consumer prices. Section 3.1 shows that there are several competitors in each of the ten countries, most of them are part of international parcel networks. Yet in only two countries, competitors run parcel shop networks that match the access network of the national USP (Germany and Austria). In the Austrian case, where the two major competitors DHL and DPD have scaled up their activities only a few years ago, the USP has reacted and considerably lowered consumer prices for domestic parcel services (2 kg) and domestic as well as international packets (1 kg). In Germany, where competition on B2C parcel markets exists since at least the nineties, the level of parcel prices is generally very low and the USP has increased domestic and international parcel prices only very slightly since 2013. In other countries where competitors do not (yet) operate parcel shop networks matching the incumbent network, consumers might not consider their services a viable alternative.

Third, increasing quality of service might justify price increases. For example, many consumer parcels now include tracking which might not have been the case in 2013. E-retailers demand faster delivery services, and many operators have invested in parcel sorting technology to cope with this need.

Fourth, the parcel services taken into account in this paper are universal services and in many countries subject to ex ante price regulation. Where public parcels are regulated as universal services, there may be other reasons to increase parcel prices, including a need to compensate falling letter revenues.

To conclude, we stress that USP's consumer prices for cross-border parcels have decreased in a number of countries. Also, there are hints that average revenues per parcel (as a proxy for business customer prices) have decreased. Overall, economies of scale and increased competition seem to have started a process towards lower consumer parcel prices. This paper has studied only ten countries within the internal market, and further research would be needed to analyze whether price trends are similar in other countries. Finally, service quality and choice for consumers have

[10]This refers to single-piece parcel products posted at the counter which fall under the scope of USO. However, universal service regulation is different in many Member States, as shown by WIK-Consult (2013), Main Developments in the Postal Sector (2010–2013), Study for the European Commission, Directorate General for Internal Market and Services, p. 129.

improved, and price increases in those countries where there was no decrease seem moderate against this background.

We ultimately conclude that there are indications that competition and economies of scale are driving prices to the right (and politically desired) direction. That said, we cannot offer strong conclusions about the speed of that drive. In light of these developments, it is difficult to forecast whether the European Commission's proposed regulatory measures (the draft parcel regulation) will still be necessary at the time it will enter into force. Despite slow progress on international parcel solutions in the years preceding the Commission's proposal in 2016, it is conceivable that cross-border parcel prices for consumers and small businesses will further decrease in the course of time, provided the cross-border e-commerce market continues to grow and e-retailers as well as parcel service providers work together to improve delivery services.

References

Claes, A and Wouter Vergote (2015), Econometric study on parcel list prices, Final Report for European Commission, DG GROW

Copenhagen Economics (2016), Principles of e-commerce delivery prices, 9 February 2016

Council of the European Union (2017), Proposal for a Regulation of the European Parliament and of the Council on cross-border parcel delivery services - General approach, 2016/0149 (COD) of 31 May 2017

DHL (2017), https://www.dhlpaket.at/de/privatkunden.html [4 May 2017]

DPD (2017), https://www.dpd.com/at_privatecustomers?mode=receive#!returns [4 May 2017]

E-commerce Europe (2016), European B2C E-commerce Report 2016

European Commission COM (2016) 285 final: Proposal for a Regulation of the European Parliament and of the Council on cross-border parcel delivery services, 25 May 2016.

European Commission SWD (2016) 166 final: Impact assessment accompanying the document COM (2016) 285 final (Proposal for a Regulation on cross-border parcel delivery services), 25 May 2016.

Ofcom (2016), The International Communications Market 2016, Post

RTR (2016), RTR Post Monitor, Jahresbericht 2015, Juni 2016.

WIK-Consult (2013), Main Developments in the Postal Sector (2010-2013), Study for the European Commission, Directorate General for Internal Market and Services, Bad Honnef, August 2013

Adjusting Rates for Quality of Service: Have Market-Dominant Mail Rates Risen Faster than the CPI-U?

Edward S. Pearsall

1 Introduction

The Postal Accountability and Enhancement Act of 2006 (PAEA) established a cap on the annual rate of increase in price of each class of domestic mail for which the U.S. Postal Service (USPS) is the market-dominant supplier. The allowable annual increase is the rate of increase in the Urban Consumer Price Index (CPI-U). The U.S. Postal Regulatory Commission (PRC) is charged by PAEA with verifying that USPS's rates for market-dominant mail comply with this cap.

The PRC's current methodology does not take into account changes in the properties of the mail. However, the PRC's monitoring has disclosed that important properties, most notably the speed of delivery, have changed over time. A reduction in the speed of delivery for a piece of mail is equivalent to a price increase with an unchanged speed of delivery.

We demonstrate how the prices used in the PRC's compliance tests may be adjusted for such changes by using fitted Hedonic Price Equations (HPEs). An HPE relates the postage for a piece of mail to variables measuring the properties of the piece such as its shape, weight, processing preparation, speed of delivery, amount of sorting and distance transported. Changes in the properties may be converted into equivalent changes in a piece's postal rate by measuring along a fitted HPE.

The views expressed in this paper are those of the author who can be reached at espearsall@verizon.net.

E.S. Pearsall (✉)
Independent Consultant, Alexandria, VA, USA
e-mail: espearsall@verizon.net

P.L. Parcu et al. (eds.), *The Contribution of the Postal and Delivery Sector*, Topics in Regulatory Economics and Policy, https://doi.org/10.1007/978-3-319-70672-6_19

The method for deriving an HPE consists of assembling a representative set of pieces of mail with different properties, calculating the postage for each piece from the postal tariff, and then fitting a regression relating the postage to indices measuring the properties of the pieces. The result of the econometrics is an analytic representation of the postal tariff in the form of an HPE.[1] Fenster et al. (2006) showed that HPEs could be successfully fit by econometric methods to past US postal tariffs. Pearsall and Trozzo (2011) used the method to estimate the effects of reductions in the frequency of delivery by USPS. Borsenberger et al. (2013) have applied it to compare the quality-adjusted prices of parcel delivery services across European markets.

HPEs were econometrically fit to each US postal tariff prevailing in the postal quarters (PQs) from FY2011 PQ1 to FY2016 PQ4.[2] Separate HPEs were fit for each of the three major mail shapes: letters and cards, flats, and parcels. The HPEs were fit to large samples comprising representative pieces from every class of mail and service. For example, a single HPE for flats in FY2016 was fit to a sample of representative pieces made up of flats with varying properties (including days to delivery) from First-Class, Periodicals, Standard mail, Priority mail and Express mail. The HPEs were specified in flexible form as restricted trans-logs and fit using weighted least-squares.

The HPEs were applied to adjust the average revenues per piece of the four major aggregate classes of USPS market-dominant mail—First-Class mail, Periodicals, Standard mail and Package Services—for changes over time in their average properties. The adjusted prices were then used to compute rates of change and to construct quarterly series of prices for an average piece with unchanged properties. Next, the price indices were compared directly to the CPI-U. The procedure approximates the compliance test specified by PAEA and applied by the PRC but uses prices that compensate for the changing average properties.

The paper is organized as follows. In Sect. 2 the methodology for adjusting postal rates for changed properties is outlined. Sections 3–5 describe how the methodology is made operational using information extracted from the public files of the PRC. The HPEs are applied to adjust the average prices of market-dominant classes of mail as described in Sect. 6. In Sect. 7 the adjusted prices are used to assess compliance with PAEA's price caps. The paper concludes in Sect. 8.

[1]In this context an HPE is just a convenient representation of an administered tariff. It has no behavioral significance that is not shared by the tariff itself. In particular an HPE alone tells us nothing about the demand for postal services, USPS's costs of supplying the services or how postal rates have been set. The advantage we gain by fitting an HPE is just the ability to estimate prices compatible with the tariff for hypothetical pieces of mail.

[2]PQs correspond to U.S. government quarters.

2 Adjusting Postal Rates

A US postal tariff is a complicated system of charges for sending different kinds of mail through the USPS network in different ways. The rate for a specific piece of mail is often calculated as the sum of the charges from several elements of the tariff. In general, the tariff is a tabulated system for deriving the postage for a piece of mail from the properties of the piece and the service it will receive.

US tariffs can be approximated analytically to a high degree of accuracy by an econometrically fitted HPE. The HPE represents the relationship between postage and properties by treating postage as the dependent variable and by using indices of the important properties such as the speed of delivery as explanatory variables.

Examples of two HPEs are shown in Fig. 1 drawn for tariffs that are 1 year apart. Each graph relates the postal rate to the days to delivery for pieces of mail that are homogenous with respect to all other properties. The dashed line graph for year 2 lies above the solid line graph for year 1 indicating that an across-the-board rate increase has occurred.

The curves both exhibit negative slopes as we would expect. On the left-hand side mail such as Express mail and Priority mail have high postage rates because they are delivered quickly. USPS takes longer to deliver First-Class mail and Periodicals so these categories are represented by points closer to the center of the HPEs while Standard mail, which takes the most days to deliver but is cheaper than the others, lies along the HPEs on the right-hand side.

Now suppose that USPS takes longer to deliver an average piece of mail in year 2 than in year 1. The vertical line through the points A and A′ is drawn at the average number of days taken during year 1 to deliver this mail. The vertical line drawn through the points B and B′ is at the longer number of days taken during year

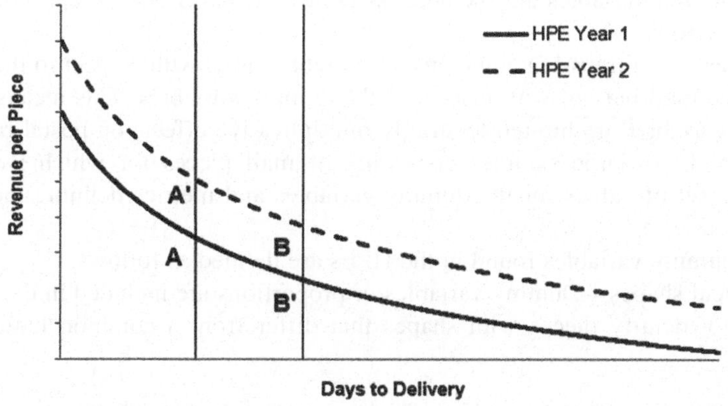

Fig. 1 Price Adjustments with HPEs

2. Point A is located at the days to delivery and revenue per piece that we actually observe in year 1. Point B is similarly located for year 2.

To correctly measure the rate of change in price we must use points on the HPEs for the same number of days to delivery such as A and A′ or B and B′.[3] However, only the points A and B are directly observable. The points A′ and B′ must be estimated from the fitted HPEs. This is done by adjusting the observed revenues per piece for changes in the days to delivery. The price at A is adjusted downward by moving along the HPE for year 1 to get the price at B′ for slower delivery; and the price at B is adjusted upward by moving along the HPE for year 2 to get the price A′ for faster delivery.

3 The Hedonic Price Equations

Our HPEs are refined versions of those employed formerly by Fenster et al. (2006) and by Pearsall and Trozzo (2011). The HPEs rely upon a combination of dummy variables and computed metrics to measure properties. The HPEs are specified as restricted trans-log equations:

$$lnP = \alpha + \sum_i \beta_i D_i + \sum_j \gamma_j lnX_j + \sum_j \sum_{k \geq j} \delta_{jk} \ln\left(X_j/\overline{X_j}\right) \ln\left(X_k/\bar{X}_k\right) + e.$$

lnP is the natural logarithm of the postage for a piece of mail from applying the tariff. The D_i are a collection of dummy variables and proportions. The lnX_j terms are logarithms of metrics that measure the piece's properties. The cross-products $\ln\left(X_j/\overline{X_j}\right) lnX_k/\bar{X}_k$ are formed by taking the logarithms of the mean-centered metrics. The mean centering was simplified by using means computed for the entire time period spanned by the samples. All possible squares and cross-products of the mean-centered variables are included in each HPE (with one exception). e is the equation error.

The restricted trans-log equations are flexible forms with respect to the properties of the mail but not with respect to the dummy variables. This means that the dummy variables are limited to strictly multiplicative effects on postal rates. The HPEs are fit to large samples consisting of mail pieces for which we have a complete set of values for the dummy variables and metrics defining the piece's properties.

The dummy variables found in the HPEs are defined as follows:

Atypical shapes—Dummy variables or proportions are included in the HPEs as needed to identify pieces with shapes that differ from a common letter, flat or parcel.

[3] Using A and A′ gives a rate of change for a forward adjustment of a price index. B and B′ give a rate for a backward adjustment. Calculating both is useful since the two will bound a rate calculated for any speed of delivery between the vertical lines in Fig. 1.

Preferential rates—Certain USPS customers qualify for preferential rates. The mailings of preferred customers are identified by dummy variables for Nonprofit Rate Periodicals, Classroom Rate Periodicals, Nonprofit Rate Standard mail and Library Rate mail.

The hedonic indices found in the HPEs are:

Preparation metric—The preparation metric is designed to capture the effects of metering, postal permits, machinability and pre-barcoding on USPS rates. The metric is based on the postage rate at the end of FY2016 for a single-piece First-Class letter weighing less than 1 oz. with the same preparation (or lack thereof).

Pre-sortation metric—Since the late 1970s US mail tariffs have included discounts offered to large mailers when their mail is submitted in ways that reduce USPS's costs of processing. To incorporate the effect of pre-sortation we rely upon a metric devised by Fenster et al. (2006). This metric is an estimate of the number of sorting passes a piece of mail will receive as the piece passes through processing stages on the USPS network.

Distance metric—The distance mail is transported is reflected in the US postal tariff in two ways. First, the rates for some kinds of heavier pieces are graduated by zones which roughly reflect the straight-line distance from origin to destination. Second, USPS offers destination entry discounts to large mailers which allow these mailers to reduce their rate by entering mail at points that reduce USPS's transportation costs. The metric devised by Fenster et al. is the estimated distance a piece travels over the USPS network in miles plus 1 to account for the "last mile" the piece would usually travel with a mail carrier.

Mailing Size metric—Fenster et al. (2006) discovered that US mail rates are functions of the size of a mailing. This can occur when rates are designed to avoid imposing user costs on single-piece mailers. Conversely, the rates may pass back to large mailers some of the saving that USPS realizes from dealing with mail in homogenous batches. Fenster et al.'s metric is an estimate of the typical number of pieces in a mailing based upon mailings sizes for 30 different categories of mailers.

Weight per piece—Aside from shape, the weight of a piece is the most important determinant of the postal rate for a piece of mail. Ordinarily, the US postal tariff converts a charge per pound or per ounce into a price in steps such as the ounce categories for First-Class letters. However, there are a few important exceptions such as Priority and Express mail flat rate envelopes where the rate is fixed for pieces of widely differing weights.

Air Weight—Weight per piece most affects USPS's transportation costs when a piece is transported by air. Consequently, the weight per piece of parcels transported by air is included separately in the parcels HPEs.

Service time—Fenster et al.'s (2006) service time metric has been replaced with estimates of the actual time taken to deliver various broadly-defined categories of mail. These times are calculated from USPS service time and variance reports made available to the PRC.

The principal refinements made to earlier work are, first, that separate HPEs are now fit for each of the three major shapes. This improvement is made possible by post-PAEA changes in USPS accounting practices that fully separate the mail stream by shape. Second, the metric for time to delivery is taken from delivery performance reports that USPS only began making regularly to the PRC in FY2011. Third, cost coverage margins have not been removed from prices as was done by Fenster et al. (2006). Fourth, previous applications used a dummy variable for automated mail whereas our HPEs include a metric that reflects different degrees of mail preparation.

4 Assembling the Samples

Samples were constructed from the public data files of the PRC for each of the 72 PQ/shape combinations from FY2011 PQ1 to FY2016 PQ4. The assembly of the samples was done class-by-class. This ordering of the process was dictated by the structure of the US postal tariff which is specialized and unique for each class. Moreover, the data that are available for assembling the samples also differ considerably in form and content by class even though all of it comes from USPS.

The samples were constructed by applying the tariff to a set of 2501 mail pieces designed to represent the entire mail stream in detail, and then separating the observations by shape. A sample was obtained for each of the 72 combinations of shapes and by applying the tariff for each PQ to the representative pieces. Standard mail revenues per piece by PQ were available from billing determinants filed quarterly with the PRC.[4] In transition quarters revenue per piece is a weighted average of the rates before and after the transition. The weights are based upon the number of business days in the quarter before and after the installation of new rates.

It was necessary to calculate or match several of the measures of properties to the representative pieces. This was done with Weight per Piece for Standard mail and with Service Time for all categories. Therefore, these measurements of properties vary from PQ to PQ and are dependent on the properties of demand in the quarters. However, this does not make these explanatory variables endogenous. It merely means that the samples for fitting the HPEs are drawn from observations that shift somewhat from quarter to quarter.

Fitting the HPEs by ordinary least-squares leaves estimates that are unbiased but problematic in two respects. First, the residual errors for light and heavy pieces all have the same standard error in logarithms, but a fit with this property turns out to be a poor representation of the tariff for very light pieces. Second, the least-squares fits exhibit the same standard error for pieces that represent both large and small components of the mail stream by volume. This is problematic because it is

[4]Billing determinants are quantities corresponding to elements of the postal tariff. For example, the billing determinant corresponding to the added charge per ounce for First-Class letters weighing more than one ounce is the total number of such additional ounces.

essential that the HPEs most accurately reflect the tariff for pieces that represent high-volume components.

The chosen remedy for both issues is weighted least-squares.[5] The following formula was used to generate the observation weights for the applications:

$$Observation\ Weight = \sqrt{\frac{Piece\ Volume\ in\ FY2016}{1{,}000{,}000 * Weight\ per\ Piece}}.$$

The weights address both problems by increasing the relative numbers of observations for representative light pieces and pieces with large volumes in FY2016. The piece volumes in FY2016 were extracted directly from the last reported billing determinants for FY2016 wherever possible. In other cases, the 2016 billing determinants were used to scale volume distributions for the sample pieces.

Some types of mail, for example FSS flats,[6] did not exist in every PQ. In other instances, primarily involving Standard mail, the reported data contained many errors and omissions that were repaired in various ways. A small number of piece types that were consistent outliers in the econometric fits were also deleted. Therefore, the numbers of representative pieces to which the tariff could be applied varied somewhat by PQ. The quarterly sub-samples used to fit the Letters and Cards HPEs varied in size from 267 to 286 observations; for Flats from 766 to 1053 observations; and for Parcels from 1073 to 1143 observations.

5 Fitting the Hedonic Price Equations

Table 1 presents a selection of 7 HPE fits for flats out of the 72 HPEs fit altogether. The selected HPEs are those for FY2011 PQ1 and for each full PQ following a major rate change. The HPEs for flats not shown in Table 1 closely resemble those selected.[7] Table 1 shows that the procedure has left HPEs that closely fit the tariff

---

[5]It is important to note that weighted least-squares is not being used here to eliminate heteroskedasticity in the equation errors. The errors obtained from an ordinary least-squares fit of the HPEs are seriously heteroskedastic and the weighting of the observations greatly reduces the heteroscedasticity, but some remains and it is unlikely that the residuals would pass tests for homoscedasticity of the errors.

[6]"FSS" stands for USPS's Flats Sequencing System, a series of specialized processing facilities for delivery sequencing flats.

[7]Each of the HPEs includes a complete set of estimated coefficients for squares and cross-products not shown in Table 1. Most of these coefficients are statistically significant at high levels. This confirms the appropriateness of specifying the HPEs using a flexible functional form. Simpler HPEs specified without the cross-products would yield significantly less accurate representations of the postal tariffs in the PQs covered by the samples.

Table 1 Selected hedonic price equations—flats

		FY2011	FY2011	FY2012	FY2013	FY2014	FY2015	FY2016
		PQ1	PQ4	PQ3	PQ3	PQ3	PQ4	PQ4
Adjusted R-squared		0.9969	0.9969	0.9970	0.9972	0.9961	0.9938	0.9942
Average standard error		0.2011	0.2002	0.1946	0.1887	0.2119	0.2747	0.2737
Degrees of freedom		734	735	743	765	922	1020	1019
Intercept	1	−0.354*	−0.339*	−0.458**	−0.679**	−0.483**	−0.960**	−1.137**
Pallet	[0,1]	−0.652**	−0.599**	−0.625**	−0.624**	−0.641**	−0.271**	−0.265**
Fixed rate envelope	[0,1]	1.698**	1.673**	1.712**	1.421**	1.355**	0.933**	1.088**
Nonprofit rate periodical	[0,1]	−0.239**	−0.213**	−0.226**	−0.258**	−0.242**	−0.299**	−0.265**
Classroom rate Periodical	[0,1]	−0.034	−0.028	−0.033	−0.056	−0.066	−0.391*	−0.350*
Nonprofit rate standard mail	[0,1]	−0.548**	−0.553**	−0.597**	−0.569**	−0.564**	−0.580**	−0.584**
Preparation metric	ln(x)	−0.461**	−0.383**	−0.562**	−0.312*	−0.317*	−1.262**	−1.213**
Presortation metric	ln(1 + x)	0.580**	0.569**	0.517**	0.535**	0.546**	0.422**	0.377**
Distance metric	ln(1 + x)	0.077**	0.087**	0.071**	0.112**	0.099**	0.106**	0.124**
Mailing size metric	ln(x)	−0.136**	−0.140**	−0.148**	−0.121**	−0.135**	−0.169**	−0.149**
Weight (lbs/Pc)	ln(x)	0.310**	0.328**	0.300**	0.276**	0.289**	0.279**	0.276**
Service time (days)	ln(x)	−0.629**	−0.598**	−0.523**	−0.477**	−0.465**	−0.167**	−0.145**

Not shown: coefficients for 21 variables constructed as cross-products of the logarithms of the mean-centered metrics, weight per piece and service time taken two at a time

*The estimate is statistically significant at a level between 95 and 99%

**The estimate is statistically significant at a level above 99%

even though the samples include pieces representative of virtually every class and kind of flat mail that USPS delivers.

The best overall index of the goodness of the fits is the Average Standard Error shown on the second line of Table 1. This statistic is the estimated standard error from the weighted least-squares fit divided by the mean of the observation weights. It is the standard error of the estimated price for a piece expressed as a fraction of the piece's price. For flats this statistic ranges from 18 to 21% before FY2015 and is around 27% afterward.[8] For letters and cards the range is 5–6%; for parcels the range is 21–25%.

The estimates of the coefficients for the dummy variables in Table 1 are mostly significant at 95 or 99% levels and present no surprises with respect to sign. The coefficients of the metrics are the marginal effects of changes in the hedonic indices taken at the values used to mean-center the squares and cross-products. These estimates are also mostly significant and unsurprising, except for the coefficients of the Preparation metric, which are unexpectedly negative. The explanation may be that USPS prefers to rely on enforcing preparation rules on large mailers rather than encouraging flats preparation through the tariff. The estimates for the mailing size metric are also noteworthy. They show that at the class-level US rates for flats are designed for commercial mailers and encourage large mailings.

The coefficients associated with Service Time are especially important for our applications because the time required for USPS to deliver the mail, particularly First-Class mail, has increased during the time period spanned by the samples. We can see from Table 1 that the coefficients for Service Time are all negative numbers and that the estimates are statistically significant at the 99% level. They are also surprisingly large numbers. This has occurred because US postal tariffs no longer offer single-piece mailers moderate-cost opportunities to improve the speed of service. The options that remain, Express mail and Priority mail, are expensive.

6 The Compliance Tests

The PRC's tests for compliance are approximated rather than exactly replicated by the methodology used here. Nevertheless, the results should repeat the results that the PRC would have obtained had it adjusted for changing properties. The tests are applied to price indices at the class level, i.e., to First-Class mail, Periodicals, Standard mail and the combined market-dominant categories of Package Services. This also differs somewhat from the PRC's tests which are applied to less aggregated classes. In addition, our tests run continuously from FY2011 PQ4 to FY2016 PQ4 while the PRC's tests are only annual.

[8]In FY2015 USPS introduced discounts for FSS destination entry of flats. The observations added to the samples for these discounts are mostly responsible for the differences in the estimated HPEs.

To adjust the average prices for changes in properties, we first sub-divide the quarterly Revenue, Pieces and Weight (RPW) report categories into sub-streams to which we apply the appropriate HPE. This usually requires some use of the quarterly billing determinants to sub-divide over-broad RPW categories that combine subclasses and shapes. Average values of the dummy variables and metrics were derived for the categories mostly by using billing determinant volumes as weights. By this process and other means values for all of the variables of the HPEs were derived for every PQ from FY2011 PQ1 to FY2016 PQ4.

PAEA's caps on postal rates are restrictions that apply to annual rates of change. To make the compliance tests operational on PAEA's terms it is necessary to adjust prices for changes in properties occurring over spans of 1 year. This has been done by calculating rates in two ways. Let $F_t(X)$ denote an HPE for PQ t with X as a vector of properties. X_i denotes the value of X in PQ i; and P_i is the observed revenue per piece in PQ i. The formulas are:

Rate in PQ t with Forward Adjustment: $R_t = [F_t(X_{t-4}) - P_{t-4}]/P_{t-4}$

Rate in PQ t with Backward Adjustment: $R_t = [P_t - F_{t-4}(X_t)]/F_{t-4}(X_t)$.

The formulas have been applied, along with the appropriate fitted HPE, to obtain annual rates of change for each class of market-dominant mail and for each of the 68 PQs from FY2012 PQ1 to FY2016 PQ4.

A simple compliance test that approximates the more complex test specified by PAEA uses a price index time series that cumulates quarterly changes measured at annual rates from a base PQ for which $i = 0$:

$$I_t = \prod_{i=1}^{t} (1 + R_i)^{1/4}.$$

The rates R_i are the forwards and backwards adjusted rates for the PQs from i up to t. The index I_t is the price in PQ t relative to the price in PQ *0*. The base PQ for all of the cumulative price indices shown in Sect. 7 is always FY2011 PQ4. This is the earliest PQ to which the rate formulas can be applied.

The series I_t adjusts each quarter for changes in the properties of the mail. The formula for I_t cumulates the price adjustments for changes in properties in exactly the same way that it cumulates the nominal part of a change in price. When we use the forwards adjusted rates we are computing a continuous series of prices for mail from FY2011 PQ4 with average properties from FY2011; with the backwards rates the average properties are those of FY2016. These rates bound the rates that we would obtain by calculating I_t using the average properties for any intervening FY. I_t may also be calculated using unadjusted rates of change in revenue per piece. This is done for comparison in Sect. 7.

The cumulative price indices are weighted averages for the domestic sub-categories of each class of market-dominant mail. The weights for the averaging are the quarterly volume proportions calculated from RPW reports and billing determinants.

For most PQs the price index I_t can be compared directly to the CPI-U also normalized to one in FY2011 PQ4. However, in the period from 26 January 2014 to 11 May 2016 the PRC permitted USPS to collect a 4.3% surcharge to make up for revenue losses suffered during the Great Recession. In order to apply the cap with the surcharge the CPI-U is multiplied by 1.043 between these dates. Compliance with the PAEA cap is tested by comparing graphs over time of cumulative price indices with the graph of the CPI-U modified for the surcharge.

The procedure is a continuous compliance test of postal rates for each market-dominant class beginning in FY2012 PQ1 and ending in FY 2016 PQ4. It differs from the test specified by PAEA in several ways. First, the procedure does not adjust the CPI-U cap for any unused space accumulated prior to FY2012.[9] Second, the procedure does not exclude from the price cap space that accumulated more than 5 years previously. Third, the procedure is a continuous quarterly test whereas PAEA only requires compliance tests that are made at the end of the FY or within 45 days of the installation of new rates. And, finally, the PRC's annual tests must average over four PQs in some fashion that our tests do not precisely replicate.

7 Compliance Tests with Adjusted Rates

Figures 2, 3, 4 and 5 illustrate the differences between USPS rates under PAEA and quality-adjusted rates for First-Class, Periodicals, Standard mail, and market-dominant Package Services. In each of the figures the rate cap is drawn as a solid

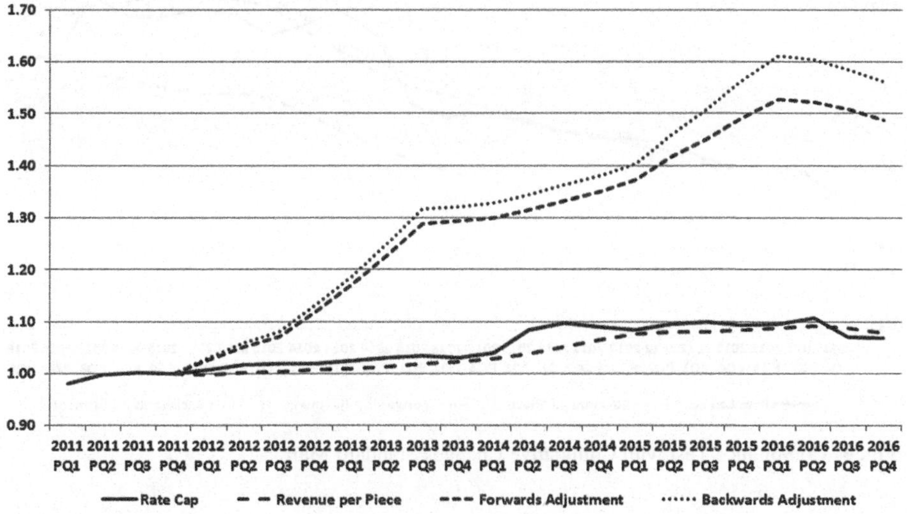

Fig. 2 Compliance Test with Cumulative Changes First-Class Mail

[9]The PRC does not keep a running public record of unused price cap space despite the fact that PAEA's rules appear to require such an inventory.

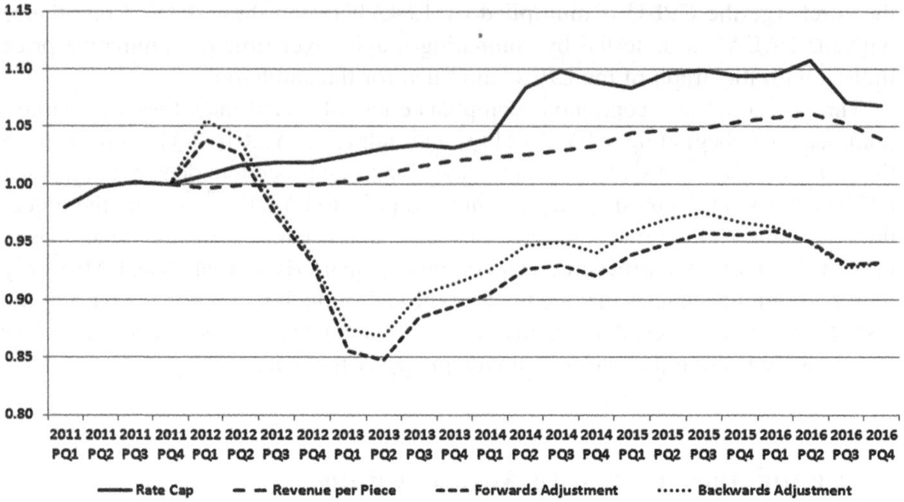

Fig. 3 Compliance Test with Cumulative Changes Periodicals

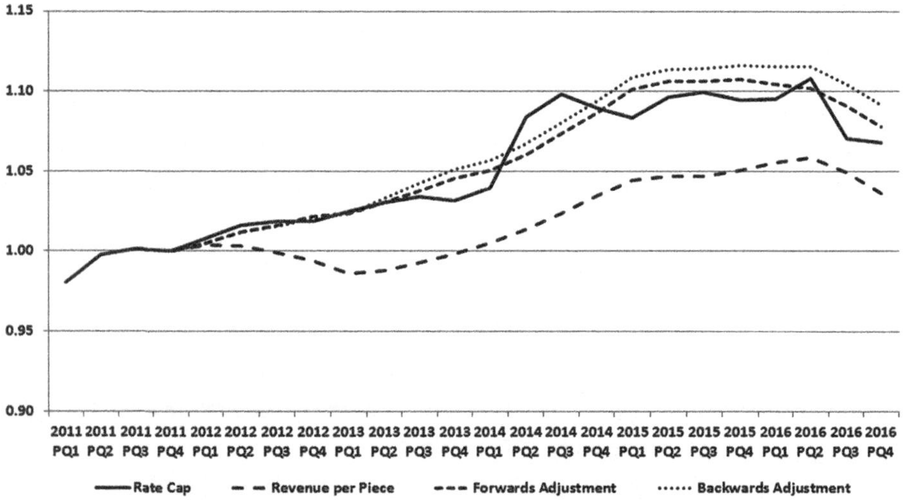

Fig. 4 Compliance Test with Cumulative Changes Standard Mail

line beginning in FY2011 PQ1 and running through 1.0 during FY2011 PQ4. The other lines are all cumulative price indices that begin in FY2011 PQ4 at 1.0. The long dashed line is the cumulative index calculated from unadjusted revenue per piece. The medium dashed and short dashed lines are the cumulative indices corresponding to the forwards and backwards adjusted rates, respectively.

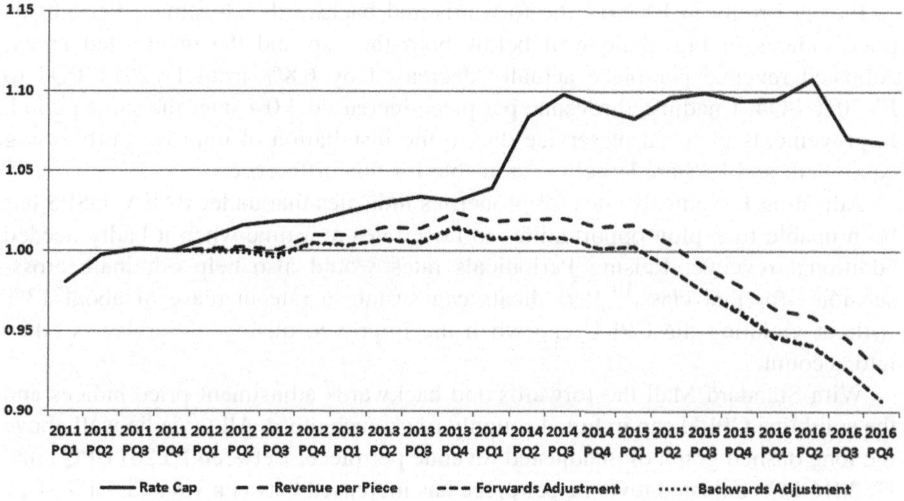

Fig. 5 Compliance Test with Cumulative Changes Package Services

The figures immediately confirm that there have been no important violations of the CPI-U cap when we follow the PRC's practice of assuming that the properties of the mail stream are fixed. With just two minor exceptions all of the revenue per piece lines in Figs. 2, 3, 4 and 5 fall below the price cap lines in all PQs since FY2011 PQ4. The exceptions are the First-Class rates in the last two PQs of FY2016. These prices exceeded the cap by minor amounts apparently because USPS did not lower First-Class rates quite enough to remain below the CPI-U when the exigent surcharge expired. This picture of overall compliance is transformed dramatically in three out of the four classes of market-dominant mail when changes in properties are taken into account.

Quality-adjusted First-Class mail rates would be considerably above rates prescribed by the PRC under PAEA. The forwards and backwards adjustment graphs in Fig. 2 both lie continuously above the price cap line. By FY2016 PQ4 the adjusted revenue per piece has increased between 48.8 and 56.1% which is far above the CPI-U cap increase of 6.8%. The increase in unadjusted revenue per piece over the same period is only 7.8%.

Furthermore, differences have occurred continuously from FY2011 PQ4 to FY2016 PQ4, as USPS reduced the average speed of delivery for First-Class mail on two occasions during this period. These reductions are almost entirely responsible for the differences between the cap and quality-adjusted prices. The HPEs equate these reductions to large changes in revenue per piece because the only ways that a First-Class mailer can buy faster service from USPS (to compensate for slower delivery) are expensive.

Except briefly in FY2012 the forwards and backwards adjustment Periodicals price indices in Fig. 3 lie well below both the cap and the unadjusted index. Adjusted revenue per piece actually decreased by 6.8% from FY2011 PQ4 to FY2016 PQ4. Unadjusted revenue per piece increased 4.0% over the same period. Improvements in speed of service due to the installation of improved processing equipment and FSS are largely responsible for this difference.

Adjusting Periodicals rates for properties indicates that under PAEA, USPS has been unable to exploit opportunities to raise rates at a time when it badly needed additional revenue. Raising Periodicals rates would also help eliminate cross-subsidies for that class.[10] Periodicals can sustain a rate increase of about 13% without violating the CPI-U cap when the improved quality of service is taken into account.

With Standard Mail the forwards and backwards adjustment price indices and the solid line CPI-U cap in Fig. 4 roughly track each other. All three lie well above the long dashed graph of unadjusted revenue per piece. Between FY2011 PQ4 and FY2016 PQ4 adjusted revenue per piece has increased between 7.8 and 9.1%. This is only slightly above the CPI-U increase of 6.8% over the same period.

When adjusted for slower service Standard mail does not offer an opportunity to raise revenue by raising rates. Unadjusted revenue per piece has risen by 3.6% since FY2011, suggesting that half the cap space accumulated since FY2011 remains unused. But this apparent opportunity vanishes when we adjust prices. Standard mail service has undergone changes in recent years including a modest reduction in speed of service. These changes eliminate all of the apparent cap space.

The graphs in Fig. 5 for market-dominant Package Services do not include the small residual of Parcel Post for which USPS is still considered the market-dominant supplier. The picture we obtain from the unadjusted prices is not materially changed by adjusting the prices for changes in properties. The graphs of the forwards and backwards adjustment price indices and the long dashed average revenue per piece do not differ very much from each other. All three lie well below the solid price cap line over the entire period after FY2011 PQ4. Altogether adjusted revenue per piece decreased about 9.5%. Unadjusted revenue per piece has decreased around 7.5%. Adjusting prices slightly increased USPS's opportunity to increase its rates for Package Services.

Despite being classified as market-dominant, Package Services actually compete fairly directly with delivery services offered by USPS's competitors in the parcel business. The declining prices shown in Fig. 5 may be USPS's response to heightened competition in parcels markets.[11]

---

[10]Periodicals revenues have not been adequate to cover the incremental cost of Periodicals services during this period.

[11]Unused cap space is not necessarily an indication that Package Services prices are set to maximize USPS's profit. USPS is not a profit maximizing enterprise and would not be likely to set prices to maximize its profits even when free to do so.

8 Conclusion

Price caps, particularly global price caps, offer a way to improve the efficiency and flexibility of postal price regulation. But price caps require some attention by regulators to the quality of service. A national postal operator may have incentives under a nominal price cap to degrade quality (Sappington 2005). Therefore, most countries adopting price cap regulation have simultaneously invested their regulators with the authority to enforce standards for postal service. However, the US Congress chose otherwise. PAEA does not empower the PRC to do much more than monitor and report quality of service.

The effects of this omission are apparent in the compliance tests exhibited in this paper. Increasing delivery times from 2011 Q1 to 2016 Q4 imply that quality-adjusted rates for First Class mail were considerably above the binding cap on USPS's prices. On the other hand, USPS may have foregone opportunities to increase postal revenues by failing to recognize that adjusted Periodicals rates and Package Services rates lay below the levels prescribed by their caps. Only the price of Standard mail conforms well to the CPI-U price cap when variations in the properties of service are taken into account.

The methodology described in this paper provides a practical and technically correct solution to the problem of accounting for changes in properties under price cap regulation. The solution is to fit HPEs, apply them to adjust postal prices for changes in the properties, and then conduct compliance tests in the usual ways with the adjusted prices.

References

Borsenberger, C., S. Breville and A. Dehais, (2013), "Price comparisons in the parcel industry: a new approach based on the hedonic price theory", in M. A. Crew and P. R. Kleindorfer (eds), *Reforming the Postal Sector in the Face of Electronic Competition,* Edward Elgar, Northhampton, MA.

Fenster, L., D. Monaco, E. S. Pearsall, C. Robinson and S. Xenakis (2006), "U.S. Postal Services as Composite Goods with Hedonic Properties", in M. A. Crew and P. R. Kleindorfer (eds), *Liberalization of the Postal and Delivery Sector,* Edward Elgar, Northhampton, MA.

Pearsall, E. S., and C. L. Trozzo (2011), "Evaluating the Demand Effects of Reductions in the Frequency of Delivery Service" in M. A. Crew and P. R. Kleindorfer (eds), *Reinventing the Postal Sector in an Electronic Age,* Edward Elgar, Northampton, MA.

Sappington, David E. M. (2005), "Regulating service quality: A survey." Journal of regulatory economics 27.2, pp.123–154.,

Simulating Cost Effective Parcel Delivery Methods for Postal Services

Michael D. Bradley, Jeff Colvin, and Mary K. Perkins

1 Introduction

Over the last decade, postal services have experienced simultaneous declines in their letter and flat volumes and increases in their parcel volumes. For example, from 2006 to 2015, the United States Postal Service's (USPS's), combined letter and flat volumes fell by nearly 30%, while package service volumes increased by nearly 80%. This change in mail mix has caused postal services to reconsider the configurations of their delivery networks. At this time, there is considerable variation among posts in the proportion of parcels delivered via dedicated routes, ranging from zero to virtually all.

Choosing the most cost-effective method for delivering parcels is a complex decision. Parcels are not interchangeable with letters and flats in the delivery process, so postal services cannot simply replace letter and flat volumes with parcel volumes on their delivery routes. For example, letter and flats may be easily delivered into curb line boxes or community mailboxes, but parcels are often difficult to deliver to those types of receptacles. In addition, parcel volumes generate different types of capacity constraints for vehicles or delivery units from

The views presented in this paper are those of the authors, and do not necessarily represent those of the Office of the Inspector General, the US Postal Service, or any other organization.

M.D. Bradley
Department of Economics, George Washington University, Washington, DC, USA

J. Colvin (✉)
USPS Office of Inspector General, Arlington, VA, USA
e-mail: jcolvin@uspsoig.gov

M.K. Perkins
Department of Economics, Howard University, Washington, DC, USA

P.L. Parcu et al. (eds.), *The Contribution of the Postal and Delivery Sector*, Topics in Regulatory Economics and Policy, https://doi.org/10.1007/978-3-319-70672-6_20

those of letter and flat volumes. Finally, parcel growth may be uneven with some areas experiencing very little growth, while other areas see dramatic increases.

This paper investigates the degree to which postal services may wish to concentrate parcel delivery on dedicated parcel routes instead of continuing to deliver them with letters and flats. Economies of scope between parcel and letter delivery support the efficiency of joint delivery. But in an era of parcel volume growth, other considerations support developing a separate parcel delivery network. These include developing the ability to deliver parcels using dynamic routing, productivity gains associated with specialization in parcel delivery, lower wage costs (because parcel delivery personnel are not required to have route-specific knowledge and do not case mail), avoiding the costs of capacity constraints (such as retraces or special stops) and the ability to utilize specialized vehicles for parcel delivery. In fact, this is not just a theoretical question because in areas where carriers deliver mail by foot, they cannot physically carry the route's parcels and some postal services perform separate parcel delivery. The question is whether this bifurcation is cost effective across a post's entire delivery network.

This paper develops a carrier delivery model that incorporates two demand-related cost drivers that help determine the choice: economies of scope between parcel and letter delivery on traditional delivery routes and economies of density on parcel-specific delivery routes. Both joint delivery of parcels and delivery on parcel-only routes are modeled. To analyze cost effectiveness, the models are calibrated with parameters chosen to represent typical postal productivities, and the conditions under which a parcel-only delivery network is the least cost alternative are identified. The model can be recalibrated for a variety of productivity and wage assumptions. Section 2 discusses the, relatively sparse, literature on this topic; Sect. 3 briefly describes current USPS parcel practice to illustrate parcel delivery options. The model is developed and calibrated in Sect. 4 and the simulation results then follow in Sect. 5. Conclusions are in Sect. 6.

2 Literature

Though there has been considerable work identifying and quantifying scope and scale economies in delivery, academic interest in the tradeoff between dedicated routes and joint delivery is recent and has followed closely upon real decisions taken by posts as they adapt to growing parcel volumes and intensifying competition. Bender et al. (2016) contains a useful summary of the empirical literature on scale and scope economies in the delivery activity, as well as an examination of the current practice by posts in this regard. Bradley et al. (2006) and Roy (1999) found evidence of scope economies, and several authors found scope economies most likely under low volume conditions (see, for example, Farsi et al. 2006). Roy (1999) also found that diseconomies of scope may prevail in integrated delivery. This will occur if the added product has a very high coverage, and therefore a lot of fixed costs to be shared, relative to the specific-fixed costs of a single product.

Bender et al. (2016) go on to examine actual postal practice on this issue, and find considerable variation in approach, varying in fact from 100% dedicated routes (PostNL)[1] to exclusive joint delivery (Royal Mail). Those posts that lie in between these extremes typically employ joint delivery in less dense areas, turning to dedicated delivery in densely populated regions. Finally, the authors investigate cost-minimizing behavior by a post under conditions of scope economies between parcels and letters on joint delivery routes and scale economies on dedicated parcel routes. They find the best path is to utilize joint delivery up to capacity on joint delivery routes, then spill the remaining parcels onto dedicated routes.

Under more flexible conditions, the optimizing post will adjust its routes such that joint delivery routes have enough spare capacity, on top of letter delivery, to meet the demand for parcel delivery. A switch point can be reached at high volume where the scale economies of dedicated delivery outstrip the savings from joint delivery. The contribution of this paper is to model explicitly the transition of parcel delivery from letter routes embodying scope economies to a delivery situation in which it is cost effective to hand off a portion of parcels to dedicated routes. The models are calibrated with parameters representing typical postal productivities, and the impacts of varying wage and productivity assumptions are examined.

3 Brief Description of USPS Parcel Delivery Options

In the U.S. Postal Service's city and suburban delivery network, parcels are delivered in one of two ways. They may be delivered on what is known as "Letter Routes" or on what is known as "Special Purpose Routes." Letter routes cover virtually all delivery points 6 days per week and the vast majority of parcels are delivered on them, concurrently with letters and flats. Letter routes have an important network characteristic in the sense that route travel is the same each day, with the carrier passing by every possible delivery point. This regularity reflects the fact that most delivery points receive mail each day and that the carriers are responsible for collecting any mail left by customers in their delivery receptacles.

On letter routes, parcels are generally delivered at the same time as other mail in order to avoid traveling the route twice. Parcels that can fit into the customers' receptacles are delivered simultaneously with letters and flats and incur very little additional delivery cost. Large parcels may cause the carrier to leave the vehicle to deposit the package at the customer's porch or stoop. In the rare case of very heavy parcels, the carrier may bypass the stop, then return to the stop after the loop is completed to deliver the parcel and letters together.

---

[1]Bender et al. (2016) note that PostNL, the post with the greatest reliance on dedicated parcel delivery (100% in 2015), plans to reintroduce joint delivery in very rural areas.

A small fraction of parcels are delivered on parcel runs (USPS 2015, pp. 7–1).[2] Parcel runs occur primarily in urban areas in which carriers are on foot and cannot physically carry parcels. They can also occur in areas with such high parcel volume that timely delivery cannot be accomplished on letter routes. Parcel runs thus correspond to the notion of dedicated parcel routes described above and costs are incurred somewhat differently from letter routes. Parcel runs are associated with an area of responsibility, and carriers visit only those delivery points that actually receive parcels. As opposed to fixed daily routes, parcel runs are usually finalized once the parcel volumes and destinations are known. The unit delivery time for parcels delivered on parcel routes is typically greater than for those delivered on letter routes because each parcel tends to generate additional driving time on parcel runs.[3] Use is made of dedicated parcel runs in urban areas where letter and flat delivery, along with small packages, is performed on foot routes (USPS 2015, pp. 7–1) in which carriers walk from delivery point to delivery point, and also during holiday season when the volume of parcels is extremely high. Though city delivery carriers have traditionally been full-time employees, USPS has recently began substituting lower-wage non-career employees, at a rate of about 3% per year over the past decade (see USPSOIG 2016, p. 8).

In rural areas, parcels are delivered on routes that are similar to city letter routes in that they have a fixed route and serve a set of delivery points. Because of the dispersion of delivery points, it is not feasible to have parcel-only routes in rural areas and we do not analyze their costs in this paper.

4 The Model and Calibration

Postal services have two current options for delivering parcels, delivering them along with letters and flats on regular letter routes and delivery on dedicated parcel routes. At historical parcel volumes, it has been cheaper to deliver parcels on regular routes and as described above, delivery on dedicated parcel routes has been limited to urban areas where carriers delivery letters and flats on foot (and thus have no vehicle) and where, on occasion, parcels need special handling due to size or the need for expediency.

However, with the growth in parcel volume, posts are faced with possible capacity constraints and other operational inefficiencies associated with handling a much higher parcel volume on traditional letter routes and the question of how to handle parcels in this environment deserves investigation. This paper accomplishes this end by investigating the cost tradeoffs between the delivery of parcels on letter routes and parcel routes and by building cost models for both types of delivery.

---

[2]Special Purpose Routes, which include collection routes and relay routes, as well as parcel routes, account for about 5% of city delivery costs. A single Special Purpose Route may also serve several functions, delivering parcels, for instance, and then collecting mail from street letter boxes.

[3]Parcel runs tend to be less than a full day because special purpose carriers also collect mail from street letter boxes and make inter-facility transportation runs.

4.1 Letter Route Model

The general model formulation will hold for both driving routes and walking routes. However, the calibration will be different as the times associated with delivery are different. There are two main cost drivers of delivery time: volume and network coverage. In the model, all volume is collapsed into two groups: letters and flats in one group and parcels in the other. This bifurcation is justified by the fact that the marginal delivery time for letters and flats is in the 2–6 s range, whereas the marginal time for parcels is in the 30–60 s range. Also, in the U.S., a typical route will deliver thousands of letters and flats in a day but deliver just 20–60 parcels.

The network cost driver is possible delivery points. It captures the network effect that delivering the same amount of mail to more delivery points takes more time. As the quadratic form has been used successfully in a variety of analyses of delivery costs (see Bradley et al. 2006; USPS 2014), this form is employed to capture the relationship between the cost drivers and total hours required for delivery.

One novelty of the approach taken here is the recognition that the traditional economies of density in the joint delivery of parcels and letters may dissipate and become diseconomies of density at some parcel volume levels. Parcels take up relatively large amounts of space, are relatively more difficult to handle and deliver, may require (on motorized routes) dismount accesses, and can be difficult to stage in a multi-use vehicle. At modest parcel volumes these difficulties are not material, but if parcel volume exceeds a particular threshold, then the additional costs associated with these factors could become material.

The model also captures the fact that the transition between normal parcel operations and inefficient parcel operations is not discrete. That is, one would not expect normal cost incurrence to take place up to say 122 parcels per day and inefficient parcel cost to arise immediately at 123 parcels. Thus, another novel feature of this approach is to model the relationship between the two parcel cost generating processes with a smooth transition function (STF). The smooth transition function appropriate for this analysis has a logistic form:

$$F(P_i) = \begin{cases} 0 : & P < P* \\ \left(1 + e^{-\gamma(P_i - z)}\right)^{-1} : & P > P* \end{cases}$$

where P refers to parcel volume and z is the critical value of the transition function.

With this transition function, the letter route model is specified as:

$$\begin{aligned} C_i^L = {} & w_i\beta_1 L_i + w_i\beta_2 L_i^2 + w_i\beta_3 P_i + w_i\beta_4 P_i^2 + w_i\beta_5 PD_i \\ & + w_i\beta_6 PD_i^2 + w_i\beta_7 LP_i + w_i\beta_8 L_i DP_i + w_i\beta_9 P_i DP_i \\ & + \left[\left(1 + e^{-\gamma(P_i - z)}\right)^{-1}\right]\left(w_i\delta_3 P_i + w_i\delta_4 P_i^2 + w_i\delta_7 LP_i + w_i\delta_9 P_i DP_i\right), \end{aligned}$$

where C_i^L denotes the cost of the ith route, w_i the wage cost incurred to deliver on the route, P_i the parcels delivered on the ith route, L_i the nonparcel volume, and DP_i the potential delivery points along the route. F takes on the value of 0 in the low volume case, where the β parameters indicate the presence of scope economies. After the transition, F becomes 1 and the relevant parameters are the sum of the β and δ parameters, indicating diseconomies of scope.

4.2 Parcel Route Model

The parcel route model is now added. Parcel "routes" or "runs" do not typically have all pre-specified stops to which the carrier must go. The carrier only goes to stops where there is a parcel to deliver. Thus, there is no network variable representing the impact of delivery points on driving costs. However, the geographic area that defines the "route's" responsibility does matter as a route covering a greater area will likely take more time. The parcel route model is thus:

$$C_i^P = \psi_i \rho_1 P_i + \psi_i \rho_2 P_i^2 + \psi_i \rho_3 SQM_i + \psi_i \rho_4 SQM_i^2 + \psi_i \rho_5 P_i SQM_i,$$

where ψ_i refers to the wage on the ith parcel route, and the square mile area of responsibility for the parcel routes is denoted by SQM_i.[4]

To investigate cost effectiveness, the model is calibrated to allow us to generate numerical solutions. Lacking access to USPS proprietary data (or any other post's data) on the number of parcels delivered on each type of route, the calibration is based on publically available, historical information on volumes and reasonable adjustments based upon volume movements in the last several years. Moreover, there is a spectrum of productivities across the postal service's delivery networks so the paper examines the implications of different calibrations for the choice between letter route and parcel route delivery.

The initial calibration for letter routes provides for an eight hour day for a route with 600 delivery points, 2400 pieces of letter and flat mail delivered (or about 4 pieces per delivery point) and 55 parcels delivered. This implies, at a $45 an hour wage and a 25% indirect cost ratio, a marginal delivery cost of parcel of 53.14

[4]Note that we specify a parcel route model with economies of density throughout the feasible range of volume. While it is conceivable that diseconomies could occur at some point on a parcel routes, this problem could be avoided by simply splitting the overly large route into two routes. Finally, the model abstracts from some minor cost considerations such as the differential cost of trucks as well as routing hardware and software.

Table 1 Letter route calibration parameters

Regime 1 parameters		Mean values		Regime 2 parameters	
β1	5	L	2400	z	100
β2	−0.00055	P	55	γ	0.1
β3	42	DP	600	δ3	10
β4	−0.075			δ4	0.2
β5	31				
β6	−0.0015				
β7	−0.000025			δ7	0.0000005
β8	−0.0001				
β9	−0.00005			δ9	0.000005
w	$45.00				

Table 2 Parcel route calibration parameters

ρ1	300	P	75
ρ2	−0.5	SQM	100
ρ3	18		
ρ4	0.0025		
ρ5	0.004		
Ψ	$45.00		

cents.[5] This corresponds to a marginal time of about 35 s per parcel. This is generally consistent with a recent Postal Service study of parcel delivery costs (Table 1).[6]

The calibration for a parcel route reflects the characteristic of parcels routes to be only part-day, so the delivery of 75 parcels takes 5 h. Once again the parameters are chosen to be consistent with analyses of USPS parcel delivery. This implies an overall average time of 4 min per parcel or 15 parcels per hour. Because of economies of density the marginal time for a parcel is less than the average time and the model produces a marginal time of just over 3 min (194 s), leading to a marginal delivery cost of $3.03 (Table 2).

At these values, the marginal delivery cost for a parcel on letter routes is just one-sixth of the cost on parcel routes. This is why USPS has historically chosen to deliver parcels on letter routes whenever possible and reserved the use of parcel routes for situations in which the regular letter carrier could not physically handle the parcel.

[5]The marginal cost includes a ratio of 1.25 for indirect costs such as supervision and vehicle depreciation.

[6]United States Postal Service, "Report on the City Carrier Street Time Study," December 2014.

5 Simulations

The analysis is designed to investigate an environment of rapidly growing parcel volumes, so examination of marginal costs at their typical historical values is not sufficient. The combination of diseconomies of density on letter routes due to large parcel volumes and economies of density on parcel routes caused by increased parcel volumes there could lead to a situation in which the marginal cost on letter routes exceeds the marginal cost on parcel routes. To investigate this possibility, we simulate the model to calculate the marginal and average incremental delivery costs of parcels on letter routes for a wide range of volumes. Figure 1 shows the actual transition function between the economies of density regime and the diseconomies of density regime for letter routes. In our calibration, the transition begins at about 60 parcels per route and is completed at about 145 parcels per route. In other words, as volume rises, the inefficiency costs grow and the diseconomies eventually overcome the economies of density.

This shift is demonstrated in Fig. 2, which plots the marginal and average incremental costs for parcel delivery on letter routes. At first, density economies cause the marginal cost to fall with volume, and then, as the shift to the inefficient regime becomes material, the marginal cost starts to rise with volume. At a relatively low level of volume, the marginal cost is below the average incremental cost but at high levels of volume, their relative position switches as expected with diseconomies of density. The result of the change in regime is a much higher marginal cost. When volume per route reaches 160 parcels the marginal cost increases to $1.43 which is 2.7 times as high as the marginal cost at 55 pieces per route.

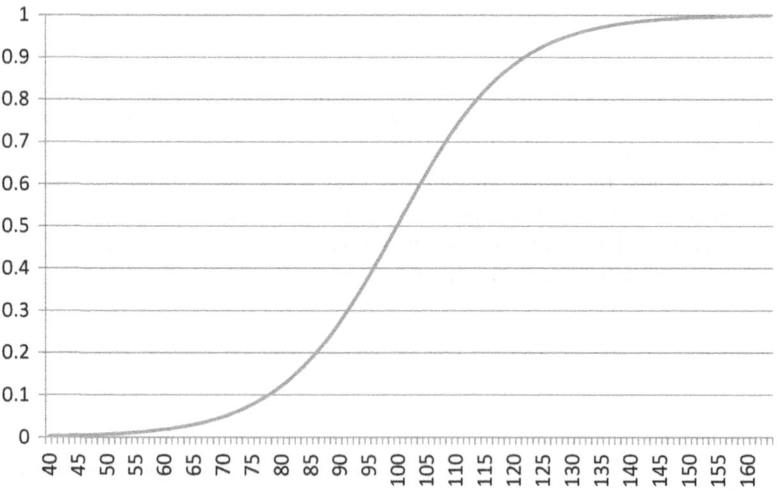

Fig. 1 Transition function

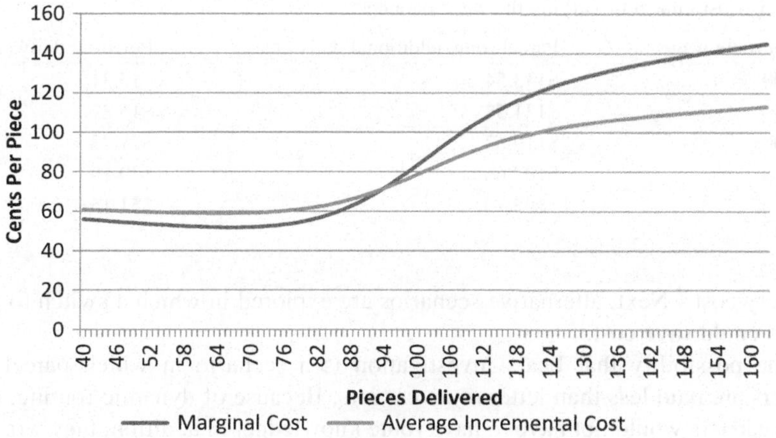

Fig. 2 Marginal and average incremental costs for parcel delivery on letter routes

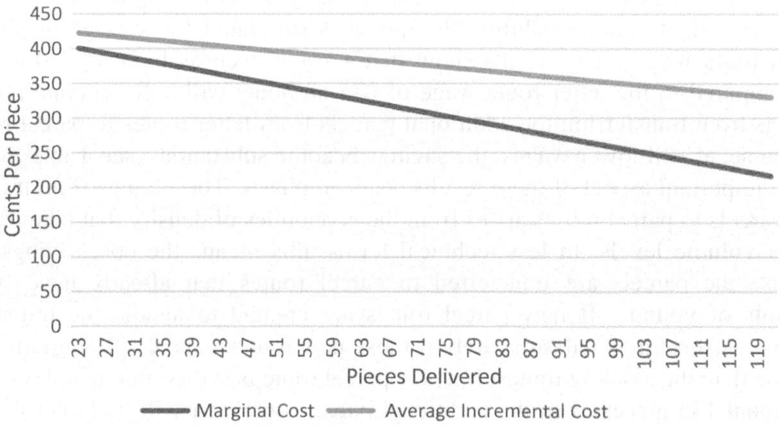

Fig. 3 Marginal and average incremental cost on parcel routes

Simulating the parcel route cost reveals a constantly declining marginal cost which always lies below the associated average incremental cost (see Fig. 3). This pattern occurs because the parcel route is assumed to have economies of density throughout its range of volume. Moreover, our calibration suggests material density economies in parcel route delivery as the marginal cost falls from $3.03 at 75 pieces delivered to $2.20 for 120 pieces delivered.

In the baseline scenario, even a tripling of parcel volume on letter routes does not indicate a switch of parcels to parcel routes. Suppose that a representative letter route had 55 parcels and the excess 105 parcels (160–55) were transferred to a parcel route. In the model, this would save $146.86 per day on the letter route but would incur and additional $213.31. Thus, the transfer drives up total parcel

Table 3 Cost impact of varying the wage parameter

Parcel route wage	Parcel route additional daily cost	Potential daily savings
$30.00	$143.54	$3.31
$27.50	$131.58	$15.27
$25.00	$119.62	$27.23
$22.50	$107.66	$39.19
$20.00	$95.70	$51.15

delivery cost.[7] Next, alternative scenarios are explored in which a switch to parcel routes could save cost.

One possibility that bears investigation is a scenario in which parcel route carriers are paid less than letter route carriers. Because of dynamic routing, parcel route carriers would not have to have route knowledge. In addition, they would not have collection responsibilities and limited in-office activities. These characteristics suggest that parcel route positions could qualify for a lower wage rate. If so, it could have a dramatic impact on the alternatives of handling increased parcel volume, as the lower wage would at least partially offset the higher time per unit.

To investigate this possibility, the model is simulated for a range of possible parcel route wages. The results show that a wage even as high as $30 an hour (as compared to the letter route wage of $45 an hour) will still generate positive savings from transferring the additional parcels from letter routes to parcel routes. Of course, at still lower wages, the savings become substantial (see Table 3).

An important aspect of these results bears emphasis. The savings from transferring parcels to parcel routes arises from the economies of density that take place at higher volume levels. In less technical terms, this means the cost savings arise because the parcels are transferred to parcel routes that already have typical amounts of volume. If new parcel routes are created to handle the transferred volume, cost savings will arise only if those new routes handle substantially more volume than the existing routes. If a new parcel route is started that handles just the additional 105 pieces, then the additional parcel route cost will be larger than the letter route savings.

Regardless of the wage applied to parcel route carriers, the base productivity of parcel routes is critical for making a cost-effective decision on how to deliver growing parcel volumes. In the base scenario, it was assumed that parcel routes would deliver, on average, 15 parcels an hour, and at that productivity, it was not cost effective to transfer parcels to those routes (at an equal wage). The paper now investigates how productive parcel routes would have to be, on average, to achieve cost savings at equal wages. The average parcel productivity at current volume

[7]This is not to say that such a transfer might not be made for other operational reasons. For example, if a route is receiving a large amount of letter and flat mail, the increase in parcels may cause the required transportation space to exceed the capacity of the delivery vehicle. In such a circumstance a transfer will take place, at least in the short run, even if it not cost effective.

Table 4 Variation in parcel route productivity

Average parcels delivered per hour at current volume	Potential daily savings
15	−$68.45
16	−$27.68
17	$4.67
18	$41.22
19	$72.16

levels is allowed to range from 15 through 19 parcels per hour to examine when cost savings would arise. As shown in Table 4, the results suggest that a productivity of 17 parcels per hour would be required.

Note that this is the average parcel per hour delivered before additional volume is transferred to the parcel route. After the volume is transferred, the average pieces delivered per hour rise to 24 because of the economies of density. As parcel volume rises in a given delivery area, parcel stops will be closer together and the number of pieces delivered per stop will increase. Both of these factors will increase measured productivity and reduce cost per piece.

6 Conclusions and Future Research

This paper undertakes preliminary analysis of the issues to be confronted by a post in designing cost effective parcel delivery methods in today's high parcel growth environment. As has been previously noted, a key issue is how best to take advantage of the well-recognized scope economies between letters and parcels. In this paper, a cost model is constructed for delivery on traditional letter routs and dedicated parcel routes. The model allows for the deterioration of economies of scope and density in parcel delivery with an increase in volume and permits the existence of diseconomies at high volume levels. The model also allow for a smooth transition between the two regimes. The model is calibrated with reasonable cost parameters and simulates the costs of different patterns of delivery. In the baseline calibration, absent changes other than volume, the simulations indicate even a tripling of parcel volume on letter routes would not generate a reduction in cost through switching the additional volume to parcel routes.

However, allowing other variables to change leads to scenarios in which dedicated parcel routes are cost-effective. For instance, a lower wage for parcel route carriers can cause the use of such routes to be cost effective. Alternatively, significantly higher productivity on parcel routes will also lead to a cost trade-off in favor of dedicated parcel routes. Finally, the existence of physical capacity constraints on letter routes could cause a post to shift parcels to dedicated parcel runs even if not immediately cost effective.

Future work might include an examination of the economics of route reconfiguration to respond to capacity constraints (e.g., weight or an 8-h workday) on letter routes, as an alternative to handing parcels off to parcel routes. The implications of volume peaks on the joint delivery-dedicated route trade-off are also of interest. Finally, it would interesting to see what information this model would provide for European postal operators, especially those that have separate parcel delivery systems.

References

Bender C, Dieke A, Niederprum A (2016) Economies of scope in delivering parcels and letters together, presented at the 24th Conference on Postal and Delivery Economics, May 18 – 21, Florence, Italy.

Bradley M, Colvin J, Perkins M (2006) Measuring scale and scope economies with a structural model of postal delivery, in M.A. Crew and P.R. Kleindorfer (eds.): *Liberalization of the Postal and Delivery Sector*, Kluwer Academic Publishers, pp 103-119.

Farsi M, Filippini M, Trinkner U (2006) Economies of scale, density and scope in Swiss Post's mail delivery, in M.A. Crew and P.R. Kleindorfer (eds.): *Liberalization of the Postal and Delivery Sector*, Kluwer Academic Publishers, pp 91-101.

Roy, B (1999) Technico-economic analysis of the costs of outside work in postal delivery, in M.A. Crew and P.R. Kleindorfer (eds.): *Emerging Competition in Postal and Delivery Services*, Kluwer Academic Publishers, pp 101-122.

United States Postal Service (2014) Report on the city carrier street time study, December 2014.

United States Postal Service (2015) Summary Description of USPS Development of Costs by Segments and Components, Fiscal Year 2015, p 7-1.

United States Postal Service Office of the Inspector General (2016) Peeling the onion: The real cost of mail, RARC-WP-16-009.

Price Elasticities and Factors Driving International Contract Export Mail Sent from the UK to Western European Countries

Frederique Feve, Thierry Magnac, Soterios Soteri, and Leticia Veruete-McKay

1 Introduction

In the economics literature traditional export demand functions in gravity models are a function of the exchange rate, economic activity and distance between countries. Models of this type provide a useful framework to examine international mail traffic. For example, Anson and Helble (2013) and Anson et al. (2014) have estimated international gravity models using econometric techniques and the latter have concluded that favorable exchange rate movements stimulated parcel dispatches within the Asia and Pacific region.

This chapter follows in the footsteps of Anson et al. (2014) and provides, for the first time, insights into the potential magnitude of UK international export price elasticities and the sensitivity of this traffic stream to changes in the exchange rate and conditions in economic activity of the destination countries. In particular, this study uses a large customer data set to model the demand for international contract export mail.[1] Furthermore, by exploring customer data disaggregated by products

The views expressed in this paper are those of the authors and do not necessarily reflect those of their affiliated organizations. We thank the editors and Frank Rodriguez for very helpful comments.

[1]This data set does not include information on smaller customer mailings, for example those using Stamp and Franking machines, and therefore these streams of traffic are excluded from our analysis.

F. Feve (✉) • T. Magnac
IDEI, University of Toulouse, Toulouse, France
e-mail: frederique.feve@tse-fr.eu; thierry.magnac@tse-fr.eu

S. Soteri • L. Veruete-McKay
Commercial and Economics Finance, Royal Mail Group, London, UK
e-mail: soterios.soteri@royalmail.com; leticia.veruete-mckay@royalmail.com

P.L. Parcu et al. (eds.), *The Contribution of the Postal and Delivery Sector*, Topics in Regulatory Economics and Policy, https://doi.org/10.1007/978-3-319-70672-6_21

and format type (letter, large letter and parcels) we also examine the extent to which we can identify differences in the estimated price elasticities by format type.

This chapter is structured as follows. Section 2 provides an overview of the data and international mail demand modelling framework. Section 3 contains empirical results and provides a range of econometric estimated international large customer export contract elasticities and Sect. 4 contains a summary and some conclusions.

2 Data and Modelling International Demand

The USA, a number of Western European countries and China are among the top ten UK export destinations, accounting for almost two-thirds of UK exports in goods and services. In line with international gravity model findings, it is therefore unsurprising that eight out of the top ten British trading partners in the world are European given their geographical proximity and relative wealth. Similarly, although to a lesser extent, Table 1 shows that a large share of UK bulk export contract mailings go to the same top ten export destinations, and that they account for 38% of total UK export mailings, of which letters accounted for 23% and parcels for 15%.

Table 1 Share (%) of UK exports by trade and mailings to other countries

	UK export destinations in 2014			UK exports mailing in 2014/2015		
	By exports			By mailings		
	Total (%)	Goods (%)	Services (%)	Total (%)	Letters (%)	Parcels (%)
1. USA	17	7	10	10	5	5
2. Germany	8	6	2	7	5	2
3. Netherlands	7	4	2	1	1	0.2
4. France	6	4	2	6	4	2
5. Ireland	5	4	2	8	6	2
6. China	4	3	1	na	na	na
7. Belgium and Luxembourg	4	2	1	1	1	0.2
8. Switzerland	4	2	2	1	1	0.3
9. Spain	3	2	1	2	1	0.5
10. Italy	3	3	1	3	2	1
Top 10 total	61	36	25	38	23	15
17 Western European countries	**54**	**35**	**19**	**30**	**21**	**9**

Source: Authors derivations based on Office for National Statistics and Royal Mail data
Notes: Letters contain both letter and large letter formats. The 17 Western European countries are: Austria, Belgium, Denmark, Finland, France, Germany, Greece, Iceland, Ireland, Italy, Luxembourg, Netherlands, Norway, Portugal, Spain, Sweden, and Switzerland

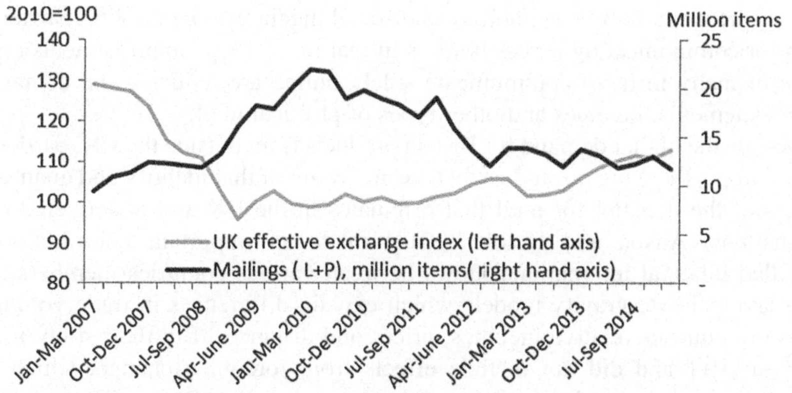

Fig. 1 Real UK effective exchange and UK mailings (letters and parcels) to Western Europe. Source: Authors derivation based on Bank for International Settlements and Royal Mail data

Demand for international mailings has been affected by various factors over the past decade, including, amongst others, the impact of technological changes such as internet shopping, economic activity, the exchange rate and the price of mail. Figure 1 displays movements in the UK real effective exchange index (2010 = 100) and mailings (letters and parcels) in millions of items sent by large customers to Western Europe.

The UK effective exchange rate is a weighted average of the UK's main trading partners, which mainly includes the euro, other European currencies and the US dollar. The value of sterling is defined with respect to this basket and several points are worth noting. First, the value of sterling has oscillated over time, falling sharply following the global recession of 2008 and subsequently gaining value particularly from 2013 onwards. Furthermore, past episodes when sterling fell have been accompanied by an increase in mailings sent to Western Europe. Similarly, periods of appreciation of sterling have occurred when mailing volume has fallen. Some of the surge in mailings could be explained by British products being cheaper during the pound depreciation but it might also be related to the increase in online shopping over time.

The growth of internet shopping has profoundly changed consumer behavior over the past few years. For many consumers, the internet is, amongst other things, a powerful new sales channel providing greater choice on what goods and services to purchase and which countries to buy from. This has led to a higher demand for British products from outside the UK and to a surge in demand for parcels from e-commerce, in particular from Europe.

Since 2010, however, mailings have followed a downward trend. This is likely to be due to increases in electronic substitution for letter volumes as has taken place with domestic letters since the mid-2000s (see, for example, Rodriguez et al. 2017). At the present time, letter traffic volumes are under constant pressure from improvements in mobile technology and social media that are eroding barriers and costs for communicating across borders in real time. These improvements and the move of many firms to communicate solely online are reducing the demand for paper statements, invoices and other types of physical mail.[2]

Despite the higher demand for British products from outside the UK, particularly from Europe, there are no studies that we are aware of that identify and quantify the drivers of the demand for mail that originates in the UK and is delivered to EU destinations. Anson and Helble (2013) made an important contribution and modelled bilateral international flows between various countries members of the UPU and estimate gravity models which explain differences in trade volumes in terms of countries relative incomes, prices and distance.[3] But their study focused only on 2011 and did not include effects from foreign exchange, which is an important factor impacting international trade and mail traffic.

In the economic literature, traditional export demand or gravity models are a function of the real exchange rate[4] and economic activity. Anderson (2011) (see, for example, Santos silva and Tenreyro 2006) surveyed this literature which consists of a vast number of studies undertaking empirical work and modelling international trade flows. It has also helped to characterize the distribution of economic activity across many origin and destination pairs to better understand the global interaction of a region. More recently, Anson et al. (2014) tested whether exchange rate movements can impact trade in the short term in the Asia and Pacific region. They estimated a dynamic econometric model for exchange rates and parcel dispatches using daily data on international postal flows. The authors found that favorable exchange rate movements stimulate trade in the short run. However, effects of mail prices or economic activity were not included in their estimations.

This paper will quantify for the first time the effect of price, GDP and exchange rates on mail flows originating in the UK and sent to Western European countries by using firm level data since December 2006. The paper proposes a framework similar to the estimation of the demand for exports, which take into account own price effects as well as foreign exchange effects and GDPs of the destination countries. Price effects are estimated using price indices of all mail products sent by firms to various Western European destinations.

We estimate demand equations for international mailings to 17 European destination countries in order to obtain new insights into the magnitude of UK international mail export price elasticities. In particular, we investigate the role of variables suggested by gravity models such as the level of economic activity of the destination countries and exchange rates (note that some of the 17 countries in our study have not adopted the euro as their currency). In addition, we also control

---

[2]However, physical letters through the post still form an important part of a well-rounded and integrated marketing campaign for firms.

[3]The first application of the gravity model to trade flows was by Tinbergen (1962).

[4]At purchasing power parity.

for changes in demand due to technology and other structural factors by including a set of unrestricted country, monthly, and product dummy variables.

The data used to undertake the empirical analysis were informed by monthly information of large customer contract mailings sending items of different format types from the UK to the Western European countries using a range of services.[5] The dataset itself contained information on the number of items, weight and value spent between 2006 and 2015 for bulk contract export mail. This dataset also identified various attributes of their mailings, for example the format (letters, large letters, parcels); speed of delivery (priority versus economy), sortation levels (high or low) and the destination country.

Rate cards provided information on tariffs for the various international mail products per unit and per kilo in a given financial year. Tariffs varied by products whose attributes are differentiated. These products can be grouped into formats which are letters, large letters and parcels, but customers can obtain volume related discounts if they send large mailings and presorted items. Among customers, some will spend more per year than others and/or use different type of products. Equally, some firms send mailings to various destination countries while others concentrate on single destinations.

Data to estimate demand models were constructed by aggregating individual customer data. More precisely, we compiled a database where the variables are observed by month t (t=1,….. T), product f, and destination country d. Using this information for volumes and values of each specific mailing to all the destination countries from 2006/2007 to 2014/2015, a price index was constructed, taking into account various attributes.[6] Dummy variables for formats (letters, large letters, parcels and no format specified), products (12) and country destination (17) were included in different models.

To deal with the varied monthly pattern of mailings, shopping online is for instance highly seasonal (e.g. increasing during Christmas) and technology and other structural changes over the period, all variables were re-centered with respect to their time means. The dependent and explanatory variables were first regressed on monthly dummy variables over the whole period and differences with respect to these estimates (i.e. differences with respect to time means) are the dependent and explanatory variables that we used in our empirical analysis. This procedure is equivalent to introducing a set of unrestricted time dummies in all the regressions estimated (see Wooldridge 2010).

Furthermore, international trade is affected by exchange rates and the size of the economy in the destination countries. To capture these factors we used monthly data on the real effective exchange rates of the 17 destination countries from the Bank of International Settlements (BIS, see, for example, Fung and Klau 2006) and GDP data for these countries from a data set supplied by Oxford Economics.

[5]In particular, this covered business customers who spend over a specified amount, equal to £5000 per annum in 2017, on a range of International Business services.

[6]Further information on how the price indices were derived is contained in the Appendix.

A log linear pooled model was estimated, based on all customer transactions for the period December 2006 to May 2015. We also tested semi log specifications but they performed less well than the simpler log linear specification, which was most convenient since the average price elasticity in the latter specification is constant. In the absence of competitor prices the real exchange rate also captures the price for substitutes of purchasing mail services and goods in the destination country. We did not include any lagged dependent variables since economic rationales for dynamics such as costs of adjustment or habit formation are of second order when examining aggregate demand by product and destination countries.

As mentioned previously, we also control for demand shifts due to electronic substitution, structural factors and other evolving environment effects by including a full set of time, country and product dummies. These dummies partly control for omitted variable bias. Internet penetration is such an omitted variable whose correlation with included variables is, we believe, very much attenuated by using country, time and product dummies.

The final specification is:

$$Ln\,Q_{fdt} = \alpha + \beta\ \ln\,Price_{fdt} + \lambda\ \ln\,GDP_{dt} + \eta\ \ln\,EER_{dt} + \\ \mu\ \mathrm{d.}Product_f + \gamma\ \mathrm{d.Format} + \delta\ \mathrm{d.}Country_d + \varepsilon_{fdt}$$

where Q_{fdt} represents the traffic for each product, f, sent from the UK to any of the 17 destination countries, d, within the Western European countries in a given month, t. That is, Q_{fdt} is the level of aggregate mail demand, which is the number of units at time t for a product f and destination d. $Price_{fdt}$ is the price index variable whose construction is detailed in the Appendix. GDP_{dt} represents the level of economic activity in any given financial year of the respective 17 Western European countries. EER_{dt} refers to the effective monthly exchange rates for the 17 Western European countries and ε_{fdt} denotes a random shock.

UK international export mail demand equation were estimated by Ordinary Least Squares (OLS), which assumes that prices are exogenous, and also by instrumental variable methods such as Two Stage Least Squares (2SLS) and General Method of Moments (GMM, see for example, Florens et al. 2007) where prices are not assumed to be exogenous. Endogeneity of prices in demand studies is pervasive since prices are usually constructed by dividing the value by the volume of each monthly mailing. This results in potential division bias if value and volume are measured with errors. Furthermore, discounts are common for large mailings and can result in the dependent variable partly causing the explanatory variable. Prices per kilo and per unit for the various products from the rate cards were used as instruments when using 2SLS or GMM. These prices are set by Royal Mail and are not affected by measurement errors or discounts.

3 Empirical Results

Section 3.1 reports estimates of aggregate UK international export mail demand models across all mail formats (letters, large letters and parcels) and Sect. 3.2 provides estimates for individual format types. Different model specifications in terms of the dummy variables were estimated which, as explained above, centered all variables with respect to time dummies in order to take account of seasonality, e-substitution and other structural factors such as evolving competition. All the models incorporated a set of product dummies, or alternatively format, and destination country dummy variables. In addition, due to changes introduced in April 2014 regarding new products and their formats, international demand for mail models were also estimated using a subsample of observations.

3.1 Empirical Results for Aggregate International Export Mail Demand

Table 2 reports the econometric results for aggregate demand functions and the estimates themselves can be interpreted as average elasticities for UK international export contract traffic across all mail formats. Results are reported only for the OLS and GMM estimators, since the 2SLS results were similar to those of GMM. Independent of the method of estimation and the specification of the demand for international mail (letters and parcels), the aggregate price elasticity of international export bulk contracts was estimated to lie in the range −0.8 to −1.1. The estimated aggregate price elasticities were statistically significant different from zero at the 5% significance level for all specifications and estimation methods and we could not reject the null hypothesis that the price elasticity is equal to unity at this same level of statistical significance.

Estimates of the effect of economic activity were less stable, ranging from 0.6 to 1.5. But note that the GDP elasticity in the specifications (1) and (4) were statistically significant only at a 10% significance level.

The estimated coefficients reported in Table 2 suggest that international demand for UK export mail traffic is highly sensitive to exchange rate movements, and elasticities lie in the range of 2.0–2.6. This implies that for each percentage point decrease in sterling relative to the Euro or other British trading partners' currencies there will be a correspondingly higher demand for the demand for UK export mailings (letters and parcels). This factor has the largest impact on the demand for UK international export mailings and implies that even when mail tariffs themselves are not modified, fluctuations in foreign exchange will lead to changes in the demand for international mail. It is possible that this large exchange rate effect is also capturing the impact of omitted macro shocks or may be acting as a proxy for the relative price of substitute products and goods or services which are being shipped.

Table 2 All traffic (letters and parcels) period Dec 2006 to May 2015

	OLS	OLS	OLS	Instrumental GMM	Instrumental GMM	Instrumental GMM
	(1)	(2)	(3)	(4)	(5)	(6)
Prices	−1.1* **(0.042)**	−1.0* **(0.027)**	−1.0* **(0.023)**	−0.9* **(0.243)**	−0.9* **(0.106)**	−0.8* **(0.107)**
GDP	0.6**	1.4*	1.5*	0.6**	1.4*	1.5*
Exchange rate	2.5*	2.1*	2.2*	2.6*	2.0*	2.1*
Dummy variables						
Format	✓	✗	✗	✓	✗	✗
Product	✗	✓	✓	✗	✓	✓
Destination country	✓	✓	✓	✓	✓	✓
R^2	0.27	0.75	0.75	0.27	0.75	0.75

Notes: * Denotes statistically significant at 5% significance level. ** Denotes statistically significant at 10% significance level. Figures in parenthesis are standard errors for price coefficients. ✗ denotes the dummy variables are absent from the regression and ✓ denotes they are present. The GMM price elasticity estimates should be preferred to the OLS estimates on the basis that this method of estimation provides consistent estimates even if the price index is endogenous

An examination of the estimated elasticities over the sub-sample period December 2006 to March 2014 yields GDP and exchange rate elasticities that are similar to those estimated when the full period is considered. The main difference between the two sets of results is that the estimated price elasticities in the sub-sample exhibit a wider range and lie between the values −0.5 to −1.3 (these results are not reported in Table 2). Furthermore, there seems to be a trade-off between the magnitudes of the central estimates for GDP versus the exchange rate, which depends on the choice of explanatory variables. For example, where GDP estimates are at the lower end of the range, the corresponding exchange rate elasticity is at the higher end of the range. This denotes a high degree of collinearity between these variables which vary across periods and countries.

3.2 Demand for Parcels and Letters

Letters represent a higher proportion of total UK bulk contract export mailings but they have been in steady decline since 2011, while parcels have started from a much lower base but have been increasing strongly over the past few years due to a surge in e-commerce. To better understand the main factors driving the demand for International mail traffic we also estimated separate demand models for parcels and letters. However, due to nomenclature changes to our data it was not possible to undertake this analysis over the full sample period and our econometric modelling examined separately the periods up to and including March 2014 and from April 2014 onwards.

Table 3 International demand by format

	Dec 2006 to Mar 2014		
	Letters	Large letters	Parcels
	GMM	GMM	GMM
	(A)	(B)	(C)
Prices	−1.5*	−1.1*	−1.5*
	(0.326)	(0.240)	(0.311)
GDP	0.3*	1.0*	3.7*
Exchange rate	2.1*	0.6*	n.s.
Dummy variables			
Peak traffic (April 2010)	✓	✓	✓
Product	✓	✓	✓
Destination country	✓	✓	✓
Seasonal variables	✓	✓	✓
R^2	0.80	0.85	0.66

Notes: * Denotes statistically significant at 5% significance level

Table 3 contains the econometric results for the letter, large letter and parcel models estimated for the period December 2006 to March 2014. The most robust estimates were those based on the GMM method and only these are reported. We observe that the price elasticity of demand for shipping all mail formats (letters, large letters and parcels) are, in absolute terms, all above unity and higher than the aggregate price elasticities reported in Table 2. However, they are not significantly larger than unity at a level of 5% since standard errors are much larger at this disaggregated level.

The magnitude of the estimated coefficients for economic activity and the exchange rate are quite different across the different mail formats. But the exchange rate effect for parcels was not statistically significant different from zero. This is a surprising result, because if the demand for goods and thus for parcels exported from the UK is responsive to the exchange rate, we would have expected a bigger impact from the exchange rate on parcels than letters. The fact that the GDP elasticity for parcels is very high suggests that this may be, in part, reflecting the upward trend of parcels traffic due to internet related e-commerce activity.

Results based on GMM estimates for April 2014 to May 2015, after the nomenclature changes to products and formats, led to poor estimates that we do not report. This is probably due to a lack of identification, in particular the paucity of price changes over such a short period of time is resulting in small price variations that are collinear with the time dummies and other macro variables. The econometric analysis reported in this section therefore suggests that the estimated elasticities for the models disaggregated by mail format type are in line but less precise than those for the aggregate mail demand models reported in the previous sub-section.

4 Conclusions

With the continued decline in letters, national postal operators have pursued other areas that could generate revenues. Parcels and international mailings have started to generate additional traffic in the UK and it is therefore important to identify their key drivers of demand and understand the extent to which they are likely to impact mail volumes and revenue.

This paper, for the first time, used econometric analysis to quantify the effects of price, exchange rates, and economic activity on demand for UK international export contract mail (letters and parcels) from 17 Western European countries using panel customer data. The estimated mail price elasticities were quite high and lie in the range −0.8 to −1.5, with the most robust estimates suggesting that the absolute value of the estimated aggregate international export contract price elasticity is insignificantly different from unity. The econometric analysis accounting for differences across firms for the products sent also identified that the most important macroeconomic factor is the exchange rate followed by economic activity.

The development of e-commerce has increased demand for parcels delivery across borders and may also have changed the nature of competition amongst operators. It also would be of interest to extend this study to examine potential interactions of price and competition taking into account characteristics of the delivery process (duration, quality, proximity of delivery). In addition, in the light of the UK vote in June 2016 to leave the EU and the substantial decline in sterling that followed, it could be of value to update this study to test whether the estimated strong impact of the exchange rate continues to hold.

Appendix: Derivation of Price Indices and Instruments

We construct a price index for each product and each destination based on Törnqvist indices.

Let p_{fdt} be the observed price of the product f at time t for destination d. For simplicity, we drop indices f and d below and we write p_t. Note that we apply the same methodology for each product f and for each country d. Denote pu_t as the unit price of the product f at time t for destination d, and let pk_t be the price per kilo of the product f at time t for destination d. These are rate card prices and are assumed to be exogenous.

Using a chained Divisia index, or its discrete approximation (a Tornqvist index), we construct this considering adjacent periods *t-1* and *t*

$$\log\left({}^{p_t}/_{p_{t-1}}\right) = \omega_t \quad \log\left({}^{pu_t}/_{pu_{t-1}}\right) + (1 - \omega_t)\log\left({}^{pk_t}/_{pk_{t-1}}\right)$$

where the weight ω_t is:

$$\omega_t = \frac{1}{2}\left(\frac{pu_{t-1}\overline{qu}_{t-1}}{pu_{t-1}\overline{qu}_{t-1} + pk_{t-1}\overline{qk}_{t-1}} + \frac{pu_t\overline{qu}_t}{pu_t\overline{qu}_t + pk_t\overline{pk}_t}\right)$$

and $\overline{qu}_{t-1}$ (respectively $\overline{qk}_{t-1}$) is the total number of units (resp. the weight in kilos) of products sent at period *t-1*.

Price indices can then be chained:

$$\log\left(^{p_t}/_{p_1}\right) = \sum_{\tau=2}^{t} \log\left(^{p_\tau}/_{p_{\tau-1}}\right)$$

We can then construct a quantity index by using:

$$\log\left(^{Q_t}/_{Q_1}\right) = \log\left(^{V_t}/_{V_1}\right) - \log\left(^{p_t}/_{p_1}\right)$$

In which V_t is the total value of items sent in period *t*.

The initial condition for p_1 can then be arbitrary and a reasonable extension of the previous expression leads to:

$$\log(p_1) = \omega_0 \log(pu_1) + (1 - \omega_0)\log(pk_1)$$

in which

$$\omega_0 = \frac{pu_1\overline{qu}_1}{pu_1\overline{qu}_1 + pk_1\overline{pk}_1}$$

Instruments

The fact that the price index is constructed using information on quantities to derive weights ω_t,that could lead to measurement errors and hence to a spurious negative correlation between quantities and prices. This in turn will overestimate the (absolute value of) price elasticities.

For this reason, we used instruments that are provided by rate cards pu_t for the unit price and the price per kilo pk_t which are set by Royal Mail in advance of future demands. These prices are revised at least every year. We also tested over-identification restrictions and they were never rejected.

References

Anderson, J. E. (2011), 'The Gravity Model' ,Annual Review of. Economics., 3(1), 133-160.

Anson, J., M. Boffa and M. Helble, (2014), 'A Short Run Analysis of Exchange Rates and International Trade with an Application to Australia, New Zealand and Japan', Asian Development Bank Institute Working Paper Series no 471, April.

Anson, J., and M. Helble. (2013), 'A Gravity Model of International Postal Exchanges', in M. A. Crew and P. R. Kleindorfer (eds). Reforming the Postal Sector in the Face of Electronic Competition, Cheltenham, UK: Edward Elgar Publishing, pp 36-47.

Florens, J.P, V. Marimoutou and A. Peguin (2007), 'Econometric Modelling and Inference', Cambridge University Press, New York .

Fung, S.S. and M. Klau (2006), 'The New BIS Effective Exchange Rate Indices', Bank for International Settlements (BIS) Quarterly Review.

Rodriguez, F., S. Soteri and S. Tobias (2017), 'E-substitution in Business Mail in the UK, Trends and Prospects', in M.A. Crew and L.P. Parcu and T. Brennan, (eds). The Changing Postal and Delivery Sector: Towards a Renaissance, Springer International Publishing. pp 35-49.

Santos Silva, JMC and S. Tenreyro (2006), 'The Log of Gravity', *The Review of Economics and Statistics*, 88(4):641-658.

Tinbergen, J. (1962), 'Shaping the World Economy: Suggestions for an International Economic Policy'. New York: Twentieth Century Fund.

Wooldridge, J., 2010, *Econometric analysis of cross section and panel data.* MIT press.

An Exploration of the Impact of Parcel Volume Growth on the Service Performance of Letter Mail

Margaret Cigno and Soiliou D. Namoro

1 Introduction

Online shopping has increased globally, leading to an explosion in parcel volumes for both postal operators and commercial delivery companies. This increase in package volume is a positive development for postal operators who have been facing long-term volume and revenue declines in letter mail. USPS' competitive products revenue, which is composed mostly of package volume, increased more than $2 billion in FY 2016, a 12.6% increase over 2015.[1]

However, whether this increase in package volume reduces service performance for letter mail should be a subject of interest to postal stakeholders and policy makers because it could impact universal service obligations and the overall financial viability of the operator. The present paper offers some theoretical perspectives on this issue and some quantitative evidence on the effect of parcel trends on service performance for letters.

In researching this topic, little previous empirical work was found. There may be several reasons for this. First, the growth in package volume is a relatively new development. Second, service performance quality is difficult to measure and may require significant resources. Third, if the service performance measurement is not

Margaret Cigno is the Director of the Office of Accountability and Compliance at the Postal Regulatory Commission. Soiliou D. Namoro is an economist with that division. The views expressed in this paper are solely those of the authors and do not reflect the views of the Postal Regulatory Commission.

[1]FY 2016 Financial Analysis of United States Postal Service Financial Results and 10-K Statement, p. 68.

M. Cigno (✉) • S.D. Namoro
Soiliou Daw Namoro 1504 Lawrence St. NE, Washington, DC, 20017
e-mail: margaret.cigno@prc.gov

P.L. Parcu et al. (eds.), *The Contribution of the Postal and Delivery Sector*, Topics in Regulatory Economics and Policy, https://doi.org/10.1007/978-3-319-70672-6_22

representative of actual service performance quality, any attempt to quantify degradation may be distorted. Fourth, many exogenous factors, such as, weather, transportation failures, and infrastructure challenges, can impact service performance quality, making it difficult to isolate a specific cause in declines in service performance.

The present paper explores possible links between quarterly service performance for First-Class and Standard letter mail and the growth in competitive volume, which is overwhelmingly composed of parcel shaped mail.[2] Using publicly available data that span from the first quarter of FY 2011 to the last quarter of FY 2016, we provide evidence that market-dominant product quality tends to be reduced, as competitive volumes increase and operating expenses escalate more rapidly.

Section 2 provides some background information and discusses the still incomplete theory of quality degradation. Section 3 presents the econometric model and the related empirical hypotheses. Our findings regarding service degradation are discussed in Sect. 4. Section 5 provides our overall conclusion.

2 Quality Degradation: Gaps in the Theoretical Underpinnings

2.1 *Background*

One potential downside to growth in competitive products volume is the deterioration of letter mail service quality. It is related to competitive pressures around speed as consumers demand overnight, and in some cases, same day delivery of parcels. Although service quality includes many characteristics of letter delivery, this paper focuses on delivery speed because it is the characteristic most likely affected by volume growth in competitive mail.

There are two aspects to delivery speed: service standards and achievement of those standards. In the United States, the postal operator, the United States Postal Service (USPS), in consultation with its regulator, the Postal Regulatory Commission (PRC), determines the expected days to delivery of all mail products. The stated days to delivery are referred to as the service standard. There are separate service standards depending on the distance the mail travels. For First-Class Mail, these standards are overnight,[3] 2-day and 3–5 day. For Standard Mail they are 3–5 day, 6–10 day, and more than 10 days. The USPS measures achievement of service standards by comparing the percentage of time the mail is delivered within the service standards to self-imposed targets for on-time delivery.

[2]Service performance for flat-shaped mail is not analyzed because of data limitations.

[3]In fiscal year 2014 the USPS eliminated overnight service for First-Class Single-Piece mail but retained it for some First-Class Presort mail.

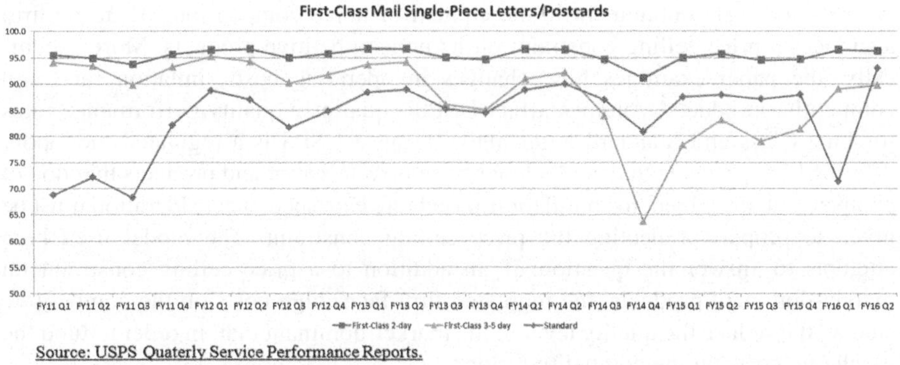

Fig. 1 Service performance results, Quarter 1, 2011 through Quarter 4 2016. Source: USPS Quarterly Service Performance Reports

To address competitive challenges in the parcel market, traditional processing hierarchies may be adjusted and fixed route delivery models may be expanded or replaced by dynamic routing or on demand delivery. These changes could lead to service degradation for non-parcel products. Figure 1 shows service performance results for First Class and Standard letters over the past few years.

Figure 1 illustrates that service performance for First-Class 3–5 day mail deteriorated significantly in quarter 4 of 2014. This was when the USPS consolidated a number of processing plants and eliminated overnight delivery for First-Class single-piece mail. The elimination of overnight delivery forced the remaining volume into the 2 and 3–5 day categories. After the consolidations, the USPS also faced transportation constraints due to the longer distance between facilities and the elimination of certain processing tours.

This led to more mail volume requiring simultaneous transportation. In the FY 2016 Annual Report, the USPS states that Single-Piece First-Class Mail (3–5-Day) "continued to provide opportunities for improvement [in service performance]" as it "balanced the air and surface transportation network due to the growth in package mail." (FY 2016 Annual Report at 16). Service performance for Standard mail has been more erratic over this time period but has generally been below the USPS's target of 90% achievement. While these trends don't necessarily reflect a reduced managerial attention to service quality, their interpretation could benefit from theoretical insights on firms' behaviors relative to service degradation.

2.2 *Theories of Quality Degradation and Related Empirical Hypotheses*

The main objective of this analysis is to estimate the potential variations in service quality that may be caused by variations in competitive volumes and their induced pressure for cost containment in the context of fierce competition, when the firm also faces a price-ceiling constraint on its noncompetitive products. More specifically, the paper examines how changes in operating costs, inflation rate, and competitive products' volumes affect USPS's quarterly quality performance rates for First-Class and Standard letter mail. Because USPS is a regulated monopoly offering both products that compete with the private sector and products that do not compete but are subject to an inflation-based rate cap, special consideration must be given to properly reflecting the price ceiling constraint. The model used here attempts to answer the question: if, in addition to a price ceiling constraint on market-dominant products, the regulated firm faces high costs on the competitive side, will it reduce the quality level of the market-dominant mail in order to fund the escalating costs on the competitive side?

To answer this question we must address a more basic question regarding the behavior of a profit maximizing monopoly, while keeping in mind that the USPS is not a profit maximizing firm (Crew and Brennan 2015). Economic theory predicts that quality levels selected by the monopoly will likely differ from the socially efficient levels (Spence 1975) and the realized bias may be positive or negative. The policy implications of these predictions are unclear, however. Hence, as pointed out by Sappington (2003, p. 356, Footnote 4), "economic theory does not even provide unequivocal guidance as to whether an unregulated monopolist will deliver more or less service quality than will a perfectly competitive firm."

In the case of a regulated monopoly, the predictions heavily depend on the specific form of the prevailing regulation. Price-regulation mechanisms and, in particular, price-cap regulation, are of special interest in the context of the present paper. Typically, price-cap regimes are designed to operate over a given time period. In the case of the USPS, acting as a multiproduct firm, an initial price vector was set in FY 2007 and the component prices are adjusted, generally on an annual basis, for inflation.

Economists largely share the view that a pure price cap mechanism—one in which, the realized earnings occurs entirely to the regulated firm—provides incentives for a profit-maximizing regulated firm to reduce quality of service (Joskow 2006). Because price ceilings are decided *ex-ante* of any cost realization, the regulated firm retains earnings above the costs it incurs (Abel 2000), and consequently has an incentive to reduce quality as it is costly to provide. The effectiveness of regulatory monitoring to counter this incentive is unclear, even if the firm will likely make some investment in quality related research and development to minimize risk exposure. Laffont and Tirole (1988, p. 35) analyzed the problem in terms of the substitutability between price and quality, stating, "If the regulator cannot monitor quality and if quality is a perfect substitute for price, everything is as if the price itself were not regulated... Any attempt at regulating pricing seems to require quality control or at least an imperfect substitutability between price and quality."

The assessment should be taken in perspective. Wiseman (2005), for example, found that the participation of a price-cap regulated firm in complementary, competitive markets, increases its investment in quality. For a firm subject to a binding price cap constraint in market X, its investment in quality in market X is increasing with its participation in a complementary competitive market Y. One explanation offered by the author in the case of telecommunication industry is that "reputation for poor quality in the provision of local exchange telephone service can spill-over to adversely affect sales in these complementary markets, wherein customers have ample choice of service providers and customer switching costs are minimal" (p. 168). The phenomenon could actually occur even if the markets are not in complementary products or services. However, concern for the possible reduction of quality by a firm subject to price cap regulation derives from the fact that, perhaps unlike USPS (Crew and Brennan 2015), the firm is the residual claimant for its costs (Wiseman 2002).

As an empirical issue, research findings seem to equally support both sides of the prediction that price cap regulation leads to quality degradation. In the telecommunication industry literature, Banerjee (2003, p. 243) reported about US retail telephone service quality that "average performance has not worsened, and has even improved, as states have moved progressively from rate-of-return regulation for ILECs (incumbent local exchange carriers) to various forms of incentive regulation." Ai and Sappington (2000) compared the impacts of several incentive regulation mechanisms on network modernization, aggregate investment, revenue, cost, profit, and concluded that price cap regulation was among the state incentive regulation mechanisms that led to greater network modernization, compared to rate of return regulation. In contrast, Uri (2004) reported that overall interstate access service quality has fallen as a consequence of price cap regulation.

The relative importance of the incentive and the disincentive of the firm to reduce quality under price cap remains, therefore, an interesting empirical question, in particular for multiproduct firms and, even more specifically, for the USPS. The focal question of this paper—whether expansion of output in a competitive market reduces quality in a price-cap regulated market—is neglected by most of the theoretical and empirical papers mentioned above, with the exception of Sappington (2003). The knowledge gap on this issue is even larger because prior theory and empirical work has looked at profit-maximizing firms, not those like the USPS. Indeed, Crew and Brennan (2015) argued that the business model of the USPS significantly differs from traditional business models of the firm.

Regarding service quality, the same authors argued elsewhere that the 2006 Postal Accountability and Enhancement Act (PAEA)[4] requirement that USPS seeks Advisory Opinions of the Postal Regulatory Commission limited the ability of the PRC to prevent reduction in quality induced by price cap regulation (Crew and Brennan 2015). In these conditions, while one may expect that reduction of service quality would be followed by the reduction in sales, it may be interesting to empirically inquire whether USPS's incentive to reduce both the costs and the quality of service has led to too little quality of its regulated products.

[4]U.S.C. 39 §§3661(b) and (c).

Further, if one considers the fact that the USPS offers both competitive and non-competitive products, the empirical inquiry is whether increases in the volumes of its competitive products and in operating expenses are negatively correlated with lower service quality for market dominant mailers, after controlling for variations in operating expenses that might trigger cost-saving measures including quality reduction. If the answer turns out to be positive and if there is enough statistical ground to interpret the relation as causal, the finding would suggest that resources that should be spent on quality maintenance (and/or enhancement) on the noncompetitive market, are used instead to increase sales volumes and shares on the competitive market.

In the absence of a strict control policy of quality or a compelling theory, whether price-cap regulation encourages the USPS to be less concerned with service quality remains an important and open empirical question. The present paper provides some answers to this question by examining publicly available data that span from the first quarter of FY 2011 to the last quarter of FY 2016. More precisely, we test the impact of competitive products' volumes on performance rates after controlling for several factors.

3 The Empirical Model

3.1 Model Specification and Data Sources

From the discussion in Sect. 2, it appeared that economic theory does not provide clear guidance regarding the likely behavior of the regulated operator with respect to reducing service performance as a means of cost control, particularly when the regulated entity operates in both competitive and noncompetitive markets. The empirical model that is considered here is, therefore, not derived from some particular economic theory. The basic econometric model that we estimate is a dynamic linear panel regression model in which the individuals are USPS postal districts and the time units are the quarters spanning between years 2011 and 2016 (24 quarters). The model is formally stated as follows:

$$
\begin{aligned}
P_{dq} = \gamma + \alpha P_{d(q-1)} &+ \beta_1 Onight_q + \beta_2 LGRROE_q + \beta_3 LGRROE_{q-1} \\
&+ \beta_4 Log\_rev\_w\_volume_q + \beta_5 Logcosts_q + \beta_6 Logrevenue_q + \beta_7 Inflation_q \\
&+ \vartheta_d + error_{dq}
\end{aligned}
$$

where the Greek letters, α, β, and γ are constant coefficients to be estimated. The subscripts d and q stand for "district" and "quarter", respectively. Hence P_{dq} denotes the quality performance of District d in the quarter q. The performance rate ranges from 0 to 100 and is actually considered in its log-odd form, i.e., it is

Table 1 Econometric status of the covariates

Covariate	Status
Lag of the Dependent (*Lag of Dependent*)	Endogenous by model specification
Indicator of overnight-mail suppression (*Onight*)	Exogenous
Log of revenue-weighted competitive volume (*Log_rev_w_volume*)	Endogenous
Log of total USPS costs (*Logcosts*)	Endogenous
Log of total USPS revenue (L*ogrevenue*)	Endogenous
LGRROE	Predetermined

calculated using the formula $\ln\left(\frac{P}{100-P}\right)$.[5] The covariates are, for most, assumed to be endogenous or predetermined. Table 1 describes the treatment of each covariate. The error term is decomposed into two components: the unobservable district-specific heterogeneity component, ϑ_d, and the idiosyncratic component, $error_{dq}$. For reasons that we discuss below, it does not include an unobservable quarter-specific component.

Cost variables enter the model in two distinct forms: relative and absolute. The relative form involves growth rates of Operating Expenses and Consumer Price Index for All Urban Consumers (CPI-U). The corresponding variable is constructed as a one-quarter lag of the difference between the quarterly growth rate of total controllable operating expenses, and the quarterly growth rate of CPI-U, both rates computed in percentages. It is labelled *LGRROE* (lagged growth rate of real operating expenses). Changes in this variable are expected to captures the speed of escalation of operating costs and are predicted to be negatively correlated with the quality performance rate. The rationale for this prediction is that ceteris paribus, the acceleration of positive changes in operating expenses should trigger cost-containment measures and, since there is a price-ceiling constraint on noncompetitive products, these measures may include the reduction in noncompetitive service quality. The absolute form of the cost variable is represented by the overall operating expenses, which, together with overall revenues, are controlled for in an attempt to isolate a potential effect on quality that is unrelated specifically to competitive volume. The variable labelled as $Logrevenue_q$ represents the USPS's total operating revenue.[6]

The timing and duration of managers' reaction to cost acceleration are uncertain, however. In particular, it is assumed that cost acceleration in a given quarter may affect the quality indexes in quarters beyond the immediately following quarter.

[5]Log odds are often used to avoid predicting performances that fall outside the defined range. As well known, a regression in which the log-odds of performances rates are the dependent variable corresponds to a logistic regression in which the performances rates are the dependent variable.

[6]These are not the revenues that were used to compute the revenue-weighted volumes. The total operating revenue covers both dominants and competitive products. The corresponding data are collected from the USPS Preliminary Financial Information (unaudited).

These considerations led to the inclusion of one lag of the variable *LGRROE* in the model. To account for the overall cost-level effects, the log of total controllable operating expenses is also controlled for and labelled as $Logcosts_q$.

The cost data were collected from the USPS Preliminary Financial Information (unaudited). These monthly data on operating expenses are averaged over every 3 months to produce quarterly data.

The variable $Log\_rev\_w\_volume_q$ relates to the volumes of competitive products and is computed as the log of revenue-weighted volumes. The competitive-volume and the corresponding revenue data are collected from the USPS's Quarterly Statistic Reports. The mail types included in the computation of the aggregate measure of competitive volumes are Priority Mail, Parcel Select Mail, Express Mail, Parcel Return Mail, International mail, and Standard Post.[7] Controlling for both the overall operating expenses and the overall revenue is an attempt to account for the interdependence that bind together the competitive and the noncompetitive aspects and environments of the firm.[8]

An additional explanatory variable is a dummy variable indicating the suppression in 2015 of overnight mails. Quarterly CPI-U data were constructed from the Bureau of Labor monthly statistics. The implementation of phase 2 of a Network Rationalization effort by USPS resulted in elimination of overnight mail service for First-Class Single Piece Letters and Cards and appears to have, at least temporarily, negatively affected service performance of other mail products as well.[9] The quarter in which this change occurred is, therefore, controlled for in the model. The corresponding variable is a dummy variable that takes the value 1 if the quarter is or follows the third quarter of 2015, and the value 0, otherwise. It is labelled as *Onight.*

The explanatory variables fall in two classes depending on whether they vary according to both districts and quarters, or according to quarters only. Due to the paucity of publicly available data, variables that fall in the second class vary only over time. They actually represent national aggregate. The first class only contains one explanatory variable, $P_{d(q-1)}$, the lagged value of the dependent variable.[10] So, while service performance data vary both over quarters and district, costs, inflation and volume data are district-invariant national aggregates.

In technical terms, the data at hand form a particular panel (or longitudinal) data set, in which each district's performances are observed over time, while costs,

---

[7]The results remain very much the same when Parcel Return Mail and International Mail are excluded from the computation of the aggregate volume.

[8]The total revenue data were also collected from the USPS Preliminary Financial Information (unaudited).

[9]Changes in business rules for entering other mail products also resulted in longer days to delivery for a portion of these products. From the third quarter of FY 2015, mail performance data on overnight First-Class Single Piece Letters and Cards were no longer available.

[10]To be more precise, it is the lagged value of the log-odd of that variable. Recall the definition of the log-odd as $\ln\left(\frac{P}{100-P}\right)$, where P is the mail performance index, which is the percentage of time the mail is delivered within the service standards.

inflation and volume variables are time-varying but district-invariant. In a regression, the latter variables can capture only temporal variation in performance rates. To also capture the variation across districts, lagged performances are used as explanatory. In fact, it seems natural to assume that current performances are the results of actions taken by district managers after observing past and recent performances. So, the inclusion of lagged performances as additional factors that affect current performances is motivated both by this learning-by-doing assumption, and by technical statistical needs, with the proviso about model identification that is discussed below.

The sample size is determined as the product between the number of districts and the number of quarters. Since the maximal number of districts is 67 and the maximal number of quarter is 24, the corresponding maximal sample size is 1608 (67×24). However, for a given quarter the number of districts considered (hence the sample size) does vary across the mail types. For example, the suppression of overnight mails in 2015 mechanically reduced to zero, the number of districts for the corresponding quarters, and the sample size decreases by 67 for each of those quarters. One particular district may also not have quality performance data for some mail type and some quarters.[11] Consideration of time-only varying explanatory variable raises the traditional identification problem—the impossibility of separating the effects of the included district-invariant covariates from those of unobservable district-invariant, but time-varying, factors. The interpretation of the estimation results relies, therefore, on the assumption that quality service performances are conditionally uncorrelated with any non-included district-invariant factors, given the included ones. In line with this assumption, the error term does not include an unobservable quarter-specific component.

3.2 Estimation Strategy

In the estimation of the model, the covariates are, for most, assumed to be endogenous or predetermined. Table 1 describes the treatment of each covariate.

We assume that the overnight mail suppression is exogenous in that the performance shocks in any given quarter are statistically uncorrelated with the entire time-series of that variable. Total cost, total revenue, and the revenue-weighted competitive volume are treated as endogenous because they result both from market forces and the firm's cost minimization efforts, which we have suspected, in the introduction and Sect. 3.2, to be non-independent of its service quality management. The cost-acceleration variable (*LGRROE*) is treated as a predetermined variable, under the contention that while current performance shocks are not

[11]This is the case, for example, for Honolulu's missing data on 2-day mail performance.

statistically related to past costs, they may affect future costs and their growth rates[12] (Arellano 2003).

Endogeneity problems are usually addressed with appropriate instruments. While finding valid instruments can sometimes be a tedious and frustrating exercise, for a class of linear panel data models, the instruments are actually determined on theoretical grounds by taking advantage of the particular structure of the model. This, of course, does not automatically guarantee that the instruments are also good. Further tests must be performed to determine their validity. Examples include Arellano-Bover and Blundell-Bond estimators. The approach that is followed here is Blundell-Bond's (Blundell and Bond 1998), which is easily implementable in the usual statistical and econometrics packages.[13]

The estimation procedures rest on the assumption that the idiosyncratic errors are not autocorrelated and the district-specific effects are uncorrelated with the earliest first difference of the dependent variable. Consequently, only the estimations, which pass the no-autocorrelation test, are retained here. A two-step estimation is first performed with the computation of GMM two-step standard errors, which are known to be biased. If the Sargan overidentification test does not reject the validity of the instruments, the equation is re-estimated subject to computing Windmeijer robust estimator for standard errors (WC-robust Std. Err.). Arellano-Bond test of zero autocorrelation is then performed and the estimation is considered to be acceptable in the case of no-rejection of the null hypothesis of zero autocorrelation in first difference of order 2, at 5% level of significance.

4 Estimation Results

The explanatory variable whose effect is mostly relevant to the question that we examine in the paper is the aggregate competitive-volume variable, *Log_rev_w_volume*. A negative and significant effect of that variable means that in the presence of intense pressure on managements for implementing cost-containment measure, service quality for non-regulated product decreases.

Tables 2, 3 and 4 show that, with the exception of Standard mail, these effects are negative and strongly statistically significant, i.e., at the level 1%, for First-Class Overnight, 2-day and 3–5-day mail service performance. The magnitude of the effect is similar for Overnight and 3–5-day mail and is larger than in the case of 2-day mail. To take the example of 3–5-day mails, a 10% increase in the competitive volumes induces about 9% decrease in service quality. The average over districts and quarters of the service performance for this mail type is 88 (over 100), with the corresponding odd of 7.33 (88/12). The 9% decrease means a

[12]Cf, Arellano (2003), p. 143, for the definition of predetermined variables.

[13]The model considered is estimated here with Stata, using the command "xtdpdsys" and the related test commands.

Table 2 First-class overnight results related to competitive volumes

logoddPerfOvernight	Coef.	WC-robust std. err.	z	P > |z|
Lag of Dependent	0.4874774	0.1000023	4.87	0
LGRROE	−0.0070343	0.0012422	−5.66	0
LagLGRROE	−0.0182601	0.001857	−9.83	0
Log_rev_w_volume	−0.6378578	0.0690121	−9.24	0
Logcosts	−2.85594	0.858155	−3.33	0.001
Logrevenue	1.003619	0.2850618	3.52	0
cons	25.42276	5.623891	4.52	0

p-value of Arellano-Bond no-autocorrelation Test: 0.5261
Sargan test of overidentifying restrictions: Prob > chi2 = 0.2232
Number of observations: 1005; Number of Districts 67

Table 3 First-class 2 day results related to competitive volumes

LogoddPerf2-day	Coef.	WC-robust std. err.	z	P > |z|
Lag of Dependent	0.5344762	0.0507969	10.52	0
LGRROE	−0.0164691	0.0016885	−9.75	0
LagLGRROE	−0.0330092	0.0013914	−23.72	0
Log_rev_w_volume	−0.3481532	0.0495373	−7.03	0
Logcosts	1.169355	0.4826576	2.42	0.015
Logrevenue	−0.4339363	0.2092276	−2.07	0.038
Onight	0.2040101	0.0383446	5.32	0
cons	−0.6994348	2.916477	−0.24	0.81

p-value of Arellano-Bond no-autocorrelation Test: 0.2446
Sargan test of overidentifying restrictions: Prob > chi2 = 0.7142
Number of observations: 1386; Number of Districts 66

decrease of the average rate from 88 to 87.07. The conversion of the estimated coefficients into corresponding reduction in the service performance rates is summarized in Table 5.

To better appreciate the magnitudes of the decreases reported in the last column of Table 5, it is instructive to refer to Table 6, which reports the target and actual performance indexes over FY 2013 – FY 2017. The decrease in the actual indexes for Overnight mail is equal to −0.14 (from 2013 to 2014), and −0.45 (from 2014 to 2015). The corresponding numbers for 2-Day mail are −0.36, −1.62, and an additional 1.38 (from 2015 to 2016). For 3–5-Day mail, they are, respectively, −3.9, −11.4, and 7.1. For the sake of comparison, the numbers in the last column of Table 5 should be interpreted as quarterly decreases, while the decreases implied by the USPS numbers are annual. Further, the decreases computed from the USPS numbers do not partial out the effects of changes that occurred in standards' definitions, such as the suppression of Overnight mail. So, although our numbers may suggest economic insignificance when compared to the standard deviations of the performances—in parentheses in column 2 of Table 5—they can, in fact, be

Table 4 First-class 3–5 day and Standard-mail results related to competitive volumes

(a) *LogoddPerf3-5-day*	Coef.	WC-robust std. err.	z	P > |z|
Lag of Dependent	0.7494126	0.0142375	52.64	0
LGRROE	−0.033672	0.0011636	−28.94	0
LagLGRROE	−0.055911	0.0010766	−51.93	0
Log_rev_w_volume	−0.956062	0.0418815	−22.83	0
Logcosts	3.06959	0.320805	9.57	0
Logrevenue	−1.188764	0.1366507	−8.7	0
Onight	0.4822844	0.0260749	18.5	0
_cons	−4.185372	1.772978	−2.36	0.018
(b) *LogoddPerfStandard*	Coef.	WC-robust std. err.	z	P > |z|
Lag of Dependent	0.3823686	0.0629557	6.07	0
LGRROE	0.0072809	0.0036772	1.98	0.048
LagLGRROE	0.0032358	0.002177	1.49	0.137
Log_rev_w_volume	0.6597728	0.168982	3.9	0
Logcosts	7.236198	1.168113	6.19	0
Logrevenue	−1.0629	0.5788957	−1.84	0.066
Onight	−0.2202304	0.0660821	−3.33	0.001
_cons	−60.28559	7.289557	−8.27	0

(a) p-value of Arellano-Bond no-autocorrelation Test: 0.9941; Sargan test of overidentifying restrictions: Prob > chi2 = 0.6789; Number of observations: 1407; Number of Districts 67
(b) p-value of Arellano-Bond no-autocorrelation Test: 0.3738; Sargan test of overidentifying restrictions: Prob > chi2 = 0.3917; Number of observations: 1088; Number of Districts 64

Table 5 Effects of a 10-percnt increase in competitive mail volumes on the mail performance index (the percentage of time the mail is delivered within the service standards) for four different mail types

Mail type	Average index	Coeff. of *log +rev_w_volume*	Percentage decrease	Resulting index	Difference
Overnight	96.00 (2.2)	−0.63786	−0.24042	95.77	−0.13
2-day	95.00 (2.1)	−0.34815	−0.16850	94.84	−0.16
3–5 day	88.00 (7.9)	−0.95606	−1.05824	87.07	−0.30
Standard	80.67(12.8)	0.659772	1.34703	81.76	1.76

considered falling within the ranges of the actual annual decrease that occurred before FY 2017, as reported by the USPS.

These findings are plausible, because First-Class letter mail and Priority envelopes are often processed in the same mail stream. Hence, as the volume of Priority, which is more time sensitive than First-Class, increases, it is not unreasonable to expect some First-Class letters to be deferred. Other competitive products, such as parcels, are processed in different mail streams using different equipment. However, transportation and delivery activities, as well as the overall labor pool, are often shared. Therefore, resource constraints may lead to deferral of the less time

Table 6 U.S. postal service FY2016 results and FY2017 targets for corporate-wide goals

Measure	FY2017 Target	FY2016 Actual	FY2016 Target	FY2015 Actual	FY2015 Target	FY2014 Actual	FY2014 Target	FY2013 Actual
Single-piece first-class mail								
Overnight	N/A	N/A	N/A	95.55	96.8	96	96.8	96.14
2-day	96.5	94.66	96.5	93.28	96.5	94.9	96.5	95.26
3–5-day	95.25	83.66	95.25	76.56	95.25	87.7	95.25	91.6

Source: USPS FY2017 Performance Targets are aligned to the U.S. Postal Service Future Ready Five-Year Strategic Plan. https://about.usps.com/who-we-are/financials/annual-reports/fy2016/annual_report2016_tech_016.htm)

sensitive or lower revenue products. The fact that the impacts are estimated to be small is also plausible given that competitive volume constitutes only 0.3% of total volume.[14]

Though the results for Standard Mail at first seem counter intuitive, on further reflection, they may indeed be plausible. Standard Mail is a bulk mail, deferrable product that is often transported between processing facilities in bundles. It is processed on some of the same equipment as competitive mail. Its service performance has generally lagged behind that of First-Class Mail. If the increase in competitive volume leads to more intra-facility transportation runs and longer mail processing equipment runs Standard Mail service performance may also benefit from these changes. Therefore, the positive correlation between Standard Mail service performance and competitive product volume growth is at least conceivable. Further research into this phenomenon seems warranted.

The effect of the cost factor, *LGRROE*, is also seen to be negative, as one would expect. Indeed, larger growth rates of inflation-adjusted operating costs can be predicted to trigger cost-containment strategies that may potentially affect service quality negatively. Inflation rates also have a negative effect, although not always significant, on service quality. The maintenance or enhancement of service quality is costly and price-adjustment to inflation does not guarantee that quality will improve or even remain the same. Overall, it seems fair to advance that competitive mail volumes have a negative impact on quality performance, after controlling for the effects of the other variables listed above.

5 Conclusion

The effect of price-cap regulation on USPS's management of service quality is an important area of policy concern and policy improvement. Unfortunately, economic theory does not provide clear guidance regarding the likely behavior of the regulated operator with respect to reducing service performance as a means of cost control, particularly when the regulated entity operates in both competitive and noncompetitive markets. The present paper is a modest contribution to a better understanding of the nature and scope of the problem. It offers an analysis of the regulated operator's incentive to reduce the quality of its noncompetitive products when facing volume increase on the competitive market, along with cost pressures, in the absence of a strict regulatory control of market-dominant product quality.

The estimation results support the hypothesis that as competitive volumes increase and operating expense escalate more rapidly, market-dominant product quality tends to be reduced. It must be stressed, however, that volumes and cost variables are national aggregates. These results are silent, therefore, about the

[14]Financial Analysis of United States Postal Service Financial Results and 10-K Statement Fiscal Year 2016 March 31, 2017, Postal Regulatory Commission.

significance and magnitude of the described trends when the cost and the volume variables are measured at the district levels. These important confirmatory studies are left for future research.

Acknowledgments We thank the reviewers for their careful reading of our manuscript and their insightful comments and suggestions.

References

Abel, J. (2000). "The performance of the state telecommunications industry under price-cap regulation: An assessment of the empirical evidence," NRRI 00-14. The National Regulatory Research Institute.

Ai, C and D.E. M. Sappington (2000): "The Impact of State Incentive Regulation on the U.S. Telecommunications Industry," Journal of Regulatory Economics, Volume 22, Issue 2, pp 133–160.

Arellano, M. (2003): *Panel data Econometrics*. Advanced Texts in Econometrics. Oxford University Press. P. 143.

Banerjee, A. (2003): "Does incentive regulation 'cause' degradation of retail telephone service quality?" Information Economics and Policy, Volume 15, Issue 2, pp. 243-269.

Blundell, R., and S. Bond. 1998. "Initial conditions and moment restrictions in dynamic panel data models." Journal of Econometrics 87: 115–143

Bremmer, D. S. (2004). "Uncertainty and Multiproduct Monopoly: Spillovers Across Unrelated Markets," Southwestern Economic Review, Vol 31, pp. 31-40.

Crew, M. A. and T. J. Brennan (2015): "Business Models: Some Implication for the USPS," in Crew, M. A. and T. J. Brennan (Editors) *Postal and Delivery Innovation in the Digital Economy,* Springer, pp. 1-15.

Joskow, P. L. (2006). "Regulation of Natural Monopoly," Handbook of Law and Economics, Volume 2, Chapter 16, 2007, Pages 1227–1348

Laffont, J.-J and Tirole, J. (1988). "The Regulation of Multiproduct Firms; Theory and Policy Analysis, October 1988, Working Papers, Department of Economics, MIT.

Sappington, D. E. M. (2003). "The Effects of Incentive Regulation on Retail Telephone Service Quality in the United States," Review of Network Economics, Vol.2, Issue 4 – December 2003. Pp. 355-375.

Spence, A. M. (1975) "Monopoly, Quality, and Regulation," Bell Journal of Economics, Vol. 6, No 2, pp. 417-429.

Uri, N. D. (2004) "The Impact of Incentive Regulation on Service Quality in Telecommunications in the United States," Quality and Quantity, Volume 38, Issue 3, pp 291–318.

Wiseman, D. L. (2002): "Is there 'Hope' for price cap regulation?" Information Economics and Policy, Volume 14, Issue 3, pp. 349-370.

Wiseman, D. L. (2005): "Price regulation and quality," Information Economics and Policy, Volume 17, Issue 2, March 2005, Pages 165-174.

The manufacturer's authorised representative in the EU is Springer Nature Customer Service Centre GmbH, Europaplatz 3, 69115 Heidelberg, Germany. If you have any concerns regarding our products, please contact ProductSafety@springernature.com

Printed and bound by CPI Group (UK) Ltd, Croydon, CR0 4YY
30/09/2026
02225566-0013